Ruskin's Maze

RUSKIN'S MAZE

Mastery and Madness
in His Art

By Jay Fellows

Princeton University Press
Princeton, New Jersey

Publication of this book has been aided by a grant from the
Paul Mellon Fund of Princeton University Press

This book has been composed in Linotron Baskerville

Clothbound editions of Princeton University Press books
are printed on acid-free paper, and binding materials are
chosen for strength and durability

Printed in the United States of America by Princeton
University Press, Princeton, New Jersey

Library of Congress Cataloging in Publication Data

Fellows, Jay, 1940-
  Ruskin's maze.

  1. Ruskin, John, 1819-1900—Criticism and
interpretation.   I. Title.
PR5264.F43   828'.809   81-47124
ISBN 0-691-06479-2   AACR2

For John Rosenberg, who showed light through dark, if not blind, mirrors

and Laurence d' A. M. Glass, Gerhard Joseph, Sean Sculley, and Marcia Stern, who know something about the territories around Cyprus Avenue, Nottinghill Gate, and Stockton's Wing.

Table of Contents

A Note on Sources   ix
Permissions   ix
Acknowledgments   xi
Preface   xiii

Part One
Strange Chords: Masterful Geometries

Introduction

A Travel Diary toward Nothing but a Dream: Shadowy
Types for Concluding Images and "The Excavations of
Silence"   3

One

Strange Chords of Incipient Orthodoxy:
Centres and Epicycles   29
  A. Cock-Robinson-Crusoe Conceit and Other Geometrically
    Central Issues   29
  B. The Parallel Advance: Panorama as Central Responsibility 38
  C. The Vantage Point of the True Centre: Problems in the
    Transcendental Altitude of the Self   45

Two

Central Men and Awful Lines: Attempts and Failures
in Mastery   60
  A. The Central Man   60
  B. The Awful Lines of Time   63
  C. Cross-References *ad infinitum*: The World of the Index 68
  D. Mastery, Makeshift and True: Glimpses of "Shattered Majesty" and
    "Stately and Unaccusable Wholes"   73

Three

The Frosts of Death   85
  A. The Man in the Middle: Mediation as Subtraction   85
  B. The "True Centre" as Condemned Space   89
  C. Juggling, Trick Riding, and the Avaricious Imagination of Repletion 98

Four

Vacancies, Kindly and Deadly: Sweet Transitions and
Jarring Thoughts   105
  A. The Syntax of Architecture: St. Peter's Divided   105
  B. Slow Travel: The Extension of Time and Space   115
  C. The Dead Spaces of Satin: Transitional Absence   120

Five

Circumferential Considerations: Lines without
Beginnings or Endings   127
  A. The Architecture of the Index: The Taming of (Museum) Centricity 127
  B. The Art of the Provinces: Suburban Efficacy   140
  C. The Garland of Thoughts: A Case for Fanciful Extension   143

Part Two
Lucent Verdure and
Asymmetrical Decompositions

Six

Labyrinths of Presence, Labyrinths of Absence:
Initial Experiences of the Superimposition of Contrasting
Designs   159
  A. The Theatre of Blindness: Items, Queries, Laws, the Bestiary, and
    Originally Invisible Dramatis Personae   159
  B. Lurid Shadow, Lucent Verdure: Early Manifestations of the
    Centripetal Maze   178

Seven

Capricious Sinuousities: Venice and the City as Mind   198
  A. White Clues: Instincts for the Exit   198
  B. Colubrine Chains: The Maze of Consciousness   205
  C. The Gothic Anomaly: Peripheral Shadows of Madness and Narrow
    Caution   212

Eight

The Excavations of Silence: Double Labyrinths and the
Architecture of Reluctant Nihilism   222
  A. The Threads of Thought: Unsystematic Intimations of the
    Centrifuged Style   222
  B. Paratactical Texts of Ripped Immanence: From Ariadne to the
    Shears and Penultimate Tablet of Atropos   240

Appendices   275

A Note on Sources

All references to *The Works of John Ruskin*, edited by E. T. Cook and Alexander Wedderburn, 39 vols., Library Edition (London, 1903-12) will appear in parentheses after quotations from the works themselves.

Permissions

Acknowledgments

I want to thank Margaret Case, Jerry Sherwood, and Robert E. Brown, whose editorial help and friendship have proved invaluable. Further, I would like to express my gratitude to John Hejduk, Robert Langbaum, and J. Hillis Miller for encouragement at various stages of the transformation of the manuscript. Harold Bloom's awareness of the blood of the text—an awareness that matches Ruskin's own—has been an inspiration which has provided courage when that was lacking. Shane Gould, who accompanied me through the streets of Arklow, showed me the path from the abyss of those right-angled labyrinths of absence. Finally, I would like to thank both Linden Arden, who involved me in the difficulties of a dark way, and Ann Douglas, whose "thread," unsevered, showed me the way out, as if to that light just before "dazzlement."

If we wish to outline an architecture which conforms to the structure of our soul . . . , it would have to be conceived in the image of the Labyrinth.

—Nietzsche, *Aurore*

Preface

Penultimately, Ruskin's consciousness (and even Ruskin himself) might be considered a double labyrinth—a three-dimensional place of cutting edges, where the double axe itself doubles.[1] Earlier, he will be concerned with a single Maze of recollected Lucent Verdure: it is as if, close to an "overlapping" Circumference, under the pressure of an impacted and exploding repletion, that single Maze had doubled in a necessitous accommodation that is part of an almost final disintegration. The design of an excessively dense coherence becomes a quasi-textual design of double labyrinthine ruins that are not entirely decipherable. For a moment, a reader may look for a translator who would render the language of a double consciousness monological, when the dialogical is only wishful understanding for the dichotomic reader/listener. Then the reader, or listener, must become a dance partner, interested in the participation of sinuous movement among the ruins rather than elucidation in the clear light of day. Certainly, close to the end, there are cutting edges that will either double or halve Strange Chords/ Cords of "intellectual" nerves, until, immediately before a White Silence, there is the counterpoint of a "marred music" that may require highly idiosyncratic lyrics.

Or perhaps it could be said that if Ruskin, one of the "lacertine breed" (XIX, 365), with the double labyrinth of his "three-dimensional" consciousness, is eventually to become a dancer without a partner (as the end may suggest)[2]—like a solitary crane[3] (in the

---

[1] Cf. W. H. Matthews, *Mazes & Labyrinths: Their History and Development* (New York, 1970), p. 34: "the great German archaeologist Schliemann, during his researches at Mycenae on the mainland, unearthed from one of the graves an ox-head of gold plate, with a double axe between the upright horns. The double axe was also the sign of the Zeus worshipped at Labraunda in Caria, country to the north-east of Crete, on the mainland of Asia Minor, where the implement was known as the *labrys*." Later, dealing with maze etymology, Matthews, without a finality that is nevertheless provocative, suggests: "The present position, then, is that the Labyrinth is the House of the Double Axe, the implication being that the Cretan example was not, as formerly believed, a miniature reproduction of the temple of Hawara, but that the latter was actually given the title by analogy with the building at Knossos" (p. 176).

[2] The design of this book, beginning with an introductory "Travel Diary" and ending with the double labyrinths of Part Two, the silence or bellowing of sacred crocodiles that are still submerged—an ending, that is, in a significant sense, an "antiphonal" response to the Part One, which is essentially preparation for that overriding "response" of contention/solution—suggests movement as well as sequence. And the shape of this book is largely dependent upon the reciprocal motion

metamorphoses of Ruskin's eventual bestiary), awkwardly stomping in front of the vertiginous reflection of a bull's-eye that is not, at least for a moment, blind to its multiplicity—he is, essentially (and close to the end), antiphonal, like Athena of the Air, who is also Athena of the Earth. With Ruskin, it is as if a compelling sense of unity, or interrelation, were being undercut, perhaps by the blades of those double axes. At times, this doubleness is lateral, between sides, as if there were a "bicameral" dialogue between the right and left hemispheres of the brain, or the labyrinthine/serpentine Antiphonal Contention that informs the mediations between the Centre and Circumference; and, at other times, this doubleness is expressed vertically, as if a buried, even "dead," creature were attempting to communicate with someone or something elevated, alive, though barely intact. Yet there is something about the Ruskinian antiphon that remains solipsistic and beyond integration—almost, it might appear for a moment, inadequate. (The crane is lonely and the eye of the bull is, more often than not, blind to everything, including itself: a blind focal point that is like the dead

---

between Centres and Circumferences that traverses a kind of geometrically informed choral space of "antiphonal contention." Furthermore, it fundamentally begins in the beginning and ends, if not at the ending, at least, penultimately. But the weight is not distributed evenly. The itinerary is directed toward the end, despite sub rosa impulses to "cross-reference *ad infinitum*": if prophecy fails, the book's gravity is nonetheless located in the "nothing but process" toward conclusion, though the final chapter fulfills—or places in context, albeit in a context of disintegration—some of the images/allusions of the "Introduction," as if imitating the spiraling, Ruskinian "language of return."

Still, while proceeding, I hope, with a critical tact for sequence, even if that sequence has aspects of the reciprocal to it, the design of *Ruskin's Maze* is not modeled after a strictly one-way phenomenological history. Ruskin's first book, *The Poetry of Architecture* (1837-38), is important close to the end of this study. What is perceived as correct in theory may well prove true in performance; Ruskin's notion of the "noun substantive," in a characteristic amalgamation of architectural design and syntax (Ruskin's language often "builds" or "deconstructs," as if language were stone, a stone that, as "white marble," will suggest solutions), is youthful dogma that becomes especially important—and practical—later. With Ruskin, and so with this book, there is a strong sense of "return," the design of the *Helix virgata* that fascinates Ruskin—even before the final return of the autobiography, *Praeterita*. And this impulse to return to first principles—though often with a significant difference (as with his shifting attitudes toward "Greek-fret" or lights against a dark background)—creates a problematical "sequence" of spirals, as if there were a logic, as well as architecture, of the snail.

[3] See Janet Bord, *Mazes and Labyrinths of the World* (New York, 1975), p. 12: "The best-known maze dance is the Geranos (Crane) dance on the island of Delos, supposedly first danced by Theseus with the companions he had rescued from the clutches of the Minotaur in the Cretan labyrinth. Some of the participants wore animal masks." The dance will reappear, as will animals *without* masks.

end of a "blind lane."[4] But what goes on vertically Between—as if a kind of "marred music" resulting from contrary superimposition—may turn out to be a kind of blindly visionary, "inner language" of extreme significance.

Close to the end, the Ruskinian "vertical antiphon" is, to the anxious reader, occasionally like an echo for a man who has become both deaf and amnesiac immediately before the sound returns. Disappointed (at least until he comes to appreciate an aesthetics of absence), he waits for phrases returning from silence that will surround the "ruins of language" with a context of sense, as if the paratactic might be restored to a condition of labyrinthine syntax in the same way that Ruskin would himself "recover" both a landscape and language lost in "error." But further, when what lies "Between," in the "horizontal antiphon," has been filled, perhaps to the extent of repletion, the antiphonal quality of Ruskin's work does not, like orthodox dialectic (or stereoscopic vision), possess a conclusion of conventional synthesis—a presumably fortunate confluence like a meandering underground river[5] rising to meet its visible and conscious counterpart. If Ruskin is eventually alone (and desertion before disconfirmation informs much of his performance), he is not, in any case, unified in his loneliness. Rather, solipsistically antiphonal, with only himself as company, he is, as

[4] Dance, the optics of the Maze, and the blindness that attends both those optics and madness itself, make a quotation, essentially anthropological, from W. Jackson Knight's *Vergil: Epic and Anthropology* (New York, 1967), p. 267, at least intriguing:

> That the "blind march" at Eleusis was a maze movement seemed almost certain, but was still an inference. Excavation has discovered no architectural maze in the telesterion there. But now the gap is filled by the Malekulan evidence, which for the first time gives a parallel to the location of a maze design at the entrance of a cave entered at death, indicating of course a change of state, from one kind of life to another. The evidence goes further still, for the Malekulans search blindfolded for the anklets which they wear when they perform maze dances at funeral rites, doubly emphasizing the principle of the "blind march," and showing that for them it belongs to the maze, at the point where the ideas of exclusion and secrecy meet.

Some sense of the panoramic encompassment of labyrinthine concerns, which, as we shall see, are Ruskinian concerns, is suggested here. Penultimately, during Ruskin's own Maze dance of broken syntax, but before either funeral rites or rebirth, there will be the "Blind Guide that had celestial light."

[5] Linking human anatomy with the earth, in an analogue of essential design that would not dismay Ruskin, Janet Bord points out that the "body of the earth does in fact contain many spirals [lines that turn to return], according to research carried out by the late Guy Underwood. Working with his divining rod, he spent many years surveying ancient sites in Britain in order to plot the underground streams, and many times his results were in the form of spirals, as illustrated in his book *The Pattern of the Past*" (Bord, *Mazes and Labyrinths*, p. 11).

if severed by a double axe, either halved or doubled, with his consciousness, like a double-tiered labyrinth that is his penultimate Theatre of Blindness, in attempted dialogical discourse with itself, which is, perhaps, Ruskin's ultimate point of failure/success.

Still, as rivers joining in a kind of fork, with black water rising from labyrinthine caves (presumably the water is not sewage, or not *yet* sewage unfit for the circumferential fish of the Middleman but rather, perhaps, "a running brook of horror" [xix, 362] for the ambiguous and daemonic crocodile, who is as demonic as he is sacred) to mingle with white water flashing in the sunlight—spume of the "angels of the lagoon" who may become the Venetian "Angel of the Sea"—Ruskin will "end" his "returning," conclusively inconclusive autobiography, *Praeterita*, with an ecstatic perception of "How things bind and blend themselves together" (xxxv, 561).[6] Yet it is at precisely this point, especially when observed, not from an autobiographical distance, but from the dislocating proximity of the unedited present tense that Ruskin (his thoughts whirling like a vortex of water, with a false presence beneath, or like a squirrel in the central Londonian cage from which he would escape) finds himself in most trouble. And it is the approach to this point of failure or textual locus of false presence, which anticipates the false presence become absence of the "end"—necessarily distressing, as language in touch with coherence moves toward a verbal condition quite different—where the reader may find his most intense experience, if not his most rewarding elucidation. If the text's itinerary is univocal, the harmonious preparation for the uncontested,

---

[6] That element of binding and blending in Ruskin can hardly be emphasized enough. His world is an elaborate construction of analogies. Categories, like his "overflowing" books, are containers that do not categorize. If there are double axes, there are also connections—Strange Chords/Cords—everywhere. The other side of the whirling of the squirrel cage is the harmonious whirling of concentric spheres, both heavenly and earthly, that would create a kind of moral orchestration. Furthermore, what is outlined in the relatively early *The Elements of Drawing* (1857) and *The Elements of Perspective* (1859), which together compose a technical manual on these subjects, goes far beyond merely technical aesthetics. Drawing correctly is a skeletal act that predicts "right" patterns in syntax, architecture, society, and the conduct of one's own life. That fifteenth volume is very much a central or model volume of "spatial form" incarnate, recollecting and anticipating a variety of performances that are elsewhere in amplified form—an amplified form which is based upon an aesthetics that is, in fact, an aesthetics of incipient morality. To draw correctly is to draw with a perspective of radiating rightness that transcends both categories and the procedures of rigid sequence. As in all of Ruskin's work, there are echoes and forebodings. Right lines of the beginning, which may be rectilinear, may return, in a line and language of return, as later "right" spirals coiling close to an end which is itself Nothing (or unreturnable), if not a new life.

the syntax of the actual travel will be described in multiple voices—
a cacophonous chorus, with disagreement of Antiphonal Contention the only available form, before even indeterminate meaning
yields the expressiveness of pathos.

A man of extraordinary influence, Ruskin possessed ideas that
shaped, to varying degrees, those of Tolstoy, Proust, Wright, and
Gandhi[7]—and even Pater, who read Ruskin antithetically. Clearly,
those ideas, as intricately conceptual examinations of often daringly
perceived problems, are not to be dismissed as the explanations/
captions of mere word paintings as illustrations.[8] Further, the biographical elements that inform Ruskin's work are also to be attended to, though the vigorous reading of biography into text can,
it seems to me, be excessively distorting. Yet the pure text is perhaps
a fiction of an immaculate conception that requires more than faith.
And if the "contaminated" text becomes a way of reading refracted
biography "backward" without the autonomy it may presume to
require, at times, it should be noted that Ruskin himself seems to
be involved in a version of this very activity, writing his own autobiography—and I do not mean merely *Praeterita*—for present
requirements, while investing heavily in certain aspects of the past
for present, if temporary, efficacy. For Ruskin's writing, as if ink
were blood (and at a point of exasperation at what he feels to be
the false distinction between language and life he will print his
pages "blood-red" [xxix, 469]), is, in some sense other than the
ordinary, his life, complete with misremembrance and editorial
reshaping. And I have attempted, with I hope unobtrusive tact, to
follow this procedure that provides an intricately informing pat-
tern/scenario for the interplay of life and language: Ruskin, transforming his own life, as onto a stage of his Theatre of Blindness,
if not through the "entrance to the pit of a theatre" (xxviii, 441),
is, after all, Ruskinian. And the drama of Ruskin's language is
indeed the theatre of his life—both blind and sighted.

[7] For Ruskin's influence on Proust, see George D. Painter, "Salvation Through
Ruskin," in *Proust: The Early Years* (Boston, 1959). Ruskin's influence as a social
reformer is suggested by Kenneth Clark, *Ruskin Today*, chosen and annotated by
Kenneth Clark (New York, 1964), p. xiv: "when, at the first meeting of the parliamentary Labour Party, members were asked what had been the determining influence on their lives, almost every one answered 'the works of Ruskin.'"

[8] For an enlightening discussion of Ruskin's ideas see G. P. Landow, *The Aesthetic
and Critical Theories of John Ruskin* (Princeton, 1971). Landow makes a convincing
case for the necessity of a reappraisal of ideas that have, in the recent past, been
too easily dismissed. And having made that case, he presents those ideas in their
proper context. Also, see Robert Hewison, *John Ruskin: The Argument of the Eye*
(Princeton, 1976), whose exploration of Ruskin's theories is also most helpful.

Yet the focus of this book, more "intentional" than either conceptual or biographical (though "shaping" ideas of "shattered majesty" will of course be considered), beginning with a discussion of orthodox and demanding perception, will be directed toward the point where coherence, as if under a terrible burden, breaks down: the phenomenological explorations of a consciousness at work will have occasions to refer back to both theory and biography, but the language will essentially have a life of its own—often a collective life, for Ruskin's texts, no matter how contradictory, overlap. And the reader, instead of involving himself in an explanation or interpretation of "biographical ideas," reaching the text (and the emerging map of consciousness) from the origin of biography and theory, must instead attempt to exist, almost passively, at least at the end, in the horizontal and especially vertical antiphonal spaces "Between" contention—the "choral spaces" of a problematic text, perhaps of an "inner language" for a dichotomic reader/listener, that is intricately orchestrated, first between clearly diagrammed concepts and a language of frequently exquisite incoherence that may be expressively "beyond" interpretation, and then between those paratactical ruins that are only occasionally visible to "Blind Guides" who cannot "see" the Exit and the buried silences that are archaeologically "below" interpretation, like an unexcavated labyrinth of sacred crocodiles. Ruskin's centrifugal solipsism, multiplying into a three-dimensional labyrinth of consciousness that is his final Theatre of Blindness,[9] as if he would play all the roles of his own drama (or metamorphose those roles he cannot play into the arcane dramatis personae of his own theatre), leads to a language of extreme pluralism.

An attempt will be made to make a case for an aesthetics of the

---

[9] Regarding the three-dimensional Maze, W. H. Matthews has this to say by way of explanation:

We may observe that a labyrinth (using this word, for convenience, as embracing "maze") may be arranged in one plane, as we commonly see it on a sheet of paper, or it may be disposed in two or more intercommunicating planes, like the Egyptian labyrinth or a block of flats. We may thus classify all labyrinths, for a start, as either two-dimensional or three-dimensional. As the vast majority belong to the first class and as, moreover, every subdivision of the first may be applied equally to the second, we need say no more concerning the latter except to remark that the complexity of a garden maze may be greatly increased, if desired, by introducing tunnels or bridges, thus converting it into a three-dimensional maze [*Mazes & Labyrinths*, p. 185].

The multiplication of Ruskinian solipsism into double labyrinths of three dimensions simply suggests an increasing complexity that would bring dark tunnels to the corridors of an already intricate consciousness before breakdown.

disintegrating Labyrinthine Penultimate, the centrifugal and paratactical textual "remains" of a vertically antiphonal double labyrinth of blind language and a silence of latent completion, immediately before the blank page, or mathematician's null-set (with
Ruskin, language, as either Nothing or next to Everything, is connected with number) of implicit madness—which is a case for certain texts that, approaching a knot of incoherence (as well as the
ultimacy of White Silence), cannot depend upon a single reading/
meaning for their flawed beauty and multiple, perhaps indeterminate, "sense." If there were a Ruskinian end before madness and
silence, perhaps it would be entangled in an Arachne-like web,
where Ruskin himself would be the one bound and blended together in a condition far from ecstatic—an unraveled, though
"knotted," victim of the woof of his own spinning thought, at a
point of failure that is like a bottomless vortex of false presence,
apparent as overtaxed imaginative faculties begin to break down.[10]
Possibly, as if before a centrifugal rebirth, he would be buried half
alive, in a mediating, if not paralyzed, condition of life-in-death.

But there are other thread-bearers who compose Ruskin's antiphon, and the emphasis will be on neither, say, Arachne's web
(except insofar as it is emblematic of the obstacle as language de-
composes into a condition beyond self-doubt) nor a tapestry of
ultimacy, but rather the labyrinthine language of "nothing but
process" that pirouettes penultimately, after the blank page of beginnings and before the blank page of Illth,[11] which is Ruskin's

[10] But of course this condition is difficult to imagine in a young Ruskin whose
theories cannot include subjunctive possibilities: "The imagination will banish all
that is extraneous; it will seize out the many threads of different feeling which
nature has suffered to become entangled, one only; and where that seems thin and
likely to break, it will spin it stouter, and in doing this, it never knots, but weaves
in the new thread . . ." (IV, 246). For an experience of radical disjunction, compare
this passage of theory with the penultimate "fabric" of fact: the weaving and spinning
of consciousness becomes more complicated toward the end, when Ruskin, as that
weaver of the mind's cloth, also becomes a centrifugal traveler/writer before he does
a concentric, pirouetting dancer/writer.

[11] Illth, as I employ Ruskin's term, is the excessive presence that becomes absence
in the postcircumferential territory of White Silence, which is to say the blind and
silent territory of Ruskin's madness. More strictly, Ruskin describes the surplus that
becomes a negative factor in terms that are economic: "A man's power over his
property is, at the widest range of it, fivefold; it is the power of Use, for himself,
Administration, to others, Ostentation, Destruction, or Bequest; and possession is
in use only, which for each man is sternly limited; so that such things, and so much
of them as he can use, are, indeed, well for him, or Wealth; and more of them, or
any other things are ill for him, or Illth" (XVII, 168). It is perhaps not entirely
inappropriate, with Ruskin, to apply an essentially economic term to the function,
and malfunction, of the imaginative faculties.

concept of the "too much" that becomes less than Nothing in the process (the "nothing but process" that is pointed beyond the null-set toward a minus category)—this, as if for an archaeologist who would find his activity a process of never-ending excavation, with site upon site, like the labyrinthine Troy,[12] or for a psychologist exploring the Maze of an extraordinarily complicated consciousness. Finally, the archaeologist and the psychologist will be like the cutting edges of a single double axe.

Briefly, although there will be anticipations and echoes within the text, just as there are in the body of Ruskin's work, the book is divided into two sections—as if by a surgeon aware of the ironic inadequacy of his severance.

It should perhaps be pointed out that the "Introduction," introducing the "beginning," also introduces, and is completed by, the turning and returning (from silence) language of the "end," almost as though the text proper were an extended digression (as *The Stones of Venice* is a digression from *Modern Painters*, if *Modern Painters* is not an "explanation of a footnote" in *The Stones of Venice* [x, xlvii]), that is, like most Ruskinian digressions, in fact absolutely central.

Somewhat reductively, Part One deals with the attempted mastery of Strange Chords (Chords of inclusion, even musical inclusion, as well as neurological Cords, as in the endings of Strange Nerves—

---

[12] Jackson Knight, in *Vergil*, momentarily approaching anthropology through mythology, finds psychological shape to anthropological repetition:

> Myth first arises from some single event of human and personal relations and act, then becomes in a sense general, as a statement of truth rather than an account of what once happened, and lastly is used as a mental container to hold the facts of some new event. . . .
>
> The principle has a firm psychological foundation, and its point is this. The mind cannot think just anything. There are certain shapes in which it must think, varying at different times, of course. In Homer's mind the events of the *Iliad* fell into a flexible symmetry according to the habits of geometric art; and that is therefore the organization of the poem. Herodotus is influenced by pedimental sculpture and Attic tragedy: his account of Peisistratus, for example, is organized by central and supporting groups, as in a pediment, and he tells the story of Cleomenes as if it were a myth of the shape of "Hercules furens."
> . . .
> The story of the fall of Troy is not less preserved in an "archetypal pattern." I think it is clear that the pattern is in some sense the "labyrinthine," and that Troy was very much a "labyrinthine" city. Accordingly, "labyrinthine" myth would be expected to provide the accretion, with the result which we find, a "labyrinthine" account of the events . . ." [pp. 215-16].

That Ruskin's "mental container"—or a significant one of them—is labyrinthine is implicit in Part Two. Troy, its labyrinthine town and games, will again occur.

Cords that will become as anatomically labyrinthine as the navel thread), and the attendant orthodox geometries[13] of both altitudinous (logo)-concentricity and fallen rectilinearity—an attempted, inclusive mastery that presents problems which it cannot solve, or, for that matter, survive. After an initial Centre of origins, there are other epicyclical locations, whose centricity anticipates the ambitions of a cross-referencing that might go on forever, like a perpetually expanding Index—an Index looking both backward to Centres of original privilege that have turned infernal and forward to a later condition of repletion that is more than unmanageable. A serpentine architecture of the museum attempts to tame an excessive plenitude, which combines concentricity and rectilinearity; but an occasional untransitional middle—the "dead spaces of satin"—threatens to bring about an unbearable condition of juxtaposition.

Part Two investigates, as Ruskin says, the serpentine and spinning problem of "the labyrinth of life itself, and its more and more interwoven occupation, become too manifold, and too difficult for me; and of the time wasted in blind lanes of it" (xxii, 452). It is as if the serpent and the arts of weaving had conspired in labyrinthine ways. Yet those ways of the labyrinth, as a superimposition of contrasting design over the orthodox and rational geometries of concentricity and rectilinearity, offer an eccentric, if not de-centred, problematically precarious solution to problems of the Centre and "ways that are straight" which are no longer tenable. If Part One deals with what might be called an Architecture of (logo)-concentricity, Part Two is concerned with an attempted salvation/solution or cure to a later discredited, or lost, logos—a cure that itself ends in the eloquent ruins of pathos.

Further, Part Two describes the lines and language of irregular, perhaps anamorphic, turn, as if upon itself, and return (as from a prolonged silence) that would attempt to counter, or "solve," a winding toward a densely "mephitic" location of central centripetence with a curvilinear, centrifugal design and an attendant syntax of "sinuousities" which appears, at times, "capricious," but which

---

[13] Aside from Ruskin's mathematics, his concern with number ("sets" of Nothing and "sets" of Everything), the relation between Ruskin and geometry, orthodox or eccentric, is rather complicated. Whereas the perfection implicit in geometric design is not encouraged, geometry, as the editors of the Library Edition point out, is a kind of "play" that is not as "bitter" as later verbal maneuverings: "Pure geometry was always a favourite study with him, and in the reduction of the elements of perspective to a series of propositions in Euclid's manner he found congenial recreation" (xv, xxxv-xxxvi).

is instead a deadly necessity—the syntax of serpentine purification. While it would be absurdly simplistic to suggest that, later, the alternating movements between Centre and Circumference are only movements between the lost central unity of a shaping, owl-eyed ("Glaukopis") mother, who perhaps able, even amid "interwoven occupation," to see in darkness the design (if not exit) of "blind lanes," would bring coherence and integration to an expanding vision, and the unimaginable integration of a post-circumferential Promise(d) Land—a land that may have been lost to be found, or only lost in order to be promised—where relativity divided to the point of excessive presence has become the absence that would replace the synoptic and where Ruskin's Rose will bloom only as a supernatural fiction, it is a point, in passing, that should nevertheless be raised.

"White clues" of fallen stone would show the way, which is a circumferential way, without itinerary or map, that is impelled by the instincts for both futurity and the exit. Being many things, the "way" of the labyrinth is like the way through not only an intestinal tract of coiling bowels, as well as travel along the birth canal, but also a way through certain patterns of thought—digestion and consciousness being indissolubly linked; it is at first perceived as a kind of solution, or cure, that is at best problematic, like Ruskin's recollection of his early run in the moonlight of the Hampton Court Maze with Adèle Domecq, who later functions as a typological figura for the (un)fulfillment of Rose La Touche,[14] with Adèle becoming more important as Ruskin's obsession with Rose increases, until it knows no boundaries—until, in fact, in spiritualistic "teachings," Rose comes from beyond the symbolical dramaturgy of the Theatre of Blindness, which is first the "unicursal" and present-tense Maze and then the interior double Maze of three dimensions that is in dialogically Antiphonal Contention. Important to begin with, Adèle becomes even more important in autobiographical retrospect. She is "re-written."

There are second thoughts about the nature of circumferential spaces. The Strange Chords of attempted mastery lead to the strange music of an eventual madness that can be no more than delayed: labyrinthine syntax predicts parataxis. Threads will be cut, if not the umbilical cord of a rebirth for a second childhood, leaving a lonely dancer, whirling blindly in a Maze, with a silence of potential meaning, in a second and submerged labyrinth, immediately below.

---

[14] It might be pointed out that Adèle was married in 1840, and that Rose died on May 26, 1875, though one could say that she "died" before and "lived" afterward.

And both parts, publicly the first part and more privately the second part, are concerned with not only concentric returns but also the significant "difference between the proper relation of the field to the city . . . which has become the principal folly and danger, alike of the citizens and countrymen in the social organization of the nineteenth century" (xxx, 156).

Despite the antiphonal impulse to return, if not "re-write" or "complete," like a potentially digressive or peregrinating commuter whose home is always where he is not, whether to the Centre of cities or the fields of the Circumference (and the urge to return is part of his strong mnemonic impulse, with memory as a kind of spiral, like the shapes of the later Transformations of the Maze), Ruskin and his shifting consciousness, as has been suggested, follow a kind of qualified sequence, which often appears to be contradictory. As the "biped" creature he will later advertise himself to be, it is as if he would be in two locations at once. And in the progressive stages of performance of the Transformation of the Maze, the initial Thesean instinct for the Exit becomes less forceful, with the later Maze taking on defensive characteristics, as if it were indeed a labyrinthine Troy that would keep the "outside" out. At the point of the Exit, between alternations and lateral hesitations, the centrifugal seems to lose some of its energy. (At times, it seems that the shaping focal point of a Ruskinian text may be organized about the vacant "pit of a theatre" [xxviii, 441] of Blindness that is of a highly idiosyncratic "negative capability," or almost paralyzed performance, with jarring, stuttering lines, perhaps improvised at the edge of incoherence, for the sake of mere perpetuation, like a juggler, with almost more than he can handle, who will lose the reason for his existence when the balls touch ground.)

Less reductively, Part One is concerned not only with the synoptic encompassment of orthodox geometries, of museum concentricity and the consequences of vacancies/absences that are either "kindly" or a kind of deadly satin with the serial, transitional middle missing, but also the rectilinearity of straight lines that can be traveled both forward and backward (which are lines that "go" economically only to "come," lines that I have concerned myself with in *The Failing Distance*,[15] especially in "The Penetration of Space" and "The Inverted Perspective"). Furthermore, Part One deals with designs, with prefigurative musical implications, of attempted mastery—an attempted mastery of Strange Chords capable of exerting considerable influence in an effort that must always fall short, despite the possibility of circularity ad infinitum or the perpetual reciprocity

---

[15] *The Failing Distance: The Autobiographical Impulse in John Ruskin* (Baltimore, 1975).

of lines that hold the embryo of second origins in their endings, as if rebirth were to be found at the gates of death.[16] Yet if mastery must always fall short, there is always the second chance—or almost always, until one runs out of drawing or writing paper, or the lines of attempted mastery are diagrammed on Atropos' tablet of the ultimate.

As an attempted mastery of inclusion, of the "wide circumference" centripetally ingested until there is nothing but a Centre that is "true" before it becomes infernally false or "mephitic," leading to "salvation" (or a kind of rebirth) through the rites of passage of either serpentine entrails or the penitent tracing of the labyrinthine *chemin de Jérusalem*, Part One is concerned with problems of an altitudinous mastery that cannot be intrinsically mastered. As a typological figura in need of creative and fruitful fulfillment (even if that final fulfillment proves, despite repletion, somewhat unfulfilling, as if that creation were somehow "stillborn"), Part One, taken autonomously, is reflexively subversive and requires complementary design and performance that is outside itself. Necessarily, the end of Part One is not closed; rather, it functions as a foundation—unlike the later, buried labyrinth of sacred crocodiles that is more problematic than firm—for the essential architecture of the book, which, in Part Two, deals extensively with Mazes both visible and invisible.[17]

Part Two, as a partial answer that is also no ending, is as labyrinthinely exclusive, or digressively "narrow-minded," as Part One, centred and altitudinous, is, or would be, inclusive. The labyrinth, beginning as a "unicursal" (or once-run) design and becoming "multicursal"[18] as it branches and doubles into the grandiose ruins

[16] Cf. Jackson Knight, *Vergil*: "On the temple gates at Cumae there was a picture of the labyrinth at Knossos, because they were near the entrance to the land of the dead, and to the City of God beyond" (p. 223).

[17] To complete the mosaic, one might say that *Ruskin's Maze*, especially Part Two, while in some obvious ways written "against" *The Failing Distance*, nevertheless, at certain points, intersects, or is contiguous with, "The Style of Consciousness: Broken Sentences" of *The Failing Distance*. What can only be touched upon in the discussion of "Broken Sentences"—"As a variation of digression, the Third Style can only be touched upon here" (101)—is amplified in Part Two of this book. It is that "touching" tangent which connects the concerns of the two books. The "Broken Sentences" of *The Failing Distance* might well be, close to the final Transformations of the Maze, Ariadne's thread broken by either double axes or the shears or nail of Atropos, leaving a Thesean Ruskin stranded in a Maze that, ironically, proves to be an architecture of defense, like a snail's shell, or a mother's uterus for a reluctant fetus who will not stretch, or make rectilinear, its umbilical cord.

[18] W. H. Matthews makes distinctions that will become important later:

We have seen that mazes and labyrinths may be roughly divided into two types as regards the principle of their design, namely, into *unicursal* and *multicursal*

of the three-dimensional Maze, is superimposed over the false presence of synoptic and (logo)-concentric geometries that have been found impossible to sustain. Part Two demonstrates an attempt to achieve temporary solution to the problems of mastery, by transforming or "anamorphically" twisting the high designs of mastery into a lower (and, in a special sense, almost pedestrian) design and syntax that is myopically curvilinear—this in an act that would exchange a transcendentally distant focal point for a focal point of eyes that are not yet "blind," at least to themselves. Achieved curvilinearity takes the form of Mazes that find themselves in a series of perpetual transformations appearing horizontally, at least initially, between the Centre and the Circumference, the city and the fields, almost as if their shifting, or progressive, functions were united in a kind of exclusively spatial mediation that is manageable, as is perhaps landscape gardening, because exterior, instead of the decomposing, verbal immediacy of the "nothing but process" (or language/consciousness in the role of the performative penultimate) that is so important to the delicate equilibrium of Ruskin's mind—his precarious sanity or sane survival, at a point just before the edge of silence and madness. The close to final Transformations of the Maze, vertical in their Antiphonal Contention rather than horizontal, are interior figurations of an antic despair beyond doubt that are based upon the faintly reassuring (and only dimly remembered) models of original exteriority.

But if Part Two would deal with attempted cure, the cure is homeopathically involved with those points of the imagination's energetic/enervated failure—points of failure along the way where an apparent vortex of presence is in fact a version of absence, like the ultimate less than nothing of Illth's excessive presence, in both miniature and in (difficult) passing. The negotiation of the labyrinth of consciousness/syntax is fraught with the pitfalls of vertiginous false presence that leaves, as we shall see, the traveler—both gracefully syntactical and stumblingly paratactical, both singly "unicursal" and equivocally "multicursal" (as well as he who would approach a Venice that is a city first of mind and then of auto-

---

types, or, as some say, into "non-puzzle" and "puzzle" types respectively. The word "unicursal" has hitherto been chiefly used by mathematicians to describe a class of problems dealing with the investigation of the shortest route between two given points or of the method of tracing a route between two points in a given figure without covering any part of the ground more or less than once (e.g., the well-known "bridge" problems), but there is no reason why we should not apply the adjective "unicursal" (= "single course" or "once run") to denote those figures which consist of a single unbranched path, using the term "multicursal" as its complement or antonym   [*Labyrinths & Mazes*, p. 184].

biography)—in a state which, "comfortless, infirm, lost in dark lan-guor and fearful silence," is at first only occasionally mad.

The "sinuousities" that at times appear "capricious" are, in fact, a life-and-death matter, as traced and retraced lines, like a cord that will become either a net or a lifeline of transition (though the threads will occasionally be "knotted"), attempt either to cover or bridge those points of failure that are vortexes of false presence. Further, the apparently frivolous is for a while a counter—and a mask—to all that is most serious. The perfect circle and "right angles" of Part One are complemented—and perhaps corrected (with Ruskin, perfection requires the correction of imperfection)— by the transforming Mazes of Part Two. And the will for farsight-edness, which is the rectilinear impulse behind "the penetration of space," is replaced by a calculated myopia before the edge of blind-ness and silence.

Those straight lines that were once useful in converging per-spective studies are now close to anathema: to see too long, or even too wide, is a problem—a problem that can be solved (temporarily, at best) by not only the narrow proximity of the present tense— and its retrospective adjunct, memory (the past seen from a cen-soring present)—but also the immediacy of exclusive space. The phenomenological experience from within the Maze (now less The-sean in its function than before) offers a sense of not only Gate, or Exit, more problematically efficacious than before, but also lines and language of turn and returning (upon themselves) which, impeding that Exit, make it only a subjunctive possibility—a "stern final purpose" that need not reach the ultimacy of Illth or White Silence beyond, where the post-circumferential new beginning is the maturation of madness, if not "the entrance to the land of the dead, and to the City of God beyond."

Still, in both the Maze and the blind theatre of occasionally "bitter play," of antiphonal response, which may, in one of its manifes-tations, be part silence and part dance, there is the spectre of Dae-dalus, and the Daedalean problem of his Maze, whose architecture is, in fact, like a theatre without a discernible fire-exit—a problem that calls for a solution that is itself a kind of exhibitionistic dance: one might say that the problem symbiotically calls for a solution, which is to say that the solution or attempted solution of even the decomposing language of the Labyrinthine Penultimate, with the hypothetical validation of its own aesthetics in question, almost seems, ultimately, to require a reason/problem in order to perpet-uate its own tenuous existence that is blind to itself, as madness must be; one might further say that a double bind has become the labyrinth's "double-blind" which, in a final twist, has achieved the mutual advantage of a kind of reciprocated double vision that will indeed see interior labyrinths in three dimensions. In any event, the Daedalean problem, with a solution that is at least partially Thesean, may be found in an ironic location "between," where the orthodox geometries of, say, the Middleman exist as problems that can themselves be solved by nothing less than his actual disappearance, and not merely his invisibility. The solution may not be found on the outside, where Theseus will discover, after his serpentine rites of passage, a new life, and where Ariadne will dance on her Daedalean-built *Choros*, but in the "process" within, as if that end beyond the Exit and its problematically implicit futurity, desired before the performance of the Maze had been transformed, were no solution at all—though what, as tenses and actuality arrange themselves, *will* come immediately before, in the doubleness of the Labyrinthine Penultimate, *were* the at least temporary solution of a kind of vertiginous defense, like the encircled or spiraling "shut" city of Troy,[19] or a spider's web inverted in function to prevent entrance.

If the present, with its reciprocity of problems and solutions, is most significantly present, what is immediately "before" ultimacy is more densely present (possibly immanent) than either a censored past or a dubious future. And the Daedalean problem-making, which, in the early stages of the Transformations of the Maze, becomes Theseus' problem before it becomes his solution, is, as has been suggested, translated into a performative act that may be even more salutary than the post-labyrinthine open spaces of the "field" for the Ruskinian claustrophobe (even though, when the curtain goes down, there are only those most temporary cosmetics of greasepaint and the echoes of applause dying toward White Silence). In any case, in much of the antiphonally solipsistic Ruskin, with his shaping double labyrinth of consciousness, there is "contention," whether naked or clothed. And just as Ariadne speaks of the "fields" beyond the Gates, so Atropos, with her shears (as well as writing tablet, on which a last page may be written or left ominously empty), which represent the process-as-threat of immediacy, of chance, signifies the vicissitudes of a present tense that may not greet the future. But in the case of either one of Ruskin's "guides," the reader (or theatregoer) is not entirely certain who or what lies

[19] Cf. W. Jackson Knight, *Vergil*: "Troy, like other places that had the name, was rather shut than shutting; and it was in all probability so called because it was at some time thought to be shut by magical power" (p. 230).

beyond the next curve (or page/curtain). If the spiral is, in some way, predictable, the empathetic reader is "blind" to what lies beyond a heterodox, anamorphic spiraling—the curvilinearity, say, of a Maze of eccentric geometries, which is perhaps informed more by the fateful immediacy of Atropos than the serial predictability (which is the predictability of surprise) of Ariadne, whose "weaving" would domesticate the necessary dangers (and initial problems) of the Daedalean labyrinth, by offering a thread-as-map. Ariadne's is, of course, the easy way out, if it is, in fact, the "outside" one finally wants.

At its most fundamental, it might be suggested that Ruskin's reason for being (as opposed to his inability to write or "live" a blank page) is the "nothing but process" of attempted Thesean solution that has been brought about both by the quintessential problem of the Daedalean Maze and the altitudinous perception of rectilinearity. Combining height with "right-angles," that problem of essential (logo)-concentricity implies a perfection and perfectibility (in a Ruskinian tense of dubious futurity) that Ruskin, who would have his "majesty shattered" (his perfection imperfect), would go to lengths to avoid. But then the ingenious Daedalus, capable of getting even himself in trouble, is also capable of bypassing trouble—or better, rising above it. His wings are more functional than those of peacocks, who cry against both the twilight (of Ruskin's sanity) and the labyrinths of inner ears that, too sensitive, are perhaps not defensively deaf, or "shut," enough.

At first, in the early stages of the Transformation of the Maze, it is as if the Centre must be merely serialized, the lines composed as either St. Paul's street "which is called Straight," or made as laterally extensive as horizontal perception. Later, both the Centre and a variety of straight lines that go along with orthodox geometries give way to serial curvature. And afterward, the serial curvature itself gives way to both the imminence of the shears, and then, penultimately, before the Exit/End of a "nothing" that is probably not so much the claustrophobe's escape or resurrection/ redemption as it is that psychically "stillborn" location without "process" or performance, to a location and condition of dreaded inactivity (as if a solitary dancer had pirouetted too long, only to collapse of vertiginous exhaustion), as well as the White Silence of "fulfilled" madness, which is a kind of demonic plenitude whose precarious condition is one of excessive presence in the act of becoming the absence of Illth.

A circumferential "play," often "bitter," of existence, of performative design, dance, and gesture, Ruskin's dramaturgy, which is internalized allegory, is acted with a supporting cast of *Dramatis Personae* that also includes a bestiary of the antithetical creatures of the air and ground, who help Ruskin stage the intricate and interior theatre of his consciousness. The cast emerges, especially in Part Two, after the attempts at mastery have given way to the adoption of a series of "guides," who may occupy a True Centre that Ruskin cannot himself inhabit for long. There is not only St. George (who will become the incarnation of a guiding society) and Athena, a Queen of the Air as well as the Earth, whose "shaping" and "spinning" guidance, transcending Arachne, is as close to Ruskin's heart as either a mother, or Morgiana's pirouettes, but also (and more to our immediate, if not final, purpose) there are both Ariadne, with her thread of "Florentine" navigation that is like a compass within a landscape of condensed curvilinearity, and Atropos, a third fate and Ruskin's Third Fors, who represents the myopic immediacy of chance that, as an itinerary which may never be traveled, can, by its very shortsightedness, render the distant prophecy of terrifying rectilinearity, implicit in the straight line, merely a "blinding" possibility, instead of the disconfirmation of post-Circumferential death and (un)-Redemption.

Involved in the various stages of the Transformations of the Maze, Ruskin himself (as well as his reader) is, if *not* Theseus, at least Thesean—especially in the beginning. Certainly, he is not Daedalus, though, as has been suggested, the instigative part of Daedalus in the problem, which stimulates further inescapable problems and contradictions, is a necessity that is both evil and good. In any case, as a more than occasional Theseus, Ruskin would, it seems, find himself ever more in a labyrinth of hesitation, as if he might double back before the labyrinth itself doubles (whether he would at, say, a middle period of the Transformations of the Maze, search more aggressively for the presumably fortunate Exit, with the guidance of Ariadne, is perhaps another matter). Still, almost always, there is at least a sense of the Exit—the Exit, presumably, at the end of Ariadne's thread, where there may be the more plural, Thesean dance of triumph, which, in turn, may be the triumph of life, or rebirth. And yet, increasingly at times, it would appear that Ruskin can endure neither the intensified awareness of the straight-lined "long shadow" of death nor the inclusive and panoramic "wide circumference" of explicit madness that lies beyond the Transformations of the Maze. Even a claustrophobic Ruskin may feel, in portions that are almost equal, Repletion and (less than) Nothing as both opposed and reciprocal problems—and all this, as we shall see, with the rectilinear Maze of "Greek fret" as part of a Daedalean problem of an unmediated "between" that anticipates Theseus' curvilinear Maze of almost blind negotiation.

Compounding themselves, problems engender a fight for solution that is a labyrinthine process of the performative penultimate fight for survival—a fight strangely like the peacock's "cry against the twilight," which may be both the vocal equivalent of the fight against the silence and blankness of an empty page, as well as a "cry" in perversely harmonious support of that page. The theatre, which will become a Theatre of Blindness, as if for the "blind march" within a labyrinth, is also a battlefield; shockingly, stage blood is, after all, real. But characteristically, categories are intermixed. Analogies multiply. Yet the solution as temporary survival may not, "finally," be found on those "fields" "outside" that might, in another lifetime, be like postnatal spaces, but rather in the penultimate "within," as if the end "outside," beyond the Exit, were something to be aspired toward, though not found—a goal to be set (if unseen), yet not, in any case, attained. Atropos' shears are as imminent as Ariadne's thread, or even the hypothetical umbilical cord for someone awaiting birth for the second time. But what is to be severed—and where—is now only problematical, though eventually of utmost importance.

Yet we must turn, or return, explicitly to language and consciousness, perhaps the *Helix virgata* language/consciousness of "return," and the Laws of (heterodox) Curvature that are informed both by shells and the "Design of Florentine Schools" of *Ariadne Florentina*—this, and a tentative aesthetics that might be culled from an antiphon that is also a morality play-as-theatre of design, gesture, and dance as it finds the appropriate syntax and voices (perhaps as stuttering as antiphonal) before the blank page of madness (or the null-set of nonexistence). And it is a blank page that would be, itself, something like a missing final act which has perhaps been dreamed, but neither written nor performed—an unacted act. The aesthetics, admittedly problematic, will be those we will come to know as the aesthetics of the (decomposing) Labyrinthine Penultimate.

Often, especially early and in the middle, one finds Ruskin absolutely sane and masterful—and in the unified vision of his masterful sanity he is, as has been indicated, perhaps more influential than any other prophet in the nineteenth century. But the extraordinarily ambitious sanity of that (logo)-concentrically encompassing vision leads to the terrifying perception of Strange Chords and raw nerves that produce, in Harold Bloom's sense, their own anxiety:

it is as though Ruskin's texts provide not only an external influence but an internal one as well, with a later self in cacophonously antiphonal combat with an earlier self, as well as multiple selves in simultaneous combat with each other—a war of multiple selves that will end in the disintegrating "selves-defeat" of madness that is, at this point of impending failure, close to inevitable.

Still, the language of that meandering, returning-upon-itself "process" toward madness has about it what Foucault calls the "lyric glow of illness." And it is the connection between the pastoral, mnemonic light of the Lucent Verdure of the Hampton Court Maze and that "lyric glow" which may well produce the heat of the yet equivocal aesthetics of the Labyrinthine Penultimate. It is a condition of heat (and light), approaching what convention would take for incoherence, that, without principles of organization, should neither be apologized for (as it has been) nor ignored. With Ruskin, there is a terrible beauty at the edge, where the embers of a truth, no less terrible, smolder with an enduring immediacy.

But the penultimate condition before collapse that is reflected in the paratactical, almost stuttering, "ruins" of an exhausted language, in which the connections of a tenuously associative logic are either severed, as if by Atroposian shears (Atropos, whose tablet is either ominously filled or more ominously vacant), or, if not severed, then buried, like a labyrinth of crocodiles who are sacred before, excavated, they are profane—that penultimate condition is one which takes language to the edge of anguish, where earned tears may eventually freeze: located there, unable to go further without the performative penultimate's becoming a disappearing act or final curtain without encore or even applause, this language is, it might be argued, one of stunning pathos, reflecting the crumbling architectonics of an uncontrolled consciousness that is capable of affecting the reader in a way which the initially rigid structures of an orthodox language (or its geometrically [logo]-concentric equivalent) cannot, nor can the later, serial, even curvilinear language given flexible shape, say, by Ariadne. Penultimately, the tenuously sinuous logic of the labyrinth that has always suggested the urgency, albeit at times qualified, of the Exit, even before the imminence of the "shears of parataxis," is close, as second thoughts predict double labyrinths, to a coherence that cannot, either tragically or fortunately, last for long.

The Strange Chords are temporarily rescued by the experience of the recollection of the experience within the Lucent Verdure of the Hampton Court Maze. Those Strange Chords of incongruously orthodox geometries are made almost familiar by the twisted and myopic designs shaped by the recollection of Lucent Verdure's curvilinearity. But even the rescuing lines of return—or labyrinthine "cords" that are both umbilical and of overworked nerves that attempt an impossible mastery—themselves return, in the penultimate condition before the minus set of the blank page, to the Strange Chords that, no longer chords of merely spatial inclusion, are a kind of "marred music." And the antiphon between the blind, paratactical "remains" of the syntax of Lucent Verdure above and the unexcavated silence, perhaps punctuated by an occasional crocodilian rumble below, is, in fact, an antiphon of music that would be as spatial, though interior, as it is aural. It is music for the "touch" of a blind man, perhaps even music for the performance of a blind, solitary dancer, whose "partner" is either lost or held tightly only in a dear recollection that may be a mnemonic fiction—the clutches of the tentative, whose grasp on the available is necessarily tight.[20] The peacocks "cry against the twilight"; the lonely crane dances, as if lost in a labyrinth it never meant to enter, searching for a mate just beyond the edge of remembrance.

With *The Failing Distance* largely about optics, their exterior efficacy that permits the penetration of space, at least before the pseudoscopic inversion that comes with the nineteenth-century Storm Cloud, *Ruskin's Maze*, organized about the internalization of exterior or excavated structures that disintegrate in spatialized interiority, is essentially about the Antiphonal Contention that takes place between not only the Centre of origins/mastery and the Circumference of ultimacy/madness, which is also the "naked contention" of a morality play, but also Blindness "above"[21]—whether sought for gastronomic comfort in labyrinthine intestines and the related comfort of consciousness for " 'blind mouths,' " or found, perhaps even calculated, by Lachesis, as concluding madness becomes close to fated—and the Silence "below." And the Silence "below" may be said to predict the White Silence beyond. If the

---

[20] With Ruskin, it is true, there is "contention" between sightless listeners and those who are blind to neither others nor themselves, and whose sight, more than either the spoken or sung word, presumably provokes actions. Theoretically, Milton's (and Ruskin's) " 'blind mouths' " should evoke more than song—or, for that matter, more than gastronomic lust. For, if not close to the end of Ruskin's "completed" work, at least close to the end of the influential *Unto This Last*, it is only the most inse⸍ ⸍ive man who "could sit at his feast, unless he sat blindfold" (xvii, 114).

[21] Still the dominating Athena, as if centrally integrated, is different—or both efficaciously "above," and, at ground level, "below," where beneficent snakes enact purification rites. And shaping, as we shall come to understand, she is far from blind: "In her prudence, or sight in darkness, she is 'Glaukopis', owl-eyed" (xix, 306).

final Ruskinian text of *The Failing Distance*, with things binding and blending, as though in a happily consummated marriage (there is, after all, in that concluding autobiographical text which also ends *Praeterita*, mention of the painting of the "Marriage in Cana"), is ecstatic, the equivalent final text of *Ruskin's Maze*, which is as solitary and unbinding as was Ruskin's brief marriage, is as infernal (or "unbishoply") as it is oddly, perhaps feverishly, ecstatic—the ecstatically centrifuged pathos of one beyond any dispute (though "naked contention" awaits beyond the final page) but the hypothetical "dialogue" with sacredly buried crocodiles, whose home—in fact, Ruskin's version of his own domestic snail shell[22]—is the appropriately spiraling labyrinth for over-sized serpents, who have become grandiose in their "fallen" condition. *The Failing Distance*'s "sight" is *Ruskin's Maze*'s "blindness"; *The Failing Distance*'s final ecstatic integration, approaching, but not consumed by, the vorticality of its vision, is the ecstatically anguished, fragmented ruins of *Ruskin's Maze*.

At the place of the cutting thread, the locus of double axes that will cut not only cords—Ariadne's thread to the "outside" (a version, perhaps, of Ruskin's connection with the postcircumferential Promise[d] Land of, among other things, Rose), where both centrifugal disintegration and disconfirmation will occur, more readily than the centrally posterior navel thread of reluctant rebirth—but also the cords of consciousness, there is the Theatre of Blindness of vertical Antiphonal Contention, which is a kind of "choral space" for an "inner language" without the conventional harmonies of a univocal synthesis. Among other things, it is an orchestrated space that is as atonal as it is, finally, alogical, and it is the result of the unmediated relation of the blind language of parataxis "above" and the remaining silence—as of final "remaining places"—of a forever latent completion "below."

Beyond that syntactical architecture of consciousness there are those ultimately vacant, circumferential "fields" of blind silence that are "after" Repletion, where even peacocks do not cry against the twilight, and the solitary crane does not attempt his postlabyrinthine dance in a failing half-light. Nothing, having come close to Every-

---

[22] The snail shell as home, with its anamorphic spirals, is an architectural version of the defensive Nest of retreat that he will return to, especially in Part Two, in a variety of ways: "The lectures are coming nice; though they're giving me sad trouble—and, in fact, I oughtn't be teased to talk about any more at my time in life, but should be left to paint snail-shells—and live in a big one . . ." (xxxvii, 4). Almost finally, it is as if a snail shell were of a uterine involution that may be an indefinite "remaining place."

thing, will become less than Nothing, like an empty snail shell (or language) of turn and return, in which present absence—perhaps Rose's, or the innocence she signifies—is intensified by former presence.

But before that, in the final Transformation of the Maze, which is more vertical, as of double-tiered labyrinths, than lateral, as with the choreographic plane of a pirouetting syntax—immediately before that paratactical disintegration reflecting interior figurations of antic despair—there is, like an antepenultimate place of temporary "remaining," perhaps like the "mental container" of Troy itself, the defensive labyrinth of the Inside, with Ruskin apparently attached to at least one cord he would not have severed: a cord, hardly Strange, of reflexive familiarity that would join him to the maternally shaping "Athena of the Dew"/"Athena of the Earth,"[23] who has also become a Centre of genesis that will only reluctantly allow the impulse of the centrifugal—those movements toward the Circumference where the "shattered majesty" of (textual) ruins, cast in the double half-lights of Lucent Verdure in moonlight and

[23] Athena, the "Queen of the Air," is many things other than a maternal principle, ranging from bird to serpent, in Ruskin's symphonic exploration of what might be called "a study of the Greek myths of cloud and storm" (XIX, 284). In any case, the part played by Ruskin's mother, Margaret, in shaping his life, need not be gone into here. The biographers have done their part. But *The Ruskin Family Letters*, vols. I, II, edited by Van Akin Burd (Ithaca, 1973), provide a necessary corrective to the precise nature of that "shaping." Probably, Athena and Margaret Ruskin are, among other things, reciprocally symbolical. With an early training in Evangelical typology, Ruskin, "doubly-minded" (XIX, 347) as of double labyrinths, often working antiphonally, even apparently contradictorily (though the contradictions may not be as Hegelian as they seem), rarely functions through mutual exclusion, even in the serial Transformations of the Maze. And the "naked contention" we shall come to know is perhaps not even mutually exclusive to a mind that will attempt to maintain the mastery of conceptual, as well as visual, simultaneity, for as long as "synoptically" possible. J. Hillis Miller has observed Ruskin's linguistic concentration of multiplicity in a "single entity" in general, and in Athena in particular—a concentration that prompts, finally, "aesthetic branchings from the central myth of Athena in *The Queen of the Air*." There is

> a recognition of the potentially endless branchings of metaphorical resemblances among these facts as represented. This leads to the insight that what he calls in *The Queen of the Air* the "living hieroglyphs" of nature and art are each a node in that network, a concentration or sublimation of multiple fact in a single entity. The final discovery toward which all his work moves is the recognition that the most comprehensive hieroglyphs are precisely the great mythological figures of Western literature, Biblical and Hellenic. The exuberantly fantastic exploration of the natural, moral, and aesthetic branchings from the central myth of Athena in *The Queen of the Air* is the most elaborate of such investigations [J. Hillis Miller, "Myth as 'Hieroglyph' in Ruskin," *Studies in the Literary Imagination* 8 (Fall, 1975): 17].

the "lyric glow of illness," lie, as though along a labyrinthine interface, before the excessive presence-become-absence of Illth, with Blind Guides pointing the way toward White Silence and the terrible solitude of multiple selves who have achieved a madness that, beyond process or travel, may manage to transcend itself in a blind "celestial light" turned infernal and no less blind in that "dazzlement" which is "night in broad daylight."

Part One

Strange Chords:
Masterful Geometries

DOMINATION OF BLACK

At night, by the fire,
The colors of the bushes
And of the fallen leaves,
Repeating themselves,
Turned in the room,
Like the leaves themselves
Turning in the wind.

Yes: but the color of the heavy hemlocks
Came striding.
And I remembered the cry of the peacocks.

The colors of their tails
Were like the leaves themselves
Turning in the wind,
In the twilight wind.
They swept over the room,
Just as they flew from the boughs of the hemlocks
Down to the ground.
I heard them cry—the peacocks.
Was it a cry against the twilight
Or against the leaves themselves
Turning in the wind,
Turning as the flames
Turned in the fire,
Turning as the tails of the peacocks
Turned in the loud fire,
Loud as the hemlocks
Full of the cry of the peacocks?
Or was it a cry against the hemlocks?

Out of the window,
I saw how the planets gathered
Like the leaves themselves
Turning in the wind.
I saw how the night came,
Came striding like the color of the heavy hemlocks.
I felt afraid.
And I remembered the cry of the peacocks.

—Wallace Stevens

Introduction

A Travel Diary toward Nothing but a Dream:
Shadowy Types for Concluding Images and
"The Excavations of Silence"

Item: the recollection of naked feet (*"Rose*mary, that's for remembrance")—"you barefoot Scotch lassies"—faultless feet, almost perfect to a pedestrian fault, with the hope, perhaps, of "no more wandering of the feet in the labyrinth like this, and the eyes, once cruelly tearless, now blind with frozen tears," both feet and caps recollected, and the caps with plumes swaying in the dark wind, three ostrich feathers, like a Thesean crest, swaying madly in the winds of confusion, while, at the same time, speaking masterfully of order and rule. One considers those "charred meanings," their still glowing significations.

And the quarreling, *that* quarreling among the "Alpine Roses"— you naughty dear—which was perhaps healed in the moonlight ("Send for the Lady to the Sagitarry," and tell her to bring her handkerchief)—the fact of that quarreling among the "Alpine Roses," the later moonlight, as if off water, and all the time Keats, like Cupid's shaft of fire, "quenched in the chaste beams," with Blake—"you stupid thing"—quite mad, though his plough, yes, his plough, adorned with "Gold and Gems," as if seeking nothing less than the arts of peace.

The key is missing and the moon, in recollection, is watery, but who can see—backward. *Rose*mary? Or Fair Rosamond in her mazy Bower?

> *Hic jacet in tumba Rosa mundi, non Rosa munda;*
> *Non redolet, sed olet, quae redolere solet.*

Certainly not failed guides, with their eyes perhaps "blind with frozen tears,"[1] whose blindness, in its incipient madness, may even

---

[1] The blindness that is so important to one concerned with what Ruskin erotically calls "the desire of the eyes" is observed in its relation to madness by Michel Foucault, *Madness and Civilization: A History of Insanity in the Age of Reason,* translated by Richard Howard (New York, 1965), p. 106:

> *Blindness:* one of the words which comes closest to the essence of classical madness. It refers to that night of quasi-sleep which surrounds the images of madness, giving them, in their solitude, an invisible sovereignty; but it refers also to ill-founded beliefs, mistaken judgments, to that whole background of error inseparable from madness. The fundamental discourse of delirium, in its con-

be blind to itself[2]—though the angels of the lagoon, surely *they* can see (as well as the postcircumferential—or posttextual—Angel of the Sea, swimming toward "floating gardens" or "Playgrounds" of the Edenic Promise[d] Land)—surely, like sea-dragons, *they* can see, as they pray for Venice in the Rialto where prayer is most needed

---

stitutive powers, thus reveals to what extent, despite analogies of form, despite the rigor of its meaning, it was not a discourse of reason. It spoke, but in the night of blindness; it was more than the loose and disordered text of a dream, since it *deceived* itself; but it was more than an erroneous proposition, since it was plunged into that total *obscurity* which is that of sleep. Delirium, as the principle of madness, is a system of false propositions in the general syntax of the dream.

Reading aspects of Ruskin covered in this book, one reads, as analogous architecture of the mind, the almost participatory descriptions of Foucault, as he appears in three French editions. The English translation is from an abridged edition. When reference to appended texts beyond abridgement are appropriate—again as sympathetic analogues to Ruskin's own condition—those editions will be noted.

[2] It is not too much to say that, for a while, Ruskin's sanity *is* his sight, and it would be difficult to think of anyone more obsessed with discerning vision than Ruskin, for whom, rather aphoristically, "To see clearly is poetry, prophecy, and religion,—all in one" (v, 333). The right kind of sight—clear-sightedness—is the awakening from a condition of blindness: "The whole technical power of painting depends on our revery of what may be called the *innocence of the eye*; that is to say, of a sort of childish perception of these flat stains of colour, merely as such, without consciousness of what they signify,—as a blind man would see them if suddenly gifted with sight" (xv, 27, note). For a discussion of the blind man in literature, see Kenneth Maclean, *John Locke and English Literature of the Eighteenth Century* (New Haven, 1936), pp. 106ff. But blindness, or a certain kind of blindness, is for Ruskin sanity's opposite. For general application, with specific significance, see Shoshana Felman's intriguing and important "Madness and Philosophy *or* Literature's Reasons," *Yale French Studies*, no. 52, edited by Marie-Rose Logan (1975), p. 206: "What characterizes madness is thus not simply blindness, but a blindness blind to itself, to the point of necessarily entailing an illusion of reason."

Ruskin's "blindness *blind to itself*" is the deception of the imagination, which is also a point of failure that is like following the branching nodal point of a labyrinth to a "blind end," that is the imaginative deception that leads to madness:

For it might be thought that the whole kingdom of imagination was one of deception also. Not so: the action of the imagination is a voluntary summoning of the conceptions of things absent or impossible; and the pleasure and nobility of the imagination partly consist in its knowledge and contemplation of them as such, *i.e.*, in the knowledge of their actual absence or impossibility at the moment of their apparent presence or reality. When the imagination deceives, it becomes madness. It is a noble faculty so long as it confesses its own ideality; when it ceases to confess this, it is insanity. All the difference lies in the fact of this confession, in there being *no* deception   [VIII, p. 58].

Ruskin would distinguish between absence and a false presence that becomes a version of maddening repletion. Put differently, Foucault will say: "madness is always absent, in a perpetual retreat where it is inaccessible, without phenomenal

(Send for the Lady, with the sprig of "sacred vervain," to the Sagitarry so that agreement can be reached rather than foul reports received—agreement as if in moonlight and among mountainous roses).

Now, with no vestige of dawn, the dawns are always dark; the eye of day is gone. "Blind, Blind, Blind, for ever." But St. Paul's eyes were opened out of the darkness of "utter mistake" on the "street which is called Straight." Yet the path is curved, though Laura's sinuous origins have fallen into disrepute.

St. Mark's horses may drown in the lagoon, as St. George's chaste bird flutters above in appropriately chaste beams, but clever Tintoret will paint them in an earthly paradise. And what is the shape of the dear doge's cap, and how large is his not entirely perfect foot?

There are no doubts about the plumes of Theseus—or how his hair is cut—and his perfect
  Naked foot
That shines like snow—and falls on earth—
or gold—as mute,
a faultless foot that will carry him, as if with white clues or celestial guides. And with naked, faultless feet he will saunter!

But it is too late now (or perhaps it is not so much too late as it is too late to stop)—¼ to one—and this lateness is just the beginning of a new kind of whiteness, a new kind of nothing.

Item: on the night of February 22, 1878—perhaps even then with the screeching of peacocks sounding in his ears, a screeching that would later signal demonic triumph, the victory of the "Evil One"—

---

or positive character; and yet it is present and perfectly visible in the singular evidence of the madness" (*Madness and Civilization*, p. 107). One might say that Ruskin's Travelogue toward Nothing is directed toward what Jacques Derrida calls the "eastern edge of absence," which, spiraling back, is close to Ruskin's concept of "Illth" that we will come upon, after much hesitation, in the conclusion of a postpenultimacy that is also postcircumferential. Here is Derrida, "Form and Signification," *Writing and Difference*, translated and edited by Alan Bass (Chicago, 1978), p. 8:

> This universe articulates only that which is in excess of everything, the essential nothing on whose basis everything can appear and be produced within language and the voice of Maurice Blanchot reminds us, with the *insistence* of profundity, that this excess is the very possibility of writing and of literary *inspiration* in general. Only *pure absence*—not the absence of this or that, but the absence of everything in which all presence is announced—can *inspire*, in other words, can *work*, and then make work. The pure book naturally turns towards the eastern edge of absence which, beyond or within the prodigiousness of all wealth, is its first and proper content. . . . It is the consciousness of nothing, upon which all consciousness of something enriches itself, takes on meaning and shape.

Ruskin, whose modified persona of Theseus without an Exit that is more than "nothing" had only shortly before, on the seventeenth, come close to being a mad Hamlet who loved his Ophelia more than "forty thousand brothers," paced cold floors (the night was bitter even for February), marching in a "condition" that was naked (shortly before, of course, close to a quarter to one, he had praised a naked foot, shining like snow), his clothes discarded with a conviction uncomplicated by full possession of his faculties. Naked, but concerned with both cap and a "Naked foot," he waited on that cold night for a conflict he knew must come. And waiting, he marched, perhaps on a "blind march," the entire night (though, years earlier, he had preferred sauntering, as if exploring Rome, and, in the process, "yielding to every impulse," as if preparing for a convenient syntax, a style of serial survival that might give way to a happy exit and the "farthest extremity" of an entirely hypothetical/problematic topography). In a "state of great agitation, entirely resolute as to the approaching struggle," he moved about his cold room, "growing every moment into a state of greater and greater exaltation." He was waiting for the Devil whose cry of victory would later sound in the voices of fowls, the screeching of peacocks,[3] as though the eyes in those fanning tails—eyes that he knew were the absolute essence of the peacock (IX, 288)—had seen what he would have his own essential, if no longer innocent, eyes avoid; perhaps, in the cold, his tears would now freeze in blindness. Yet because of the incipient "contention," he needed his vision, he needed to see the Evil.

He waited from sometime after a quarter to one until a gray dawn broke, after seven, when he walked to the window. Gesturing toward the weak light, he saw a large black cat spring from behind

---

[3] If not the silence of the end, the sounds of the peacocks are nevertheless beyond words:

> During my first illness of wild delirium—for I have had several such attacks, but the first was by far the worst—the voice of the fowls was an inexpressible terror to me. Ridiculous as it may seem, my madness took the form of my ever being in conflict, more or less personal, with the Evil One. I had at that time an old peacock who was good for nothing—and bad for very much; for at that season of the year the weather was abominable, and he was for ever foretelling rain with his ugly, croaking voice. I was lying ill upstairs, and so quickly flew my thoughts . . . that every time he croaked I thought I was in a farmyard and that I was impelled by the tyrant Devil to do some fearful wrong, which I strove with all my might and main to resist. But my passionate efforts were of no avail; and every time I did the wrong I heard the voice of the Demon—that is, the peacock—give forth a loud croak of triumph. And it was more terrible than words can express   [XXXVIII, 172].

a mirror that might have been the dark mirror of his own double consciousness's double blindness. His waiting was over, the vigil ended. Darting toward the cat, he grabbed it with both hands, holding it with all the strength that was left after the cold night of entirely resolute, if "blind," marching, and threw it to the floor. The cat did not move. The struggle had been resolved. Swaying over the dead cat, he understood that he had triumphed. The peacocks would scream with a different kind of triumph, as though perversely applauding Ruskin's own private failures, while sacred crocodiles, from subterranean labyrinths, would perhaps issue a muffled response of antiphonal ambiguity. As he swayed in naked victory, the black cat—flung against the cold floor with "might and main"—was defeated in the "dull thud, nothing more" of its death. And finally, "worn out with bodily fatigue, with walking and waiting and watching," his "mind racked with ecstasy and anguish," his "body benumbed with the bitter cold of a freezing February night," he collapsed upon the bed, which had not been slept in during the night of awaited contention, and he was found in the morning entirely "bereft" of his senses (xxxviii, 172)—an authentically mad Hamlet, who, in shifting allusions and tones, had only shortly before scolded Blake in that final diary entry before the White Silence of "nothing" (or less than "nothing"):

> And when Gold and Gems adorn the plough!
> Oh—you dear Blake—and so mad too—
> Do you know what Titians good for *now* you
> stupid thing?

Diary entries record the centrifugal trip to the Edge of the twenty-second of February, to the Edge or "Cumaean Gate" and the blank page beyond—a blank, perhaps blind or blinding in its "dazzlement" that is "night in broad daylight," page of White Silence that, compelling and horrifying, as well as absent in its presence, is another version (in fact, an inversion) of the "magnificent blank" (xxxvii, 38) Ruskin had noted as potential that might be employed to his own advantage. The recorded trip to the Edge of the twenty-second (beyond which there is no rational performance, perhaps no immediate performance at all, though there is the Dream) is the centrifugally quintessential Travel Diary through a syntactical topography of consciousness toward the less than "nothing" of White Silence's excessive presence, which is the verbal equivalent of the movements we shall come to know as the breathless and vertiginous experience within a Maze that is both perpetually transforming itself, even as the serial (and submerged) logic begins to break up—movements that, in those last entries, shift from Ophelia, who is obsessively Rose-like (without Mary), to Laertes transformed from a brother into a Bishop, whose " 'unbishoply' " fingers are at the diarist's throat, to, shortly later, Edward Burne-Jones, a "Black Prince," who is concerned with a cap "plumed with three ostrich feathers,"[4] like the crest of Theseus, whom Ruskin, metamorphosizing identities even as Mazes are transformed, will himself almost become.

Item: Eight years later, he writes to a friend: "Isn't that a nice amusing categorical, catalogueical, catechismic, catcataceous plan" (xxxvii, 566). And one year before the vigil (that contention which ends in a failure punctuated by triumphant screeching), it occurs to him while writing the same correspondent, Susan Beever, that he would rather "purr" his letter than write it—at least for a "cat-cataceous" moment: "St. Theodore's horse is delightful—and our Venetian doggie—and some birds are coming too! This is not a letter—but just a purr" (xxxvii, 218). Yet this is hardly surprising. Not only does he possess a "cat's eye in the dark" (xxxvii, 224), as he may also possess the eye of a bull, but, loving to tease, as well as observe, he is "wholly cattish" (xxxvii, 234). Finally, writing Susan Beever he signs himself simply and perhaps reasonably, "Cat."[5]

Furthermore, one year before that "Good Friday" of the twenty-second of February, Ruskin considers the fitness of flying from an examination of Psalters to the company of both Susan Beever and peacocks—neither of whom presumably, at this point, is prepared to predict anniversary silence: "The feathers nearly made me fly away from all my Psalters and Exoduses, to you and my dear pea-cocks" (xxxvii, 224). Yet if he cannot fly, he can nevertheless send his regards to a creature that later amplifies infernal performance: "My grateful compliments to the peacock" (xxxvii, 231). At the least, the cast of characters is versatile, if not vertiginous; their performances are as self-divided as Ruskin's own: beneficence and maleficence are separated only by a serpentine interface that may be a moebius strip of what will finally emerge, reluctantly, as a kind

---

[4] See *The Brantwood Diary of John Ruskin*, edited and annotated by Helen Gill Viljoen (New Haven and London, 1971), p. 122. References to the diary will appear in parentheses as *Brantwood Diary*, followed by page number. Mrs. Viljoen's annotations are invaluable.

[5] See R. H. Wilenski, *John Ruskin: An Introduction to Further Study of His Life and Work* (London, 1933), p. 146.

of "inner language." The "Evil One," unlike Poe's one-eyed black cat that *is* the demonic self that it *sees*, is of no certain "categorical" category, beginning or demise. The vantage point aspires toward the affiliation with a focal point (at least before the focal point "returns" the reflection of an eye of evil) that possesses, initially, before mirrors, a fond, perhaps nostalgic, memory of original peace. Yet seeing anticipates unpredictable activity, even a reversed or inverted activity, given the shapelessness of a blank page of "nothing" by forces that may be, among other things, devilish.

Sometimes a letter writer who is a cat and sometimes a letter writer whose enthusiasm for peacocks seems other than feline and less than sinister, Ruskin, beyond the categories of bestiaries, also signs himself *Master*—and with considerable justice. Historically, he was, after all, a sage, a prophet, and a moralist: a man most emphatically to be reckoned with—mostly on his own terms. Occasionally, he was a man who wrote books while asking questions that were ultimately directed toward his most demanding audience, that single audience of the self in search of the master of answered questions[6] Yet he was also a man who, when addressing others, made pronouncements unqualified by even the slightest tone that would admit either interrogation or qualification. And in both the interrogations leading toward tentative solution and those pronouncements gone authoritatively public, he was a wise man, a good man—a sane, if energetically dogmatic, man.

But wrestling with, rather than interrogating, aspects of a self that could use questions to detonate explosive energy instead of forcing that energy toward impacted contention—those "categorical, catalogueical, catechismic, catcatacious" aspects apparent in the fifty-ninth year of his life—Ruskin was quite mad. It is likely he had experienced the "strange intellectual chords" of almost impossible mastery that Turner, as we shall see, both perceived and conceived—Strange Chords/Cords of dazzling interrelation whose comprehension necessarily requires the almost angelic (those farsighted "angels of the lagoon") altitude of a difficult-to-maintain mastery and whose effects, depending upon the condition and power of an observer who may also be a composer, can be either paradisiacal or infernal. Still, he signed himself, called himself "Master." It was something he insisted upon, that sense of mastery. Contention would be wistfully directed towards the moral control

---

[6] See *Deucalion* (xxvi) and *Proserpina* (xxv) for what amounts to a syntax of interrogation and process, a syntax without distance or control—a syntax of almost autonomous immediacy.

of battling skies: "At the moment, whistling wind, calm luminous sky and black Devil cloud all contending for mastery."[7] Frequently, the control was in nomenclature only. During the illness of 1881, at Brantwood, he rushed at his cousin, Joan Severn, "shouting, 'I will be Master in my own house'! to which I [Joan Severn] answered 'If you are incapable of being master—I *must* be mistress['] & had just time to escape into my room—. . ." (*Brantwood Diary*, p. 548).

As in 1881, Ruskin, in 1878, wrestling with the black cat "reflected" within himself in a match that was also a "sifting examination" of "all the dark sides and in all the dark places" (XXXVII, 247)—a wrestling match punctuated by the applause of devilish peacocks who were, only shortly before, more "dear" than mocking—then, as later in 1881, Ruskin was neither his own Master nor anyone else's. He was mad. Perhaps in the strictest sense, it was for the first time. Seven years earlier at Matlock, he had suffered from a delirious fever brought on by internal inflammation. Yet what happened at Matlock was not the same thing that happened on the Good Friday of the twenty-second of February, and it was not the same thing that would happen six times in fewer than ten years.[8]

At Matlock, Ruskin dreamed. At Brantwood, dreaming what he would afterward call "the long Dream" (XXXVII, 246), he also performed. In a letter, Joan Severn describes the 1881 version of the movement between attempted control, which would be the momentary mastery of madness, and the circumferential resignation of that control, signalled by the shattered glass of potential reflection, like a mirror that might have been broken by a black cat:

> On Sunday morning he was tolerably quiet—tho' he smashed another pane of glass in his bedroom exactly next to the former one—when later on, he came into my room—& seemed tolerably himself (completely dressed) I asked him *why* he had done it?—and he said "it was a signal to be given at Windsor Castle—of breaking a spell of witchcraft"—but, added he, "I've killed the third witch at last"—I said "that was a good thing—& there was the end of it—& she wouldn't bother him any more [']—to which he said "he was'nt so sure of that—& he might have yet to suffer a great deal for having done it" so I comforted him—& begged him to promise he would not break

[7] Diary entry for August 16, 1875, as quoted in R. H. Wilenski, *John Ruskin*, p. 125.

[8] See John D. Rosenberg's *The Darkening Glass: A Portrait of Ruskin's Genius* (New York, 1962), p. 179: "[the Matlock vision] was the obverse of the waking nightmares which were to plague him during the later episodes of madness."

any more windows—I was so afraid of his catching cold—(and he never has since) then he became *almost* himself—& said he was tired—so Arthur with my persuasion got him to lie down on the sofa beside me (I being in bed—) & wrapt him up—& he fell fast asleep—how I thanked God for that!—he woke much refreshed in about half an hour—wandering a *very* little—calling me "mama"—& himself "a little donkey boy"!—but quite calm & sweet—& went to his room saying he'd come back & have tea—which he did in about 1/2 an hour & enjoyed it, with Arthur & me—in my room—(I being in bed, with my sprained ancle[)]—then I got him to lie down again on the sofa—& Arthur left us quietly alone—& the poor Darling lay quite still for an hour & a half—& *may* have slept a little—he was *so* much himself that he had tea-dinner at 7:30 with Arthur, Laurie, & Martha Gale in the dining-room—(wandering a little but not much[)]—then they all came up, & for an hour I read "Ormonde" (Miss Edgeworth's) aloud—& he seemed to enjoy it & spoke very sensibly about Ireland as it was, & now is—then about 9:30 he went to bed—*would* be alone—& wouldn't take his draught—& had a pretty quiet night—

All Monday he insisted upon being master in his own house—& would have no orders obeyed but his own—   [*Brantwood Diary*, p. 547].

By 1883, the arena of Ruskin's madness has been considerably reduced. At Brantwood in 1878, with a "catcatacious" Ruskin insisting upon playing all the roles, the ambitious vision of madness encompasses nothing less than the panoramic breadth of a morality play—good contending with evil, and Ruskin, all the while, fighting for a precarious sanity beyond ethical categories. The focus has narrowed. Moral contests, in both cosmic and zoological incarnations, are reduced to a "demoniacal vision" that, despite intimations of the infernal, is "quite narrowed"—and finally to sad autobiography that includes not much more than the autobiographer's father:

Well—the first thing to be noted of those three illnesses, that in the first there was the great definite vision of the contention with the Devil, and all the terror and horror of Hell—& physical death. In the second, there was a quite narrowed demoniacal vision, in my room, with the terrible fire-dream in the streets of London; in the third, the vision was mostly very sad & personal, all connected with my Father [*Brantwood Diary*, p. 297].

As madness becomes an infernally recapitulated habit, instincts toward narrowness, toward a perception of limited encompassment, replace the horizons of panorama—the ambition of breadth, which creates the optical tug of the potentially dangerous and inclusive vision of Strange Chords: the interrelation of "things in general." If the self in its relation to the world is fast becoming unmanageable, style *or* syntax (as we shall see), as a means of establishing that relation on terms that permit the suggestion of manipulation, becomes increasingly important. Still, panorama, as the interrelation of "things in general," may, at times, be more the solution to the problem than the problem's origin. Retreating toward not only things in specific, but, most specifically, the self alone,[9] Ruskin's consciousness is moving toward a frighteningly personal confrontation with a self—as if that self had seen the reflection of a large black cat—for whom madness has become a periodic (perhaps February) way of life. Overextended, Ruskin may well find that the retreating focus to specific selfishness or self-

[9] Briefly, and among other things, Ruskin's madness is his own uncensored autobiography—an autobiography unrefracted by the distances and prisms of memory, an autobiography before *Praeterita*. Subjectification creates claustrophobic spaces. There is no sense of otherness. The world is reflexive, unbearably selfish. There is nothing outside the prison of the first person:

—this illness, having been one, continued vision to me of my selfishnesses, prides, insolences, failures, written down day by day, it seemed to me, with reversed interpretation of all I had fondly thought done for others, as the mere foaming of my own vanity   [xxxvii, 244].

With the world as a version of the self, Ruskin, standing large, stands alone. The way to counter the solitude of the self, which is selfishness, is through work. Objectification, or selflessness, occurs not with a labor of consciousness, which, with "reversed interpretation," turns the world into a mirror reflecting the "catcataceous" self, but with the labor of dextrous hands:

Well, I am so alone now in my thoughts and way, that if I am not mad, I should soon become so, from mere solitude, but for my *work*. But it must be manual work. Whenever I succeed in a drawing, I am happy, in spite of all that surrounds me of sorrow. . . . But we are in hard times, now, for men's wits; for men who know the truth are like to go mad from isolation.
. . . the few of us now standing here are there, alone, in the midst of this yelping, carnivorous crowd, mad for money and lust, tearing each other to pieces, and starving each other to death, and leaving heaps of their dung and ponds of their spittle on every palace floor and altar stone,—it is impossible for us, except in the labour of our hands, not to go mad   [xxviii, 206-7].

Or again, despairing:

. . . as soon as I see or hear what human creatures are suffering of pain, and saying of absurdity, I get about as cheerful as I should be in a sheepfold strewed hurdle-deep with bloody carcases, with a herd of wolves and monkeys howling and gibbering on the top of them   [xxxvi, 417-18].

consciousness, while it avoids the central—or, as will become apparent, "polygonal"—responsibilities of mastery, may also be an advance toward a mirror that, reenforcing the infernal both by reflection and exposure of the "nakedness" behind, would in retrospect also be avoided:

> The actual illnesses of which accounts, to my great regret and inconvenience, go to the papers, are fits of, sometimes trances, sometimes waking delirium, which last their time, like a fit of the gout . . .—only, with each fit, more cautious of plaguing, or even interesting myself about things in general. . . . And it is quite possible that the sense of languor is rather because I have withdrawn from that work to forms of selfish study, than because my strength is materially abated [xxxiv, 598].

The focus narrows, and narrowing, it spirals inward like a devouring whirlpool toward what is private and entirely insular, concluding in an act close to self-consumption that, in the end, leaves nothing but the "ripped immanence" of a deafening silence. And in anticipation of final things, there is the Medusa-like horror of a "nothing" in miniature—the blank page of false presence that poignantly follows the gymnastic and privately allusive writing of February 22, 1878. As an example of the language of the Transforming Maze (an example concerned with naked feet, blindness, and madness) there is the solipsistically antiphonal writing of the Travel Diary toward an emptiness that is only followed by the recollections of a dream, though the dream is itself long, like certain ominous shadows of encroachment. Afterward, there are the increasing periods of silence. The last eleven years of life are endured in a condition that is a version of dubious peace either beyond speech or before a speech that has not yet returned—a silence that may be the result of Strange Chords, of having both seen and given too much. But close to the Edge and before Nothing, there is always something and that something is extraordinary. And because, with Ruskin, the Preface to silence is always better than the Addendum, it is perhaps possible to suggest a general aesthetics of stress—an aesthetics prompted by the terrible density of centripetal (logo)-concentricity—while at the same time avoiding what might become a suspicious and melodramatic rationale for madness. Clearly, to be mad is not to be great. But just as clearly, great madness—the madness of genius, as that genius watches itself go mad—is more than interesting.

Ruskin's madness, dreaming or performing, is an eventual part of his later greatness. Ruskin is himself almost aware of this: "no great man ever stops working till he has reached his point of failure: that is, to say, his mind is always far in advance of his powers of execution, and the latter will now and then give way in trying to follow it" (x, 203). But Ruskin's points of failure, as the branching nodes of a "multicursal" labyrinth that leads to the pathos of a kind of "honourable" self-defeat and decomposition, are not merely those of execution, but also, as will become apparent, of the imagination taken to the repletively explosive edge of breakdown.

The point of failure of the great man's mind is what would concern an aesthetics of stress, a penultimate stress of repletion, or what might be called the Labyrinthine Penultimate. Here, he is concerned with the beauty of "almost the last thing": "I wrote a rather pretty bit about Ophelia almost the last thing before I fell ill, which I think is really better than I could have done if I hadn't been goind crazy—. . ." (xxxvii, 247).[10] Beyond the page, the black cat beaten against the cold floor at dawn is the result of a consciousness that operates desperately in the face of both public and private central stresses—stresses of centricity that would be eased by dangerously masterful performances and that are often, instead, intensified by a terrible awareness of time's limitations, or rather by the straight-lined awareness of the limitation of Ruskin's own allotted time—and this even at the age of twenty-eight: "Death casts its long shadow towards me, and seems to reach me across the mirage of years."[11] Intensifying the stress of incipient centricity, the farsighted awareness of the "long shadow"—with rectilinear length brought terrifyingly near rather than being extended in an outward-bound optical awareness that will penetrate space—makes the panoramic (and, at the same time, [logo]-concentric) inclusion of Strange Chords even stranger. Further, the "long shadow" makes the responses of an acrobatic, sometimes multiple consciousness even more acrobatic, as that juggling consciousness strives to maintain a balance of precarious sanity on the Edge for an audience who may be no more than a solitary writer.

An aesthetics of the penultimate must necessarily possess a profound sense of the Edge, where balance is necessary for survival. And with a highly associative consciousness that is at once wide-

---

[10] The passage according to Cook and Wedderburn, never published, is no longer available. But Ophelia is, at this point of Ruskin's madness, much on his mind. See my later section "Paratactical Texts of Ripped Immanence: From Ariadne to the Shears and Penultimate Tablet of Atropos."

[11] *The Diaries of John Ruskin*, selected and edited by Joan Evans and John Howard Whitehouse (Oxford, 1956-59), p. 354. References to the diaries will appear in parentheses after the quotation as *Diaries*, followed by page number.

ranging and myopic in its tightrope performance, the centrifugal response to the stress of centricity, occurring finally on the circumferential Edge, might well yield a style that, as the essential diction and syntax of a Travel Diary toward Nothing but a Dream, would not only tightrope close to that Edge, but juggle at the same time, as if by tossing allusions into the air—as if, in fact, by verbally perpetuating itself, an obscure exit from terrible pressures might be temporarily found in the mere extension of language. An aesthetic of the penultimate, initiated by pressures of the orthodox geometries of centricity—or better, (logo)-concentricity, as the outer circles of potential density centripetally become a form of repletion—would prompt a response from the Edge that, in the form of a style which is "nothing but process" (xxv, 216), would be considerably more than language in search of appropriate paginal space.

Especially private and especially allusive, sometimes almost frantically so, as if something might be lost in public dispersal, Ruskin's diaries—those edited by Joan Evans and John Howard Whitehouse, but even more so *The Brantwood Diary* edited by Helen Gill Viljoen—often make no concession to "things in general," or, more accurately, an audience "in general." Wrestling with himself, that black demonic "catcataceous cat" (his grasp on his sanity is, after all, "in the labour of . . . hands"), and having himself seen "spittle on every palace floor and altar stone," Ruskin is writing not only for himself as reader—he will say, "It is a great bore to keep a diary but a great delight to have kept one" (*Diaries*, p. 129)—but also for himself as writer. His language, becoming explosively replete as it moves toward the "nothing," or minus category, of excess presence, becomes a process of Antiphonal Contention—as if between either a "calm luminous sky and a black Devil cloud" or a double labyrinth of blind language and a silence of latent completion—that aspires not so much toward the retrospective mastery implicit in reading as toward the linear extension and survival of the writing itself.

Watching this language of contorted, labyrinthine release—language whose inevitable exit will finally be confined only by the edges of a blank page—there is the compelling sense that words have been taken there by someone whose failure to control language is as spectacular as the command that is finally lost is awesome; and that, afterwards, there is simply nothing left to say: the Travel Diary toward Nothing is a performance which cannot be followed. There is only the blank page, the blind silence of the ineffable—and the *Dream*. And that "nothing," which may at first be merely the mathematician's "null-set," is ultimately not only as horrifying as a vacuum but as austerely elegant as uncontaminated potential.

But the silence, the "nothing" of an implicitly "honourable [self]-defeat," must be justified in the perhaps stuttering "nothing but process" of the essentially vertical architectonics of the Labyrinthine Penultimate. Language taken too easily to an Edge of decomposition is itself "nothing"—certainly not the "earned" absence of textually horrifying elegance, as of the postcircumferential Illth predicted by versions of the *"mise en abîme,"*[12] which is, among other things, the condition of false presence/points of failure of intermediary transitional difficulties that are the difficulties along the way of the syntactical traveler. The inevitable release from the compounding of concentric and centripetal stress—even if it is inevitable—must be fought against, twisted, perhaps transformed from the rectilinear into something both more myopically contorted and spatially economical, like his "Helix virgata" (xxviii, 551): the distance of curved immediacy, which is the "blind distance" of a proximate transcendence, becomes prized. To go with easy grace is not to go in significant style. Mastery, the rational performance both "of" and "from" the Centre, must be established before its opposite can achieve significance—before the circumferential Edge can be approached, albeit with anguished pathos, by a self either painfully and intricately pirouetting before a mirror or experiencing what we shall come to see as the no less agonized and more inclusively important intricacies of a Transforming Maze that would avoid, even if only for a while, the horror and elegance of the empty page. Before Ruskin can sign himself "Cat," even with the screams of peacocks resonating in the paradigmatic labyrinths of his ears, he must be able to sign himself "Master" (though any

---

[12] Hillis Miller, discussing both heraldry and an impasse in language that must also be, in some sense, trespassed or transgressed, describes something like an excessively retraced presence that lurks vertiginously over an abyss that is, after all, a false presence: "Since it is a question of the abyss of the absurd of the grounding or the filling of that abyss, one may borrow from the French an inexhaustible name for the enigma of the nameless, the impasse of language, *'mise en abîme.'*" He goes on to note the paradox of the *"mise en abîme"*: "without the production of some scheme, some 'icon,' there can be no glimpse of the abyss, no vertigo of the underlying emptiness. Any such scheme, however, both opens the chasm, creates or reveals it, and at the same time fills it up, covers it over by naming it, giving the groundless a ground, the bottomless a bottom." "Stevens' Rock and Criticism as Cure, I," *The Georgia Review* (spring 1976): 11-12. Ruskin's own points of failure, which are often overlayered by the "crincle crankle" of syntax, serve as a verbally woven net of false presence over/before the "bottomless." They reveal even as they cover the experience of the vertigo of that chasm of "nothing" at all but a profound absence anticipating the negatory excesses of Illth.

entirely rational mastery of Strange Chords must indeed be "make-shift"). A shortcut would bypass the territory of difficulty, of unmediated contention or the vacancy between "difference" that results in the desperate stylization of vortical and labyrinthine language at its performative limits as it is (mis)-shaped by terrifying pressures—pressures, both phenomenological and metaphysical that might be politically analogous to those caused by the thoroughly modern, Venetian "system of centralization that brought humble friends lower still" (xxiv, 412).[13]

Defining categories of the Pathetic Fallacy, Ruskin comes close to both locating points of imaginative failure and defining the tensile strength of potential, or evolving, disequilibrium between true mastery and the blank page of madness that is like an abyss of White Silence beyond the Edge. The Pathetic Fallacy is itself the result of disequilibrium between the self and a perceived object. Bulking large, overbearing yet curiously inadequate, the early Ruskinian self interprets what it sees on terms that are strictly its own. The result of both the projection of the observer's emotions on a hollow, transcendental landscape and a reflexive awareness that would judge an inadequate landscape autobiographically, the Pathetic Fallacy is, in certain circumstances, something other than fallacious. For example, the rhetorical avoidance of the Pathetic Fallacy by one who had seen something infernal—something more devastating, say, than the heaps of dung and ponds of "spittle on every palace floor and altar stone"—would be no virtuous mastery but a sign of the death's emotions: the entirely objectified condition, say, of the Crystal Palace automaton with whom a curiously fascinated Ruskin liturgically plays chess.[14] To perceive and bear the perception of the most intense kind of grief with a sympathetic identification that might become the transference of the Pathetic Fallacy would suggest at once a greater disequilibrium and a lesser strength of mind than might occur in a landscape that could be read as an autobiography of the observer's emotions.

Nevertheless, the Pathetic Fallacy, no less than the blank page—or, more precisely, the labyrinthine and penultimate trip to the circumferential Edge, beyond which paper is necessarily empty—is a condition that must be earned if it is to express something other than easy emotions that should best be kept by the self to the self. Those who, in the highest or strongest sense, interpret the world

---

[13] It should be pointed out, as will become apparent, that the problems of "altitude" present another kind of "antiphonal contention," and are for later, when a case for the "pedestrian" can be made.

[14] *Diaries*, pp. 841-42.

as a kind of autobiographical adjunct, are people who, "strong as human creatures can be, are yet submitted to influences stronger than they, and see in a sort untruly, because what they see is inconceivably above them. This last is the usual condition of prophetic inspiration" (v, 209). It is, in fact, the inspiration of the prophet of Israel as he attempts to master or govern the description of the "destruction of the kingdom of Assyria"—an inspiration that "dashes him into a confused element of dreams," "there being . . . always a point beyond which it would be inhuman and monstrous if he pushed this government, and, therefore, a point at which all feverish and wild fancy becomes just and true" (v, 215). And that demanding "point," which as a point of earned failure that is further the success of the heroically impossible, is a version of an equally demanding Centre that is also "true"—or at least before its altitude, proving angelic, also proves to be infernal.

In any case, often prophetic, Ruskin—unless the desertion of his guides signals a sub rosa unwillingness to confront the possibilities of disconfirmation—is not his own prophet, or rather would fail to prophesy his own end. And the difficulty of the way to the White Silence of the blank page is never advertised as a process of difficulty toward an earned, if unsought, absence that will signal greatness at the point of an overworked imagination's disintegration. But the later narrowing of Ruskin's scope in madness possesses the inherent integrity of having come from a panoramic vision of public engagement that may, at its most theatrical and demanding, yield the raw nerves of Strange Chords/Cords—a public engagement, as opposed to early theorizing, that results finally in the most severe kind of disconfirmation: a disconfirmation originating close to "prophetic inspiration" and described by a self-perpetuating language in proximity with the circumferential Edge, as if a language of at least attempted mediation or transformation might be a momentary consolation or substitution for the space of disconfirmation—or experienced difference—between theory and enacted performance.

Yet as Ruskin travels toward a condition of "nothing" that is also a White Silence interrupted only by a triumphant, demonic screaming, the mind that has itself broken loose from the gravitation of both orthodoxy and responsibility is a mind that once possessed the energy and strength of prophetic vision. No straight line, the movement has been not only considerable but difficult. Unlike the ominous rectilinearity of the "long shadow"—ominous because of the self's farsighted awareness of an Edge that is the end—the

Travel Diary describes a condition of labyrinthine myopia that is in the "process" of going "blind." But the prophecy (or itinerary), no matter how inspired, has gone wrong in the act of externalization (just as, oppositely, the labyrinthine structures either as elaborate topiary or architecture, when internalized as solution/cure, lead to the further problems of the doubling and then disintegrating blind theatre of the three-dimensional Maze), and the vision gone wrong possesses the sighted fact of an altar-defiling spittle and dung. Still, the contention between prophetic "answers" presented in orthodox syntax and the eventually absolute (dis)-quietude of "nothing" beyond even nostalgia is not a conflict that is easily resolved. The potentially mediating space "between" becomes, instead, a battlefield (before it becomes an intermediary "nothing"/abyss beyond any negotiation but a wistful retracing of lines that might once have become the threads of a net to keep one from falling too hard)— this mediating space "between," in any case, is also a labyrinthine travelogue of perpetual transformation that will end, finally, in the transformation of what once might have been "magnificent" in its blankness but which is now merely compelling, in the anguish of pathos itself taken too far and the vertiginous horror of prospective presence met at the "broken promises" of absence.

The power and integrity of the Travel Diary toward Nothing is, like the Pathetic Fallacy of certain prophets (a Pathetic Fallacy that is an infernal autobiography even when written from a position of painful strength), in the energy of the contention—that embattled energy Ruskin would shape into the mediating tensile strength of an attempted coalescence between rational and perhaps even masterful procedures, and the inevitably alarming consequences of a vantage point of pathos amid "bloody carcasses" and a focal point of dung and spittle on both palace floor and altar stone. In any case, contention predicts mediation—or at least an attempted mediation before the "difference" implicit in disconfirmation yields the antiphon of a "marred music," as of screeching peacocks, before White Silence. With Ruskin, the space of negotiation is the transforming space of brave delay, a stuttering delay that would hold the imagination together for as long as possible. And the myopic, almost blind to itself, style of attempted mediation, which itself knows no prediction or future in its intricate unraveling, is a style, more serpentine than panoramic, that incarnates the vestiges of equilibrium and rational survival in its economically contorted elongation. On the page—and as we shall see, even in the city (especially a city of the Centre that is like a mind capable of autobiography)—

the serpentine line, as long as it is unsevered, is nothing less than a lifeline, though whether that line is prospective or retrospective is beyond our immediate purposes.

Theoretically dealing with the essential energy of mastery, as well as the intermediary (if unmediated) space and style of transforming mazes and the "nothing" of the blank and silent page of madness beyond the disintegrating, if "overlapping," Edge, for which we have been presumably prepared by the possibility at least of intervening vortexes of false presence, we may find it more useful, instead of speculating with naive confidence on the specific reasons for the blank page, like Ruskin's early biographers, to examine— as tentatively we consider a decomposing aesthetics of the Labyrinthine Penultimate, with tenuous, serpentine lines predicting points of failure—a number of the general pressures that, provoking response, result in some of Ruskin's finest and most moving pages: pages of "earned pathos."[15]

Even if confidence about the reasons for the blank page were possible, language asked to survive and even perform before "long shadows" and Strange Chords (and not dubious speculation about

---

[15] Nevertheless, it would be irresponsible not to mention the part played by Rose La Touche in Ruskin's approach to the blank page of February, 1878. Rose, in fact, transformed into a variety of personages, as well as being an (un)fulfilling version of Adèle Domecq, who seems to anticipate Rose, dominates Ruskin's digressive, meandering syntax. She is like Ariadne in that she is postcircumferential, beyond the Transformations of the Maze while still a part of them, the thread of her own life severed by Atropos before the disconfirmation of full maturation in a Promise(d) Land that would, perhaps, be avoided. Ruskin would have his innocence, or rather her innocence, "frozen" in time. Hawthorns that are "vital" in the transforming Maze fall over a dead Rose. On May 26, 1875, when Rose died, Ruskin was "away into the meadows, to see buttercup and clover and bean blossom, when the news came that the little story of my wild Rose was ended, and the hawthorn blossom, this year, would fall—over her" (xxxvii, 168). He writes Charles Eliot Norton: "*Mere* overwork or worry might have soon ended me, but it would not have driven me crazy. I went crazy about St Ursula [identified in his mind with Rose] and the other saints,—chiefly young-lady saints—and I rather suppose I had offended the less pretty Fors Atropos" (*Letters of John Ruskin to Charles Eliot Norton*, edited by C. E. Norton, 2 vols. [Boston, 1904], i, 148-49).

Attention to various stresses is one thing. But clearly, psychopathological analysis for the reasons of Ruskin's madness is beyond the scope of this book. Even expert medical opinion would do no more than create a case-study. Ruskin's own language is more helpful. In an earlier letter also directed to Charles Eliot Norton, he is explicit as to the origins of madness: "Upon my word, I haven't been afraid of going mad, all through my sorrow; but if I stay much in Switzerland now I think my scorn would unsettle my brain, for all worst madness, nearly, begins in pride, from Nebuchadnezzar downwards. Heaven keep me from going mad *his* way, here, for instead of my body being wet with the dew of Heaven, it would be with tobacco spittle" (xxxvi, 582).

the origins of psychopathological behavior) is, after all, our over-riding concern: the language and syntax of madness, returning as from Foucault's "archaeology of silence," calls more urgently for participation in the experience of equivocal signification than a psychoanalytical (or even exegetical) elucidation/explication of words organized, or disorganized, in a particular way. In any event, it is a curious language with references that are almost always ex-tensive (not words about words, and not often words posing as objects)[16]—sometimes so astronomically, if personally, extensive that it is a language which appears, contradictorily, to be part of a hubristic solipsist's dictionary, consulted as he writes a world encyclopedia. But if so, the world is nothing less than the self, like a mirror faced at dawn (or the Contrasting Mirrors of his own consciousness), and the encyclopedia is a form of ambitiously uni-versal autobiography.

Though at times the language of the filled page appears cos-mically hermetic (oxymoron of the self-effacing egotist), it is not ultimately—or better—only, reflexive or self-referential. Essen-tially, he is without the economy of the narcissist whose space is confined by mirrors. With Ruskin, there is a kind of doubleness involved in the relation between symbol and self. He is both "there," in a world of naturalistic and mythological otherness, and "here," in an autobiographical topography that would take himself as his own subject. And the response—both verbal and spatial (a verbal style that immediately reflects not only architectural but horticul-tural obsessions)—is at first a potentially implosive structure, or a series of tenuously held together structures that, as incipiently dan-gerous versions of that vortical vision capable of ecstasy, cannot easily be separated from the provoking pressures that give original shape to a final art which spectacularly breaks loose, as if those impacted pressures had built to a point sufficient to cause an abrupt reversal of direction, in a sudden "lyrical explosion."[17]

One of the pressures that can only be outlined here[18] is Ruskin's pervasive feeling of claustrophobia, which can be seen in both his

[16] Occasionally, with Ruskin, words become a kind of architecture, as if aspiring toward a condition beyond print or page—a condition of three dimensions and weight. See, for instance, Ruskin's description of St. Mark's (x, 82-83) for an example of words as autonomous re-creation, the word as stone, if not "paint."

[17] Moving from the compacted implosive to the centrifuged explosive, I have borrowed Foucault's term for a description of Ruskin's eventual burst of "marred music." *Folie et déraison. Histoire de la folie à l'âge classique* (Paris, 1962), p. 537.

[18] But see my *The Failing Distance, passim.* As has already been suggested, *Ruskin's Maze* will attempt to make a complementary case for the Inside—an Inside nec-essarily, if not entirely felicitously, experienced by even the claustrophobic Ruskin.

attitudes to the problems of the self (his impulse not only towards pseudonymity but also toward the contradictory presentation, at first camouflaged, of an exaggerated, performative first person) and his fear of the inversion of recessional space, the turning of the sacrosanct third dimension "outside in"—a crucial act that would eliminate both psychic space and the world of options in an even more incisive fashion than the maddening transitional absence of the interrupted series of infernal two-dimensional juxtaposition. And what Ruskin almost always requires, especially in the early stages of the Transformations of the Maze, is a sense of the exit, the possibility of an "escape forward" (IV, p. 83) from a densely unrefracted selfhood. Most dramatically, the claustrophobic conflict between selfhood and collapsing space can be seen not only in Ruskin's early and vigorous defense of Turner's painting of Juliet and the "mysteries of lamplight and rockets" that had been attacked in *Blackwood's Magazine*—a defense prompted by a "black anger" that finds release at first in an unpublished article and then in the five, widely ranging volumes of *Modern Painters*—but also, later, in Ruskin's own paradoxical attack on Whistler's "The Falling Rocket," an attack, finally, that is not merely based upon aesthetic judgment but is also an assault on himself, forty years earlier, as the defender of Turner. With neither future nor a failed distance left, Ruskin, almost always insisting upon playing all the available roles, circles back, like his language of "return" to become the antagonistic reviewer from *Blackwood's*.[19] Self-division becomes, for a moment, a form of solipsistic unification that is not entirely satisfactory.

More obviously, perhaps, and in less need of explanation, Ruskin responds to the pressures resulting from the imbalance between interior, imaginative designs and their exterior potential—an imbalance between schemes that exist imaginatively as an almost self-

[19] Perhaps inverting what is an extremely complex problem by making the response the reason for the response, Ruskin seems to suggest that patterns of light and dark—patterns emphatically employed in both Turner and Whistler—aggravate a mind that is already in a weakened condition: "the endurance of monotony has about the same place in a healthy mind that the endurance of darkness has: that is to say, as strong intellect will have pleasure in the solemnities of storm and twilight, and in the broken mysterious lights that gleam among them, rather than in mere brilliancy and glare, while a frivolous mind will dread the shadow and the storm" (x, 211). But often the equilibrium of a Ruskinian mind that is "healthy" seems largely the result of the precise locations of those "broken and mysterious lights"— the way they affect Ruskin's autobiographical claustrophobia: the contradictory attitudes of a "distanced intimacy" toward the emergence of a potentially present and performing first person.

fulfilling form of inner pastoral, but which, as they are externalized from theory toward practice (and the inside and the outside are not finally kept separate), become in the process infernally humiliating. Vision, as has been suggested, anticipates eventual disconfirmation—unless, that is, "guides" have been called upon to fail prematurely. The St. George's Guild exists as a fine idea, an agrarian release from, among other things, centripetal burdens—a circumferential answer, flirting with notions of the Redemption not only of landscape but of language (and with Ruskin the one can "speak" for the other), to the engineering of sewage, where truth, as we shall see, is replete with eventual danger.[20] But Ruskin, who later, with his instinct for the Exit, will search for circumferential space, is unable to tolerate the empty space between theory and practice, ideas and implementation. With little of the medieval respect for fences—a respect that is expressed by the fifteenth-century artist's "always dwelling especially on the fences; wreathing the espaliers indeed prettily with sweetbriar, and putting pots of orange-trees on the tops of the walls" (v, 260)—Ruskin, breaking down boundaries in an act closer to a vaulting transgression that would attempt to ignore the "difference between" rather than explore either mediation or transformation, underscores, in his failure to arbitrate, an imbalance that is, at times, without even a fulcrum of transition.

And with Ruskin, the terrible imbalance—the lack of correspondence between "inside" and "outside," between theory and practice—is apparent, finally, to almost everyone, even Ruskin himself: "I went mad because nothing came of my work" (xxix, 386).[21] The works of the early pseudonymous Kata Phusin of *The Poetry of Architecture* (1837-38) and that of the anonymous "A Graduate of Oxford" of the first volume of *Modern Painters* (1843) were to be read, but their authors neither seen nor identified. Yet as a virtually invisible voyeur, who looks to learn and learning would "become,"

---

[20] Two years after the Good Friday of contention, in 1880, he will be explicit about the dangers of the Centre. The quotation is a significant amplification of one already employed: "the illness which all but killed me two years ago, was not brought upon by overwork, but by grief at the course of public affairs in England, and by affairs, public and private alike in Venice [during his visit of 1876-77]; the distress of many an old and deeply regarded friend there among the humbler classes of the city being as necessary a consequence of the modern system of centralization, as the destruction of her ancient and religious buildings" (xxiv, 412).

[21] Ruskin's point is also, with qualifications and precise dating, R. H. Wilenski's: "Disappointment at the contrast between his grandiose plans and the actual results of his activities in the 'seventies was a factor in the 1878 collapse . . ." *John Ruskin*, p. 118.

he soon turns toward action and demonstration (even as he assumes his own name), emerging in the process as a highly visible first person, whose theoretical assertions are simply prefaces for later undisguised, even dangerously exhibitionistic performances. Nevertheless, there is that discrepancy between vision and fulfillment. And it is a discrepancy of an unnegotiated open space that is not yet postcircumferential—an open space/abyss having analogues in syntax/parataxis and an antiphonal consciousness at the point of the imagination's breakdown—that would temporarily be spanned by the penultimately tightroping language of a bridge, as if of twine, emanating from an origin (which may even be an unacknowledged point of awareness that "nothing" will come of one's work) only to arrive at the centrifugally replete double labyrinth of blind language "above" (a language of problematic "Blind Guides") and the silence of latent completion "below" (as if buried sacred crocodiles [perhaps "sacred" before "profane" in excavation that will anticipate its own repetition] might make "sense" if they could only be heard) that predicts the inevitable "nothing"/absence of a Travel Diary's ultimate page of White Silence. It is as if the double labyrinth's blindness "above" and silence "below" were a preparation for the despair of the disconfirmation of visionary blindness, as of "night in broad daylight," and the silence of confirmed madness "beyond."

But according to Ruskin's doctors, it was not the open space of "nothing" having come of his work that prompted the long February night vigil—that cold night of moral contention and "Naked foot." It was not "nothing," they were certain, that provoked the stress, but "too much" instead, as if, as we shall see, concentricity had been made unnaturally dense by centripetal tendencies: "I must allow myself a few more words of autobiography. . . . The doctors said that I went mad, this time two years ago, from overwork." Yet permitting himself autobiography, Ruskin also permits himself a certain skepticism. He is unconvinced by medical opinion: "I had not been then working more than usual, and what was usual with me had become easy" (xxix, 386). Still, beyond permitted skepticism, there is the repletion of centripetal stress that may come from the assumption of excessive synoptic responsibility on polygonal sides, perhaps from an exaggerated sense of panoramic and organic inclusion (a sense that can be the result of having lived too long in a landscape of Strange Chords that is "central" in either its density or its altitude). In any case, the (logo)-concentric and centripetal stress of that unrefracted repletion, if not the work itself, is real enough, as is the later penultimate repletion that doubles labyrinths before the Circumference: "Oh me! do you recollect when you first made me read *Past and Present*? It was the only book I could get help from during my illness, which was partly brought on by the sense of loneliness—and greater responsibility brought upon me by Carlyle's death" (xxxvii, 361).

The stresses, then, are there—the pressures of the attempted mastery of Strange Chords grotesquely perceived (as well as the rectilinearity of the "long shadow," a shadow of death that, as time's final Edge, compounds the repletion of those things either imagined or rightly observed)—the stresses, if neither the actual reasons for madness nor an ironically developed basis for a decomposing aesthetics of the Labyrinthine Penultimate's "shattered majesty" (x, 191), are there, as well as the responses that are all-important for our purposes: some, as we shall see, that are immediately visceral and visual, without time for calculation, and some, delayed, that are strategic enough to create and chart areas of pastoral in a world where, otherwise, dung has touched the altar.

It is probably not enough to say, even as a kind of economically necessary and aphoristic shorthand, that Ruskin's madness, part of his greatness, is partly the result of his essential sanity—that, with Ruskin, discriminations are not easily made and surgery, or better, the vivisection he so despised, is always difficult. Things bind and blend. Both R. G. Collingwood and Graham Hough,[22] while not connecting the results of centripetal stress with greatness—a combination which creates a kind of meta-presence that anticipates the dangerous Illth of the pathos of an overreaching imagination—have convincingly indicated the rational and deeply humane impulse toward a kind of moral coherence and unity that is the organizing principle behind most of Ruskin's attempted performances. It is even, or perhaps especially, the principle that informs those activities from which "nothing" comes—a shaping vision reflected in the intricately organic "Nature of Gothic" chapter that lies at the centre of *The Stones of Venice*, as well as his panoramically inclusive attitudes toward art, society, and economics that may end in the all-too-often disconfirming "something" of a venture, as a highly visible point of failure, gone painfully and embarrassingly public. And what is perceived is, theoretically, to be perceived by a self—hopefully neither "double" nor "treble" (xxxvii, 246)—no less whole than the unified vision. It is a need—this impulse for interrelation and organic harmony—that finally

---

[22] R. G. Collingwood, *Ruskin's Philosophy* (London, 1919), p. 16; Graham Hough, *The Last Romantics* (New York, 1961), p. 14.

becomes the ecstatic binding and blending of all things as Ruskin, mnemonically and imaginately, enters Siena in an act of concluding autobiography, equipped with those paginal distances and tenses which still permit even hazardous mastery without a vortical difficulty that will prove eventually maddening (xxxv, 561-62).

Yet beyond the fictive reconstructions of ecstatic autobiography, the necessary revisions which make the first person presentable, if not entirely agreeable, that impulse toward the dazzling, if neuropathic, interconnection of Strange Chords/Cords, with no oases of vacant pastoral possible and nothing excluded from "polygonal" responsibility, brings about a condition of "too much" that is ultimately intolerable. And that whole self, finally, is a self whose wholeness involuntarily brings about a downfall in the form of disintegration—a disintegration which becomes the multiplication that yields the "double, or even treble" self who experiences, in the rectilinear face of the "long shadow," a "Dream" that is also "long." But if that blank page—the Nothing that comes, at least in part, from "nothing" having come—is to be successfully avoided, or more accurately, if its arrival is to be delayed, there must be strategic responses to the centripetal stresses of repletion and "polygonal," or (logo)-central, responsibility. A centrifugal response must be tried that, before the impacted self splits under central pressure into multiple fragments, will attempt to divide, of its own accord, the Strange Chord's burden of an almost impossible wholeness and interrelation, which is the burden of the attempted centripetal mastery of "too much." The entirely sane and humane vision of the "binding and blending" of all things, if it is unseparated by the distinctions/separations of tenses (distinctions that are like "kindly oases" for the overreachingly "avaricious imagination"), anticipates a vision that, neither sane nor humane, is the vortical vision of meta-presence gone infernally wrong immediately before it spirals into "nothing."[23]

Both the stresses and responses that lead "to" the blank page (in the skeletal role of the Travel Diary toward Nothing) take the shape, in Ruskin's essentially spatializing consciousness, of verbally

---

[23] Both the vortical "nothing" and the centrifuged "nothing" of White Silence are immediately preceded by the "lyrical explosion"—much coming just before the "nothing" at all of madness. Foucault's analogue to the Ruskinian condition is at the least recognizable: "Joining vision and blindness, image and judgment, hallucination and language, sleep and waking, day and night, madness is ultimately nothing, for it unites in them all that is negative. But the paradox of this *nothing* is to *manifest* itself, to explode in signs, in words, in gestures. Inextricable unity of order and disorder, of the reasonable being of things and this nothingness in madness!" *Madness in Civilization*, p. 107.

described design in which exterior and interior architectures reciprocally inform each other. And those stresses and responses are located at both Centres that are the locations not only of centripetal mastery but "polygonal" responsibility, where Strange Chords are conceived as well as perceived, and Circumferences that are, for a while, suburbs of potentially sane, centrifugal dispersal, where perception and responsibility are divided, as if by that surgical act of apparent Ruskinian heresy the pressures of unmitigated repletion might be conquered. This, for a time, is at least the "Hope" before the "lyric explosion" of a myopic (patho)-eccentricity.

And in between, connecting density with dispersal, everything with nothing, mastery with madness, there is, superimposed over the orthodox geometries of (logo)-concentricity and rectilinearity, the decentering transformations of a Maze that is, incarnated in language, the diction and syntax of the initially Thesean Travel Diary toward Nothing—a Maze (meant for naked feet shining like snow) that also, as both a style whose extent and elongation is its doomed survival and a path going either toward a somewhere of extreme hypothesis or toward the more likely White Silence beyond repletion, would attempt to fill the open space or Middle of difference/disconfirmation with something other than the meta-presence of vortical vision—fast talk, say, as of even felicitous quarreling among Alpine Roses, or writing that is as unpremeditated and labyrinthine as we shall find the winding "clues" of white marble that connect Venice's Centre with her Circumference. In any case, the centrifugal Travel Diary toward Nothing (as well as the less than Nothing of an absence without remembered echo)—not only dense and opaque along the way, but also highly associative and allusive (even as the Diary's transforming style attempts, with its necessarily contorted myopia, to avoid the rectilinear consequences of the "long shadow")—represents, in its "nothing but process," an agonizing account of struggle, resistance, obstacles, and finally the "honourable defeat" (x, 191) of decomposition before and within the Theatre of Blindness of the Labyrinthine Penultimate that, in its "shattered majesty," immediately precedes the earned absence of madness and White Silence that stands as austere and final punctuation (the boundaries of an empty page) to intermediate points of failure along the way. And it is an account, the eccentric pathos of which might not even be lost on failed, blind guides, without "celestial light" (that "dazzlement"), whose tears may eventually freeze, like the white, winter ice of rectilinear canals, which themselves might be called "Straight."

Yet Ruskin's way toward madness is not St. Paul's way to the

Kingdom of God, though, curiously, Redemption, whether het-erodox or not, is in either case close to a promise that might be kept. Unrectilinear, Ruskin's peregrination is one of characteristic centrifugal digression that, at the point of verbal dissolution, is transfigured in an agonized attempt at an articulation that would be a fallen "error's" still fallen "recovery," as if the "recovery" of a lost tongue could aid in a landscape's elevation, and this in a highly idiosyncratic version of that anonymous, universally re-pressed lexicon of pathos and *"folie"* mentioned by Foucault which would include, above all, "those words deprived of language whose muffled rumbling, for an attentive ear, rises up from the depths of history, the obstinate murmur of a language which speaks by itself, uttered by no one and answered by no one"[24]—after which, with Ruskin, there is only the return to White Silence beyond even the fiction of Redemption, if not the occasional revisitations of sanity.

[24] Michel Foucault, *Histoire de la folie*, "Préface" to the original edition (Plon, 1961).

Chapter One

Strange Chords
of Incipient Orthodoxy:
Centres and Epicycles

A. *Cock-Robinson-Crusoe Conceit and*
Other Geometrically Central Issues

In the beginning, Ruskin is at the Centre, a Centre of implicit
decomposition, which is nevertheless strong enough to be not only
his point of origin but furthermore his point of inaugural departure
as well. Later, after much travel, it will also be a point of return
that itself embodies the oscillations of redeparture. The act will not
be one of becoming reacquainted with the recognizable. But to
begin with, he is at the Centre—an unfallen Centre of original
innocence—and there he possesses virtually no density, no opacity.
As if unbound by gravity, he is virtually incorporeal. At the most,
preoccupied by sight, he is an eyeball, as later, approaching a kind
of reflexive blindness that is also an awareness of the multiplicity
of selves, he will be the eye of the cat observing the eye of a bull,
as if in contrasting mirrors. But seeing, he is himself now invisible.
Simply, it is as if he did not exist. Yet he is at the Centre, as though
on a stage that is yet to be part of a Theatre of Blindness. With no
sense of self, he is nevertheless self-centered: "and, having nobody
else to be dependent upon, [I] began to lead a very small, perky,
contented, conceited, Cock-Robinson-Crusoe sort of life, in the
central point which it appeared to me, (as it must naturally appear
to geometrical animals,) that I occupied in the universe" (xxxv,
37). And he is happy with his Centre, his privileged space. Still, his
universe—the walled garden at Herne Hill—is small, "seventy yards
long by twenty wide" (xxxv, 35-36). His "central point" is the Centre
of almost nothing. Shrewdly, he understands that he must make
the most of what he has. Making his Centre important by an act
of focus, he, like most children, will set

> all the faculties of heart and imagination on little things, so as
> to be able to make anything out of them he chooses. Confined
> to a little garden, he does not imagine himself somewhere else,
> but makes a great garden out of that; possessed of an acorn-

cup, he will not despise it and throw it away, and covet a golden one in its stead: it is the adult who does so. The child keeps his acorn-cup as a treasure, and makes a gold one out of it in his mind [xx, 249-50].

But Ruskin's original "central position" is different from those special, if not always happy, locations that follow as experience is translated into autobiographical history. In fact, the first Centre is entirely different from the second. Privileged by the virtue of its innocence, the original "central point" is not a Centre of inclusion and mastery. Like its young occupant, it is without density. It weighs nothing. Essentially, it is a Centre without information or responsibility; it is without plenitude of any kind. Instead, there is only the shaping conceit of an innocent eye. And just as he rules what amounts to a model landscape from a throne of naive centricity, expanding his domain by a willfully proximate focus, as if his eyes were magnifying lenses curiously unqualified for or disbarred from distant focus, so, without a past and no feeling for the future, the young Ruskin also inhabits a tense of immediacy—a tense that is, in fact, every bit as central, or perhaps "between," as his "Cock-Robinson-Crusoe" location: "I remain in a jog-trot, sufficient-for-the day style of occupation—lounging, planless. . . . I am beginning to consider the present as the only available time. . . . I spend my days in a search after present amusement of what I have not future strength to attain" (I, 435). Time, like his early Herne Hill space and the later glass that concludes his "naked contention," is a mirror. There is only a kind of narcissistic immediacy—what refers directly to the unrefracted self. Without history, his world is without serial consequence. Cause and effect are fictions for the convenience of others. A gesture is autonomous, self-referring, and without echoes. Even death's "long shadow," apparent soon enough, cannot at first penetrate a world framed by his partitioned present tense: "I was sorry that my aunt was dead, but, at that time . . . I lived mostly in the present, like an animal, and my principal sensation was—what a pity it was to pass such an uncomfortable evening—and we at Plymouth" (xxxv, 71)!

Yet Centres, like an autonomous present tense that will become a tense of ambitiously digressive indulgence, a painfully intimate autobiography of consciousness, have the potential to be embarrassing in the same way that excessive time spent in front of the mirror can be heretical for a reluctant first person, whose vanity has, until then, been merely theoretical. The child's Centre of naiveté is the charming pastoral of egotism before reflection. But the

Centre of a more tested self-love is a public location, where the
exaltation of the first person, beyond charm, is close to madness:

> The following letter is an interesting and somewhat pathetic
> example of religious madness. . . . The writer has passed great
> part of his life in a conscientious endeavor . . . but his intense
> egotism and absence of imaginative power hindered him from
> perceiving that many people were doing the same, and meeting
> with the same disappointments. Gradually, he himself occu-
> pied the entire centre of his horizon; and he appointed himself
> to "judge the United States in particular, and the world in
> general" [xxviii, 312].

Ruskin's movements back and forth between a "central position"
(an original vantage point not long blessed by either a childish
naiveté or optics that are innocent, but soon characterized instead
by his own brand of idiosyncratically "intense egotism") and, after
the farsighted penetration of space, the more selfless and less dense
Circumference that is a version of the background (a background
of dispersal where "suburban" real estate has yet to become the
infernal space of the confirmed claustrophobic) are the essential
movements of Ruskin's consciousness. Yet these reciprocal movements—traveling back and forth in three-dimensional space—are
concerned more with panorama than a conventional depth that is
straight ahead, or any rectilinear distance but that announced by
the perception of the "long shadow." And the history of Ruskin's
attitude toward Centres, starting "perky," undergoes transformations that reflect his responses to pressures and responsibilities that
are, finally, no less "conscientious" than those of the Central Judge
of the "world in general" who, in the middle of his own panorama,
is not entirely sane.

The "central position" of the child, with his Cock-Robinson-Crusoe conceit, is more self-centered than masterful, more concerned
with the examination of self than the extensive observation of either
the recessional space of backgrounds or the panorama of an inclusive peripheral vision. But then, surrounded by the Edenic walls
of his Herne Hill garden, he has neither background nor sufficient
panorama to challenge his egocentricity with a notion of "otherness." Still, shortly after conceit, comes shame—a mild shame, to
be sure, that arrives as a feeling that he may not be entirely worthy
of his geometrically "central position." It is the shame of the youthful, anonymous author of *Modern Painters I*, who employs the first
person in print, if at all, with grave reluctance. The child's position

of naive egocentricity is discarded by the anonymous author who has come to understand that he must earn the right to both signature and use of the first person. But earned egocentric signature and pronoun—only possible when a sense of "otherness," located either in distance or panorama, has been experienced—are anticipated by respect for a different kind of centricity.

Observed Centres—rather than central vantage points of private conceit that, as examples of reflexive space, reinforce the sense of a self which exists merely as a prefigurative shadow of a first person to come—begin to flourish. With a newly acquired awareness of a past that may itself be new, history (both personal and public) is interpreted by crisis, privileged time—central moments that, like enclosing circles, are turning points:

> The painter's vocation was fixed from that hour [xii, 311].

Or about the Pre-Raphaelites:

> I believe that these young artists to be at a most critical period of their career—at a turning point from which they may either sink into nothingness or rise to very real greatness [xii, 319].

Still, if most histories can be interpreted by the perception of crisis—

> One saw in a moment that the painter was both powerful and simple, after a sort. . . . And one saw in a moment that he had chanced upon his subject [xxii, 309]—

Ruskin would always wish to be even-handed enough to point out those patterns that are not revealed in privileged time:

> in the earlier scenes in the life of Moses, by Sandro Botticelli, you know—not "in a moment," for the knowledge cannot be so obtained [xxii, 398-99].

Uninvolved in either the self-conscious search for the abstracted and autonomous moments of the Aesthetic School—of, say, Gabriel Dante Rossetti's "Silent Noon" from "The House of Life," Pater's "Conclusion," or the "instant made Eternity" of Browning's "The Last Ride Together"—Ruskin nevertheless chooses to see an art whose essence is not so much aesthetic and momentary detachment as it is an essence with societal ramifications: Gothic art consolidated in a flashing instant that overcomes rude, "intermediate" spaces. There is, Ruskin insists, a privileged, almost epiphanic, pause in that public history:

> And it is in this pause of the star, that we have the great, pure, and perfect form of French Gothic; it was at the instant

when the rudeness of the intermediate space had been finally
conquered. . . . That tracery marks a pause between the laying
aside of one great ruling principle, and the taking up of another. . . . It was the watershed of Gothic Art. Before it, all
had been ascent; after it, all was decline; both, indeed, by
winding paths and varied slopes; both interrupted, like the
gradual rise and fall of the passes of the Alps, by great mountain outliers, isolated or branching from the central chain, and
by retrograde or parallel directions of the valley of access. But
the track of the human mind is traceable up to that glorious
ridge, in a continuous line, and thence downwards. Like a
silver zone. . . .

And at that point, and that instant, reaching the place that
was nearest heaven, the builders looked back, for the last time,
to the way by which they had come. . . .

Up to that time, up to the very last instant in which the
reduction and thinning of the intervening stone was consummated, his eye had been on the openings only, on the stars of
light. . . . It flashed, out in an instant, as an independent
form [VIII, 89-91].

Unsurprisingly, it is not merely a decidedly unmomentarily
Gothic Art that can be understood by a shrewd grasp of the pause
of central time. Italian Art is also an art whose essence can be
revealed by a keen comprehension of its historical Centre. The
altitude of an adolescent "high ground" gives way to a "spot"—
albeit a special, selected "spot"—and plural, swollen moments that
collectively become a privileged "hour":

Now so justly have the Pre-Raphaelites chosen their time
and name, that the great change which clouds the career of
medieval art was affected, not only in Raphael's time, but by
Raphael's own practice, and by his practice in *the very centre of
his available life.*

You remember, doubtless, what high ground we have for
placing the beginning of human intellectual strength at about
the age of twelve years. Assume, therefore, this period for the
beginning of Raphael's strength. He died at thirty-seven. And
in his twenty-fifth year, one half-year only past the precise
centre of his available life, he was sent for to Rome, to decorate
the Vatican. . . .

And he wrote it thus: On one wall of that chamber he placed
a picture of the World or Kingdom of *Theology* presided over
by *Christ.* And on the side wall of that same chamber he placed

the World or Kingdom of *Poetry*, presided over by *Apollo*. And from that spot, and from that hour, the intellect and the art of Italy date their degradation [xii, 148].

As if with a centripetal motion whose gravity is given its coherence by a still "spot" of privilege, Centres, like Chinese boxes—or the Monte Rosa Society within St. George's Guild—further dissolve into Centres that are increasingly interior, as if imaginatively protected. History becomes a design of centripetal (logo)-concentric circles, with special significance attached to a diminishing diameter, as privilege aspires toward the spatial economy of a "spot" that is either the altitude of "high ground" or—at sea level—the Centre itself. But as accounts become increasingly ambitious, moving from biography to public history, private moments, taking on a communal aspect, become hours. And in the process, history submits to a form of temporal optics—a "kind of focus of time"—that defines the Centre of nothing less than the Middle Ages:

> it seems to me that there is a kind of central year about which we may consider the energy of the Middle Ages to be gathered; a kind of focus of time, which, by what is to my mind a most touching and impressive Divine appointment, has been marked for us by the greatest writer of the Middle Ages, in the first words he utters; namely, the year 1300, the 'mezzo del cammin' of the life of Dante. Now, therefore, to Giotto, the contemporary of Dante, and who drew Dante's still existing portrait in this very year, 1300, we may always look for the central medieval idea in any subject [x, 400].

As a location of special moments, of spots, pauses, instants, the Centre, translated from substance to the attributive, comes paired with adjectives that describe their descriptive partner as much as the noun toward which they are directed. The connection between a "high ground" that is the beginning of intellectual maturity and centricity—a "high ground" before it becomes "too" high, like the meta-presence that will lead to a vortical vision spiraling toward absence—is familiar:

> We now enter on the consideration of that central and highest branch of ideal art [v, 111].

But not only is what is central "highest," it is also, at this point, good for you—"healthy":

> none of the three are a healthy or central state of man [vii, 424].

Predictably, to be central is to be extraordinary:

> he has expressed the power in what I believe to be for ever a central and unmatchable way   [vi, 364].

And what is "unmatchable" is at least close to greatness:

> And I claim the personal honour of presenting to the Museum the great central work of Turner's life   [xxx, 37].

Further, central location demands that certain standards be met:

> I am at a loss to know why this picture is in a central position; it possesses no special merit of any kind   [xiv, 128].

Special, the Centre is curiously not always central. It is not limited to circumferential middles. Too important to be merely "central," the Centre is at times, as with Ruskin himself, at the etymological "beginning"[1]—or at least at a beginning that is like a seed or root whose originally centred concentricity, having extensively branched as toward the limbs of labyrinthine meaning, will be discovered later, as if in a memory that would, in an act of nostalgic impossibility, attempt to recentre what has become, as the ecstatic best that a dissymetrically surviving pathos has to offer, epicyclical or circumferential. More to the immediate point, the beginning—the root of the matter—is as central as an original innocence that knows its appropriate "height" (if not depth):

> we have thus got to the root of it, and have a great declaration of the central medieval purpose   [v, 280].

With Ruskin, if not only space can be central but also a time defined by an optical "focus" of space, so, too, the cast of characters who inhabit those dimensions can have a representative of the Centre. Before there is a Ruskinian Central Man, there is Dante, who is nothing less than "the central man of all the world" (xi, 187).

Going public, Ruskin replaces the vantage "point" that is also central with space to include more than a self curiously amalgamated as a conceited "Cock-Robinson-Crusoe." The vantage point that is close to a focal point within the Herne Hill garden is enlarged to include European cartography:

> It seems that just in the centre of Europe, and at the point where the influence of the East and West, of the old and new

---

[1] Much concerned with "first ideas connected . . . with names," Ruskin nevertheless cautions that "etymology, the best of servants, is an unreasonable master" (xxv, 242).

world, were to meet, preparation was made for a city which was to unite the energy of the one with the splendour of the other; and the Sea, which in other countries is an Enemy as well as a Servant, and must be fought with to be enslaved—or else, as to us in England, is a severe tutor as well as protector, was ordered to minister to Venice like a gentle nurse, and to nourish her power without fretting her peace—to bear her ships with the strength of our English seas, but to surround her palaces with the quietness of the Arabian sands [x, 15-16].

Yet just as central moments of biography are expanded to include hours and years, just as a single person, a conceited self, becomes a first person plural, then part of public history, so that "conceited" vantage point becomes not merely a central city but "central cities." After initial models, there is an almost inevitable multiplication. Not only is Venice located "just in the centre of Europe," but Rome is the Dante of cities, "the central city of the world" (xiii, 426). As if establishing a cartography, or perhaps gravity, of epicycles, instead of the design of concentric circles that he also diagrams, Ruskin discerns as many Centres as there are subjects. It is as if Centres, once seen from the "conceited" vantage points of orthodox geometries, of incipient (logo)-concentricities, have now become the prescient bull's-eyes of focal points:

> I am surprised to find what a complete centre of the history of Europe, in politics and religion, this lake of Lucerne is, as Venice is a centre of the history of art   [vii, xxxii].

Once living in a Centre, surrounded by the four walls of his Herne Hill garden that compose an enclosed Circumference of reflexive, if naive, egocentricity, Ruskin, shortly afterward situated at a vantage point which has no privilege conferred upon it by his own dubious presence that is characteristically next to an at least qualified absence—either anonymous or pseudonymous (he cannot, after all, sign his own name)—observes Centres elsewhere: elsewhere and virtually everywhere. But accumulating both knowledge and experience that is an efficacious plenitude before becoming infernally replete, he begins to reconsider the value of immediacy, of the ground beneath his feet. His Herne Hill garden, his version of childish and geometric pastoral, is a type predicting a city that is also a vantage point of privilege, like a nest that is essential to national greatness—"preserve your eagles' nests" (xxix, 71)—a vantage point that is precisely as much his own, like "nests of pleasant thoughts" (xxii, 262), as those that occupied his Herne Hill garden:[2]

> This London is the principal nest of the men in the world; and I was standing in the centre of it   [xxii, 164].

As he does with Raphael, noting the centrality of his life, so Ruskin does with himself. Observing pauses, he observes not the ground beneath his feet but the middle-ground of his life:

> The fact being that I am, at this central time of life's work, at pause . . .   [xxviii, 403].

Further, perceiving Centres everywhere—beneath his feet, in the autobiography of his movement toward the "long shadow," and where he looks—he prospectively determines to write a life's work that is also central:

> and, after turning the matter hither and thither in my mind for two years more, I resolved to make it the central work of my life to write an exhaustive treatise on Political Economy   [xvii, 143].

Yet after the fact, during lectures given at Oxford in 1877, the central book becomes not *Munera Pulveris*, which was to have been the "exhaustive treatise on Political Economy," but instead *Unto This Last*:

> Next, I will read you the passage nobody has cared about, but which one day many will assuredly come to read with care, the last paragraph, namely, of that central book of my life   [xxii, 514].

Ruskin's movement toward the new Centre—a location of privilege beyond Cock-Robinson-Crusoe conceit—is also a movement toward responsibility. It is a movement toward a Centre of density in which plenitude in the form of the concentrated responsibility that also holds the seeds of mastery—the centripetal mastery, say,

---

[2] Nests prefigure the shells that inhabit the second part of this book. For a phenomenology of nests (and shells) see Gaston Bachelard's chapter, "Nests," in *The Poetics of Space*, translated by Maria Jolas (New York, 1964). By way of introduction, he says: "With nests and, above all, shells, we shall find a whole series of images that I am going to try to characterize as primal images; images that bring out the primitiveness in us. I shall then show that a human being likes to 'withdraw into his corner' and that it gives him physical pleasure to do so" (p. 91). The defensive labyrinth, in the later stages of the Transformations of the Maze, has some of the features of both nest and shell.

later suggested by both altitude and the manipulation implicit in indexes—is at first an uncomplicated good, a single and central beneficence which is also a fiction that can survive the experience of disconfirmation ("nothing" having come of grandiose plans) only temporarily. But then there is something temporary about the location of Ruskin's consciousness: its history can be seen as a process of sophisticated and labyrinthine commutation between a changing Centre and a Circumference that is, at least at first, close to being a decentralized Herne Hill garden—an earthly, almost suburban paradise that is, nevertheless, no pastoral for egocentric and "geometrical animals." Still, that is for later. Now, de-centred, circumferential concerns have no more than a potential existence. The possibility, or necessity, of a Promise(d) Land has not entered the realm of consciousness. And the Centres of agreeable plenitude flourish, as if the possibility of "too much" were an entirely tentative condition locked in a future tense that would, perpetuating its centrifugal futurity, never become present.

B. The Parallel Advance:
Panorama as Central Responsibility

Beginning, Ruskin is at the Centre, though a Centre that is in topographical fact suburban. And that Centre has only a small Circumference, or more accurately, no Circumference at all—not because his youthful world is without limits, but rather because it is all limits: necessarily, he attends to what he has—an immediate and present foreground. But when he leaves the walls of Herne Hill, he is obsessed with vistas, space, an extensive dimension in which he can find a place to lose the self-referring energy of early "conceit." Yet this is only one aspect of Ruskin's space—an efficacious aspect of a space that, retreating, is as recessional as an orthodox third dimension should be. Further, it is essentially a private, rectilinear space, organized about a private perspective, where the impulse to explore would achieve the immaculate privacy of self-annulment.

But even as this is occurring, this exploration that is the discovery of how to lose the "conceit" of an excessively "geometrical" self, there is an understanding of what is happening at the side—an awareness of what is occurring along a public, horizontal perspective that, avoiding loss at all costs, would include as much as might be handled by either a well-developed peripheral vision or a panoramic social conscience. And if loss becomes a possibility, condensation—as we shall see—is the solution. Lateral vision, accommodating more than autobiography in search of an erasure, includes public history—a sense of the intricate implication and extent of public issues, a sense, involving self with world, that is never eliminated for long by Ruskin's contradictory urge to ride the straight lines of converging orthogonals toward the focal point as vanishing point of transcendence.

With the panorama of a surface perspective brought about by the aggressive exercise of peripheral vision, Ruskin's existence, if not his "conceit," is momentarily assured by a publicly horizontal extension that emphatically establishes lateral connections as if for the buoyancy of a public-spirited self, rather than bringing about the depth perspective's disappearing act for a private and reluctant self. But the existence shaped by the perception of the horizontal, surface perspective will often be, as optical inclusion yields "polygonal" responsibility, an existence of terrible contention, of variations of the experience of cold floors and screaming birds. And it is an existence that cannot be separated from what the Centre is to become. Panorama and Centres are locations that are not in necessary conflict; instead, they are places that deal with the same fundamental energy, which is an energy that, at its most extreme, emanates from the perception of the interrelation of Strange Chords.

The original Centre of Cock-Robinson-Crusoe "conceit" is private. But the later Centre—a Centre of privilege and attempted mastery—is as public as the horizon of lateral focus. The intuition—it is more that than an explicit point—is not merely Ruskin's idiosyncratic organization of space and self. Merleau-Ponty, exploring the differences between perspectives, suggests that lateral vision involves public inclusion, whereas depth implies a more limited relation between a single self—the observer—and world. With the horizontal perspective, the emphasis is on the public history of the world; with depth perspective, the emphasis is on the private autobiography of the self. So Merleau-Ponty can say: "It [depth] announces a certain indissoluble link between things and myself by which I am placed in front of them, whereas breadth can, at first sight, be taken as a relationship between things themselves in which the perceiving subject is not implied."[3] Still, there are differences. Merleau-Ponty's "perceiving subject," observing horizontal breadth, is as invisible—or "not implied"—as Ruskin's explorer of the farthest depths of the third dimension. Perceiving laterally, Ruskin certifies—perhaps even justifies, though Ruskin is impelled by far

[3] M. Merleau-Ponty, translated by Colin Smith, *Phenomenology of Perception* (New York, 1962), p. 256.

more than guilt in search of justification—his own public-spirited existence, an existence that requires an audience, though not necessarily its applause.

When the depth perspective has been explored and found wanting except for its ability to "lose" Merleau-Ponty's "things" and Ruskin's self, when the vanishing point has been sought for a privacy that becomes the final solipsism of a lost self, when a failing transcendence is the initial failure of a foreground of naive immanence, in which for a short time there is virtually no optical distinction between self and the world (the early whole "conceited" self being the whole world), then what is left, the next step—or better, the next adjustment of the eye—is off to the side, in those peripheral areas that have a public existence which will become central in an economically inevitable act of consolidation.[4] The redistribution of a failed distance precipitates a sense of interconnection, the lateral and organic perception of a self who would include the world rather than have an excluded self disappear. That Ruskin's refocusing of consciousness (the optical shift from an exclusive depth perception to one of lateral inclusion) is closer to public history than idiosyncratic autobiography is suggested by Hillis Miller, whose reluctant Victorian God, disappearing, is involved in the same performance as Ruskin's "conceited," if not egomaniacal, first person—a first person whose necessary goal in life is the death of self-consciousness at a point where the centrally "geometrical" animal might be reborn with peripheral vision: "When God vanishes, man turns to interpersonal relations as the only remaining arena of the search for authentic selfhood. Only

---

[4] It should perhaps be pointed out that the side—those peripheral areas that will become the Centre of the social critic's concern—is also below. Penetrating recessional space, moving toward the Nothing of the circumferential background in an act that anticipates the centrifugal movement toward the blank page of the Travel Diary, Ruskin explores, with narrow intensity, the transcendental topography of a "Mountain Glory"—a landscape formulated by both an aesthetic of the Infinite and a keen attention to the structure and beauty of a benign and uncomplicated version of Wordsworth's nature. But after this transcendental exploration, which occurs largely in *Modern Painters I* and *II*, what is below is taken increasingly into account, included, explored—the "Mountain Gloom" that is part of a fallen condition that does not have either energy for, or interest in, the Infinite. The vision, both inclusively lateral and low, can be, for example, of inhabitants of an Alpine village, connected to Ruskin by an agonizing awareness of the indissolubility of the horizontal perspective, who are:

... obscured by an unspeakable horror—a smoke, as it were, of martyrdom, coiling up with the incense, and, amidst the images of tortured bodies and lamenting spirits in hurtling flames, the very cross, for them, dashed more deeply than for others, with gouts of blood   [vi, 388-89].

in his fellow men can he find any longer a presence in the world which might replace the lost divine presence."[5]

The accommodation of the horizontal is no small shift of focus or concern. Potential autobiography, without fear of eventual erasure, is substantiated by those peripherally extensive concerns of the incipient social critic, whose self will be found, not in the private vanishing point of recessional space, but in the public "interpersonal relations" of panorama. Once, the attempt to limit areas of concern, to contain the horizontal aspect of the "lateral range" (III, 642), led Ruskin to dismiss paintings whose ambition lay in breadth considered excessive—that lateral "interpersonal" dimension which might happily be ignored by someone who, given half a chance, would trade the possibility of a publicly supported autobiography (the account of an "authentic selfhood") for immediate self-annulment. Once, the panoramic inclusion of serial extensions was, at the least, undesirable:

> Hence it appears, that all such paintings as Stothard's Canterbury Pilgrimage are panoramas, not pictures. In the Royal Academy, two years ago, there was a very sweet bit by Landseer—Highland drovers crossing a bridge; and if the picture had been confined to the breadth of the bridge itself, and a white Shetland pony looking into the water, which was the chief light, all had been well; instead of this, we had a parallelogram of about seven feet by one, with a whole progression of figures, extending from one end to the other, the bridge in the centre, and the picture was altogether ruined [I, 241-42].

Furthermore, just as panorama was a suspicious dimension, so a version of the panoramic, extended until it became a kind of enclosing Circumference, was also considered a little unworthy. The early Ruskin, whose only knowledge of the Centre was one of youthful conceit and who manipulated both consciousness and self (the two not always being the same) along a perspective of depth that was so personal the self might become invisible in the process, could only think of the peripheral territory at the edge of vision as, at best, a diffuse and watered-down rendition of the Centre. The Circumference was not only less than the Centre but lower. Then unperceived as a version of the background (a location of both the pastoral dispersal of selfhood and public responsibility), the Circumference of a series of concentric circles that were held together by the almost feudal organization of central privilege not

[5] J. Hillis Miller, *The Form of Victorian Fiction* (South Bend, 1968), p. 33.

only *could* be ignored but, because of the implications of its eccentric location and lack of altitude, *should* be ignored. At first the Circumference is not the transcendent territory of "Mountain Glory." Instead, like "Mountain Gloom," it is a fallen landscape for fallen judgment and perception:

> The question [of judgment] is not decided by them, but for them; decided at first by a few; by fewer in proportion as the merits of the work are of higher order. From these few the decision is communicated to the number next below them in rank of mind, and by these again to a wider and lower circle; and each rank being so far cognizant of the superiority of that above it, as to receive its decision with respect   [III, 80].

But now, the Centre is connected with a panorama that is virtually circumferential. There is the feeling that, aside from the naive Centre of Cock-Robinson-Crusoe "conceit," there is no Centre that is without a strong sense of the horizontal, which is to say an awareness of the "interpersonal" inclusion of the social critic, whose selfhood must be supported by public concern. And Ruskin's progress toward the new Centre beyond the rectangle (the implication of "right angles" will soon become apparent) of the four walls of Herne Hill is a campaign conducted on a broad front, with nothing to be left out, as if the peripheral were potentially central. Perhaps the concentric circle farthest removed from the self's starting point will prove to be a circular Edge of penultimate, if replete, privilege before the "nothing" beyond. In any case, lateral perception has achieved the condition of a significant reality, albeit a panoramic reality that has to be divided in order to be perceived/expressed:

> . . . any student of intelligence may perceive that one inherent cause of the divided character of this book is its function of advance in parallel columns over the wide field . . .   [XXVI, 273].

Ruskin has become very much aware of his earlier tendency to dismiss the "wide field," to employ the early narrowness of depth perspective as the most economical dimension for the solitary penetration of space:

> . . . but Norton saw all my weaknesses, measured all my narrownesses . . .   [XXXV, 522].

His "weaknesses," measured in "narrownesses," do not support substantial selfhood. He decides that breadth must be cultivated; language, imitating his new attitudes toward space, becomes a form of elastic:

I use the word in a far wider sense . . .   [xvii, 317].

Or again:

. . . I carefully extended my definition of a roof so as to include more than is usually understood by the term   [x, 239].

Yet advancing "in parallel columns over the wide field," Ruskin understands that the "wide field" is beyond his control, even as he divides to perceive: encompassed, like an "overlapping" Circumference, the "parallel columns" cannot be mastered. Anticipations of the problems of the rectilinear, the problems of the gardener-critic of straight lines, are already apparent. Chances, which may later prove to be curvilinear digressions of the early Transformations of the Maze, must be taken:

. . . the labour of a critic who sincerely desires to be just, extends into more fields than it is possible for any single hand to furrow straightly. . . . It is not possible to extend the range of work thus widely, without running the chance of occasionally making mistakes   [v, 6].

But the inability to control the "wide field" does not dissuade him. The same intensity that he once employed in the narrow exploration of recessional space he now uses for the horizontal extension of his "lateral range":

I shall endeavor to make the courses of my University lectures as wide in their range as my knowledge will permit. The range conceded will be narrow enough   [xx, 39].

Further, even when a certain kind of limitation becomes necessary, as in the process of a limitation necessary in order to keep the cries of peacocks from infernally assaulting the ears, a sense of width is required:

I have been endeavoring this morning to define the limits of insanity. My experience is not yet wide enough   [xxxvii, 13].

As Ruskin advances toward a new Centre that is neither a vanishing point's bull's-eye (this, before the multiplicity of mirrored reflection) nor solipsistically "conceited," the safe limitation that would eliminate "the chance of occasionally making mistakes"—or far worse—is uncharacteristic. Even close to the beginning, he suspects that containers are meant to overflow as much as hold:

I have only to express, in conclusion, my regrets that it has been impossible to finish the work within the limits first proposed. Having, of late, found my designs always requiring enlargement in process of execution, I will take care, in future, to set no limits whatsoever   [v, 13].

Without limitations, Ruskin will find greatness beyond himself at the side even as he has found extinction in depth—either loss of not only "conceit" but selfhood, or the terrifying, farsighted awareness of death's "long shadow." And if sublimity, an important ingredient of the Aesthetics of the Infinite that shapes his early transcendental organization of space, is dependent upon a sense of width as well as a perception of distance—

All the size and sublimity of nature are given, not by the height, but by the breadth of her masses   [iii, 564]—

then the Parallel Advance stakes out a peripheral territory that is not, in fact, the wasteland charted by the early Ruskin, who saw the outer reaches of concentric circles as a circumference of fallen, even "gloomy" landscape. The peripheral Circumference—the "breadth" of the "wide field"—is resurrected as a territory, which will later be seen as a kind of Promise(d) Land, that can only be perceived from the Centre. One might say that the "wide circumference," as a dimension of privilege, achieves its status by the optical virtue of its connection with the central vantage point, just as, fundamentally, any "contention" between Centre and Circumference, as with the later vertical antiphon of double labyrinths, is a "contention" based upon reciprocity and interrelation. Competition is neither a relation that is parasitical nor one of mutual exclusion; rather, it is a condition of symbiotic survival.

The Central Judge, who is more than merely centrally "conceited," occupies the middle of his own "wide field," as if the "winner," which is to say "loser," of Gaston Bachelard's "*plains test*."[6] But the horizontal perspective is to be seen, not lived amidst. If the rectilinear movement along the depth perspective anticipates the loss of self in the devouring distances of recessional space, the self's occupation within the extremities of the "lateral range" predicts

---

[6] Provocatively, Bachelard suggests: "In the realm of images, there can be no contradiction, and two spirits that are identically sensitive can sensitize the dialectics of center and horizon in different ways. In this connection a sort of *plains test* can be used" (*Poetics of Space*, p. 203).

another kind of "nothing"—the blank page of madness. Yet at first, Ruskin does not become what he sees. And perspectives—both depth and horizontal—are straight lines of spatial organization that are to be seen, but lived neither "along" nor "within." For Ruskin to enter into the intricate designs of his shaping *The Elements of Drawing* and *The Elements of Perspective* is for him to lose the location of both his self and his sanity. At this point, the efficacy of Ruskinian perspective, which is informed by the intricate "right angles" of Greek fret, requires that the observer not be manipulated by the space he would, guideless, himself organize—and study. But this will be subject to change.

C. The Vantage Point of the True Centre:
Problems in the Transcendental Altitude of the Self

Almost always, Ruskin is the traveler, whose itinerary is not often his travel diary, and whose prophecy is not often confirmed. Faced with the rectilinear, he will often digress. If he continually watches, he often continually watches while moving. At any rate, the necessarily troublesome movement toward a point that must be as "earned" as the Travel Diary's blank page, a point from where the horizontal perspective or its curved, three-dimensional equivalent, the Circumference, can be discerned—a point which is nothing less than that vantage point of central privilege which, without naive "conceit," permits not only the distanced "study" of perspectives but also the organization of experience and knowledge—is like moving toward another kind of Centre. It is, in fact, like early movement toward Venice. Often, Ruskin's travel through the topography of his consciousness is a reflection of an earlier movement through external landscape: design, as well as the maneuvering among and through designs and shapes that may be of architecture, landscape, or the more self-conscious landscape of horticultural concern, is reflected in the later negotiations between syntax (as well as parataxis and an ultimate "inner language" that would twist insides out) and consciousness, as with the final Theatre of Blindness that is osmotically both "inside" and "outside." One might say that gardening, or walking through a garden, was preparation for writing that is at least temporarily efficacious.

In this case, the journey is a process of peregrination through a landscape of stifling flatness—a landscape that, with the exception of an occasional tower, is without a hint of altitude, without any means for the traveler to judge his position, to get his bearings that will locate his temporary, "in progress" vantage point. The move-

ment toward the Centre is a blind proposition, as of Blind Guides—
a proposition that, like later travel through dark and labyrinthine
syntax directed toward the Circumference, is undertaken without
maps, without paths, and without comfort:

> The scene is often profoundly oppressive, even at this day
> . . . but, in order to know what it was once, let the traveller
> follow in his boat at evening the windings of some unfre-
> quented channel far into the midst of the melancholy plain;
> let him remove, in his imagination, the brightness of the great
> city that still extends itself in the distance . . . and so wait, until
> the bright investiture and sweet warmth of the sunset are with-
> drawn from the waters, and the black desert of their shore lies
> in its nakedness beneath the night, pathless, comfortless, in-
> firm, lost in dark languor and fearful silence . . . and he will
> be enabled to enter in some sort into the horror of the heart
> with which this solitude was anciently chosen by man for his
> habitation   [x, 13].

Or, more centripetally concentric, the progress of Ruskin toward
a position of central organization may be similar to the movement,
within that central city, toward St. Mark's, which provides both
towering altitude and the potential for mastery and clarity in the
middle of a densely urban confusion that is itself like the "windings
of some unfrequented channel far into the midst of the melancholy
plain." But Ruskin's journey toward St. Mark's is more claustrophobic than merely oppressive. There is too little space rather than
the too much of the "melancholy plain." Simply, there is no room
for the "parallel advance":

> We find ourselves in a paved alley, some seven feet wide
> where it is widest, full of people, and resonant with cries of
> itinerant salesman—a shriek in their beginning, and dying
> away into a kind of brazen ringing, all the worse for its con-
> finement between the high houses of the passage along which
> we have to make our way. Overhead, an inextricable confusion
> of rugged shutters, and iron balconies and chimney flues,
> pushed out on brackets to save room . . .
> We will push fast through . . . into the shadows of the pillars
> at the end of the "Bocca di Piazza," and then we forget them
> all; for between those pillars there opens a great light, and, in
> the midst of it, as we advance slowly, the vast tower of St. Mark
> seems to lift itself visibly forth from the level field of chequered
> stones; and, on each side, the countless arches prolong them-

selves into ranged symmetry, as if the rugged and irregular houses that pressed together above us in the dark alley had been struck back into sudden obedience and lovely order.
. . .

And well may they fall back, for beyond those troops of ordered arches there rises a vision out of the earth, and all the great square seems to have opened from it in a kind of awe, that we see it far away   [x, 80-82].

Just as the horizontal perspective has central implications, so does altitude: perhaps animated more by privilege than pathetic fallacy, the tower of St. Mark's lifts itself—or seems to—from the maze of streets, where space is so precious that "brackets" are employed "to save room." Elevated, striking back the claustrophobic "rugged and irregular houses that pressed together above us in the alley," St. Mark's, in that position of central elevation, masters the winding path of Ruskin's circuitous progress. From the tower, that progress, which is confused at street level, suddenly becomes clear. From the animated central tower of the city that is itself central, there is perceived not only a "ranged symmetry," but also a "sudden obedience and lovely order." It is as if gaining (or better, earning) knowledge and experience, Ruskin would achieve the altitudinal vantage point of St. Mark's tower in order to make retrospective sense of previous patterns—patterns that, giving meaning to experience (perhaps the experience of labyrinthine movement), were invisible in the process of approach either across the oppressive plain, or within the dense contortions of the city's labyrinthine space.

The altitude of the Centre—not an observed but an observing central altitude which would make the vantage point as transcendent as the infinite focal point that is itself nothing less than the vanishing point of the anonymous depth perspective—is not only an altitude from where the horizon can be either summed up or accommodated. It is also a transcendent, extracted position that, in its synoptic extrication, both includes the peripheral extent of the Parallel Advance and predicts its later serpentine exit—a centrifugal exit that may well be in the form of intricately pedestrian lines of white marble that are, as we shall see, like the transforming syntax of the Maze as its essential locus penultimately coils toward the Edge of the blank page. The vantage point of distanced and altitudinal transcendence, coming after the transcendent, and always instructive, focal point of the self-annulling depth perspective, anticipates the perpetual self-transcendence of a labyrinthine immediacy. But anticipations are fulfilled with the arrival of later tenses. The blood of the circumcision is only the shadowy type of a more substantial blood-letting that will come as the "long shadow" becomes shorter.

Fascinated by labyrinths—his later "fallen" performances, as will become apparent, shaped by early time spent in the Lucent Verdure of the Maze—he is also, antithetically, preoccupied by heights. The experience of the one brings about the desire—even need—for the other. With Ruskin, antithesis, if it is not in "contention," "naked" or antiphonal, yields symbiotic advantages, as later dialectic does not. Transcendental disengagement permits serial mastery. But it is an extracted mastery that would be impossible without the information and sense of engagement that comes from the fallen, and essentially temporal, experience of the Maze. Further, the exclusive awareness of either is an optical impossibility; with reciprocal needs, height requires the labyrinth in the same way that the Centre requires the Circumference, and in the same way that a vantage point requires a focal point. Yet with Ruskin, the vantage and focal points shift, perpetually reversing themselves, and an original love of the labyrinthine brings about a later need for the extractions of altitude, where room to breathe is also room from which to see.

Ruskin arrives at (or centripetally "winds" his way toward) St. Mark's as narrowly as possible, in an approach that is as serpentine (and appropriately "fallen") as the inevitable "unwinding" of his expressive departure. But narrow "arrival" is a rare occasion. More often, it will be the Parallel Advance that will move toward the necessary central altitude—an altitude where, with a short-lived privilege predicting repletion, what will be required is the sinuous release of the Parallel Advance's condensed horizon. And after both Parallel Advance and the masterful altitude of the Centre, there is the Maze—the labyrinthine and circumferential style of Theseus, whose obsession, after dealing with Minotaurean centricity, is with the open, even circumferential, space beyond the exit, as if that might prove a solution to intricately fallen problems.

Organized by a need to take into account the public, horizontal perspective that includes public "interpersonal" relations rather than the private erasure of the penetration of space's antiautobiography, and, at the same time, impelled toward the Centre of density and inclusion (and, very possibly, an "inextricable confusion" that even Strange Chords cannot master) by a further need to organize what has been taken into account, Ruskin, apparently at his destination, may discover that "there" is in fact only halfway "there." Yet if the high centrality of the apparent "there" is in the middle, it is not the middle of the Central Judge's vantage point that is also, in the more orthodox guise of those who do not inhabit their own perspective studies, the central focal point of the horizontal perspective.

The central goal may, in fact, be disconcertingly close to the starting point, with less room than expected for either "study" or travel. Just as the transcendental altitude of St. Mark's—between the advance of experience and the exit of presumably meaningful expression—at first appeared to be a goal of mastery, bringing order and open space to the claustrophobic and unparallel approach of streets that wind like suburban channels, so Centres in general are nearer to being halfway structures of synoptic altitude than the final destination of ultimacy. More often than not, the elevated Centre, closer to middle than end, is "between." Hence, the location of Ruskin's conditional traveler, who is like Ruskin himself, as he resumes *Modern Painters* after ten years' absence:

> In taking up the clue of an inquiry, now intermitted for nearly ten years, it may be well to do as a traveller would, who had to recommence an interrupted journey in a guideless country; and, ascending, as it were, some little hill beside our road, note how far we have already advanced, and what pleasantest ways we may choose for farther progress [v, 17].

Here (characteristically with Ruskin), altitude is sought in the middle or Centre. The extricated observation of movement through a "guideless country," as if following the "windings of some unfrequented channel," makes a kind of sense out of both past and prediction (if not the prophecy that will lead to desertion and disconfirmation) that is at least sensible. The "little hill" between the "intermitted" ten years separating *Modern Painters II* from *Modern Painters III* is the textual equivalent to the tower seven miles outside of Venice that Ruskin, anticipating the more ambitious and masterful altitude of St. Mark's, would ascend at evening:

> On this mound is built a rude brick campanile, of the commonest Lombardic type, which if we ascend towards evening (and there are none to hinder us, the door of its ruinous staircase swinging idly on its hinges), we may command from it one of the most notable scenes in this wide world of ours. Far as the eye can reach, a waste of the wild sea moor . . . with the corrupted sea-water soaking through the roots of its acrid weeds, and gleaming hither and thither through its snaky channels [x, 17].

A map substantiates what someone who is "guideless" intuits: that altitude is central by virtue of its ability to accommodate the Circumference; to be elevated is to occupy a Centre. The raised gardens of Turin, offering an inclusive vision that is a geographical version of the Parallel Advance, compose a representative vantage point of central elevation:

> . . . these gardens often gave me a good deal to think about. They are . . . on the slope of the hill above the city, to the east; commanding therefore, the view over it and beyond it, westward—a view which, perhaps, of all those that can be obtained north of the Apennines, gives the most comprehensive idea of the nature of Italy. If you glance at the map, you will observe that Turin is placed in the centre of the crescent which the Alps form round the basin of Piedmont; it is within ten miles of the foot of the mountains at the nearest point; and from that point the chain extends half round the city in one unbroken Moorish crescent, forming three-fourths of a circle [XVI, 194].

After the egotistical Centre of childish naiveté and the subsequent concern for the foregrounds and backgrounds that organize both Ruskin's depth perspective and the private, almost anonymous penetration of space, the particular energy that gives idiosyncratic shape to his landscape is the intense concern for privileged space, usually central, which is either an observable location of primary privilege by virtue of its own density and plenitude, or which is central not so much because of what it is or what can be observed of it, as what it sees. This secondary Centre—the Centre of transcendental altitude—becomes, because of observed essences, reflexively central. The success is optical. Instead of the vantage point aspiring toward the condition of the focal point, the focal point retroactively confers privilege by its special nature. If not a pile of rocks, the point of elevation may be no more than a single rock, a "piece of crag, with its blue and prickly weeds," whose singularity is the result of what is conferred upon it by the reciprocity of its focal points:

> Now, I do not think that there is any rock in all the world, from which the places, and the monuments, of so complex and deep a fragment of the history of its ages can be visible, as from this piece of crag, with its blue and prickly weeds. For you have thus beneath you at once, the birthplaces of Virgil and of Livy, the homes of Dante and Petrarch, and the source

of the most sweet and pathetic inspiration to your own Shake-speare; the spot where the civilization of the Gothic kingdoms was founded on the throne of Theodoric . . . You have the cradle of natural science . . . the central light . . . the chief stain . . . the birthplace   [xix, 19, 434].

Seeing specially, Ruskin sees "at once," bringing both the burden and privilege of the Centre's implicit simultaneity to the altitude of "rock" or "crag." And what is seen is a landscape that, like the interrelations of Strange Chords, is a slice of past time that is not only "complex and deep" but also a series of precisely original and temporal locations consisting of "homes," a "source," a "spot" for the founding of a "throne of Theodoric," as well as a "cradle," a "central light," a "chief stain," and, either finally or firstly, a "birth-place." Discerning origins, as if from the primary point of concentric circles that is itself ambitiously involved in expanding, centrif-ugal aspiration, Ruskin would make historically (logo)-concentric sense of a rock that, after the sense making, is no mere rock. An observed history of beginnings makes an otherwise forgettable space entirely memorable. Furthermore, the "Now"—as in the "Now, I do not think"—becomes as reflexively important as the rock's immediate vantage point, which translates into the "this" of a proximate "piece of crag." Significance is brought home.

Historically, in the "complex and deep" slice of time that presents a characteristically Victorian perspective on landscape preoccu-pations, Ruskin's topographical obsessions—perhaps exaggerated by his intrinsic concern with the reciprocal relation between optics and landscape, at least until primary concern becomes submerged assumption—are more representative of a time than eccentric to it. Or rather, they represent a characteristically Victorian response to what is seen as a fundamentally Victorian problem. The modern landscape inhabitant of *Modern Painters* is writing an early version of the gardening sections of *Praeterita*. The gardens or architecture of Ruskin's mind—the sense of design formulated in horticulture or stone that organizes primary gesture—is based upon the instincts toward an organic interrelation that can most easily be satisfied by altitude. Wholeness of either perceived landscape, or reflexively, the perceiving self, is, despite peripheral vision, close to an im-possibility at ground level.

The attempt to get an overview, to get to the elevated gardens that are either within or permit sight of the equivalent of the "centre of the crescent"—gardens that enable the observer to discern pat-terns in both past, private experience and a present society that is more apparently fragmented than "interpersonal"—is largely an attempt to get a position of potential synthesis amidst the growing, assembly-line specialization of an age that, at least initially, is reluctant to treat width as an organically inclusive dimension. The Victorian horizon is originally seen as a model of the assembly-line that Ruskin will talk about in "The Nature of Gothic" chapter of *The Stones of Venice*, where the disconnected and repeated acts of unintegrated activities necessarily breed a specialized and relativistic series of vantage points whose only fallen comfort resides in the calculatedly unambitious narrowness of their vision.

But there are varieties of comfort. And perfect narrowness can also be seen as dehumanized limitation. So, promoting what Ruskin with his initial optical bias and peripherally inclusive ambitions assumes, someone as representative of an age as Arnold—or, more accurately, his blind Homer, with a properly Hellenic, if not Daedalean, regard for the organic whole rather than mechanistic parts—sees (if one can interpret poetry as a rhetoric for optics and direction) with an insistently panoramic awareness that is the blind sight of the visionary, who brings the possibility of a wide solution to original problems:

> Who prop, thou ask'st, in these bad days, my
>   mind?—
> He much, the old man, who clearest soul's
>   of men,
> Saw The Wide Prospect. . . .
>   ["To a Friend"]

And like Homer's blind, synthesizing (synthesizing because blind) sight, Goethe's panoramic scope—or at least Arnold's version—has the potential, if summoned, to provide a ground-level coherence where only the multiplicity of agitation exists. Reversing what will later become Ruskin's response to width, Arnold's replete "too" can be slackened by the extension and accommodation of horizontal vision, which, with Arnold, yields a space that is as "calm" and "luminous" as those early distances of Ruskin:

> Too fast we live, too much are tried,
> Too harrassed, to attain
> Wordsworth's sweet calm or Goethe's wide
> And luminous view to gain.
>   ["Stanzas in Memory of
> the Author of 'Obermann' "]

Yet if the results are finally different—and the differences are largely those of chronology—the need for the "Wide Prospect" is essentially the same.

More striking than Arnold's desired ground-level panorama or either Ruskin's "little hill" of his conditional traveler, who would make sense of a "guideless country," or Tennyson's more aspiring "empyreal heights" that permit the poet to catch the "deep pulsations of the world" ("In Memoriam," VC) is the vantage point of Newman—privileged by altitudinal virtue—that enables him to find coherence not only "behind" him, in the immaculate history before schisms, but "below" him. Still, coherence is "below" only because he himself is "above." The tower of a church may be as useful as the pulpit's elevation:

> I say then, if we would improve the intellect, first of all, we must ascend; we cannot gain real knowledge on a level; we must generalize, we must reduce to method, we must have a grasp of principles, and group and shape our acquisitions by means of them. It matters not whether field of operation be wide or limited; in every case, to command it, is to mount above it. Who has not felt the irritation of mind and impatience created by a deep, rich country, visited for the first time, with winding lands, and high hedges, and green steeps, and tangled woods, and everything smiling indeed, but in a maze? The same feeling comes upon us in a strange city, when we have no map of its streets. Hence you hear of practised travellers, when they first come into a place, mounting some high hill or church tower, by way of reconnoitering its neighborhood.
> [*The Idea of a University*, Discourse 6, Section 7].

The potential perfectability of the mind resides in its ability to "ascend" to a position where "command" and generalization of specific and separated information lead to the probability of "real knowledge." It is a position, like St. Mark's, that would master the "winding lanes" and "high hedges" of what is, essentially, a Maze, a Maze that, despite apparent smiles, irritates—at least at ground level.[7]

---

[7] Yet, prefiguratively, it is important to note the ground-level efficacy that Ruskin himself will find in the Hampton Court Maze. The Maze, in fact, would not be mastered from "above." Altitude, the special dimension of the attendant, is not Ruskin's later solution. Newman's "irritation" will become Ruskin's ecstasy. The "rostrum" will not be sought. Here is W. H. Matthews on the relation between Mazes and altitude generally, and Hampton Court, specifically:

> If the maze is intended to be seen at all from above, some attempt should be made to introduce a symmetrical and artistic element into its design. Usually

Finally, in its broadest aspects and most auspiciously, it is New-man whom the Victorian Parallel Advance greets, as lateral exten-sion becomes an enveloping Circumference. And it is most clearly Newman who rises to an occasion of necessity and problem by rising above it. Explicitly, Newman self-consciously advertises and pro-motes what is assumed (and so, almost submerged) in Ruskin's own optical organizations. Both an intellect, which has achieved the heights (not necessarily "empyreal") of synthesis, and an eye, per-ceiving with panoramic inclusion, have central locations—if only because of what they receive. And that Centre, with its awareness of at least "interpersonal relations," which are as fundamentally organic as the unvivisected body of a "whole self," is nothing if it is not "true":

> That only is true enlargement of mind which is the power of viewing many things at once as one whole, of referring them severally to their true place in the universal system, of under-standing their respective values, and determining their mutual dependence. Thus is that form of Universal Knowledge, of which I have on occasion spoken, set up in the individual intellect, and constitutes its perfection. Possessed of this real illumination, the mind never views any part of the extended subject-matter of Knowledge without recollecting that it is but a part, or without the associations which spring from this rec-ollection. It makes every thing in some sort lead to every thing else; it would communicate the image of the whole to every separate portion, till that whole becomes in imagination like a spirit, every where pervading and penetrating its component parts, and giving them one definite meaning. Just as our bodily organs, when mentioned, recall their function in the body, as the word 'creation' suggests the Creator, and 'subjects' a sov-ereign, so, in the mind of the Philosopher, as we are abstractly conceiving of him, the elements of the physical and moral world, sciences, arts, pursuits, ranks, offices, events, opinions, individualities, are all viewed as one, with correlative functions and as gradually by successive combinations converging one

---

some vantage-point is available from which an attendant or expert can observe and direct over-bewildered visitors, but if this point be accessible to the visitors themselves the hedges should be provided with pinnacles or balks, here and there, to prevent the observer from solving the puzzle by unfair means. This is the case with, for instance, the Saffron Walden maze; at Hampton Court, where there are no balks, only the attendant is permitted to mount the rostrum [*Mazes & Labyrinths*, p. 189].

and all, to the true centre.   [*Idea of a University*, Discourse 6, Section 6].

Newman's True Centre, anticipating the (logo)-concentricity implicit in the vision of Strange Chords, is close to Ruskin's early altitudinal aspirations—aspirations for the transcendentally elevated vantage point. And as we shall see more explicitly later, with the Central Man, the inhabitants of those locations have much in common. Not only does Newman's extraordinary man see with an ambitious sense of spatial apprehension, but the nature of his altitude also permits him to see temporal relations:

> And therefore a truly great intellect . . . is one which takes a connected view of old and new, past and present, far and near, and which has an insight into the influence of all these one on another; without which there is no whole, and no centre. It possesses the knowledge, not only of things, but also of their mutual and true relations . . .   [Discourse 6, Section 5].

Similarly, here is Ruskin's early man of privileged altitude—in this case, as in most cases with Ruskin, he is a type of Turner—who also, as both historian and prophet, makes connections that are as temporal as spatial:

> He stands upon an eminence, from which he looks back over the universe and forward over the generations of men. Let every work of his hand be a history of the one, and a lesson to the other. Let each exertion of his mighty mind be both hymn and prophecy . . .   [III, 631].

But the reader can become Turner. Or at least, from a position of textual eminence and in retrospective aspects, Ruskin invites the reader to become like Turner. And like Newman's "practised travellers," both writer—at least the first time through the text—and the reader, who is not a rereader, must get a sense of their context, which, specifically, is a sense of their paginal history:

> . . . and we shall therefore pause on the threshold of this final change, to glance back upon, and gather together, those fragments . . .   [x, 301].

> . . . I believe the reader may both happily and profitably rest for a little while beneath the first vault of the arcade, to review . . .   [x, 365].

Fundamentally, it is the writer as the "practised traveller," who must employ the pause of "textual eminence" to see not only history but make sensible prediction:

> The reader remembers, I trust . . . and I must anticipate . . . [x, 359].

Like Turner, the Ruskinian writer, even more than his most ambitious reader, must be able to look back over the textual equivalent of "the universe and forward over the generation of men."

Textual pauses of "eminence" are necessary because both history and prophecy, past and future, can be accommodated by a version of altitude that confers the privilege, when it is that, of (logo)-concentricity upon those pauses which compose a kind of series of "still centres" that are like oases of broad comprehension—Chords that are "true" before they become Strange. But the textual eminence of both writer and reader fails to answer more demanding requirements. Avoiding peacocks that are yet to be a problem, Ruskin will nevertheless become a bird—or rather, he would have the knowledge of the optics of a variety of birds:

> Now, I want to know what the appearance is to an eagle, two thousand feet up, of a sparrow in a hedge, or a partridge in a stubble field. What kind of definition on the retina do these brown spots take to manifest themselves as signs of a thing eatable . . . ? And then tell me, farther, does it see only a square yard at a time, and yet, as it flies take summary of the square yards beneath? [xxii, 201].

What is needed is a farsighted optics of generalization through altitude—that high and wide accommodation of the organic whole. Ruskin suggests levitation by an act of imaginative supposition:

> We must now proceed to obtain some rough idea of the appearance and distribution of the palace itself; but its arrangement will be better understood by supposing ourselves raised some hundred and fifty feet above the point of the lagoon in front of it, so as to get a general view . . . [x, 331].

Exploring the optics of birds, he would be like Pater's zoologically ambiguous Sebastian van Storck, whose vaulting ambition is his preference "for those prospects *à vol d'oiseau*—of the caged bird on the wing at last":[8]

---

[8] Walter Pater, *Imaginary Portraits* (London, 1910), p. 89.

I must do what I can, by the help of a rough plan and a bird's eye view, to give him the necessary topographical knowledge . . . [x, 329].

Yet ultimately Ruskin is closer to pragmatic map making than to Sebastian with his vaguely Platonic philosophy of abstract extinction. To draw a map is to assume Newman's commanding and "connected view of old and new, past and present, far and near." Making maps—or, as in the "Of Map Making" chapter of *The Laws of Fésole*, demonstrating how maps are made—Ruskin's altitude is at least birdlike. But the vigorous changes in geographical nomenclature announced in "Of Map Making"[9] suggest an altitudinal ambition that would render the consideration and exploration of the bird's-eye view entirely obsolete. It is, in fact, as if he were creating a new world. Looking down on the cartographer—and his "modern science"—he would also look down on birds, even those in flight. Simply, as if from a True Centre that had become portable, he would be "above"—almost angelically:

The charts of the world which have been drawn up by modern science have thrown into a narrow space the expression of a vast amount of knowledge, but I have never yet seen any one pictorial enough to enable the spectator to imagine the kind of contrast in physical character which exists between Northern and Southern countries. We know the differences in detail, but we have not that broad glance and grasp which would enable us to feel them in their fulness. We know that gentians grow on the Alps, and olives in the Apennines; but we do not enough conceive for ourselves that variegated mosaic of the world's surfaces which a bird sees in its migration, that difference between the district of the gentian and of the olive which the stork and the swallow see far off, as they lean upon the sirocco wind. Let us, for a moment, try to raise ourselves above the level of their flight, and imagine the Mediterranean lying beneath us like an irregular lake . . . [x, 186].

[9] "I wish my students to call these circles, severally, the St. James' circle, the Arabian circle, the Venetian circle, the Christian circle, and the Fern circle. On . . . the St. George's circle, opposite the Venetian, will mark the mid-quadrant, reminding the student also, that in far South America there is a Gulf of St. George; the Thule circle will pass close south of the Southern Thule; and the Blanche circle (*ligne* blanche, for French children) [will] include, with Mounts Erebus and Terror, the supposed glacial space of the great Antarctic continent" (xv, 443).

Beyond Ruskin—perhaps above him—there is of course, as always, Turner. Ambitious, the "grasp" inherent in map making is one thing; more than merely ambitious, renaming a world's cosmology suggests a hubristic aspiration that would have Ruskin become as exalted as Turner, or almost, with an important distance between aspiration as calculated fiction and aspiration as potential fact. Newman's perception of "mutual and true relations," observed from his True Centre, which is Ruskin's avian, even at times angelic, altitude, only anticipates the visionary expression of Turner, who, creating the organic interrelation of "strange intellectual chords," is involved in actually making what a privileged Newman only sees:

> Every touch in these plates is related to every other, and has no permission of withdrawn, monastic virtue, but is only good in its connexion with the rest, and in that connexion infinitely and inimitably good. The showing how each of these designs is connected by all manner of *strange intellectual chords* and nerves . . . pathos and history . . . [xv, xxiv, italics mine].

But the Strange Chords of Turner—that "broad glance" and "connexion infinitely and inimitably good," which is an anatomical cord, perhaps the bundle of fibers called the corpus callosum that connects the brain's right and left hemispheres, before it is a musical chord—may be Ruskin's only in aspiration or retrospect. For him, those Chords may be unlivable in the present tense, where the possibility of Newman's "connected view" that in Ruskin's memory is the ecstatic binding and blending of all things is more likely to underscore the necessity of transcendental discrimination and separation than a vortical union of immanent proximity. Possibly, with Ruskin the present fact of the matter requires more distinction than connection. Possibly, the Strange Chords of attempted mastery and potential madness, as well as the rectilinear stress of death's "long shadow," become "infinitely and inimitably good" with Ruskin only in the penultimate response they elicit. Perhaps his livable version of Turner's Strange Chords is a "fine grotesque," which is the condensed, privileged space, not of the creator, but of the beholder, who is left to make his own, presumably less burdensome, chords that are not so strange—at least not at first, before the necessity of the transforming response, when Ruskin, as the vantage point gets emphatically closer to the focal point, must himself turn from merely looking to performing, describing ("in any verbal way"), or making. But for now, it is likely that, after an altitudinal truth approaching meta-presence (the True Centre on its way to becoming an even more elevated and inclusive epicentre), those

Strange Chords of increasingly articulated (logo)-concentricity, which will become only stranger until there is an asymmetrical, if not dissymmetrical, labyrinthine attempt to make their "strange orthodoxy" familiar in a superimposing act of crucial reversal or inversion, are for the time no more than ambitiously "grotesque":

A fine grotesque is the expression, in a moment, by a series of symbols thrown together in bold and fearless connection, of truths which it would have taken a long time to express in any verbal way, and of which the connection is left for the beholder to work out for himself; the gaps, left or overleaped by the haste of the imagination, forming the grotesque character   [v, 132].

Chapter Two

Central Men and Awful Lines:
Attempts and Failures
in Mastery

A. *The Central Man*

If with Ruskin, there is a strong sense of the Centre, an obsessive conviction that it is a territory, after original naiveté, not only worthy of observation but from which it makes sense to observe, there must also be a population, probably select, of the Centre—people, beyond the singular if archetypical Turner, who are something more than either the urban dwellers of central cities or that Central Judge who, in his intense egotism, occupies the central position of his own horizon. In fact, there must be both a population actively engaged in the mastery of centricity and a population of the Centre whose privilege, informed by the optics of disengagement, is in what they see. But then with Ruskin, the observed becomes the observer, with the consequence that the problems implicit in the focal point are acted out in the vantage point. Role playing is largely a matter of a sequence that becomes increasingly dangerous.

In what might well be called the central chapter of *The Stones of Venice*, "The Nature of Gothic," Ruskin moves toward an explicit examination of the character and performance of the Central Man—an examination that, condensed, recapitulates some of the scattered altitudinal situations that Ruskin, with his conditional aspirations toward both centricity and a syntax of eminence, also experiences, as if in preparation for his own habitation of privileged landscape. But the Centre explored in "The Nature of Gothic," if not like the later Middle Man's corrupt Centre of a parasitical "between," which is itself *not* the penultimate "choral space" of the antiphonal double labyrinth, is closer in design to the horizontal middle of the Central Judge's vantage point than Ruskin's essentially sane and more characteristic radiating Centre that cannot be considered without its surrounding Circumference. Still, as a persona of inclusion, Ruskin's Central Man might be observing in three dimensions from Newman's True Centre of meta-presence. And with Newman's synthesizing authority, the Central Man is a man of the middle, whose greatness, which is at least initially not the

Central Judge's madness, occupies a position of "between,"—a position that is at once transcendental, as if with the altitude implicit in any truth that would aspire to be "whole," and mediating:

> Men are universally divided, as respect their artistical qualifications, into three great classes; a right, a left, and a centre. On the right side are the men of facts, on the left the men of design, in the centre the men of both.
>
> The three classes of course pass into each other by imperceptible gradations. The men of facts are hardly ever altogether without powers of design; the men of design are always in some measure cognizant of facts; and as each class possesses more or less the powers of the opposite one, it approaches to the character of the central class   [x, 217].[1]

But the approach is only flirtation. Peripheral opposition is not cultivated. Central inclusion is privileged mediation and accommodation. Essentially, both right and left go their own ways. The tendency of the sides is partial and exclusive. The shift from aesthetics to morality—and with Ruskin the shift is necessarily slight—underscores the "uncontamination" by inclusion of the peripheral: "Those on the right perceive, and pursue the good, and leave the evil," while those on the left, with no less single-minded determination, "perceive and pursue the evil, and leave the good." Yet in that condition of "between," in a continuum "edged" not by a Circumference but "sides," there is a small population whose peripheral vision includes the mutually exclusive: "those in the centre, the greatest, perceive and pursue the good and evil together, the whole thing as it verily is" (x, 221).

The Central Man possesses an instinct for the panoramic unimagined by those on the "right" and "left," whose partisan vision is narrow enough to permit pursuit uncomplicated by either qualification or inclusion. Perhaps impelled by an ambition that will eventually yield Strange Chords, those in a beneficent Centre that is "between" render all that they see in nature unhesitatingly, with a kind of divine grasp and government of the whole, sympathizing with all the good, and yet confessing, permitting, and bringing good out of the evil also . . ." (x, 222).

The Central Man, capable of the "divine grasp and government of the whole," is what Ruskin calls a "Naturalist." His view is not merely passively peripheral, it is actively synthesizing. His vantage

---

[1] It should perhaps be made explicit that we are here only dealing with a version of concentricity. The circle has become a continuum with a mid-point, a two-dimensional "between."

point is not merely elevated; it may, as an epicentre immediately above a True Centre that will eventually radiate vortical disturbance, be beyond both birds and maps: "But the great Naturalist takes the human being in its wholeness, in its mortal as well as its spiritual strength. Capable of sounding and sympathizing with the whole range of its passions, he brings one majestic harmony out of them all; . . . he casts aside the veil from the body, and beholds the mysteries of its form like an angel looking down . . ." (x, 226). Just as Newman's True Centre, as if from the elevation above the Maze of the attendant's "rostrum," summons synoptic order, reason, and a version of symmetry from a condition of fallen labyrinthine irritation, so the angelic altitude of the central Naturalist permits the accommodation of the "whole range." Yet central sympathy with "the human being in its wholeness" does not make the Central Man's vantage point readily approachable. Rather, his sympathy is part of his altitudinal distance: "there is nothing which he is reluctant to behold, nothing that he is ashamed to confess; with all that lives, triumphing, falling, or suffering, he claims kindred, either in majesty or in mercy, yet standing, in a sort, afar off, unmoved even in the deepness of his sympathy; . . ." (x, 226-27).

Ruskin's Central Man, whose horizontal perception permits a "grasp" of situations and information that is nothing less than "divine"—he is, after all, capable of "embracing both horizons" with a single "glance"[2]—is the only Ruskinian persona, who, "exactly throned on the summit of the crest," is either blessed or damned (and in time he is both) by a vantage point that permits the simultaneous and three-dimensional equivalent of what is Ruskin's ultimate, if perhaps "subjunctive," stereoscopic ambition: to see, if not paint, St. Paul's from both ends of London Bridge at once (xv, 215).

Yet as a practical matter, the embracing of either "both horizons" or both ends of London Bridge at the same time is excessively ambitious, even for Ruskin's Central Man, who would, above all things, be rational about his mastery. That optical chord is too strange to entertain, much less maintain, for long. In the "Of Greatness of Style" chapter of *Modern Painters III*, a no less extensive "Grasp," capitalized if not "divine," is the result not so much of

---

[2] With Ruskin, the concentric circles of "orthodox geometries" are at least familiar. There are circles within circles, and centres within centres. And a scheme of defined hierarchy rules over—and "above"—all. Not even many Central Men have exactly privileged vantage points: "Few men, even in that central rank, are so exactly throned on the summit of the crest that they cannot be perceived to incline in the least one way or the other, embracing both horizons with their glance" (x, 217).

elevation as a special kind of economy. The Central Man is a type of the "great painter," who necessarily has something of the "Naturalist" about him:

> as a great painter is always attending to the sum and harmony of his truths rather than to one or the other of any group, a quality of Grasp is visible in his work, like the power of a great reasoner over his subject, or a great poet over his conception, manifesting itself very often in missing out certain details or less truths (which, though good in themselves, he finds are in the way of others), and in a sweeping manner of getting the beginnings and ends of things shown at once . . . [v, 61].

The Central Man's "both horizons" at once become the painter's "beginnings and ends of things shown at once," as if lines, like transcendental altitude, could tell time, even as simultaneity is approached.

B. *The Awful Lines of Time*

Though the "embracing of both horizons with their glance" may be a perfectly orthodox theoretical performance for the optics of "exactly throned" Central Men, the great artist's economy "of getting the beginnings and ends of things shown at once" would seem at first to be somewhat heterodox. After all, since the extensive "grasp" of the stereoscopic vision does not translate to the canvas, there is no reason to suppose, after the dogmatic and discriminating assertions of Lessing's *Laocoön*, that beginnings and ends belong in the same picture. The illustrated events of history should be multiple. If not, they are for such curiosities as Sienese narrative paintings or the emblems of simultaneous activity of, say, Whitney. Drawn lines of interconnection create potentially Strange Chords that are necessarily spatial. But presumably, extended time on canvas—beginnings and ends, causes and effects—is not merely strange, but anathematic.

Yet specifically, beyond theory—or rather, before it, in concrete particulars—Ruskin will make a case not merely for the artist's spatial interrelation, but for the potential of a kind of temporal interrelation. If every touch on the plates of Turner's *Liber Studiorum* is "related to every other," so too those Chords of spatial accommodation include a kind of narrative—the "history" of at least "this old English country of ours," and at most "the history of European mind from earliest mythology down to modern rationalism and irrationalism" (xv, xxiv). Without reintroducing the heresy implicit in pictorial narrative techniques—the technique of the condensed mural—Ruskin, as if determined to transcend conventional limitations, would bring to line a serial time more extensive than an autonomous present tense. There is, after all, always the potential fulfilled by Giotto, whose "mastery," though "uninformed," is "the mastery of mental expression by bodily motion, and bodily motion, past and future, by a single gesture," which is the result of emphasizing the "right line" (XII, 222). Further, pictorial moments are only privileged if they are more than moments, more than a present tense without either a sense of history or prediction. An example of a painter without "right line" is Copley Fielding, whose moments lack temporal implication: "it often grieves us to see how his power is limited to a particular moment, to that easiest moment for imitation, when knowledge of form may be superseded by management of the brush, and the judgment of the colourist by the manufacture of a colour; the moment when all form is melted down and drifted away" (III, 399).

Above or before grief and opposed to Fielding's paintings of claustrophobic tense, expression that touches even the most innocent eye necessarily transcends the depicted moment. If it is not larger than life, it is larger than particular time. Ruskin's spectator of the two-dimensional, with the structure of perspective that implies the third—in this case, the spectator of Holman Hunt's "The Awakening Conscience"—requires a dimension after recessional space to carry him beyond the grief of claustrophobic limitation: "I suppose that no one possessing the slightest knowledge of expression could remain untouched by the countenance of the lost girl, rent from its beauty into sudden horror; the lips half open, indistinct in their purple quivering; the teeth set hard; the eyes filled with the fearful light of futurity, and with the tears of ancient days" (XII, 334). And beyond the frames of two dimensions, sculpture— "central in every respect," even if only because the mobile spectator is nothing less than an enveloping Circumference[3]—condenses time to the grotesque point before repletion where masterful design, given shape by Right Line, "submits to all the laws of the past, and expresses all the hopes of the future" (XXIV, 170).

Despite being perceived in Lessing's reflexively condensed and essentially spatializing tense,[4] objects beyond canvas or the sculpted

[3] In point of fact, the sculpture Ruskin is talking about—"the last Florentine work in which the proper form of the Etruscan tomb is preserved, and the first in which all right Christian sentiment respecting death is embodied"—is temporally ambitious even for an art object already launched into a third dimension: "But this, as a *central* work, has all the peace of the Christian Eternity" (XXXIV, 170).

[4] Any discussion of Lessing and the reaction to the earlier dictum, *ut pictura poesis,*

stone of, say, Laocoön nevertheless have both a past and a future. And like elevated Centres, even pictorial truths have not only breadth and height but an almost heretical sense of the potential of time as panorama. Those truths must occupy a tense that is as transparent and extensive as a window pane: "It ought further to be observed respecting truths in general, that those are always most valuable which are most historical; that is, which tell us most about the past and future states of the object to which they belong" (III, 163). More specifically, Ruskin's version of Turner—a man whose mastery is his truth—describes history by painting a present tense which transcends itself in a fashion that, in situations outside the canvas, is characteristically Ruskinian in both intention and performance. For Turner "is never altogether content unless he can, at the same time that he takes advantage of all the placidity or repose, tell us something either about the past commotion of the water, or of some present stirring of the tide which its stillness does show" (III, 546-47). Any contentment that is Turner's is contradictorily beyond contentment's implied limitation. One at a time—at least at first—is not nearly as good as "at the same time."

Turner's Right Line, like Giotto's, takes truth from transcendence, becoming in the taking process the linear, as well as "right," incarnation of a "transcendent truth" that would not so much displace the accuracy of specificity—after all, to look at a Turner is to experience the landscape—as to organize the interrelations of parts. Ruskin would have Turner's "transcendent truth" become nothing less than a "whole truth." Making much of the specific, Turner appears to make even more out of the accumulated parts that, like "transcendent truth," increase in truthful significance as Turner, as if employing an ambigious mathematics, transforms serial addition into a curious form of multiplication that is finally close to economical subtraction. Parts, in their transcendent interrelation, become a "whole truth" that has the capability of changing the careful observer of Turner's drawings—his Right Lines—into the occupant of Newman's True Centre:

> In fact, the great quality about Turner's drawings which more especially proves their transcendent truth is, the capa-

---

if it is to be accurate, must avoid the shorthand I am employing here. Lessing's spatializing tense is only a tense for the plastic arts, not verbal narration. Too simply, Lessing is making a distinction between the extensively temporal dimension of poetry and language and the spatial dimension of painting and line. For an important and amplified discussion of the problem, I refer the reader to G. P. Landow's "Ruskin's Version of 'Ut Pictura Poesis,' " *The Journal of Aesthetics and Art Criticism*, 26 (summer 1968); 521-28.

bility they afford us of reasoning on past and future phenomena, just as if we had the actual rocks before us; for this indicates not that one truth is given, or another, not that a pretty
or interesting morsel has been selected here and there, but
that the whole truth has been given, with all the relations of
its parts; so that we can pick and choose our points of pleasure
or of thought for ourselves, and reason upon the whole with
the same certainty which we should after having climbed and
hammered over the rocks bit by bit   [III, 487-88].

Somewhat paradoxically, the Central Man's aesthetics of the
whole may actually be closer to a kind of condensed economy than
a mathematics of multiplication—an economy of condensed privilege that synoptically understands the temporal implications of
serial continuity. From a topography that itself both grotesquely
condenses and masters serial extension—or, for that matter, in
front of a drawing by Turner that is shaped by nothing less than
Right Line—the privileged observer can perceive the "whole truth"
of a lengthily elaborated line. Precisely, he can see, by virtue of an
extracted or transcendent vantage point, what is denied the palsied
maker of glass beads on his assembly line that is in fact closer to
the vivisectionist's table for the operations of a soon to be divided
self—an assembly line of divided and multiple perception on which
the "narrow caution" of compartmentalized activity and optics becomes as narrow and deadly as the edges of a double axe.[5]

It is as if, either with the perception of given Right Lines or from
the transcendental vantage point of an elevated Centre, the entire
series of the continuum-as-Circumference (the assembly line, say,
extended infinitely until it returns as an enveloping circle) might
be grasped "with all the relations to its parts"—that economical
grasp which approaches the simultaneity of the absolute interrelation of Strange Chords: the simultaneity in fact of the "whole
truth" seen "at the same time" from a transcendentally privileged
altitude of (logo)-concentricity. Simply, the entire assembly line,
aspiring at least in the end toward wholeness, cannot be seen from
the fallen landscape of the assembly line, and all parts cannot be
apprehended from a point of view that is itself nothing but a point
of "parts." The Circumference must be seen from the Centre, but

---

[5] Again, see "The Nature of Gothic" chapter of *The Stones of Venice*. "Narrow
caution" (x, 191) refers more to restricted performance than vision. But with Ruskin,
there is no restricted performance without, in the beginning, a restricted vision.
The maker of glass beads, involved in perfect repetition, is not permitted to indulge
in an inclusively peripheral vision.

the Centre achieves its privileged status by taking the extensive lines of the Circumference and making them densely, even grotesquely, "Right" on terms that are entirely central and presumably rational. The landscape of densely economical privilege cannot retain its altitude without a fallen—or at least lower—landscape of serial slack, where open space organizes the consecutive.

The man of aesthetic inferiority, an inferiority that speaks of a more generalized inadequacy, sees only circumferential "parts," either as if things were "standing still," or as if a single act were being performed on an assembly line that takes the interrelation out of serial procedure; he fails to see what the Central Man—the "wise man" of *The Elements of Drawing*, who knows "how things are going"—draws: "the change or changing in them [things] . . . the animal in its motion, the tree in its growth, the cloud in its course, the mountain in its wearing aways" (xv, 91). As an artist, the Central Man turns line—Right Line, which is as rational as the "right angle" we shall come to know is eventually maddening—toward an extensive rather than reflexive tense. The man whose vision, after having explored the private perspectives of recessional space, can also accommodate a surface perspective with a lateral sense of peripheral spaces, requires a temporal equivalent to the spatial perspective studies of both depth and breadth—Right Lines that are "awful" in not only their history but their "futurity": "Try always, whenever you look at a form, to see the lines in it which have had the power over its past fate and will have power over its futurity. Those are its *awful* lines; see that you seize on those, whatever else you miss" (xv, 91).

Already explored and charted, depth, in the private and self-annulling penetration of transcendent space, and panorama, in the publicly parallel advance of the space of horizontal engagement, require still another dimension in order to make truth entirely "whole." The Awful Lines of Time are "right" insofar as they complement, with the temporal accommodations of both "past fate" and "futurity," the intricately schematic diagrams of his perspective studies. The Central Man's position of synoptic privilege is not the anonymous and self-transcendent focal point (and eventual vantage point) of recessional space, but a transcendental vantage point of (logo)-concentricity and elevation that promotes, by separation, both the self's importance and a meta-presence that will become dangerous.

From that position of privilege (and removed from an assembly line which is like a continuum-as-Circumference that is at first, before later considerations, seen as a slack and fallen landscape), the Central Man finds implicit extension and interrelation in an unwritten but assumed temporal "perspective study" of those Awful Lines that are time's equivalent of Strange Chords. And the entire arrangement of Lines and Chords, as a "whole truth," includes a variety of past and future tenses, as well as not only Centres and Circumferences, but, as we shall see, the significantly intervening (if not always mediating) procedures of a labyrinthine, Antiphonal Contention that is lateral before it is vertical.

C. *Cross-References* ad infinitum: *The World of the Index*

In a letter to Carlyle, Ruskin amuses himself, in a problematical tense that is both past and conditional, with the notion of having a starting point in history, one of the "beginnings" that fascinates Ruskin even as "endings" begin to appall—a "beginning," in fact, absolutely authenticated by documents that possess no intervening time between event and record. He would have documents of immediacy in order to resurrect a history that is as close to actuality as possible. But with the vast information of immediate documents close to the source (documents unfiltered by the Ruskinian golden stains of time, which are the mnemonic stains of "The Lamp of Memory" that have their own efficacy), the problem of repletion—and, implicitly, that of simultaneity—is introduced. What is required—all in this entirely speculative tense that, indulging historical fiction, predicts future "fact"—is a method of organization that will reduce the dangers of repletion. Writing to Carlyle, Ruskin would rather have live indexes than dead horses: "Fancy, papa, what times you and I should have had if those beasts of aristocrats, instead of spending all their money in horses, had set up printing presses, and printed all the first documents of their own history (the worthless dish-washings that they are)—and nice Indexes!" (xxxvii, 214).

But like the multiplication inherent in the printing of even "first documents"—after all, printing does involve a "present fury" (xxix, 483)—indexes, which are Centres of textual mastery (paginal True Centres, more pronounced than "pauses of eminence," that hold the possibility of a grotesquely condensed information), also multiply.

It is as if soon there may be nothing but privileged textual space, the space of economically stored information with a potential mastery that is far more significant than the more circumferential syntax of mere eminence. In any case, there are Centres within

Centres; predicting the landscapes of Borges, the text becomes a landscape of concentricity, before it is modified by the vertiginous. Perhaps an entirely graphocentric world can be created that will have an index for indexes. Yet before that, Ruskin will have an index for his central city. He will do nothing less than assemble a "Venetian Index," in which he will name "every building of importance in the city of Venice, or near it" (xi, 355). But one index calls forth another, with a centrifugal motion that would not disperse itself so much as encompass previous territory. In fact, the "Venetian Index" is only the fourth, if most ambitious, of a series described in the first three editions of *The Stones*:

I. Personal Index
II. Local Index
III. Topical Index
IV. Venetian Index   [xi, 355, n.]

Expanding centrifugally, indexing can also be a process of concentric regression, of centripetal movement. Within the indexes, there must be another index—an interior index: "Alphabetical Indices will, however, be of little use, unless another, and a very different kind of index, be arranged in the mind of the reader" (xi, 356).

From the index of even a central city, Ruskin's indexes move inward. "Alphabetical Indices" of cities lead to special, centripetal indexes more interior—or at least more immediate—than that within even the reader's mind, whose interior text is itself an anticipation of the later indexing of the writer's own mind. Instead of indexing others, Ruskin will index himself, bringing mastery from a central city to a self whose texts deal with subjects in a fashion that is regretfully "desultory." Indexing will become a form of privileged autobiography, with the slack of digression left out: "The index closing this volume of *Deucalion*, drawn up by myself, is made as short as possible and classifies the contents of the volume so as to enable the reader to collect all notices of importance relating to any one subject, and to collate them with those in my former writing. That they need such assemblage from their desultory occurrence in the previous pages, is a matter of sincere regret to me" (xxvi, 273).

But then (though far from finally), Ruskin would go from text to texts—still his own—from *Deucalion* to the texts of his life. He would index not a book but all the books he had ever written. Perhaps if he could write the index to his life, he would not write *Praeterita*—at least not with the pretense (and there is little) of accurately recording the information of his life. In a letter of 1877, with little left to say, with no future aside from a future of re-phrasing and censored recapitulation, he writes: "I've no more to say, I believe, now on any subject . . . if I knew all I *had* said and could index it" (XVII, xx). Perhaps ill-considered, his autobiograph-ical index would be as dangerously inclusive as *Praeterita*, with its distancing retrospections that are in fact hiding places, is not. But conditionally further, perhaps an autobiographical index would be the paginal essence of a kind of fictional, or textual, self-control, which might offer—at least temporarily—satisfactions that its op-posite, the annulment of self at an infinite vanishing point, would not. Total control of self might be even better than the dispersal of circumferential loss. But this is the whimsical 1877 speculation on an autobiographical index that is an emphatically conditional "if."

In fact, indexing, textually prefiguring the responsibilities of excessive privilege (or being in the position to experience vortical meta-presence or repletion that renders "too" meaningless until it becomes less than "nothing") is not easy beyond conditional tenses—especially an autobiographical index that would require one to examine one's own unrefracted essence, without those slack oases of hiding places. Ruskin warns a friend about the nature of the world of indexes: "Mind you do not work too hard at this index world; it may not be unamusing, but it is trying" (XXXVI, 326). And more to what proves to be the eventual point: "I find index-making more difficult and tedious than I expected, and am besides bent at present on some Robinson Crusoe operations of harbour-dig-ging" (XXVII, 505). The antithetical Robinson-Crusoe "harbour-dig-ging" does not occur at the centre of Cock-Robinson-Crusoe conceit because the new Centre, now transformed by ambitious wisdom, is the centripetal working space of the Index World. "Harbour-digging" is play, as digging is generally for Ruskin, but good "index-making" is like good broom-making without adequate materials. Neither the index nor the broom can easily deal with loose "odds and ends" that cannot be ignored: "This unlucky index. . . . It is easy enough to make an index, as it is to make a broom of odds and ends, as rough as oat straw; but to make an index tied up tight, and that will sweep well into corners, isn't easy" (XXVII, 553).

The kinds of demands imposed upon the maker of the Index World can be as strangely depressing as Turnerian Chords are potentially "strange"—and for some of the same reasons. Ruskin had arranged Turner's sketches (1857-58), as if from the altitude of a masterful True Centre that is in fact the replete space of a museum's too-well-stocked storage room—a fallen, but dense, "altitude" that either permits him to see or requires that he see "unfolded the whole career of Turner's mind during his life" (VII, 5). After such arrangement, Ruskin finds that his response to the demands of attempting to write not an Autobiographical Index but a kind of "biographical index" of Turner's life is nothing less than perhaps strangely and certainly terribly "violent": "I have had cloud upon me this year, and don't quite know the meaning of it; . . . I believe there is something owing to the violent reaction often after the excitement of the arranging of Turner's sketches" (XXXVI, 292).

If it is difficult for Ruskin to arrange Turner, to write his biographical index, the control and accommodation necessary to see autobiographically the unfolding of one's own "whole career" is in fact still more demanding than is suggested in those conditional tenses of indulgence ("if I knew all I *had* said and could index it"). Finding biography easier, though less inevitable, than autobiography, Ruskin would have someone else create his Index World. He will play Turner to someone else's Ruskin, and have a biographical, rather than "auto"-biographical, index. It is almost as if he were Nabokov's John Shade in search of Charles Kinbote. He will be "arranged" by another. In 1879, he writes a letter to Miss Sara Anderson: "Did I never explain in the least what I wanted by the arranged index? I want you to find out all my wisest bits and choose the wisest of the wise, and then put all the other bits that are like it, round it—or in a row beside it—and then, when you've quoted the pretty ones, say 'compare' the others up and down the books" (XXXVII, 281).

Though Ruskin can be arranged and compared by another, he exists on the original page alone. He is responsible for his texts. Yet resenting the mirrors that he is also drawn toward, Ruskin, having written *Fors Clavigera*, may not return to the text as reader. Certainly, he will not make a Forsian Index World. Still, that does not mean that there should not be an index to *Fors* "arranged" by another. The thought is intriguing. And intriguing Ruskin, it also intrigues another—in this case, J. P. Faunthorpe, who understands that the Forsian Index World he has "arranged," with an eye toward "intimate, and what seemed to me at the time to be superior, connection," might well have become a kind of enclosed, paginal infinity: "No one who admires *Fors Clavigera* will, I think, object to the length of the Index, nor to the numerous cross-references,—which, indeed, might have been multiplied almost *ad infinitum*" (XXIX, 605).

But if Ruskin, along with Faunthorpe, can conceive of no one objecting to a Forsian Index World that, cross-referenced *ad infi-nitum*, might be larger than the work indexed, he has not yet taken into account, as he does in a diary entry, the virtually insatiable appetite of an Index World that is a monstrous void masquerading as an empty stomach: "Wild wind and rain, for welcome back after a fortnight of troublesome work in London. Index to *Fors* swallowing all up" (*Diaries*, p. 748).

But then gastronomics, as well as meteorology (both aspects of Ruskinian autobiography), has always been a problem for Ruskin. An appeased appetite anticipates both repletion and the later labyrinth of entrails and myopic vision. While claiming that he requires "space more than food" (xxviii, 19), Ruskin nevertheless eats his way (or thinks he does) toward not only indigestion but the failing sight of amaurosis,[6] as if the appeased appetite of the stomach could in some way make up for the lost desire of failed eyes, or as if he had in fact ingested the intervening and transcendental space necessary for both optics and creation. At any rate, the Index World, bringing clouds ("I have had cloud upon me this year"), is as ravenous as another cloud, a variation of *The Storm-Cloud of the Nineteenth Century*: "To-day, a fairly bright sky, overcast every five minutes by drift of the ragged cloud, white, but evil-minded as usual, and soon I doubt not to swallow the day" (*Diaries*, p. 863). The Index World is a world of appetite, clouds, and dense space—a world in which the lines of "intimate, and . . . superior connection," which might eventually be criss-crossed (or "crinkle-crankled") "*ad infinitum*," threaten to become nothing at all. As convoluted as a labyrinth without discernible beginning or end (a labyrinth without the attendant's rostrum), the intricate infinity of the Index World predicts the blank page of silence and madness.

Bringing more than clouds, existence for any prolonged period in the Index World is precarious. In fact, existence there requires the ability to rise above clouds in order that someone very much like the Central Man may avoid the "swallowed," interior life of a Jonah, whose centricity is described more by gastronomy than the altitude of a True Centre. What Ruskin has done—especially in the three volumes of *Fors Clavigera*—is to create a syntactical topography which is an enclosed, but potentially *ad infinitum*, version of the recessional space of *Modern Painters* that, knowing no bounds, moves toward the infinity of a focal point that is also a vanishing point. Infinity has been contained by three volumes whose cross-referencing might never end. That vertiginous graphocentricity of

---

[6] See *The Failing Distance*, p. 153.

the Index becomes both its own infinity and a web of language that might prevent injury to a tightrope walker, whose false presence has become his own abyss. Still, the Indexer may be "swallowed" between book covers as easily as the Ruskinian traveler vanishes—in search of that species of escape which is to be found in "Escape, Hope, Infinity" (IV, 83)—in the third dimension. Yet a version of the enclosed infinite, which combines centripetal mastery with centrifugal exploration and "play," has been brought home in the intricacy of an anticipating and echoing cross-referencing that is nothing if it is not a prophecy of the transformation of the recollected, single Maze of Lucent Verdure into the penultimately replete and vertically antiphonal, three-dimensional double labyrinth to come: the graphocentric Index World is preparation for both the Theatre of Blindness and the blank page of maddened "dazzlement" beyond. And the repletion of an infinite but enclosed Index further predicts, if only as a temporary solution, the double tiers of a blind paratactical language "above" and the silence of a forever latent completion "below," whose only negotiations will be the problematic discourse of a twisting "inner language."

D. Mastery, Makeshift and True: Glimpses of "Shattered Majesty" and "Stately and Unaccusable Wholes"

An Index requires a text, perhaps a library: something to order. Similarly, the Centre needs a Circumference. But that space, the serial space of circumferential slack, will be properly introduced later, and it will be an introduction coming out of dire necessity, with the urgency of oxygen for a drowning man: or conversely, it will come as oxygen for a man whose altitudinal aspirations have become angelic. But the Centre, in its incipient doubleness, must be reckoned with first.

And if the child is born there, without anything to catalogue or index but perceptions that are too innocent to require organization or to permit comparison, the adult—still dealing with first things first (or second Centres second)—requires a kind of transportation. In the same way that Newman searches for the appropriate altitude for his True Centre, so Ruskin searches for a Centre that is more explicit in its significance than the altitudinal centricity of St. Mark's—a Centre that is fraught with not only announced political implication, but, finally, as the self takes on public dimension, perhaps more personal meaning as well. In any event, once the naive Centre has been left, gravity appeals to "first duty." If a True Centre cannot be immediately found—and as a "first duty" it cannot—then one should find, as if impelled by centripetal motion, a True Master: "the first duty of everyman in the world is to find his true master, and, for his good, to submit to him" (xix, 129).

Born centrally, or egocentrically, the child, to become an adult, must move toward a new Centre, one that is outside himself, beyond his most immediate vantage point, which is the foreground of autobiography that is happily, to begin with, without personal history. Yet at first, the child may not be ready for the initial, centripetal movement toward his True Master. Or rather, having been mastered as a child, the young man may later find himself unable to perceive the kind of gravitational pull that would permit him to move toward central authority. It is as if he were on the Circumference of a maelstrom, spinning in the eccentric vortices of innocence, without that later vortical vision of meta-presence, unaware of an inevitable centricity which is also a responsibility that may prove as ultimately bottomless as it will first appear altitudinous: "the ceaseless authority exercised over my youth left me, when cast out at last into the world, unable for some time to do more than drift with its vortices" (xxxv, 46).

But then, decidedly and politically, Ruskin is not "everyman in this world." Always, he learns by looking, and, when he has an option, he will look either "into" or "from" a distance. Unsurprisingly, the True Master can be seen with characteristic farsightedness from a distance. Yet with Ruskin, the intervening (and eventually reciprocal) optical space between vantage and focal points always collapses, and that collapse is the success of Ruskin's performance. To find a True Master and then become one himself, he must leave the circumferential lip of the vortex behind and approach a "first duty" that has something in common with St. Mark's. Among other things, what is required of the True Master is an optics of inclusion—a sense of the surface perspective of the horizon, the perspective that accommodates the Parallel Advance. Like Newman, he must have a vantage point that is as public and grotesquely inclusive as the child's perspective, both egocentric and myopic, is itself exclusive. To be able to condense the serial information of the Circumference, he must determine to leave those eccentric, drifting "vortices" that on their own are without either the potential for central gravitation or transcendental altitude. The information of circumferentially drifting water, no matter how initially naive, is worth bringing to an eventually replete point of danger that may be like a whirlpool's Centre—a vortical Centre of masterful presence whose vertiginous centripetence covers, at least for a time of excessive interrelation, a sense of inevitable absence.

The relation between the Centre, which is either grotesque or privileged (or rather, privileged because of the grotesque density of its received information), and the Circumference, which is the space of oxygen and a serial, rather than simultaneous, perception—a relation at first between the altitudinous One and the submissive Many—is, with Ruskin, more political than Platonic. The geometry of concentric circles incarnates the potential of power. And Ruskin directs his secondary attention, if not his ultimate sympathy, toward the One of political Mastery. Describing the exercise of power, which for him is the substance of the relation between Centre and Circumference, Ruskin, dealing with number and elevation, describes two kinds of government:

> A Government may be nominally vested in an individual; and yet if that individual be in such fear of those beneath him that he does nothing but what he supposes will be agreeable to them, the Government is Democratic; on the other hand, the Government may be vested in a deliberative assembly of a thousand men, all having equal authority, and all chosen from the lowest ranks of the people; and yet if that assembly act independently of the will of the people, and have no fear of them, and enforce its determinations upon them, the Government is Monarchical; that is to say, the Assembly, acting as One, has power over the Many, while in the case of the weak kind, the Many have power over the One   [XII, 552].

Yet if Ruskin, an eventual Master whose self-control is at times a promoted fiction, would have political power located centrally, instead of having pressure exerted from the Circumference, he would also, as one preoccupied by both the antithetical and the reciprocal, have that essential power working against itself—or, more accurately, if not quite against itself, at least with a fundamental concern that is neither reflexive nor selfish: central concerns are not for the "head" at the Centre, if that Centre is "true," but rather for the circumferential "body" of the Many, who, located far from privilege, may not feel the gravitational necessity of "first duty." After concentric "first duty," Ruskinian desire is *from* the Centre, but "for" the circumferential Many, whose case, to give geometrical design a syntax, is objective and whose tense is, or should be, passive:

All true and right government is Monarchical, and of the head. What is its best form, is a totally different question; but unless it act *for* the people, and not as a representative of the people, it is no government at all; and one of the grossest blockhead-isms of the English in the present day, is their idea of sending men to Parliament to "represent their opinions." Whereas their only true business is to find out the wisest men among them, and send them to Parliament to represent their *own* opinions, and act upon them. Of all puppet-shows in the Satanic Carnival of the earth, the most contemptible puppet-show is a Parliament with a mob pulling strings   [XII, 552].

For the most part, the right kind of government is good composition. Design incarnates morality. "Right lines" are "good." As has been suggested, the technical *The Elements of Drawing* (1857) is an illustrated version of the "Nature of Gothic" chapter of *The Stones of Venice* (1852):

Composition, understood in this pure sense, is the type, in the arts of mankind, of the Providential government of the world. It is an exhibition, in the order given to notes, or colours, or forms, of the advantage of perfect fellowship, discipline, and contentment. In a well-composed air, no note, however short or low, can be spared, but the least is as necessary as the greatest: no note, however prolonged, is tedious; but the others prepare for, and are benefited by, its duration: no note, however high, is tyrannous; the others prepare for, and are benefited by, its exaltation: no note, however low, is over-powered; the others prepare for, and sympathize with, its humility; and the result is, that each and every note has a value in position assigned to it, which, by itself, it never possessed, and of which, by separation from the others, it would instantly be deprived   [xv, 162].

The world of composition, aspiring toward a condition of inclusion that will incorporate the panorama of the horizontal plane, is a world that does not promote the contradictory third dimension as a space of pseudonymity in which an irresponsible and solipsistic Ruskin would lose both himself and his signature. There is, in fact, a politics of composition. And the Ruskinian world of composition is without those open spaces that, encompassing the possibility of both tyranny and tedium, are virtually immoral—an immorality of "unfelt" space that, predicting both the parasitical space of the Middleman and the triptych's space of transitional absence, might prove, if it were to be cultivated instead of either ignored or misused, a guarantee against the future trip to the blank page of silence and madness.

With an ideal political structure in mind—a model that will later be transformed from something between fiction and vision to the tenuous fact of his St. George's Guild—Ruskin understands that the actual nature of the relation between the Centre and the Circumference, which is also the relation between the Master and the Operative, is the key to the most apparent of social and political problems. The essence of that "relation" is a distance that is too much like the unfelt space of immoral composition. The "relation" is too often separation unbridged by sympathy. There are no "reciprocal interests" (xvii, 28) in the dehumanized geometry of existing political design. The sense of interrelation—the organic structure of society that is like moral design—has been lost, as competition has replaced the Gothic cooperation of affective space. The vocabulary "of," and the view "from," the Centre of mastery are no longer those of the operative's Circumference—and there are no interpreters for the differences between: "Obstinately, the masters take one view of the matter; obstinately the operatives another; and no political science can set them at one" (xvii, 27).

Discerning the coherence of an order over unfelt space that is moral by virtue of connection and reverberating consequence, Ruskin would make universal application of an order that is also a design. In a world tending toward interrelation, composition—precisely, what is diagrammed and discussed in the technical and theoretical *The Elements of Drawing* and *The Elements of Perspective*—has, as has been suggested, political, as well as moral implications. And they are almost, but not quite, democratic—as if mastery should be a position of reluctant permanence, with Masters, in search of truth, prepared occasionally to leave their landscapes of mastery:

> . . . it is very difficult to say which is the principal note. The A in the last bar is slightly dominant, but there is a very equal current of power running through the whole; and such passages rarely weary. And this principle holds through vast scales of arrangements; so that in the grandest compositions, such as Paul Veronese's Marriage in Cana, or Raphael's Disputa, it is not easy to fix at once on the principal figure [xv, 166].

At first, or rather "at once," the Principal Figure involved in implication and consequence is not apparent, in more or less the same way that the Ruskinian Master will necessarily prove only temporary. Notions of centricity must be eventually relinquished, if only to prepare for a return trip.

In any case, at least politically, one cannot now leave the Centre for the Circumference—or the other way around—and not so much on account of a lost, Thesean thread as a lost mediating labyrinth of "right relations between master and operative"—this though "all their best interests, ultimately depend on these" (XVII, 28). It is as an examination of the distance between "relations" that would be "right" if they were in fact "interrelations"—an examination that is further developed and expanded in *Unto This Last* (1860)—that Ruskin writes the central, but embryonic "The Nature of Gothic" chapter of *The Stones of Venice* (1852). And he writes the chapter as if he were an agoraphobe suffering terribly from a vision of the void, a horrifying sense of moral and political vacuity that at least language, well-chosen, might partially fill. "The Nature of Gothic" becomes a mediating labyrinth of exhortation—a series of pronouncements and directives aspiring toward the bringing together of a previously missing sense of "reciprocal interests" by the exploration and establishment of "right relations," which we will find quite different from the rectilinearity of "right angles." Later, with the "capricious sinuousities" of language, straight statement gives way not only to the style and syntax of curvilinear performance— the language of turn and return—but to the topography of a consciousness that is more surprising than predictable.

The landscape of the Circumference is at first inexpensive real estate. It is a topography of extension, as opposed to one of condensation, and, although distance is prized, sought, and penetrated by loving and intricate perspective studies, suggesting a romance of vista, the economics of space fails to place a high premium on the outermost of concentric circles. Either to see or be seen, unless with angelic altitude (or from central elevation), the Circumference—the landscape of the Operative—requires multiple, perhaps relativistic, vantage points. As we by now know, sight, with Ruskin, anticipates performance. And the product of the Operative, given his limited and highly specialized "second duty," which is the duty of the assembly line, is the result of an act as divided as that circumferential perception which sees only the fallen and eccentric landscape that "irritates" Newman's traveler, who may approximate the Everyman of the nineteenth century. Briefly, just as sight anticipates the performance, the performance *is* the performer. The eye is the man (if not the bull or the cat). And multiple vantage points—or more emphatically, a single, circumferential vantage point among many directed toward a single goal—lead to a divided man, who cannot possibly be "at home" in a True Centre, where there is only room for one whose largeness is his presumably unified diversification as well as his centripetal mastery (and even he may find the True Centre only a temporary abode): "We have much studied and much perfected, of late, the great civilized invention of the division of labour; only we give it a false name. It is not, truly speaking, the labour that is divided; but the men:—Divided into mere segments of men—broken into small fragments and crumbs of life" (x, 196).

The Operatives—and the nomenclature would seem to be entirely unkind, cruel, except that it is more likely the brutally clinical language of an ill-disguised empathy—are broken men, divided men, who perform activities that are as disconnected as the Circumference is from the Centre, before the Maze, in an attempt to mediate a version of Antiphonal Contention, is transformed into the connecting stones of white marble. The division of men is a history that can be read in the history of ornament: for ornament, as an architectural expression beyond the restrictive demands of structure, is the portrait of the man who produces it. And what is important in the nature of ornament is the freedom with which it is executed. Self-expression, though not self-indulgence, is the Operative's relatively felicitous autobiography. But tyranny from the Centre—ornament as someone else would have it—is instead the Master's biography written, as if by proxy, from the Circumference.

With sympathy for the Circumference, Ruskin is masterful enough—though in a passive syntactical construction—to be dogmatic in division. Essentially, there are three kinds of ornaments that hold the types of three kinds of personal history, ranging from what might be called a biographical tyranny, which, like the use of transparent glass, suggests ornamental play as the dictated expression of another, to an autobiographical freedom that permits the relativistic circumferential indulgence of a self-expressive ornament that is not so much like a transparent glass as the self's looking glass:

> . . . it was noticed that the systems of architectural ornament, properly so called, might be divided into three:—1. Servile ornament, in which the execution or power of the inferior workman is entirely subjected to the intellect of the higher;— 2. Constitutional ornament, in which the executive inferior power is, to a certain point, emancipated and independent, having a will of its own, yet confessing its inferiority and rendering obedience to higher powers; and 3. Revolutionary ornament, in which no executive inferiority is admitted at all   [x, 189].

Servile decoration, according to Ruskin's unfelicitous history of ornamentation, is the result of the inability of the centrally located (or elevated) Master to endure either the imperfection of the Operative or the fallen condition of the extensive Circumference. As Ruskin would have his idiosyncratic history, the Greek Operative is dehumanized by a limited expectation that would yield nothing more than the abstraction of a deathly geometry of "right angles" that are not always morally "right"—an abstraction of "absolute precision" that is itself without life: "The Greek master-workman was far advanced in knowledge and power above the Assyrian or Egyptian. Neither he nor those for whom he worked could endure the appearance of imperfection in anything; and, therefore, what ornament he appointed to be done by those beneath him was composed of mere geometrical forms,—balls, ridges, and perfectly symmetrical foliage—which could be executed with absolute precision by line and rule, and were as perfect in their way, when completed, as his own figure sculpture" (x, 189). Yet symmetrical foliage, without imperfection, is without life. And perfect, the Greek Operative is also dead—or rather, he is living a life of death as only a perfect slave can. Ruskin's classical Circumference is not only fallen—occupied by those "beneath"—but it is as full as an old graveyard. Without the Gothic hope of the reciprocity of affective space, the interchangeability of vantage and focal points, the Centre and the Circumference have between them only the distance of central domination that oversees, as if with rectilinear precision, the circular outskirts of the Greek death.

But the untraveled space of the Greek death, which predicts the absent transitions of the triptych, is the potentially employed space of Gothic life. The nature of Gothic ornamentation implies the possibility of bridges, of an empty space that may be filled, even as the diction of exhortation darkens the pages of "The Nature of Gothic." Ruskin's Christianity, his Gothic Christianity, accepting imperfection—the fallen or "beneath" condition of vital man—includes a fallen Circumference that is an extensive and slack landscape without an aspiring altitude that might itself be above mortal oxygen. The chance to fail is as humanizing as the failure to be given that chance is not. The Gothic Circumference, tending toward the Centre as if impelled by a "first duty," is an entirely habitable curved landscape because of its ability to recount the tendency in a necessarily imperfect autobiography—self-expression that will live, perhaps rising from "beneath," in the admission of its failure. Ruskin's own sympathy for the Circumference becomes an empathy for life, a movement away from the death-defying because life-denying world of symmetry that is geometrically perfect, and perfectly elevated. The acceptance of the organic relation or "interrelation" of Gothic architecture—necessarily a scheme of transgression when compared with the previously straight and un-reciprocated space of an almost mechanical Greek death—tran-scends single failure by enlarging its focus to include the greater unity of a whole that is both "stately and unaccusable." The Gothic Circumference becomes a landscape that, fallen fortunately, will be resurrected by intricate paths over a space which is without a history of either transgression or connection:

> . . . slavery is done away with altogether; Christianity having recognized, in small things as well as great, the individual value of every soul. But it not only recognizes its value; it confesses its imperfection, in only bestowing dignity upon the acknowl-edgement of its unworthiness. . . . And it is, perhaps, the principal admirableness of the Gothic schools of architecture, that they thus received the results of the labour of inferior minds; and out of fragments full of imperfection, and betray-ing that imperfection in every touch, indulgently raise up a stately and unaccusable whole   [x, 190].

The history of ornamentation has an application that is entirely present, a story that is unhistorically present in tense. Mostly, Rus-kin's investigation of the past, unlike Pater's nostalgic, past-tense fictions, is a way of getting a perspective on an accurate, if occa-sionally idiosyncratic, present: "the modern English mind has this much in common with that of the Greek, that it intensely desires, in all things, the utmost completion or perfection compatible with their nature. This is a noble character in the abstract, but becomes ignoble when it causes us to forget the perfectness of the lower nature to the imperfection of the higher" (x, 190). The right kind of attitude, which is also the correct altitude, is the result of the right kind of fault—or rather it is the result of an aspiring dramatic failure. And in that failing, the fallen Circumference rises as noth-ing so much as a "whole" that is "unaccusable" in its imperfection.

In any case, Ruskin is certain that a choice must be made, a choice between the dehumanized perfection that follows from the Centre's masterful control over a circumferential Operative and the hu-manizing imperfection of an Operative possessed of the freedom to fail, which is the freedom to find his own flawed altitude, or the "imperfection of the higher":

> You must either make a tool of the creature, or a man of him. You cannot make both. Men were not intended to work with the accuracy of tools, to be precise and perfect in their actions.

If you will have that precision out of them, and make their
fingers measure degrees like cog-wheels, and their arms strike
curves like compasses, you must unhumanize them. All the
energy of their spirits must be given to make cogs and compasses of themselves [x, 192].

Perfection comes very close to being altitudinally "lower" than
imperfection. Because it is a landscape that both admits and accommodates failure, Ruskin's Gothic Circumference is capable of
resurrection, almost as if a lost paradise were to become a Prom-
ise(d) Land. And, essentially, that failure, with the vertical potential
to rise "stately and unaccusable," is the result of the chance-taking
in horizontally inclusive ambitions and responsibilities:

> while in all things that we see or do, we are to desire perfection,
> and strive for it, we are nevertheless not to set the meaner
> thing, in its narrow accomplishment, above the nobler thing,
> in its mighty progress; not to esteem smooth minuteness above
> shattered majesty. . . . But, above all, in our dealings with the
> souls of other men, we are to take care how we check, by severe
> requirement or narrow caution, efforts which might otherwise
> lead to noble issue [x, 191].

With panorama as the perspective for the Gothic Circumference—a perspective that will be nothing if not inclusive—Ruskin,
rejecting "narrow accomplishment" and unlikely, at this early time
(before even the initial stages of the Transformations of the Maze),
to be constrained by "narrow caution," would transform the circumferential man-machine, who is merely an "animated tool" (x,
192), composed of "cogs and compasses," into a man capable of
tending, if not assiduously cultivating, the garden of his soul. He
would be a man whose own "progress" might lead to neither the
solipsistic self-annulment of the vanishing perspective nor the ty-
rannical perfection of the Greek death-in-life that is imitated, in
the present, on assembly lines of perfect division, but rather to the
"noble issue" of a "shattered majesty" that is "noble" because it does
not finish until the point of failure—a "shattered majesty" that
predicts the final ruins of Ruskin's own architectural and archaeological syntax/parataxis.

With that characteristically overriding sense of "interrelation"—
a vortical perception that can and will lead, first, to the grotesque
and replete logic of the Centre, and then, in an act of centrifuged
reversal, which will itself be qualified by moments of vortical centripetence, back to the suburbs or fields "beyond," as an impossible

density uncoils itself on the way to the Edge of the blank page—Ruskin dramatically expands the responsibility for the Circumference's modern landscape condition. Simply, he turns his reader—or if not the reader, the reader's friend—into a slave trader. The living room becomes part of the debased and accused architecture of division, an architecture organized (or disorganized) only by the open, and openly unsympathetic, spaces of pathless separation. The living room, as an extension of the assembly line, becomes an "unliving" room:

> The Men who chop up the rods sit at their work all day, their hands vibrating with a perpetual and exquisitely timed palsy, and the beads dropping beneath their vibration like hail. Neither they, nor the men who draw out the rods or fuse the fragments, have the smallest occasion for the use of any single human faculty; and every young lady, therefore, who buys glass beads is engaged in the slave trade, and in a much more cruel one than that which we have so long been endeavouring to put down   [x, 197].

If the living room threatens to become unlivable because of those Greek rules that promote both the deathly distance of separation and perfection—and the threat is there with both conscience and gun—then Ruskin would have that distance transgressed, the distance between Centre and Circumference, not only in sympathy but in performance, and not merely for the sake of the Circumference but for the Centre as well. The "whole" that is "unaccusable" is not only "interrelated" but interdependent. The adhesion is the necessity of reciprocity ("best interests" are, after all, "reciprocal interests") and the curvilinear path through Gothic space, imperfectly constructed without the aid of geometric measurement, is to be traveled not one way, but from opposing directions. Instead of a kind of parasitism, what is required is a mutually inclusive symbiosis: "We are always in these days endeavouring to separate the two; we want one man to be always thinking, and another to be always working, and we call one a gentleman, and the other an operative; whereas the workman ought often to be thinking, and the thinker often to be working" (x, 201).

The True Master must be able to relinquish his mastery. Often, Ruskin is only too glad to do so. He will be the object of another's "first duty" only temporarily. He will not for long be composition's easily discernible Principal Figure: "if any persons trust me enough to obey me without scruple or debate, I can securely tell them what to do, up to a certain point, and be their 'makeshift Master' till they can find a better (xxix, 197). Further, pride that cannot be given up is as false as perfection that is slavery: "no master should be too proud to do its [the profession's] hardest work. The painter should grind his own colours; the architect work in the mason's yard with his men; the master-manufacturer be himself a more skillful operative than any man in his mills" (x, 201).

With a Master whose essential truth is dependent upon the "second duty" of his being more "makeshift" than permanent, altitudinal aspiration returns to an originally fallen condition. Aspects of the Centre are translated to the Circumference, even as aspects of the Circumference become central; "perfection" is necessarily imperfect just as elevation predicts its own fall. The separation and competition that make living rooms undeserving of the name would be (or rather *must* be) replaced by the bridging (the bridge being closer to an intricate path through foliage than a span over the Thames) cooperation of that affective, symbiotic space of Gothic reciprocity, architectural and societal (if there is a difference), which has the capacity to transform the accused rooms of individuated perfection into a structure of "shattered majesty." And that "shattered majesty" of a "stately and unaccusable whole" is like a composition of implicit morality in which the Principal Figure is so dependent upon surroundings that he is as "makeshift" as a True Master—or, for that matter, a word in a poem that is effective only because of its retrospective and anticipatory contextual implication: "in a good poem, each word and thought enhances the value of those which precede and follow it; and every syllable has a loveliness which depends not so much on its abstract sound as its position. Look at the same word in a dictionary, and you will hardly recognize it" (xv, 162).

Chapter Three

The Frosts of Death

A. The Man in the Middle:
Mediation as Subtraction

The affective and symbiotic space of Gothic reciprocity—a two-way, "vegetative" path of cooperation rather than the cannibalism of a competition which would deplete the existing store toward the "nothing" which horrifies—is a felt, and perhaps sinuous, space which links, with either God's speed or the Devil's speed,[1] the Centre and the Circumference. Further, it is part of an essentially (logo)-concentric design that has not yet taken into account an unfortunate and entirely rectilinear geometry of the Middle, which, despite its straight lines, is no more Classic than Gothic. The Middle between diametrically opposing arcs of the Circumference is the Centre, but there is another Middle that is between the Centre and Circumference, the function of which is to mediate between the two locations. And just as the Centre has its Man, its very select population, so this Middle is not without its Man. And he is a Man whose "interests" are more reflexively selfish than emotively reciprocal. If there is a True Centre, perhaps there is a False Middle, which is a dark version of the later problematic "choral space" of Antiphonal Contention—a False Middle perhaps dominated by a full-length mirror that might, at a crucial moment, become transparent glass, as though for a quick exit.

Reconciling or translating neither Centre nor Circumference to the advantage or interest of either, the Middle Man robs both to give to himself. Rather than being in any way symbiotic, he is, as a sometimes invisible False Master, a Janus-faced, double parasite. His "mediatorial function" (XXVIII, 31), which is mediation as sub-

---

[1] Ruskin, talking about the eloquence of the spiral that we shall come to know more about, equates it

with endless symbolism, representing the power of the winds and waves in Athenian work, and of the old serpent, which is the Devil, and Satan, in Gothic work; or, indeed, often enough of both, the Devil being held prince of the power of the air—as in the story of Job, and the lovely story of Buonconte of Montefeltro, in Dante: nay, in this very tale of Theseus, as Chaucer tells it,— having got hold by ill luck only of the later and calumnious notion that Theseus deserted his savior-mistress, he wishes him Devil-speed instead of God-speed [XXVII, 405-6].

traction, anticipating the final "difference" or open spaces between syntax as it becomes parataxis, as well as the excessive presence as absence of Illth beyond, is to fix prices for the (un)-mediatorial profit of his own pocket—a pocket that will not, like those of the members of Ruskin's St. George's Guild, be made of clear glass for the purposes of economic frankness (xxviii, 528). He will buy the Circumference, without regard for the felt space of Gothic reciprocity, in order to peddle it to the highest bidder of a radically new kind of Centre, where appetites, as well as bodily functions in general, are increasing alarmingly.

But the Circumference, fallen though it may be, would seem to be able to meet central needs. A correspondent, in "Letter 38" of *Fors Clavigera*, which is titled "Children, Have Ye Here Any Meat," points out a circumferential plenitude not of meat but of fish: "in the North Sea it is always harvest-time" (xxviii, 33). Qualifying circumferential plenitude, which is also original plenitude, Ruskin introduces St. Peter, as a "true monger of sweet fish," in order to lead into a discussion of both fish and the man of the middle, who, as a "false fisher for rotten souls" (xxviii, 36), inhabits a space of mediation that is closer to a self-interested vacuum than a space of sympathetic coordination. Concerned with the economics of an infernal Middle—an economics that inverts the notion of ungeometrically Gothic "right relations"—Ruskin invokes the morality of a "simple clergyman's wife," who describes the activities of both Centre and Circumference in connection with a Middle that threatens, arithmetically, to become a versatile location of both multiplication and subtraction: " 'The poor fishermen who toil all through these bitter nights, and the retail dealer who carries heavy baskets, or drags a truck so many wearying miles along the road, get but a poor living out of their labour; but what are called "fish salesmen," who by reason of their command of capital keep entire command of the London markets, are making enormous fortune' " (xxviii, 32).

Moving, the Ruskinian Middle moves shrewdly, if not morally, toward Nothing, as if the very act of transportation were also one of disappearance. Those paradoxically "mathematical" fishermen of the Middle, who are halfway from the ironically introduced St. Peter, would transform fish into, if not outright sewage, at least a manure that might know a Second Coming—this rather than the selling of the fish of a vital Circumference at a price made justifiable by available plenitude. Ruskin's correspondent continues: " 'When I told our fishmonger about it, he said I was quite right about the "big men" [the Middle Men] in London, and added, "They will not let us have the fish under their own prices; and if it is so plentiful that they cannot sell it at all at that, they have it thrown away, or carted off for manure; sometimes sunk in the river" (xxvIII, 33). Transforming the extensive and "plentiful" Circumference, the Middle Man would also, if economically necessary, condense it— make it less than it in fact is—even before the Centre's collective stomach has performed its reductive digestion. Disastrously, there is that Middle-act of disappearance, which is the showpiece of the economic magician. And dead fish from a vital sea create a city's dead river—a Dead Sea of sewage for the "false fisher of [inevitably] rotten souls."

The poor are highly visible. The vacancy of their stomachs commands attention. But if the vacancy of empty stomachs is apparent, the Man in the Middle, commanding capital even as the Central Man attempts to master Strange Chords and Awful Lines, is, despite the fact that he is "big," virtually invisible except in the effect of his economic power. His presence is his price. His size is the immorality of what he charges. Otherwise, he does not exist. The reductive performance of the Middle Man is a gesture of legerdemain that, if visible, would be worth regarding as a step preliminary to the purgation of the Middle. To "see" the Middle Man, and seeing him, also understand him, would be to render him, finally, both morally and effectively invisible—without even the opacity of price, the density of his multiplying pounds and pence. The disappearing act would be "of" the Middle, not "in" the Middle. Simply, if the Middle Man could be "seen," he would cease to exist:

> But what's to become of the middleman?
> If you really saw the middleman at his work, you would not ask that twice. Here's my publisher, Mr. Allen, gets tenpence a dozen for his cabbages; the consumer pays threepence each. That is to say, you pay for three cabbages and a half, and the middleman keeps two and a half for himself, and gives you one.
> Suppose you saw this financial gentleman, in bodily presence, toll-taking at your door,—that you bought three loaves, and saw him pocket two, and pick the best crust off the third as he handed it in;—that you paid for a pot of beer, and saw him drink two-thirds of it and hand you over the pot and sops,—would you long ask, then, what was to become of him? [xxIx, 21-22].

Yet if that False Middle has been "seen" somewhere in a location of economically "mediatorial function," the perception of its process, knowing no Gothic reciprocity (the curvilinear paths, say, bordered by vegetation, that can be traveled both ways), has failed to lead to its banishment in London. With heavenly cities, as we shall see, in his mind's eye—cities close by Dead Seas that are far from London's river of sulphur and dead fish—Ruskin, who, promoting the elimination of the False Middle, would also eliminate not only "rotten souls" but "false fishers," looks to the "city of the Lily," Florence, which, if not as bridelike as we shall find an ironically introduced New Jerusalem, is at least middleless. Florentine "mediatorial function" is invisible because it no longer exists, and the "apostolic succession" of new St. Peters is not, in the mathematics of importation, a process of subtraction:

> The profession of middleman was then, by civic consent, and formal law, rendered impossible in Florence with respect to fish. What advantage the modern blessed possibility of such mediatorial function brings to our hungry multitudes; and how the miraculous draught of fishes, which living St. Peter discerns, and often dextrously catches—"the shoals of them like shining continents" (said Carlyle to me, only yesterday)—are by such apostolic succession miraculously diminished, instead of multiplied; and, instead of baskets full of fragments taken up from the ground, baskets full of whole fish laid down on it, lest perchance any hungry person should cheaply eat of the same [xxviii, 31].

But London, many things, is not Florence. And "fishes"—and with them, perhaps, those men who are the "true monger[s] of sweet fish"—are swallowed by the Londonian Middle, where circumferential plenitude is transformed into vacuity by an economics that would make a virtue of the metamorphosis of fish into manure and a Thames decorated with white fish bellies. The False Middle, as a double parasitical place of "mediatorial" subtraction unlike in intent that at first carefully orchestrated "choral space" of concluding Antiphonal Contention which is lateral before it is vertical, aspires toward the centripetally unified parasitism of the Centre's bull's eye, which might be a vanishing point for anything but the reflection in the eye of a Minotaur. The new Centre, which is unshaped by Athena, evolving (or degenerating) in its characteristics, is in the process of no longer requiring the Middle for pernicious disappearance. That Centre will be its own vanishing point. The importation of the Circumference to the Centre is now an act of terrible concentration that will lead not only to the destruction of the Circumference, but to the condemnation and loss of those central spaces as well. For the fictions of orthodox pastoral are now beyond the potential of even fantasy; the shepherds have fled. And ancient hills have been defaced "with guilt of mercenary desolation, driving their ancient shepherd life into exile, and diverting the waves of streamlets into the cities which are the very centre of pollution, avarice, and impiety" (xxii, 531). The death of the Circumference anticipates—or better "is"—the death of the Centre. The "mercenary desolation" of both Circumference and Centre has essentially the same (un)-"mediatorial" economic/mathematical effect of Janusian parasitism as the mostly invisible False Centre, where there is not only the subtraction of food but the multiplication of a "desolation" that is infernally interdependent on both the circumferential Outside (where water for fish is not as "Straight" or rectilinear as we shall find it for travel in an autobiographical Venice) and a concentric Inside, where circular design predicts a final zero which is not unlike either the bottom of a vortex or a blank page that is also final in its madness. At first, the Whole is "shattered" by the False Middle. Yet the False Middle stands—and, visible or not, it stands "accused," by one who will later be led for a while by Blind Guides of the Rialto, who themselves possess, at times, "celestial light" before the blinding "dazzlement" of pathos.

B. The "True Centre" as Condemned Space

If not already in fact changed, the valuation of locations is in the process of changing. The double parasitism of the False Middle, as the (un)-"mediatorial" function of Antiphonal Contention in its heterodox and most subversive aspect, aids in the metamorphosis. Originally, before compositional/political morality and before the Middle Man's double-faced transactions-as-subtraction, there was the substantial geological morality of centripetal and centrifugal "tendencies": "Note of yellow quartz. . . . Of moral and immoral tendencies, the centralization of power which hits the apex neatly, and the irregular dispersion of it, seem two of the most distinctly opposed" (*Diaries*, p. 630). If the centripetal movement had not yet arrived at a True Centre, it was at least winding, like the tendency of a vortex, toward the presence of a moral "apex," as opposed to the immoral unwinding and "irregular dispersion" of the centrifugal. Yet there is perhaps a bottomless absence beneath vortical presence, and things in general have changed. The centripetal now has to move through a Middle devoid of ethics. And morality will not necessarily meet at the "apex." Principal Figures should not be "too" principal. Mastery may well be more "makeshift" than permanent. Now, it is as if opposing territories have something in common, even if it is only the commonness of both being "entirely otherwise": "You will find it entirely otherwise, gentlemen, whether of the suburb or centre" (xxviii, 30).

A Centre may be "true," but an aspect of its truth resides, finally and most importantly, in its being a landscape of almost perfect privilege that can be left without regret. Then again, there are not only "centres" and "suburbs," there are Centres and centres. And there are risks inherent in centricity. The journey from the (logo)-concentricity of the True Centre as transcendental vantage point, above the irritations (at least, Newman's irritations) and, more significantly, the serial "interrelations" of the Maze, toward a potentially irritating focal point that is like the labyrinthine "cross-references" of the urbanly dense Index World, translates terrifyingly into the political and economical consequences of not only "The Nature of Gothic" but the fulfilling *Unto This Last*. Further, this journey, it is becoming increasingly apparent, is one that, if more than a visit from a place of dispersal to a Centre as potentially replete as a city, is possibly not so much a process of "mediatorial" subtraction as of dangerous multiplication. If fish are lost in the Middle's rectilinear importation, something—or, in fact, nothing less than too much—may be gained in that same impulse toward centricity.

Yet not only can one leave the altitudinous vantage point for the "apex" or focal point of a central city, one can also leave an altitudinously central vantage point, like a True Centre, for another Centre that is also, as we shall see, as labyrinthine as what has been located customarily "below": "the labyrinth of black walls, the loathsome passages between them, which now fills the valley of the Thames, and is called London" (xxi, 104).[2] But more conventionally and after an originally childish and geometrically perfect egocentricity, the progress (if it may be called that), as if impelled by an inaugural geological morality, is from circumferentially dispersed "suburbs" to a Centre that is at first only secondarily laby-

---

[2] London as a labyrinth is a concept with a history. W. H. Matthews, in *Mazes & Labyrinths*, comments on a quotation from Spenser: "As Spenser says ('Faerie Queene,' iii, 9):

'For noble Britons sprange from Trojans bold
And Troy-Novant was built of old Troyes ashes cold.'

If any reliance could be placed on this old story the Corporation of London might do well to embody the Labyrinth, or Troy-town, in their armorial bearings, for what symbol could better typify the complexities of our metropolis?" (p. 140)

rinthine, though that secondary significance becomes a kind of later salvation. And the trip, geologically moral in "tendency," but now potentially dangerous and with the added complication of the paradoxical mathematics of a False Middle, which adumbrates the excessive presence become absence of an ultimate Illth, may be from a "suburb" of profligate "dispersal" to an alternative Centre (within a city which is also central) that has lost much of its truth in transit. It is as though one might move toward the innermost heart of an already corrupt matter, prompted, perhaps, by the False Middle's essentially rectilinear energy that has all the force, if none of the integrity, of Ruskin's Imaginative Penetrative (IV, 270):

> In the very Centre of the City, and at the point where the Embankment commands a view of Westminster Abbey on one side, and of St. Paul's on the other,—that is to say, at precisely the most important and stately moment of its whole course. . . . .
>
> . . . .
>
> The place is worth your visit, for you are not likely to find elsewhere a spot which, either in costly and ponderous brutality of building, or in squalid and indecent accompaniment of it, is so far separated from the peace and grace of nature, and so accurately indicative of the methods of our national resistance to the Grace, Mercy, and Peace of Heaven   [xx, 256-57].

But now, the urban heart, no longer a more or less naive location of privilege—an achieved Centre from which collected information can be morally "dispersed," as if with all of the early Cock-Robinson-Crusoe arrogance and some of the innocence—has become a corrupted heart. And corrupt, fallen by the failed virtue of excessively ambitious density, that territory is at present, in the middle of Ruskin's life, without the elusive peace that he will seek, both fastidiously and passionately, until the end, when it will be partially achieved at the expensive cost of White Silence.

Still, beyond occasional appearances—or more likely "before"—there is the untarnished focal point for those "suburbs" that are the limbs of the topographical body. And, at least "from" a condition that is itself not yet overtly corrupt, the Suburbs do not see a Centre of "ponderous brutality": "In all healthy states, the city is the central expression of the national religion, the throne of its legal authority, and the exponent and treasure-house of its artistic skill" (xxx, 156). From the circumferential Suburbs, which is a landscape without either the central vitality of a beating heart of its own, or, as we shall see, the abrasions of an intricate and contorted hawthorn that is no less "vital," the eye is turned with admiration inward, not with reflexive autonomy, but toward "expression," within far-flung limbs, that is "central": "To such a city, the country people in the district look, as the brightest standard of the national faith, the guardian of justice and peace in their social life, the arbiter of their relations with foreign states, and the treasure-house of all that has been most admirable and is most active in the national genius" (xxx, 156).

But "central expression" is not, in fact, always healthy expression. And the impulse toward centralization, after the fact or peak of "national genius," as the forces of either rectilinear or centripetal concentration move toward the eventual revelation, below the vertiginously interrelated surface of apparent mastery, of the vortex's final nil point of absence (or absent vitality), reoriginates, as we know, at a location of former plenitudinous privilege, as of "sweet fish" that are souls to be saved, if bellies cannot be filled—a circumferential location that, far from predicting the death of Centres, fallaciously anticipates only further "truth" that has a life of its own. After all, that Centre, as a shaping place of synthesis and inclusion, has been an ideal landscape from which to watch the lateral horizon of Parallel Advance, before that panoramic advance yields claustrophobia and repletion next to Illth. Nevertheless, inevitably, there is corruption at the Centre. Yet if that central corruption begins at the topography of the urban heart, it does not at first seem to. Appearance suggests that it is, in fact, entirely "otherwise"—that corruption comes not from the Centre but rather from the Suburbs. Still, appearance is only a false "cause" seen after the original effect. The "frost of death" is initially perceived from a True Centre, perhaps for false masters, that is only belatedly understood to be a faltering heart. Blood is centrifugally pumped fitfully to the extremities. And "suburban limbs," at least this time around, go first because they are secondary:

> The decay of the city of Venice is, in many respects, like that of an outwearied and aged human frame; the cause of its decrepitude is indeed at the heart, but the outward appearances of it are first at the extremities. In the centre of the city there are still places where some evidence of vitality remains, and where, with kind closing of the eyes to signs, too manifest even there, of distress and declining fortune, the stranger may succeed in imagining, for a little while what must have been

the aspect of Venice in her prime. But this lingering pulsation has not force enough any more to penetrate into the suburbs and outskirts of the city; the frost of death has thus seized upon it irrevocably, and the grasp of mortal disease is marked daily by the increasing breadth of its belt of ruin   [x, 36].

At times an expression of "national genius," urban Centres, as points of "pulsation" that linger, can also be expressions of national corruption. The problem becomes one of tense. In Ruskin's history of the Suburbs and Centre, the Centre, centripetally invaded by the "frost of death," that tightening "belt of ruin," has descended into present corruption—a fallen condition of corruption that is entirely without anything fortunate except the possibility of an exit that might lead back to the dead limbs of the Suburbs, where decrepitude is at least completed before the dying anguish of the Centre. In any case, Ruskin's present tense has become a tense that interprets the Centre as a landscape that is more imprisoning than privileged: "Tales of the prison-house . . . Londonian and Parisian misery . . . the punishment of reckless crowding in cities . . ." (xxxiv, 276).

The locus of the National Genius, once attempting to pump blood to the topographical body's limbs that, as "farthest extremities," Ruskin himself will make an effort to attain, has become not only a prison but a bloated stomach that is unable to support its appetite. The stomach-genius requires suburban aid. "Central expression" is a gastronomic art. And the stomach-genius looks beyond the infernally diminishing Middle to a Circumference whose "belt of ruin" has already been tightened: "over the whole country the sky is blackened and the air made pestilent, to supply London and other such towns with their iron railings, vulgar upholstery . . . and other means of dissipation and dishonour of life. Gradually the country people cannot even supply food to the voracity of the vicious centre; and it is necessary to import food from other countries, giving in exchange any kind of commodity we can to attract their itching desires" (xxviii, 136). Creating the Frosts of Death as it sucks circumferential life, the "vicious centre" caters to a hunger that is at the least voracious—and perhaps more.

But the hunger is not only of the stomach. Ruskin, "honoured by the receipt of a letter from the Bishop of Manchester," and alluding to Revelation 18.3 in his evaluation of the nature of the focus of Centres, in "Usury: a Reply and a Rejoinder," rejoins, as if to suggest not only an immorality of consumption at the Centre but also of multiplication. Centres have now, in fact, become "foci" of "fornication":

At the close of your letter, my Lord, you, though in measured terms, indignantly dissent from my statement of the power of great cities for evil; and indeed I have perhaps been led, by my prolonged study of the causes of the Fall of Venice, into clearer recognition of some of these urban influences than may have been possible to your Lordship in the centre of the virtues and proprieties which have been blessed by Providence in the rise of Manchester. But the Scriptural symbol of the power of temptation in the hand of spiritual Babylon—"all kings have been drunk with the wine of her Fornication"—is perfectly literal in its exposition of the special influence of cities over a vicious, that is to say, a declining, people. They are the foci of its fornication   [XXXIV, 414-15].

First as heart, then descending as stomach in turn yields to the focus of fornication, the falling anatomical centricity of the city anticipates later and perhaps final bodily functions that are not regenerative. Density, which historically suggested an achieved Centre of fortunate plenitude in which eager anticipation was part of centripetal concentration, has become, outside of history, a claustrophobic condition. Such a condition is also the landscape equivalent of the perception of repletion that comes after the appetite of the eyes has been surfeited by the panoramic fact of the Parallel Advance. Inhabited by too many, Centres are becoming no longer habitable except for those without choice. No longer even close to "true" in Newman's sense, no longer a position of privilege, the Centre, having become a voracious stomach that would turn the "outside in," like a monstrous prisonhouse or a gastronomically ambitious parenthesis,[3] threatens to become "true" only as a "Cloaca Maxima." Culinary arts will become "Fimetic" instead: "The Rhone still runs, too though I think they will soon brick it over at Geneva, and have an 'esplanade' instead. They will then have a true Cloaca Maxima, worthy of modern progress in the Fimetic Arts" (XXXVII, 408). Once perceived as the essence of National Genius and later as a heart attempting to counter the suburban Frosts of Death, even if only with "lingering pulsation," "central expression" is closer to centripetal sulphur than the attempted animation of the topographical extremities. The "tendency" of the heart is now directed through the "foci" of "fornication" toward the labyrinthine entrails of the bowels that are a centripetal version of the later centrifugal unwinding of Athena's umbilical cord, as the new Central Man

[3] See "Outside In: The Antithetical Architecture of the Parenthesis," in *The Failing Distance*, pp. 117-26.

becomes more like a Middle Man than his originally "true" self. In fact, it is now as if the villainy of the False Middle is only an anticipation of a "central expression" of central villainy.

But before the heart is irrevocably translated into urban bowels in a metamorphosis that predicts a process of self-cannibalization, which will finally leave nothing but a cesspool, and as the "belt of ruin" tightens, the citizens of a dreadfully achieved Centre, once possessing a kind of inherent "truth," are not only virtually without food but also without space, whether it be the immaculate "Truth of Space" of *Modern Painters I* or not. And Ruskin, fond of food, has always, as we know, preferred space to food: "I do not care where the land is, nor of what quality. I would rather it should be poor, for I want space more than food" (xxviii, 19). But if food for a while—even with the river full of white fish bellies—can be imported, space, it would appear, cannot. Circumferential spaciousness cannot easily be sucked by the vortex of the Vicious Centre. That aspect of the Circumference will not come easily; it will not come without a certain amount of guile. Yet, terribly, there are the Frosts of Death, and the closing "belt," tending toward no moral "apex."

Still, if the Circumference—its spaciousness, not its exported and diminishing food—will not come to the Centre, perhaps the Centre will go to the suburban Circumference. The Centre has become a version of infernal pastoral—a marsh that is a malarial brew of potent putrifaction in which breeding becomes a form of multiplication that mocks the original urge toward plenitude: "the iniquity of the tribes sinks by instinctive drainage into a slime-pit of central corruption, where sin reacting upon sin, and iniquity festering upon iniquity, curdle and coagulate into forms so monstrous, that the eye hath not seen, nor the ear heard them" (xxx, 156). As if with the immoral dispersion of geology, the pollution of the Centre spreads outward, back to where the Frosts of Death are originally apparent. It is as if the sewage of the Cloaca Maxima had backed up, creating a sulphuric, eccentric, and centrifugal reverse of the "tendency" of the whirlpool. It is as if the Centre had become, not simply a sewer, but a malfunctioning sewer. If the Vicious Centre, a "slime-pit of central corruption," is "where all the principal follies of the nation excite themselves into fraternal fury, and all the principal vices of the nation knot themselves into the loathsomest alliance," that "instinctive drainage" spreads itself "over the length and breadth of land soon to be left desolate, and through the innocent places of peace, soon to be overthrown" (xxx, 156).

Without space, there is nothing to eat. But with a density which denies even that space, there is, more importantly, nowhere to go; the Centre has become the nation's topographical bowels—bowels without the later efficacy of labyrinthine entrails—just as the inhabitants will become squirrels in a cage of foul concentricity. If the suburban Circumference were once dependent upon the Centre for a moral "tendency" that was also part of the gravitation toward National Genius—a "tendency" as centripetally moral as the central "apex" of yellow quartz—now that Circumference, which has hitherto been composed of "innocent places of peace," is being invaded by the momentarily immoral centrifugal movement[4] of a whirlpool given "reverse motion" by the failure of the central cesspool's "instinctive drainage." But if the Frosts of Death, originating centrally, arrive centripetally only to have the "loathsome alliance" of the centrally located "principal vices of the nation" disperse themselves centrifugally, the Centre's citizenry is involved in a hell that goes, in fact, almost nowhere—a hell whose space has been reduced to an infernally futile circularity that may revolve infinitely, as tight revolutions that lead an idle company nowhere:

> The tendency of the entire national energy is therefore to approximate more and more to the state of a squirrel in a cage, or a turnspit in a wheel, fed by foreign masters with nuts and dog's-meat. And indeed, when we rightly conceive the relation of London to the country, the sight of it becomes more fantastic and wonderful than any dream. Hyde Park, in the season, is the great rotatory form of the vast squirrel-cage; round and round it go the idle company, in their reversed streams, urging themselves to their necessary exercise. They cannot with safety even eat their nuts, without so much "revolution" as shall, in Venetian language, "comply with the demands of hygiene." Then they retire into their boxes, with due quantity of straw; the Belgravian and Piccadillian streets outside the railings being, when one sees clearly, nothing but the squirrel's box at the side of his wires. And then think of all the rest of the metropolis as the creation and ordinance of these squirrels, that they may squeak and whirl to their satisfaction, and yet be fed [xxviii, 136].

The citizen of the Centre has become a squirrel, whose "revolution" is the futile circularity of a point that is eternally re-beginning—a circle of futility that is close to the centricity of an "apex"-become-

---

[4] Later, with the Transformations of the Maze, centrifugal movement will be not only moral, but as necessary as life itself. Centripetence will be the dance of death.

Cloaca-Maxima that, unable to import circumferential spaciousness, exports the excess of the "slime-pit's" corruption.

Confined within the "very centre of the mother city," performing "squirrellian revolutions," the squirrel-citizen finds its mother-to-be ironically prepared as the New Jerusalem—a bride, as revolution yields Revelation 14.2, whose gates will open perhaps too quickly, wantonly, as if a focus of fornication, or as if to consume the extensive outside where both space and food were once plenitudinously available. Acting like the geometrician who, with significant qualifications, he is not, Ruskin maps the area of a "very centre" that is also the squirrel-cage of infernal re-beginnings:

> Measure the space of its [the squirrel's] entirely miserable life. Begin with that diagonal which I struck from Regent Circus to Drury Lane to St. Giles' Church, look into Church Lane there, and explore your Seven Dials and Warwick Street; and remember this is the very centre of the mother city,—precisely between its Parks, its great Library and Museum, its principal Theatres, and its Bank. . . . This is the thing they have produced round themselves; this their work in the world. When they rest from the squirrellian revolutions, and die in the Lord, and their works do follow them, *these* are what will follow them. Lugubrious march of the Waterloo Road, and the Borough, and St. Giles'; the shadows of all the Seven Dials having fetched their last compass. New Jerusalem, prepared as a bride, of course, opening her gates   [xxviii, 137].

Yet if even re-beginnings are necessarily infernal, the bride opens gates to the Seven Dials that, approaching eternity, have formed their last shadows, "fetched their last compass." And finally, the momentary geometrician, measuring the "space of . . . entirely miserable life," measures next to (if not less than) "nothing"—that central portion of a mother city, whose potential lovers are in fact "death mongers" (xxviii, 137), and whose womb, not far from a focus of fornication, is a vacuity that will not successfully be made into a location of reproduction by a swift and erotic transformation of a now barren mother into a new and aggressively open bride[5]—

---

[5] The bride of urban centricity—the Bride as the New Jerusalem of orthodox geometry—is, in some way, "saved" by the later, heterodox Transformations of the Maze. Yet perhaps it is the penitent way to the original Jerusalem that is represented by the Maze within the Cathedral of Amiens. Centricity, as if it were a fallen woman or a fallen city, is rescued by the labyrinthine. The "way" is not "Straight." Here, in any case, is Matthews, in *Mazes & Labyrinths*, on the labyrinth at Amiens: "the labyrinth was known as a '*Chemin de Jérusalem*,' '*daedale*,' or '*meandre*,' terms which

a transformation that would in fact be a cruel travesty of the laterally antiphonal relation, in Ruskin's consciousness, between a centrally "shaping" mother and a postcircumferential Rose, whose New Jerusalem is in a Promise(d) Land that is too late even for broken promises.

The anatomical metamorphoses and decline of the Centre—from head and heart, to stomach, to bowels, to the focus of fornication, to dead womb—chart an attendant landscape change. The Cloaca Maxima has become solid sewage. What was shortly before a dead-river version of the Dead Sea has become, in the process of a kind of "land-change," a "central expression" that is a memorably Fimetic wasteland informed by the Nation's Bowel Genius and given "shapelessness" by the hollow womb of death, which "Athena of the Dew"/"Athena of the Earth" would herself, in any of her manifestations, never permit:

> For these streets are indeed what they have built; their inhabitants the people have chosen to educate. They took the bread and milk and meat from the people of their fields; they gave it to feed, and retain here in their service, this fermenting mass of unhappy human beings,—news-mongers, novel-mongers, picture-mongers, poison-drink-mongers, lust and death-mongers; the whole smoking mass of it one vast dead marine storeshop,—accumulation of wreck of the Dead Sea, with every activity of it, a form of putrefaction. [xxviii, 137].

C. Juggling, Trick Riding, and the Avaricious Imagination of Repletion

Later, as if Theseus, Ruskin, in a different kind of "mediatorial function"—involved with lateral Antiphonal contention—will become a fortunate version of the parasitically Janusian Middle Man. Concerned with the mathematics of neither subtraction nor multiplication, Ruskin, leaving the Centre, will then negotiate the Middle for an entirely different effect. But before he leaves the Centre, there are aspects of centricity that must be explored. The Ruskin who understands that the location of dual vantage points on either end of London Bridge to create stereoscopic depth in a painting of St. Paul's is a fiction that will never approach fact is the same Ruskin who would not "violate one of the most essential principles

---

need no explanation. The centre was called *'ciel'* or *'Jérusalem.'* The labyrinth formerly in the nave of Amiens Cathedral was larger than that at Chartres, being 42 ft. in diameter" (p. 60). Compare with Ruskin's *Bible of Amiens*, Chap. IV.

of nature" by representing "that as seen at once which can only be seen by two separate acts of seeing," which would be telling a "falsehood as gross as if we had represented four sides of a cubic object visible together" (III, 321). But the Centre, or the condition of being surrounded as if by a Circumference, requires, as we shall see, accommodation. The approach toward what becomes a central simultaneity of perception, even if it cannot create depth on canvas, is called forth by a kind of panoramic awareness: "They talk of my inconsistency because they cannot see two sides at once; all people are apparently inconsistent who have a wide range of thought, and can look alternatively from opposite points" (XII, li).[6]

The efficacy of being surrounded by "opposite points" "at once," like a Centre surrounded by a simultaneously perceived Circumference of varying information, is developed and advertised in order to answer the charges of inconsistency and self-contradiction that result, Ruskin is certain, from the extension of the lateral focus to encompass the "wide range of [his] thought": "among the various modes in which the architects, against whose practice my writings are directed, have endeavoured to oppose them, no charge has been made more frequently than those of their self-contradiction; the fact being, that there are few people in the world who are capable of seeing the two sides of any subject, or of conceiving how the statements of its opposite aspects can possibly be reconciled" (XII, 44). And when the lateral focus extends too far into apparently opposing and peripheral areas, attempting to include too much, the textual focus breaks apart in order to present contradictory information. But opposing texts, like the right and left side of the Central Man, guard the integrity of a third and central textual focal point. Predictably, Ruskin's model for the central texts of truth is the Bible: "It will be found that throughout the Scriptures there are on every subject two opposite groups of text; and a middle group, which contains the truth that rests between the two others. The opposite texts are guards against the abuse of the central texts—guards set in opposite directions" (V, liii).

Still, there is the implication that if the "wide range of thought" were extended far enough to accommodate all three texts, that panoramic and inclusive focus would aspire toward the geometry of an enveloping continuum-as-circumference, as though reconciliation, in the extended process of becoming a circle, were possible

---

[6] Less concerned with the problems of "at once," Ruskin in the same vein will say that "the more I see of useful truths, the more I find that, like human beings, they are usually biped; and, although, as far as apprehended . . . balance on opposite fulcra" (V, 169).

on the far side of a "wide range of thought." With the conjunctive—
or anticontradictory—impulse implied, Ruskin approaches the far
curve of a circle, where dichotomic contradiction, "describing two
contradictory aspects of both minds," moves toward the hypothetical reconciliation that is like the twisting, möbius logic of his penultimate "inner language." If, metaphorically, the problem is that
"you divide two balls into red and blue—look at them from one
side—and one is blue and other red; and look at them from the
other, and the first is red and the second blue," then what is required
to make connection, as opposed to underscored contradiction, is
extensive "expanding and explaining." There are, Ruskin knows,
"many subjects which involve this species of reversed light before
you can work them out thoroughly" (v, 431). With opposition and
contradiction expanded in order to be explained, central texts are
approached by a widely ranging—and twistingly circular, as though
cast in a "species of reversed light"—process of thought.

In the same way that a straight line eventually aspires toward the
eternity of a circle, so opposing extremes extended lengthily in
opposite directions aspire toward the dim location of circular meaning where contradiction becomes a potentially profound paradox,
a language of dialogical condensation, or antiphonally dichotomic
listening, in which different messages are received simultaneously.
The problematic circular "meaning" of paradox as a kind of dialogue that may be profound anticipates the later Antiphonal Contention of the three-dimensional double labyrinths of Ruskin's final
architecture, his Theatre of Blindness—this, as syntax becomes
parataxis and meaning, uncompleted by the labyrinth of silence
below, becomes both indeterminate and multivocal. But for now,
it is enough to suggest that just as the intensity of stereoscopic
depth is dependent upon the distance between twin vantage
points—the distance of the bridge of the nose between perceiving
eyes—so a truth, not necessarily of depth, is also dependent upon
a similar distance between opposed, though finally coordinated,
perception; the greater that distance, the greater "the security given
to the conclusions arrived at . . . in consequence of the breadth of
the basis on which the reasoning is founded" (xxxiv, 474). Unsurprisingly, Ruskin's antithetical but reciprocal Gothic architecture
is a structural model for the strength of his (stereo)logic in a way
that is no different from the political, even universal, coherence
provided by the key implications of *The Elements of Drawing* and *The
Elements of Perspective.* And again, right design incarnates morality
and truth: "The multiplicity of subject, and opposite directions of
investigation, which have so often been alleged against me, as if

sources of weakness, are in reality, as the multiplied buttresses of the apse of Amiens, as secure in allied result as they are opposed in direction" (xxxiv, 474).

But the inclusion of apparent contradiction in a panorama of "wide-ranging thought" becomes a process that is more demanding than a mere accommodation of diversity and multiplicity. If he has not yet come to telling a "falsehood as gross as if we had represented four sides of a cubic object visible together," he has at least dealt with two sides—one red and the other blue—that might well be seen, without canceling each other, at the same time. After all, Ruskin has already done more than suggest that he sees "two sides at once" (xii, li). What is anticipated is either a divided self or multiple selves. Too broad a forehead—too much distance between eyes, which is perhaps too much "breadth of the basis on which the reasoning is founded"—may lead neither to the unity of a circle nor the dim location where contradiction becomes the "stereo-scopic" or antiphonal logic of a certain kind of paradox, but to what is at least the intimation of a fragmentation beyond mere calculated division:

> Perhaps some of my hearers this evening may occasionally have heard it stated of me that I am rather apt to contradict myself. I hope I am exceedingly apt to do so. I never met with a question yet, of any importance, which did not need, for the right solution of it, at least one positive and one negative answer, like an equation of the second degree. Mostly, matters of any consequence are three-sided, or four-sided, or polygonal; and the trotting round a polygon is severe work for people any way stiff in their opinions. For myself, I am never satisfied that I have handled a subject properly till I have contradicted myself at least three times [xvi, 187].

Falsehood may be the perception of four sides at once, but now "matters of any consequence" are "three-sided," or "four-sided, or polygonal." And if "the trotting round a polygon is severe work for people any way stiff in their opinions," the simultaneous perception of the polygon must be too much for one person. There may be a truth of cubism, but it is a demanding truth, as of Strange Chords. With problems that are potentially polygonal, multiple measures are required. In the "Affairs of the Master," from *Fors Clavigera*, Ruskin trades in his first person for an objectified third, and, in the process, becomes a juggler: "and it is quite certain that he can't continue to ride so many horses at once, or keep so many balls in the air" (xxix, 248). The self-as-juggler, or the mind as the juggler's air-borne balls—"I'm perfectly overwhelmed under the quantity of things which must be kept in mind, now, going like a juggler's balls in the air" (XXXVII, 227)—is, in either case, an appropriate image for a Ruskin who would have his texts move through the presses seven abreast, as if with the simultaneous expression of a "wide range of thought": "But this, I beg my readers to observe, will be the seventh large book I have actually at this time passing through the press" (XXVIII, 444). Yet another kind of press—the "press of coincident thought," which becomes a "thousand things in my head pushing each other like shoals of minnows" (*Diaries*, p. 923)—begins to define limitations to both the trick riding of his consciousness and the number of balls he can keep in the air at once: "I can see that I am defeated only because I have too many things on hand: and that neither rabbits at Coniston, road-surveyors at Croydon, or mud in St. Giles, would get any better of me, if I could give exclusive attention to any one business" (XXVIII, 205).

Still, he cannot easily give attention that is single and exclusive. Working against the deadline of the point where the "long shadow" becomes the dark substance of death, he understands, at the age of fifty-six, that to rid himself finally of one thought or project— to work it out to its ultimate end—is to leave something else behind, probably forever. The "press of coincident thought" becomes a "pressing arithmetic" of the End—an inevitably premature End that will prevent the completed building of what might have been a "many-towered city":

> —I begin to ask myself, with somewhat pressing arithmetic, how much time is likely to be left me, at the age of fifty-six, to complete the various designs for which, until past fifty, I was merely collecting materials.
>
> Of these materials, I have now enough by me for a most interesting (in my own opinion) history of fifteenth-century Florentine art, in six octavo volumes; an analysis of the Attic art of the fifth century B.C., in three volumes; an exhaustive history of northern thirteenth-century art, in ten volumes; a life of Turner, with analysis of modern landscape art, in four volumes; a life of Walter Scott, with analysis of the general principles of Education, in ten volumes; a commentary on Hesiod, with final analysis of the principles of Political Economy, in nine volumes; and a general description of the geology and botany of the Alps, in twenty-four volumes.
>
> Of these works, though all carefully projected, and some already in progress,—yet . . . it does not seem to me, even in

my most sanguine moments, now probable that I shall live to effect such conclusion as would be satisfactory to me; and I think it will therefore be only prudent, however humiliating, to throw together at once, out of the heap of loose stones collected for this many-towered city which I am not able to finish, such fragments of good marble as may perchance be useful to future builders; and to clear away, out of sight, the lime and rubbish which I meant for mortar [xxvi, 95-96].

The humor of the middle paragraph—if self-mockery met of desperation can be called a brand of humor—is perhaps not entirely apparent, for the multiplication of either projected work, or works in fact in progress, threatens to become not the desired infinity of an anonymous depth perspective but an infinite and disintegrating surface perspective of thoughts so widely ranging as to require the aid of either proxy delegates, themselves with peripheral vision, or a self with not merely polygonal ambitions but polygonal performance.

In a Middle that is as central as the "middle group" of central, Scriptural texts, Ruskin, as now a beneficent Middle Man of (logo)-concentricity incarnate, for whom Janusian parasitism would be an unthinkable fiction, finds even the accommodations of his polygonal consciousness under attack. He might be a St. Sebastian whose arrows are ideas or projects:

> I wonderfully well, and slept well; but to-day trembling and nervous with too much on my mind—all pleasant; but Minerals, Turner's life, the Saints, and Oxford Lectures, with instant *Proserpina*—five subjects, like this, with poor me in the middle.

> [xxxiii, 1]

An architectural "shattered majesty," like the ruins of the Theatre of Blindness, can anticipate the condition of a too inclusive mind that leaves language, at a point of pronounced failure, in a state of extreme decomposition. But the "press of coincident thought" that is like the convergence of arrows is equally ominous.[7]

With its logic at least plural before it may be alogical, Ruskin's

---

[7] Later we shall see where polygonal ambitions can lead: "I never understood the meaning of that phrase before, but indeed I was a double, or even treble, creature, through part of that dream" (xxxvii, 246).

polygonal consciousness, attempting to accommodate an excessively "wide" variety of demands by juggling without itself disintegrating, is a mind that, perhaps anticipating a penultimately replete syntax verging on parataxis, is nevertheless an imagination of potentially "morbid hunger." In fact, that consciousness represents ambitions of an aspect of an imagination of a double mind, as of double labyrinths, which rarely works through mutual exclusion, even in the face of self-destruction at a point of failure that is the imagination's "shattered majesty"—a condition of self-destruction arrived at by the imagination's overly ambitious multiplication and branching "*ad infinitum*." At least this is the case until the vacuum of Illth is reached, when it is already too late. Rarely is a question of the imagination's choice involved that would reduce the "biped" to the "uniped," any more than stereoscopic vision would be replaced by the depthless sight of the Cyclops. Ruskin would turn division against himself into a double advantage.

As if in a location of vicious centricity, where it is not so much the demands as the performances that are excessive, there is an avaricious imagination whose appetite, a kind of "morbid hunger" that is as devouring as condemned central space, brings about a condition of repletion—a condition that is, in fact, a point of failure without "noble issue," in which a greedy plenitude is as deathly as a Dead Sea covered with the white bellies of floating fish that, like souls beyond Redemption, are no longer "sweet":

> . . . and it is necessary to be very careful how we deaden this faculty of finding sublimity in things comparatively small by over-indulgence in the excitement of greater magnificence. For though it is the nature of the imagination to rouse itself with little help, yet it will never start but from the highest point it can reach; its ambition is insatiable; it always fixes on the largest thing it has in sight. . . . And this avarice of the imagination increases with the stimulus . . . and it may be pushed at last into a morbid hunger, in which it has nearly lost its own inherent power but craves an increase of external excitement— and at last dies of repletion   [v, 436].

Chapter Four

Vacancies, Kindly and Deadly: Sweet Transitions and Jarring Thoughts

A. The Syntax of Architecture:
St. Peter's Divided

Always a Central Man, Turner, now that the Centre is in trouble, presents possible problems. Turner, also involved in circumferential, if not suburban, backgrounds—distances that, by an effort of both brush and palette, will not fail—is further, in his instincts toward centricity, concerned with number. His imagination is in danger of being subject to a "morbid hunger." In fact, he might find it dying of an avaricious imagination—an imagination seduced not so much by the "largest thing it has in sight" (v, 446) (like his perception of a St. Peter's that will be optically divided in order to be conquered) as the number of things in sight. A Turnerian death of repletion will be a numerical death:

> Quantity takes the place of mass. Turner has also ascertained, in the course of his studies, that nature was infinitely full, and that old painters had not only missed pitch of hue, but her power of accumulation. He saw there were more clouds in any forest, more crags on every hill side; and he set himself with all his strength to proclaim this great fact of Quantity in the universe [xiii, 129].

Even Ruskin, who, before repletion, finds pastoral in plenitude, can be overwhelmed by what he calls Turner's "numerical superiority" (vi, 353). Turner's painting, "The Bay of Baiae," is an example of mass ineffectively transformed into the "great fact of Quantity." In this case, number leads to no superiority. As in Ruskin's concept of "Illth," which, as we know, is wealth disastrously beyond use (xvii, 89, 168), more is simply too much, and too much is, finally, less than nothing. The way to investigate properly "The Bay of Baiae" is by an uncharacteristic method of limitation and division:

> The main fault of the composition is, however, in the over-indulgence of his new triumph in quantity. . . . The following

procedure will, I think, under these circumstances be found serviceable. Take a stiff piece of pasteboard, about eight inches square, and cut out in the centre of it an oblong opening, two and a half inches by three. Bring this with you to the picture, and standing three or four feet from it, according to your power of sight, look through the opening in the card at the middle distance, holding the card a foot or two from the eye, so as to turn the picture, piece by piece, into a series of small subjects. Examine these subjects quietly, one by one; sometimes holding the opening horizontal, sometimes upright, according to the bit you are examining, and you will find, I believe, in a very little while, that each of these small subjects becomes more interesting to you, and seems to have more in it, than the whole picture did before   (XIII, 134].

The whole is replete by the failure of any virtue to be found in the numerical IIIth of too much/less than nothing. But pasteboard, with the Centre cut out, necessarily reduces Turner's central repletion to a serial perception—"a series of small subjects"—which is the examination of objects observed "piece by piece" and "one by one," either as if from within the curvilinear Hampton Court Maze that, biographically important early, will later, becoming autobiographically more important, act as a shaping mnemonic model, or as if Turner's plenitude had been turned into a mural to be "read." The problem is not so much one of composition as it is that point of failure of a "numerical superiority" which predicts intensely experienced interrelation—the kind of repletively intricate connection that leads toward, and is syntactically reflected in, the language (perhaps vortical before centrifugally reversed) of the Travel Diary toward Nothing, which is the journey to the Edge where peacocks scream in infernal triumph:

> It is of course both a merit and a marvel, that these separate pieces should be so beautiful, but it is a great fault that they should be so put together as to destroy their interest: not that they are ill composed, but there is simply a surfeit of material. No composition whatever could render such a quantity digestible; nay, the very goodness of the composition is harmful, for everything so leads into everything else, that without the help of the limiting cardboard it is impossible to stop—we are dragged through arch after arch, and round tower after tower, never getting leave to breathe until we are jaded   [XIII, 134].

To be within certain of Turner's paintings is not only to be among the interrelation of Strange Chords—"everything so leads into everything else"—but it is also to be within a kind of self-canni-balizing Piranesian vortex[1] (or Hall of Contrasting Mirrors), with-out essential design, motion, or available exit: "we are dragged through arch after arch, and round tower after tower, never getting leave to breath." Yet the missing Centre of a pasteboard can, bring-ing "nothing" to plenitude, halve the vertiginous interrelation of numerical repletion, impeding the serial process so that one is moving with comfortable ease, as though in the calculated "slow travel" we shall soon come across, rather than being dragged head-long out of control.

Turner's error of excess is precisely one of imposing upon his observers an exaggerated, perhaps burlesque, version of the Index World. Yet every man is not an Indexer capable of indexing ad infinitum. In fact, perhaps no one is. For the plenum is God's bounteous good, but man's apprehension is necessarily his own. Further, it is his "fallen" own. "Everything" so leading into "every-thing" is a system of grotesquely inhuman intensity that can only be perceived from angelic altitudes or Newman's True Centre, which is a Centre that is a figure for the fulfillment of another's condemnation:

> . . . he [Turner] erred finally, and chiefly, in *quantity*, because in his enthusiastic perception of the fulness of nature, he did not allow for the narrowness of the human heart; he saw, indeed, that there were no limits to creation, but forgot that there were many to reception; he thus spoiled his most careful works by the very richness of invention they contained, and concentrated the material of twenty noble pictures into a single failure [XIII, 130].

Man cannot take Nature entirely to his narrow heart; the heart is densely central and Nature plenitudinous, but privileged location and "numerical superiority" are not interchangeable commodities.

If the "human heart" is defined by a "narrowness" that limits the

[1] J. Hillis Miller, in "Thomas De Quincey," *The Disappearance of God* (Cambridge, Mass., 1963) pp. 67-68, speaks intriguingly of what he calls the "Piranesi effect" as "the power which the mind has to sink into its own infinite abyss, not by emptying itself out but by becoming trapped in some form of thought or mental experience which is repeated forever. This produces a vertigo like that caused by the endless multiplications of a single face in a hall of mirrors." Hillis Miller's notion of the "Piranesi effect," which is a spiraling version of what he has also called the "Quaker Oats box effect," anticipates his explorations of the *"mise en abîme."* Ruskin's vortical/ centrifuged vision, spiraling either over nothing, as a false presence, or repletively toward White Silence after the decomposition of the Labyrinthine Penultimate, would seem related to these vertiginous effects that further may have something in common with the will and result of cross-referencing *"ad infinitum."*

observer's heartfelt "reception" of the plenum, the imagination described by Ruskin, which is also vulnerable to surfeit, can be jaded as easily as a heart with human limitations:

> Another character of the imagination is equally constant, and, to our present inquiry, of yet greater importance. It is eminently a *wearable* faculty, eminently delicate, and incapable of bearing fatigue; so that if we give it too many objects at a time to employ itself upon, or very grand ones for a long time together, it fails under the effort, becomes jaded, exactly as the limbs do by bodily fatigue and incapable of answering any farther appeal till it has had rest   [v, 182].

The "limbs" of the imagination become as weary as the human, or even urban, heart if "too many objects" are encompassed simultaneously. Again, what is required is the pasteboard serialization of a plenitude that has become the infernal repletion of the "wide circumference" ingested.

The serialization of the Centreless pasteboard yields rest in the face of vertiginous Strange Chords, whose strangeness may even go so far as the self-cannibalizing interrelation of eventual disappearance. Simultaneity has always predicted problems. "Too much at once" is more dangerous than simply "too much." What is required is a place empty enough for the imaginative "limbs" to lie down in. If plenitude anticipates repletion, Ruskin, once horrified by a *horror vacui*, can develop the tentative aesthetics of a prone agoraphile. Imaginatively unused horizontal space assumes the ability to provide rest:

> . . . in consequence of that other great character of the imagination, fatigableness, it is a great advantage to the picture that it need not present too much at once, and that what it does present may be chosen and ordered as not only to be more easily seized, but to give the imagination rest, and, as it were, places to lie down and stretch its limbs in   [v, 186].

The unused horizontal space of the imagination is a vacancy— or, more precisely, plural and "kindly vacancies" that will beguile the imagination "back into action, with pleasant and cautious sequence of incident; all jarring thoughts being excluded, all vain redundance denied, and all just and sweet transition permitted" (v, 186). The "jarring thoughts" of infinity condensed to an Index World are banished. Instead, the serial activity—"all just and sweet transition"—that counters the simultaneity and repletion of the Strange Chords of condemned central space is promoted. If "everything so leads into everything else," perhaps *"ad infinitum,"* Ruskin would have it do so slowly, with the imaginatively horizontal oases of "kindly vacancies" between. Death by the repletion of "too much at once" can be delayed by the occasionally benevolent "nothing," where the prone position of rest can be assumed for a while before death's similar but more permanent position.

Once, pasteboard was not required. There was no problem of plenitude to be solved. Repletion did not require the extension of serialization. But then there were no Centres of dung and central rivers of death, swollen with the white bellies of once "sweet fish." Instead, there was naively central conceit. Still, the "once" before pasteboard anticipates the situation after pasteboard. In *Praeterita*, Ruskin talks about a childish focus that brings happiness before the received consequences of panoramic inclusion has been felt in the Strange Chords of condemned central space. Early on, even as later, with penultimate repletion, less is "good," and the early enveloping walls of his childhood might have been made of pasteboard, instead of brick:

> . . . that great part of my acute perception and deep feeling of the beauty of architecture and scenery abroad, was owing to the well formed habit of narrowing myself to happiness within the four brick walls of our fifty by one hundred yards of garden   [xxxv, 132].

"Narrowing" himself "to happiness" in childhood, Ruskin establishes an early model for the comfortable wisdom of maturity. By 1883, returning with not only experience but the meaning of the original experience of *Modern Painters II* (1846), Ruskin finds consolation in conclusions that are neither daring nor panoramic— conclusions that might be the entirely sane result of a centreless pasteboard or the optical limitation of brick walls: "I . . . believe that the conclusions arrived at are safer in their narrowness than they would have been in pretending to include the total field of investigation" (IV, 222). Limiting the "total field" in 1883, Ruskin, even in the beginning and with a distance of futurity that will be more dangerous than safe, understands that conventional, perhaps (logo)-concentric success, not to mention a rational survival that would avoid the problematic decomposition of "pathos" on what Derrida calls the "eastern edge," depends upon the avoidance of repletion:

> Among these three virtues, it seems to me, that men in general least feel the full scope and bearing of Temperance; . . .

At least, in the particular branches of study into which I have been led, I find that Providence seems through various symbols and in more various ways to insist upon the need of temperance far more than that of other virtues. I find in art, power and success depending continually upon a "Not too much" [v, 437].

If recessional space for a solitary traveler will first be explored with enthusiasm—an enthusiasm that, more or less (and the "less" predicts the later impulse for the curvilinear and the language of turn and return), lasts as long as the distance holds out—the peripheral, almost from the beginning, is an inclusive territory that should be approached "Not too much" at one time. The simultaneity of the Parallel Advance can overwhelm. And the imagination, in that inevitably replete process, no matter how "avaricious," can die—a "morbid hunger" leading to the imagination's gourging itself to death.

Having originally narrowed himself to happiness, Ruskin would return to that naive condition unencumbered by panoramic and central ambition. He would find a solution to the Strange Chords of attempted mastery that have come to occupy a condemned space of excessive interrelation. It is not simple. As poignant reminder, the diction of limitation and economy is everywhere. But fundamental discursiveness—the syntactical urge to fill the blank page with a verbal plenum—is not easily discouraged. Further, the enemy appears in various guises: it can be either claustrophobically dense or frantically allusive, with vast open space—even spaces for the imagination to lie down in—between. Still, the reminders are constant. The directions are urged more upon self than reader. The One—as prototypical model—will be more important than the plural and confusing Many:

More progress in power of judgment may be made in a limited time by the examination of one work, than by the review of many [xx, 34].

And again:

I should also attach the greatest importance to a severe limitation of choice in the examples submitted to him. To study one good master till you understand him will teach you more than a superficial acquaintance with a thousand [xvi, 182].

But the limits that Ruskin sets are themselves almost without limit. By constant reminder, he will attempt to avoid the consequences of excessive interrelation. Yet the repetition of reminders, approaching the Piranesian and potentially infinite cross-referencing of self in a Hall of Contrasting Mirrors, where multiplication is next to disappearance, is itself almost another version of what might be called the Strange Chord's interrelation *"ad infinitum."* Endlessly, he would remind himself to limit himself. Matching experience with meaning, he understands that, under certain circumstances, not only does "everything so lead[s] into everything else," but that the dimensions of the human heart might well be more accommodating than in fact they are. Understanding much, he understands the essential "narrowness of the human heart," as well as the potential dangers of panorama—especially a panorama that, in parallel lines, advances. Coached by Temperance, he will not transgress: "I cannot, of course, within the limits of this paper, proceed to any statement" (xvi, 151). He is determined not to travel to the next "planet or nebula" in search of the final implication of the tennis balls of Harry the Fifth.[2] Like "vacancies" that are "kindly," limitation offers a kind of peace in the midst of the necessarily dense controversy of Strange Chords.

Yet it is not the early garden-variety of brick delineated peace that is offered—the naively narrow happiness of hubristic and inexperienced exclusion. Rather, it is the peacefully narrow dimension of self-conscious awareness. Heeding his own direction, Ruskin advertises his responsibility: "Nevertheless, lest the direction which I have been led to give to my discourse, and the narrow limits within which I am compelled to confine the treatment of its subject . . ." (xix, 163). In fact, he is pleased, perhaps aided by his pasteboard sense, to have developed a nose for limitation: "The limit to practically useful discovery is rapidly being approached" (xxii, 168). Further, he shares his Temperance with others; immodestly, he will direct modesty elsewhere: "But, if you were discontented with the limit I proposed for your sciences . . ." (xxii, 168). And finally, in the "simplest order" of an exhibition of art objects, which is the simplest order of "cautious sequence" and "sweet transition," what is important is that number should not become "confusion" at the expense of "best advantage." The limits will be "resolute": "the collection must never be increased to its own confusion, but within resolute limits permanently arranged, so that every part of

[2] "But if I wrote a parenthesis of that length every now and then, the entire book would overlap into the next planet or nebula; and if I began putting notes to explain, or confirm, I should probably write a new book on the trotting of Centaurs and Lapithae, or the riding of Bellerophon, or the crawling of the tortoise of Aegina, or the flying of Harry the Fifth's tennis balls" (*Diaries*, p. 1136).

it shall be seen to the best advantage in the simplest order" (xxx, 54).

Architecture, like a collection of art objects, must have an order of perception, though not necessarily a "simplest order." In the same tentative way that Ruskin, by employing the centreless paste-board, would almost have a painting by Turner extended to a mural or divided and multiplied into a Sienese narrative painting, so architecture must not be—cannot be—encompassed by the eye "all at once." The tendency to do so is dangerous. Temporal series, for a narrow and perhaps Gothically human heart, must be brought to single objects in space that might otherwise be viewed from the True Centre of what we shall see to be Daedalean heights with that undivided simultaneity apparently dreaded by Ruskin, who, with his occasionally polygonal consciousness, knows better than most the implications inherent in the perception that "everything so leads into everything else."

But the theory comes before both experience and significant meaning. The early *The Poetry of Architecture* is a poetry that would have the spatiality of a building "read," as if it were the left to right progress of language on a page: "The building itself should be low and long, so that, if possible, it may not be seen *all at once* [italics mine], but may be partially concealed by trunks or leafage at various distances" (i, 70). The view from one end of Ruskin's early divided building gives no clue of the other end; final shape is revealed more by serial perspectives extended in time than the simultaneity of an overly ambitious polygonal consciousness. What is required is "slow travel" from one end to another. With Ruskin's architecture, nothing can be taken for granted. It must be unpredictable, an architecture whose future cannot be discerned in the present at a terribly privileged moment of "all at once":

> Only one general rule can be given, and that we repeat. The house must not be a noun substantative, it must not stand by itself, it must be part and parcel of a proportioned whole: it must not even be seen all at once; and he who sees one end should feel that, from the given data, he can arrive at no conclusion respecting the other [i, 187].

Ruskin's early trip to Rome, outlined in *Letters to a College Friend*, is, among other things, a study of architecture as an intricately serial and unprophetic syntax, as opposed to a composition of autonomous "noun substantives," connected, presumably, only by intransitive verbs. Reading architecture assumes the temporality of movement. Often, we find Ruskin in his role of traveler; his vantage point is mobile. And walking through the Vatican is a process that would leave the consciousness triumphantly unpolygonal. Multiple perspectives, extended in time, yield a sanely single mind. The "all at once" of a "truly privileged" perspective—the perspective of Strange Chords—is not encountered in an architectural syntax that would avoid the dangerous model of the Noun Substantative. The optical negotiation of the Vatican is a process of "cautious sequence" rather than prophecy. Single statues, requiring attention, are like perceptions through a centreless pasteboard, or the careful, word-by-word reading of a page: "I have been much pleased with the Vatican, which takes about an hour's quick walk to get you through from one end to the other, passing a statue for every second, and such statues!" (I, 433). Statues "every second" are foci of "sweet transition."

Like the Vatican in particular, Rome in general is not a place for privileged vantage points that would reciprocally yield privileged focal points. In fact, "express points of lionisation," approached with "excited expectation," are anathema. But Rome, if approached the way one writes an unpredictable syntax, "yielding to every impulse," becomes entirely admirable. Like a house about which "no conclusion" can be reached from simply one end, Rome requires the unpremeditated division, as if by pasteboard, of both slow and impulsive travel:

> In the city, if you take a carriage and drive to express points of lionisation, I believe that most people of good taste would expect little and find less. The Capitol is a melancholy rubbishy square of average Palladian—modern; the Forum, a good group of smashed columns. . . . But if, instead of driving, with excited expectation, to particular points, you saunter leisurely up one street and down another, yielding to every impulse, peeping into every corner, and keeping your observation active, the impression is exceedingly changed. There is not a fragment, a stone, or a chimney, ancient or modern, that is not in itself a study, not an inch of ground that can be passed over without its claim of admiration and offer of instruction, and you return home in hopeless conviction that were you to substitute years for the days of your appointed stay, they would not be enough for the estimation or examination of Rome [I, 380-81].

Impulse defeats the privilege of "particular points." Sauntering leisurely extends and opens up the potentially dense and overlapping spatial-temporal coordinates. Rome is not to be seen from a

True Centre. It is to be experienced from within, where multiple perspectives emanate from a single consciousness, whose imagination is not threatened by a death of infernally privileged repletion. As we shall see, time and space are not to be "killed."

If the proper model of Rome is not the Vatican (and it may be), then it is St. Peter's in "fifty fragments." The "whole" of St. Peter's is less than the sum of its parts; it may even be less than a single part, a part that is itself greater than St. Paul's. Like certain cottages, it should not be seen "all at once." It is as if Renaissance (or Daedalean) addition were, in fact, subtraction. And the final figure is in a minus category—or rather the "nothing but a ballroom" of St. Peter's as a whole:

> And as a whole, St. Peter's is fit for nothing but a ballroom, and it is a little too gaudy even for that (inside I mean, of course). But the overwhelming vastness of every detail, and the magnificent solidity and splendour of material are such that, in walking through it, you think of St. Paul's as of a pasteboard model—a child's toy—that the wind may blow away like a pack of cards and nobody the wiser. And the exquisite feeling and glorious art brought out in every part and detail are so impressive that, were St. Peter's dashed into fifty fragments, I would give our St. Paul's—and Ludgate Hill into the bargain—for any one of them. As a whole, I repeat, it is meagre outside and offensive within   [1, 380].

An example of architectural repletion, St. Peter's, if unpredictable, is also altogether excessive. But the optics of division—of the multiple perspective that comes from "walking through it"—conquers. "Slow travel," or perhaps even "an hour's quick walk," eases the demands of both perception and an imagination that threatens to die of repletion. Ironically, an approach to the privileged perception that we have come to expect from a True Centre, which may result in "such feelings as we can have only once or twice in our lives," comes instead from the kind of limitation that a centreless pasteboard might provide:

> I have not made up my mind about St. Peter's: there is certainly a great deal too much light in it, which destroys size . . . but if you go into its details, and examine its colossal pieces of sculpture which gleam through every shadow, the thorough *get up* of the *whole*, the going *whole hog*, the inimitable, unimaginable art displayed in every corner and hole, the concentration of human intellect and of the rarest and most beautiful

materials that God has given for it to work with, unite to raise such feelings as we can have only once or twice in our lives. The value of intellect and material concentrated in one of the minor chapels of St. Peter's would have built Cantebury or York [i, 432].

It could be said that even the divided interiority of St. Peter's—"one of the minor chapel's of St. Peter's"—is almost, if not quite, too much: while "meager outside," it is "offensive within." Inverting his informing organicist maxim, Ruskin would have the syntax of this decidedly un-Gothic structure great only in the formed humility of the almost vivisectional division of its detail, which is to say great as the language of the Noun Substantive approaches the disconjunctive condition of parataxis—though Ruskin's parataxis, taken as a whole, is an "honourable defeat" (x, 190), a defeat of "shattered majesty" that a more perfect and unfallen St. Peter's can never aspire toward. Nevertheless, St. Peter's stands, and, as a "whole," it stands "accused."

B. Slow Travel:
The Extension of Time and Space

The Letters to a College Friend is a kind of ocular autobiography; the letters are, in fact, obsessed with optics—the problem of Ruskin's Desiring Eyes.[3] But they are also about travel—more precisely, the coordination of travel and optics. If to see is not necessarily to travel, to travel, with Ruskin, is necessarily to see. And to see is to construct the specific groundwork for generalization. Laws occur after movement and sight have joined in significance. As a child, we recall, there is no place to go. Ruskin is in an ambiguous Centre, with the naive conceit of an infernally geometric Cock-Robinson-Crusoe. Yet he has run out of things to see. He must leave. At the age of twenty-two, he announces a new mobility. The drifting water of the vortex's Circumference, which may later become a "winding" of information, summons him: "but I have none of my old childish contentment and am restless and wandering—always wanting to get to any part of the coast than that I have reached; unable to stand and watch, as I once could, in happiness of hours" (*Diaries*, p. 160).

Again in *The Letters to a College Friend*, Ruskin, complaining of his friend's geographical agility, might be receiving a letter instead

[3] See "The Desire of the Eyes," *The Failing Distance*, pp. 1-23.

of sending one: "I have just read your letter over, which leaves me in a very uncomfortable doubt of your being in any particular point of space, and possessed of an exceedingly indistinct notion of your state of existence, as you date from three places and profess an intention of going to two more" (I, 448). Yet close to the beginning, mobility is something that is earned, not given. Space is linked to time by established ratio; and it cannot be negotiated without an interval that is extended, as though by a slow gear. Neither space nor time is condensed. Mobility is paid for in extended time. Here is a description of original travel:

> In the olden days of travelling, now to return no more, in which distance could not be vanquished without toil, but in which that toil was rewarded, partly by the power of deliberate survey of the countries through which the journey lay, and partly . . . or, from the long hoped for turn in the dusty perspective of the causeway . . . hours of peaceful and thoughtful pleasure, for which the rush of the arrival in the railway station is perhaps not always, or to all men, an equivalent,—in those days, I say, when there was something more to be anticipated and remembered in the first aspect of each successive halting-place, than a new arrangement of glass roofing and iron girder . . . [x, 3].

But the coordination of travel and optics has not achieved a satisfactory conjunction in the present. Now, both travel—the fast travel, say, of a quick assembly line—and optics seem jointly bent upon an immoral "apex" of simultaneity that would, with false economy, join the dimensions of time and space. And altitude and horizontality create similar problems: in the same way that looking from the elevated Centre can cause a vertigo of "too many," so fast lateral traveling, which exhausts the eye by a too swift mobility rather than synoptic privilege, leads to the condition of the "jaded" observer. Fast movement, beyond the easy accommodation of the eye, is merely a prefiguration of simultaneous central repletion. The result is optical exhaustion and the momentary death of the imaginative faculty that has led a briefly avaricious existence:

> And this is the real nature of the weariness which is so often felt in travelling, from seeing too much. It is not that the monotony and number of the beautiful things seen have made them valueless, but that the imaginative power has been overtaxed; and, instead of letting it rest, the traveller, wondering

to find himself dull, and incapable of admiration, seeks for
something more admirable, excites and torments, and drags
the poor fainting imagination up by the shoulders: "Look at
this, and look at that, and this more wonderful still!"—until
the imaginative faculty faints utterly away, beyond all further
torment, or pleasure, dead for many a day to come; and the
despairing prodigal takes to horse-racing in the Campagna,
good now for nothing else than that [v, 183].

"Seeing too much" leads to another kind of fast travel—"horse-
racing in the Campagna," which is no solution to a fainting imagination overcome by too swiftly perceived multiple subjects. Like
a "numerical superiority" that finally is the inferiority of the IIIth
beyond repletion, a series speeded up—a series without pause or
momentary oases, a series without the gesture of a "kindly vacancy"—is a vertiginously Piranesian procedure that ignores its
own built-in healing qualities, which are the qualities of limited
perception and expression, both of which emanate from unperiph-
eral optics shaped by a narrow but very human heart.

To move with too much alacrity is to reduce, not only space, but
the tenses on either side of the present. Fast travel both condenses
the space transgressed and decreases anticipation and memory.
The creation of an optical, spatial-temporal IIIth, traveling too fast
is like going nowhere at all. It is like life at a condemned Centre,
where condensation has led to a deadly repletion. Once, "the distance could not be vanquished without toil"—the "toil" of life—but
now, the foolish would conquer, if that is the word, not only time,
as if blindly sprinting to greet the "long shadow," but also space,
which, as we know, is advertised as being more necessary to Ruskin
than food:

There is always more in the world than men could see, walked
they ever so slowly; they will set it not better for going fast.
And they will at last, and soon too, find out that their grand
inventions for conquering (as they think) space and time, do,
in reality, conquer nothing; for space and time are, in their
own essence, unconquerable, and besides did not want any sort
of conquering; they wanted using. A fool always wants to
shorten space and time: a wise man wants to lengthen both.
A fool wants to kill space and kill time: a wise man, first to gain
them, then to animate them. Your railroad, when you come
to understand it, is only a device for making the world
smaller [v, 381].

Traveling, Ruskin would push concentric beginnings and endings as far apart as possible. He would become a new kind of Middle Man, who instead of cheating Centre and Circumference by the vanishing act of the Middle, would save both beginnings and endings (as well as memory and anticipation) by an elaboration and extension of the Middle. The world that fast travel makes small—and eventually claustrophobic—by condensing the time-space ratio, Ruskin would enlarge.

As the Middle Man transformed (or better "reformed"), Ruskin would neither subtract fish in transit nor would he himself become invisible; instead, by an act of linear elaboration, he would stretch the Middle even as he avoids the ends. To protract that Middle, which becomes True in its visible elaborations, is to court surprise with the same intensity with which Ruskin avoids the deadly end of familiarity become claustrophobic monotony. But the marriage of surprise to a perpetual travel that would avoid monotony is, finally, more than disappointing:

> Again the influence of surprise in producing the delight, is to be noted as suspicious. . . . Observe, my pleasure was chiefly when I first got into beautiful scenery out of London. . . . I find that by keeping long away from the hills, I can in great part still restore the old childish feeling about them; and the more I live and work among them, the more it vanishes. . . . There is no cure for this evil, any more than for the weariness of the imagination already described, but in patience and rest; if we try to obtain perpetual change, change itself will become monotonous [v, 369].

"Perpetual change" is the equivalent of the repletion of fast travel; the act of changing perpetually, as a creation of optical Illth, is an act that, at best, changes nothing of consequence.

As the reformed and elaborating Middle Man, Ruskin never takes two things at the same time, when he can take one. He would "kill" neither space nor time. And taking two things at once is to approach, as we shall see, the dangerously spaceless (and timeless) condition of museum-juxtaposition—a necessarily concentrated and potentially contaminated condition that Ruskin will attempt to domesticate, to make "lookable," if not livable (though one is tempted to suggest that Ruskin could always live where it was possible to look—that eyesight is life, despite the fact that later, he will have to survive in a kind of "blindness").

Once involved in plenitude on its way to becoming repletion, now Ruskin would multiply not objects—or even Turners—but perspectives. The man who would surround and explore St. Peter's with a circumference of divided arcs understands the advantage, even necessity, of both the "numerical superiority" of perspectives and the limitation—or slow travel, the "proper train"—of change: "I say, first, to be content with as little change as possible. If the attention is awake, and the feeling in proper train, a turn of the country road, with a cottage beside it, which we have not seen before, is as much as we need for refreshment; if we hurry past it, and take two cottages at a time, it is already too much" (v, 370).

Extending time and space, rather than centripetally killing or concentrating it toward an "apex" of terrible privilege, Ruskin establishes his own speed limits. "Change," if "perpetual," must be slowed to the accommodations of the narrow dimensions of the Gothically human heart: "hence, to any person who has all his senses about him, a quiet walk along not more than ten or twelve miles of road a day, is the most amusing of all travelling; and all travelling becomes dull in exact proportion to its rapidity" (v, 370). Traveling fast, one does not operate under one's own volition. Things are out of control. It is as if, even in this early volume of *Modern Painters*, Newman's True Centre of elevation were becoming Yeats's integrated Centre of nostalgia; centrifugal pressure breaks the binding of original geological morality. With the fast travel of railroads, the gravitational Centre represents, in the chapter from *Modern Painters III*, "The Moral of Landscape," a forgotten morality: "Going by railroad I do not consider travelling at all; it is merely 'being sent' to a place, and very little different from becoming a parcel; the next step to it would of course be telegraphic transport" (v, 370).

A landscape of morality is a landscape over which time has been taken. The time-space landscape ratio, killed by the immorality of condensation, must be cultivated like the early garden at Herne Hill. The moral continuum becomes landscape pastoral perfect for both slow travel and a decidedly unambitious series of multiple perspectives. As if with "kindly vacancies" or occasional "refreshment," such perspectives, within the Antiphonal Contention of Centre and Circumference, will oppose the inevitable consequences of an avaricious imagination bent upon the suicide of repletion. If there will always be, with Ruskin, points of failure, as of excessive presence become absence, there will also be the attempt, poignantly opposite and eventually doomed, to create points of conjunctive success, as of a "sweet transition" that would both negotiate and elaborate the labyrinthine Middle and span those abysses of vortical Centres that prefigure White Silence.

C. The Dead Spaces of Satin:
Transitional Absence

Writing to Charles Eliot Norton about the emerging design of *The Laws of Fésole* (that enormously significant book about drawing and perspective which makes Right Line as political, economical, and moral as it is aesthetic), Ruskin again emphasizes familiar procedure. Organizing *The Laws* is like looking at St. Peter's the correct way: "The scheme is too large for arrangement. I must do it piece by piece" (xxxvii, 69). But in the middle of *The Laws*, Ruskin is suddenly uncertain of the result of the "sweet transition" of series. The "End" that had been delayed by the extension of the Middle becomes too important. But the End can be made less ominously important by bringing some of the significance of the epiphanic End into the present tense or Middle. It is almost as if final consequences of "cautious sequence" were as potentially dangerous as the vortical interrelation and concentration of the Index World:

> I find this book terribly difficult to arrange; for if I did it quite rightly, I should make the exercises and instructions progressive and consecutive; but then, nobody would see the reason for them till we came to the end; and I am so encumbered with other work that I think it best now to get this done in the way likeliest to make each part immediately useful. Otherwise, this chapter should have been all about right lines only, and then we should have had one on the arrangement of right lines, followed by curves, and arrangement of curves [xv, 381].[4]

Still, despite questions of "progressive and consecutive" design that may lead to a privileged and perhaps repletive End (for the moment, we will not concern outselves with the differences between the Ultimate and the Penultimate), the experience with *The Laws* is not itself a law. More often, there are "steps" or "stages" in serial advance or unraveling that bring the meaning of the End to the immediacy of the present, and this is a harmony of "orderly succession" that is closer to the pastoral experience of slow landscape travel than the waiting, as in *The Laws of Fésole*, for the revelations of the End: "there is a unity of Sequence, which is that of things

---

[4] In keeping with the problematic spirit of the quotation, it should perhaps be pointed out that, if not "right lines," which are always Right, the Orthodox Geometries of "right angles" of Part One of *Ruskin's Maze* are followed, in Part Two, by precisely that *Helix virgata* "arrangement of curves." The rectilinear is "corrected" by the curvilinear, just as severely concentric design is transformed into the spirals of moral connection.

that form links in chains, and steps in ascents, and stages in journeys; and this, in matter, is the unity of communical forces in their continuance from one thing to another; and it is the passing upwards and downwards of benevolent effects among all things, the melody of sounds, the continuity of lines, and the orderly succession of motions and times . . ." (iv, 94-95).

Moving "upwards and downwards"—or sauntering leisurely through Rome, avoiding "expressed points of lionisation"—the traveler cannot tolerate even the illusion of being stationary, which is the illusion of sequence brought to a standstill by monotony and repetition. The unity of sequence requires not only change, but the appearance of change, which brings at least the necessary fiction of autonomy:

> Another important and pleasurable way of expressing unity, is by giving some orderly succession to a number of objects more or less similar. And this succession is most interesting when it is connected with some gradual change in the aspect of character of the objects. Thus the succession of the pillars of a cathedral aisle is most interesting when they retire in perspective, becoming more and more obscure in distance. . . . [But] If there be no change at all in the shape or size of the objects, there is no continuity; there is only repetition— monotony. It is the change in shape which suggests the idea of their being individually free, and able to escape, if they liked, from the law that rules them, and yet submitting to it [xv, 170-71].

There must be distinctions in the Middle, distinctions between what is linked by "orderly succession." With Ruskin, there must always be an apprehension, even if that apprehension is only an illusion of "Escape, Hope, Infinity" (iv, 83). Repetition, as if of glass beads that are the product of a Victorian slave trade, suggests both claustrophobic confinement and a Greek perfection that will never know "shattered majesty." "Orderly succession," without the need for perpetual retinal readjustment, becomes a dead stop in dead space.

Yet moderate repetition is not always unextended claustrophobically dead space; repetition can also be a version of "kindly vacancies" rather than a cell without retiring perspective or distance. Familiarity can breed response:

> In general, through Nature, reflection and repetition are peaceful things, associated with the idea of quiet succession in events; that one day should be like another day, or one history

the repetition of another history, being more or less results of quietness, while dissimilarity and non-succession are results of interference and disquietude. Thus, though an echo actually increases the quantity of sound heard, its repetition of the note or syllable gives an idea of calmness attainable in no other way [XIII, 73-74].

"Orderly succession," which is the serial "yielding to every impulse" in the exploration of a central city, is itself a form of rest from the disquietude implicit in repletion. And the confrontation of sound with sound, as in an echo, is not so much a variation of an infernally reflexive Ruskinian self-portraiture as it is a soothing adumbration of an elusive but understandable peace that is not to be found in dead space.

As with sound, so with sight. Visual repetition is not necessarily a reflexive monotony that creates a kind of reciprocal spacelessness. If not exact, repetition—or repetition with a difference, like a spiral, perhaps, or the later "language of return"—can approach a condition of repose that is more vital than stultified. Further, visual "echoes," which proceed in "orderly succession," are far closer to "sweet transition" than the "jarring thoughts" of juxtaposition which occur in breathless space that has been foolishly "killed"— or more accurately, killed by the foolish. Echoes, whether heard or seen, bring both a soothing sense of successive order and repose, without the jolting confrontation that occurs in dead space. Unremarkably, Turner exemplifies Ruskin's theory:

It is quite curious to see the pains that Turner sometimes takes to echo an important passage of colour; in the Pembroke Castle, for instance, there are two fishing boats, one with a red, and another with a white sail. In a line with them, on the beach, are two fish in precisely the same relative positions; one red and one white. It is observable that he uses the artifice chiefly in pictures where he wishes to obtain an expression of repose [XV, 168].

Yet against "sweet transition," which permits no unkindly vacancies of dead space that, interrupting "orderly succession," would create "jarring thoughts," Ruskin characteristically makes a case for an opposite activity that bypasses series. If "sweet transition" is as "kindly" as those vacancies which permit rest amidst potentially insane intensity and grotesque interrelation, that serial process is perhaps more restful than informative: education proceeds through comparison. And Ruskin, manufacturing "laws" with the same en-

ergy and sense of self that he uses to create geographical nomenclature in "Of Map Drawing" (xv, 445), manufactures a law of
"Contrast," which is based on the concept of a Missing Middle.
While sequence buffers, the Missing Middle, without "sweet transition," exposes:

> Of course the character of everything is best manifested by
> Contrast. Rest can only be enjoyed after labour; sound to be
> heard clearly, must rise out of silence; light is exhibited by
> darkness, darkness by light; and so on in all things. Now in art
> every colour has an opponent colour, which, if brought near
> it, will relieve it more completely than any other; so, also, every
> form and line may be made more striking to the eye by an
> opponent form of line near them; a curved line is set off by
> a straight one. . . . and in all good work nearly double the
> value, which any given colour or form would have uncom-
> bined, is given to each by contrast   [xv, 191].

It should be pointed out that, even while law making, which comes
uncomfortably close to the "system-mongering" that is often a malediction, Ruskin would add qualifying addenda to laws that might
be otherwise dogmatic. He cautions against a "too manifest use of
the artifice [which] vulgarizes a picture. Great painters do not commonly or very visibly, admit violent contrast. They introduce it by
stealth, and with intermediate links of tender change; allowing,
indeed, the opposition to tell upon the mind as a surprise, but not
a shock" (xv, 191).

As with the notion of "sweet transition," the Law of Contrast,
elaborated upon in *The Elements of Drawing*, had first been touched
upon as naive theory supported by an essentially "innocent eye."
If at first serial procedure is a single line that does not double back
like Newman's irritating Maze that surrounds his True Centre, and
neither repetition nor recognition is known—if at first everything
is a beginning without comparison and no echoes are either heard
or seen, still, even then, Ruskin can make an incipient case for a
theory, if not law, of Contrast. As early as his pseudonymous existence as the Kata Phusin of *The Poetry of Architecture*, he sees a
world organized about theoretical Contrast that will become, albeit
with qualifications, law: "to compel the eye to expect something
from the building itself, a gentle contrast of feeling in that building
is extremely desirable" (i, 17). Desirable, Contrast can also lead to
aesthetic pleasure, for there is always the possibility of "such a
contrast of feeling as bestows on it a beauty" (i, 17). Further and
more surprisingly, Contrast, bringing delight, can also bring the

"rest" of something like "kindly vacancies": "Thus, the eye rests with delight on the broken mouldings of the windows, and the sculptured capitals of the corner columns, contrasted, as they are, the one with glassless blackness within, the other with the ragged and dirty confusion of drapery around" (I, 23). At times, it appears that *The Poetry of Architecture* is nothing more than the Poetry of Contrast.[5]

Yet the emphasis on Contrast is a luxury that is not always—especially later—an agreeable poetry. Before he knows enough to have perceived and received the Parallel Advance, before he has suffered from the repletion of a horizontal perspective that has become condemned central space, Ruskin has enough sense of "vacancy" to be able to welcome the Missing Middle, to be able in fact to afford the development of a theory, connected with an entirely problematical Law of Contrast, that would eliminate precisely those horizontal "kindly vacancies" that make the theory originally possible, even sound. "Opponent form," assaulting the observer, also informs him. Removing objects from "sweet" and "cautious" sequence, the function of Contrast as Juxtaposition is to teach by startling and shocking:

> In looking through the collection any careful and thoughtful student or visitor will learn much from the juxtaposition of works of art presenting entirely opposite qualities. Thus, having had his attention directed in the last thirteen pieces to the simplicity of Greek outlines and the parallel simplicity of Greek execution and of modern processes rightly founded on it, he will, I hope, be at first considerably startled and shocked by the petty, crinkly, winkly, knobby and bumpy forms of Albert Dürer, and by execution which devotes a day to a dog's ear and a week to a weed   [XXI, 184].

But juxtaposition, if often startling and shocking, is rarely as gentle and agreeable as the original Contrast of *The Poetry of Architecture*, which, after all, has implicit in it those "links of tender change." Reading newspapers can be an experience of juxtaposition that is cruel—what might be called an "unfine" grotesque.[6] The parallel descent of newspaper columns causes the eye to range "from one to the other." No longer concerned merely with sight and agreeable Contrast, as in *The Poetry*, Ruskin finds the verbal

---

[5] In fact, Contrast, in *The Poetry of Architecture*, comes close to felicitous incantation. For example: "and contrast with the horizontal lines of the flat roofs and square walls" (I, 26); "now, white, which is intolerable with green, is agreeably contrasted with blue" (I, 27).

information presented to him to be visually more than striking. If "parallel columns," as though "advancing," educate, they also horrify:

> (November 12, 1851.)—I was rather struck yesterday by three paragraphs in Galignani—in parallel columns—so that the eye ranged from one to the other. The first gave an account of a girl aged twenty-one, being found, after lying exposed all night, and having given birth to a dead child, on the banks of the canal near (Maidstone, I think—but some English county town); the second was the fashions for November, with an elaborate account of satin skirts; and the third, a burning to death of a child   [x, xl].

"Sweet" and "cautious" sequence missing, the middle column, like the Missing Middle of a continuum, is a frivolous vacancy of sorts, the central inconsequence of which emphasizes terrible social inequities. Dead children surround satin skirts. And essentially, the information of this descent in "parallel columns" is the same information brought in the horizontal, surface perspective's Parallel Advance.

Whether advancing or descending, parallel extension, with the Middle missing because the fashions of "satin space" yield neither transition nor gravity, tells us too much too fast about dead children. And that information, at times when "vacancies" are more desperately necessary than merely "kindly," is not to be wrapped (or "centred") in "satin skirts." Beginning as agreeable and gentle Contrast, parallel advance/descent now has for its Middle the dead space of unmediating satin as a location for a kind of vacuous irresponsibility, whose guilt is balanced between commission and omission—this, rather than the space of "sweet transition," whose absence is now apparent with pain. Though it is of course possible that in the midst of this absence which could be taken as a kind of home space for a man of essential disappearance, the rarely visible but Janus-faced Middle Man might be on the point of making an appropriately parasitical appearance in the guise of the insane Cen-

---

[6] Marshall McLuhan, tentatively approaching the newspaper for different reasons, suggests the discontinuous and "fearless connection" (the term is Ruskin's) of newspaper format by quoting from *Modern Painters V*, p. 132: "A fine qrotesque is the expression, in a moment, by a series of symbols thrown together in bold and fearless connection of truths which it would have taken a long time to express in any other way, and of which the connection is left for the beholder to work out for himself, the gaps, left or overleaped by the haste of the imagination, forming the grotesque character." "Joyce, Mallarmé, and the Press," *The Literary Criticism of Marshall McLuhan* (New York, 1969), p. 17.

tral Judge who, we recall, occupies the Centre of his own horizon, as if waiting to be borne forth, in Parallel Advance and with knowledgeable "conceit," at the crucial moment for the coronation of a False Master.

The absence of transition in dead satin, or the wrong kind of parallel presence, has the potential to exact a toll that can be considerable. It is in fact a lateral version of the pseudoscopic reversed relief of three dimensions, with foreground and background changing places in an incisive act that excruciatingly eliminates the intermediary dimension of depth.[7] Dimly, Ruskin hears the echo of a peacock's scream.

[7] See "The Inverted Perspective," *The Failing Distance*, pp. 127-57.

Chapter Five

Circumferential Considerations:
Lines without
Beginnings or Endings

A. The Architecture of the Index:
The Taming of (Museum) Centricity

Peripheral columns about dead children that threaten to invade the Middle of inconsequence are to be neither seen nor heard—not if one is to endure the screeching of peacocks, not if the naked vigil is to last beyond the cold dawn, not if one is going to survive to assume the identity of the assaulted and killed "Cat."

Yet if specifically dead children, along with "bloody carcases" (xxxvi, 418), are neither to be seen nor heard for the sake of precarious sanity, they nonetheless exist in a parallel perception that will not go away, a perception that would be, if possible, accommodated by both integrity and sanity. And if not only "bloody carcases" but dead children are to be admitted into the public panorama of a private person's vision, they cannot be effectively separated by the dead space of satin. There must be an entirely different Middle—one that will make the potentially "unfine" grotesque of an infernal Parallel Descent, which is a kind of Newspaper Fall into a condition of wastefully plenitudinous print, at least livable. Simply, there must be a version of oxygen (or room to breathe, and breathing see), no longer of extricated altitudes, but within the Middle—an oxygen, one might say, that would bring a kind of transitional sanity to even an unmediated "choral space" of Antiphonal Contention. Since survival on the rational side of madness is most likely desirable, though perhaps not a blind and silent necessity, the immoral texture of satin must be exchanged for something "sweeter," if not smoother—something "sweeter," if not in fact that easy transition which will be finally and effectively as conjunctive as a pastoral landscape of Lucent Verdure, where moral fertility will promote a horticultural design of efficacious negotiation.

As areas of collection and privilege, Museums and Libraries are Centres of special interest to Ruskin, who, concerned with making the juxtaposition implicit in density other than maddening, would create an architecture to tame or domesticate an area that has the potential to become either entirely condemned or unfortunately grotesque. Within the Centre, there must be some form of "sweet transition" that would make less infernal the effect of that terrible triptych of dead children, in which the central panel is present only in its moral and transitional absence. Museums must be something other than graveyards, triptychs of death—or, more broadly, "slime pits" of central putrefaction. Like cities importing the circumferential wealth of food that is as valuable as space is to the Ruskinian claustrophobe—a transaction/translation of subtraction conducted, we recall, originally under the legerdemain direction of the invisible Middle Man—Museums gather, or import, the only art that is truly worthwhile, which is the art, as we shall see, of that same Circumference.

If the Museum is, in ways of densely labyrinthine plenitude, like the vertiginous repletion of a city, it is also like an externalized mind with both a considerable memory for detail and a plethora of future plans: there is little slack. But instead of a dream-gifted memory, brooding over and sorting out images of the past, Ruskin, himself playing curator, performs a sorting process that, if less magical than the processes of the Imagination, is more easily discerned. It is a process that intrigues the later Ruskin, who, in his "Master's Report, 1884," addressed to the members of his St. George's Guild, expresses the concerns of a Master for things inevitably central. As Master, his "first duty" will be the creation of a "storehouse":

> But we need immediately, beyond all other needs, a store-house for our property on our grounds: and I have, therefore, on the final rupture of negotiations at Sheffield, requested Mr. Robson to adapt the design he had prepared for the museum in that town, to this immediate purpose on our ground at Bewdley, where the air is free from smoke, and the soil dry. It became quite clear to me, during the various debates about the Sheffield building, that my first duty to the Guild was to provide them with this treasure-house in pure air, so that all books and drawings purchased by us might at once be put in safety in a known spot   [xxx, 76].

Writing the reports of a Master who must attend, before all other things, to a "storehouse" that is like those "storehouses" of a great poet's "unindexed" but "dream-gifted memory," Ruskin, in search of a "known spot" in "pure air," conceives of the plausibility of

Centres on the Circumference—of epicyclical Museums which are as provincial as an art that, attached by an unsevered root to its circumferential context, has a chance for greatness. And the Museums of the Circumference will be without that dangerous density which might lead to the unrelieved parallel perception of dead children—a vision of a kind of Strange Chord—that is separated only by the space of "satin skirts." It is as if, instead of importing the Circumference to the Centre, with the aid of the sleight of hand of the Middle Man, Ruskin will instead export or unwind centricity to suburban eccentricity, where, after all, "the air is free from smoke."

Or if condemned centricity cannot always become the quasi-pastoral of eccentricity, if the air, with the nineteenth-century storm-cloud hovering, cannot always be absolutely "pure," it is perhaps at least possible to make those "storehouses" of architectural privilege, which are like great minds, less privileged and perhaps less perfectly—the term will become meaningful—Daedalean. With Ruskin, privilege has always been as much a problem as perfection. If the Many finally becomes the Illth of repletion, the One is too few. Ruskin would multiply the central specificity of the British Museum, creating, as with St. Peter's, divided and multiple versions. For a moment, it is as though he would majestically shatter the British Museum's undeniably True Centre into "fifty fragments": "the founding of museums adapted for the general intrusion and pleasure of the multitude, and especially the labouring multitude, seems to be in these days a farther necessity, to meet which the people themselves may be frankly called upon" [xxx, 53]. Locations of privileged idiosyncracy would be replaced by public, perhaps fallen, places for the "labouring multitude." Ruskin would have "The Nature of Gothic" inform "storehouses" as once that "Nature" gave shape to cathedrals.

Like the fragmental vantage points of St. Peter's, circumferentially eccentric "storehouses" of the multitude are necessarily multiple. They are places of fallen copies, almost like happily imperfect Gothic tracery. Unsurprisingly, the as yet uncondemned British Museum, which is the Architecture of the Index, is an architecture of both "higher privilege" and essentially unreproduced singularity: "The British Museum ought to contain no books except those of which copies are unique or rare. All others should be arranged in smaller public libraries for familiar use with excellent attached reading-rooms, and access to the Museum reading-room should be a matter of higher privilege" [xix, 220]. Also, education must be distinguished from history. History is a central concern, a concern of "higher privilege" that is finally removed from context. But the multiple Museums of education are for those whom Ruskin addresses in *Fors Clavigera*—"The Workmen and Labourers of Great Britain": "Farther, every one of our principalities ought to have a permanent gallery of art of which the function should be wholly educational, as distinguished from the historical and general purposes of the collections in the British Museum and National Gallery" [xix, 221]. History is an intense burden even for the Centre, but there is a "permanence" that may not be entirely historical for the fallen and eccentric world of copies.

Yet if there are common copies, or permanent though lesser originals, in Museums for purposes of education, there must not be too many. Dealing with something other than privilege, Ruskin will not promote plenitude. Curiously, "popular teaching" and "superabundance" are at odds. "Too much" is a form of "disorder" for those problematic "Working Men and Labourers of Great Britain." Their Museums, as opposed to the British Museum's potentially replete Architecture of Index, will be Museums of economy: "In all museums intended for popular teaching, there are two great evils to be avoided. The first is superabundance; the second, disorder. The first having too much of everything. You will find in your own work that the less you have to look at, the better you attend. You can no more see twenty things worth seeing in an hour, than you can read twenty books worth reading in a day" [xxvi, 203-4]. For Museums that are neither "storehouses" nor places of privilege, less is better than the "too much" of "superabundance." Less, like the slow travel that is the right kind of "mediatorial function," focuses the attention on the transitional condition of "between."

With ambitious versatility, Ruskin's Sheffield Museum is two Museums in one. It is not only central but circumferential. Accommodations are made for both the "higher" privileged and the underprivileged. The Museum's "principal room," which is the space of essential privilege, is the equivalent of the Museum for Masters that is untempered by eccentric slack—the imperfection and amateurism of "popular teaching" and public learning that thrives in "pure air":

> Necessarily the books will fall into two very distinct classes. The first will consist merely of standard literature in good editions for general use; and these I should wish to be placed in a separate apartment, with convenient seats and reading desks, and under the care of an obliging and intelligent at-

tendant. . . . But the principal room, or rather gallery of the library [within the Sheffield Museum] will contain all illustrated works of high value, rare copies of classical books, and MSS.; for all which I hope to institute methods of exhibition and use not yet seen in anything like complete operation   [xxx, 35].

Always, with the "biped" (or antiphonal) Ruskin, who would divide himself for his own dialogical advantage, in an act that creates both intervening space that might be breathed and apparent contradiction, there should be at least "two very distinct classes," just as there is the Centre and the Circumference, the vertical and the horizontal, the abyss and repletion—categories that symbiotically inform each other. Undiscriminated sameness—the claustrophobia of an all-too-familiar homogeneity—horrifies more than the vacuum does even when plenitude is the ideal. Yet in Ruskin's Sheffield Museum, the "two very distinct classes" are brought together— though not made the same—in an act of amalgamating economy, which comes close to recalling the introduction of the intricately serial labyrinth into the Centre of Minotaur-dominated London.

But the relation of either the multitudinous or special student to the Museum reduces to no easy formula. For the "general student," who is something more than either underprivileged or the product of a teaching that is entirely "popular," the National Gallery—a Museum of the unadulateratedly compacted Centre—is not easily dispensable. Still, apparently paradoxically, the expert—privileged at least in his hopefully unDaedalean or imperfect expertise—is to avoid rooms that are "principal" in favor of the slack (or "pure air") of a kind of eccentric authenticity that permits original and provincial growth: in fact, the expert would be well advised to return to the roots of context, which are apparent before Strange Chords or the maddening parallel juxtaposition of dead children. One goes home to study seriously—not to one's own home, but the provincial home, as we shall shortly see, of a piece of art. "Magnificent rooms" might well be the plural of a "principal room," but magnificence, too much for "popular teaching," is not enough for privileged study: "the magnificent rooms of our National Gallery; without question now the most important collection of paintings in Europe for the purposes of the general student. Of course the Florentine School must always be studied in Florence, the Dutch in Holland, the Roman in Rome . . ." (xxxiv, 451).

Nevertheless, there is, as we recall, something special about the spacelessness of the Centre. The observer of "superabundance," if not overwhelmed by "disorder," can be shocked and startled toward understanding by "parallel juxtaposition." Among other things, the Centre is a locus of comparison that achieves its effect by the plucking of provincial objects from their eccentric soil: "but to obtain a clear knowledge of their relations to each other, and compare with the best advantage the characters in which they severally excel, the thoughtful scholars of any foreign country ought now to become pilgrims to the Dome—(such as it is)—of Trafalgar Square" (XXXIV, 451). But despite the information made available by central collection, only old art—the art of dead masters, amputated from context by time, like a garland of dead thoughts— should be brought together for the business of comparison. Only the old, which is cut off by age from the home-growth of the soil of the Circumference, belongs in the centrally public arena where "parallel juxtaposition" can bring public information for those able to profit by superabundance, even as it moves toward the penultimately replete Edge: "So then, generally, it should be the object of the government, and of all patrons of art, to collect, as far as may be, the works of dead masters, in the public galleries, arranging them so as to illustrate the history of nations, and the progress and influence of their arts; and to encourage the private possession of the works of living masters" (XVI, 81).

Living art, the art of living arts and eccentric soil, does not immediately belong with the public at the Centre of both privilege and death, where central truth is located and rivers are white with fish bellies. Art that is mobile, separated from the roots of its context like a gathered bouquet, must be dead, but dead with the potential of immortality. Only dead (and immortal) art can be translated to the central, if falling, parallel spaces of an untransitionally deadly satin, where, in another context, one might say that the "rudeness of the intermediate space had been finally conquered" (VIII, 224). Circumferential art must remain in the suburbs of relative privacy until it shifts into a past tense that is as large as the "vast storehouse" of mnemonic superabundance. In that past tense, immortal art is economically both privileged and contaminated by a centrality constructed out of a selective process requiring centripetal mobility in order to achieve a dense, and inevitably "jarring," quality. With Ruskin, who would himself be involved in either a perpetual penetration of space, or a "nothing but process" of perpetual self-transcendence (a process that is always moving, even if only with the serpentine confines of something like Newman's irritating and labyrinthine landscape), the movement of art objects approaches the failure of the sense of integrity that would keep things, other than the perhaps too-traveling self, in a context or soil that is usually either private or circumferential. Independent of all place, portable art is, for the most part, ignoble:

> . . . so far from Decorative art being inferior to other art because it is fixed to a spot—on the whole it may be considered as rather a piece of degradation that it should be portable. Portable art—independent of all place—is for the most part ignoble art. . . . It is, indeed, possible that the portable picture or image may be first-rate of its kind, but it is not first-rate because it is portable; nor are Titian's frescoes less than first-rate because they are fixed; nay, very frequently the highest compliment you can pay to a cabinet picture is to say—"It is as grand as a fresco" [xvi, 320-21].

Ruskin's posture toward the centralization of art, its portability and the problems of a Middle, whose immoral presence is the absence of transitional sanity, along with the attendant problem of "parallel juxtaposition," anticipates those attitudes of Valéry, Benjamin, and Malraux.[1] The inclination toward a detached disposition, cut off from eccentric soil, that would place the work of dead masters on the walls of a home that might have, instead, if not unportable frescoes, at the least the work of living artists, is an assumption of private privilege. But in addition to privilege, it is an attitude of corruption in an "unliving room"—an attitude that smacks more of an aesthetic detachment from eccentric context than the central corruption of a "slime-pit's" Illth.

The growth of aestheticism, as described by Ruskin, is the result of the achievement and refinement of special skills—skills that themselves imply the kind of separation necessary for portability. These skills lead at once to a sacrifice of the art object and an elevation of the self at the object's expense. The resulting attitude is that of the Museum, which has eliminated a sense of the Circumference, the sense of both connection and a context that cannot be avoided in the case of those objects that are "as grand as a fresco" in their suggestion of permanence. At the Centre, there is a condensed amalgam without either imported space, which is like food, or the roots of context—a spaceless amalgam that is the result of

---

[1] Joseph Frank is generally instructive on the subject. Here, for example, he quotes Valéry describing something like Ruskin's "opponent form," though to Valéry, as often to Ruskin, the equivalent of "opponent form" is more cannibalistic than symbiotically informative about relations: "I can well understand why neither the Egyptians, the Chinese, nor the Greeks, all wise and civilized peoples, were familiar with this system of juxtaposing productions that mutually devour each other." As quoted in Frank's "Malraux's 'Metaphysics of Art,'" *The Widening Gyre* (New Brunswick, 1963). See especially pp. 100-4.

an essentially reflexive attention focused on skilled hands rather than the created object and its surroundings:

> And thus, the more skilful the artist, the less his subject was regarded; and the hearts of men hardened as their handling softened, until they reached a point when sacred, profane, or sensual objects were employed, with absolute indifference, for the display of colour and execution; and gradually the mind of Europe congealed into that state of utter apathy,—inconceivable, unless it had been witnessed, and unpardonable, unless by us, who have been infected by it,—which permits us to place the Madonna and the Aphrodite side by side in our galleries, and to pass, with the same unmoved inquiry into the manner of their handling, from a bacchanal to a nativity [xi, 131].

The "parallel juxtaposition" of the "Madonna and the Aphrodite side by side in our galleries" is Valéry's cannibalistic juxtaposition— the juxtaposition separated by dead space which is parallel comparison only possible when the observer is overwhelmed by "absolute indifference" and "utter apathy." As if an antithetical version of the excessive interrelation of the vortical vision, detached aestheticism, no solution to the meta-presence hovering over the abyss and without attention to either "sweet transition" or what Ruskin elsewhere—and in a different context—calls the "roots of Honour" (xvii, 25-42), seems to celebrate the paradigmatically eclectic triptych in which the central panel of dead, untransitional space is flanked by a "bacchanal" on one side, and a "nativity" on the other.

The experience of the Museum is almost always disappointing. But the fault is occasionally not the fault of the spectator jaded to the point of "utter apathy." The paintings may themselves fail. More precisely, religious paintings may have failed:

> What single example does the reader remember of painting which suggested so much as the faintest shadow of these people, or of their deeds? Strong men in armour, or aged men with flowing beards, he *may* remember, who, when he looked at his Louvre or Uffizi catalogue, he found were intended to stand for David or for Moses. But does he suppose that, if these pictures had suggested to him the feeblest image of the presence of such men, he would have passed on, as he assuredly did, to the next picture,—representing, doubtless, Diana and Actaeon, or Cupid and the Graces, or a gambling quarrel in a pothouse,—with no sense of pain, or surprise? Let him med-

itate over the matter, and he will find ultimately that what I say is true, and that religious art, at once complete and sincere, never yet has existed   [v, 87].

Conjunction is here the problem, as serial breakdown will later be. The Museum is potentially a syntax in trouble. If the art were successfully expressive, "sequence" would necessarily be "cautious." And instead of being startled and shocked to understanding, the spectator would feel the "pain" of severed roots.

Ruskin's own love of art does not have its origins in anything that can be transplanted by Parallel Advance toward the Centre of detached aestheticism, where the triptych of initial Bacchanal is fulfilled by a panel of the Nativity, in a kind of infernal typology. His initial attention is focused entirely on the provincial Circumference, where the objects to be represented have their honorable roots. At first, he does not concern himself with either the agile skills of artistic refraction or imaginative interpretation:

The beginning of all my own right art work in life depended . . . not on my love of art, but of mountains and sea. . . . I would pass entire days in rambling on the Cumberland hillsides, or staring at the lines of surf on a low sand; . . . and through the whole of following life, whatever power of judgment I have obtained in art, which I am now confident and happy in using, or communicating, has depended on my steady habit of always looking for the subject principally, and for the art only as a means of expressing it   [xxii, 153].

Ruskin, as far as his own perception of art is concerned, is at least certain that the focal point of his own attention has not centripetally regressed from the honorable roots of eccentric soil (where, in fact, the extensive lines of the potential labyrinth, as a circumferential plenitude of the linear, may at first exist) to an autonomous aestheticism of a Centre that is capable of metamorphosing privilege into infernal concentration.

Still, it is something very much like this regression of the focal point that, eliminating an inclusive peripheral vision which takes context into account, makes existence within the Museum possible. In fact, the Museum cannot afford the eccentric soil that holds the "roots of honour." Ruskin's calculated "utter apathy," permitting the "parallel juxtaposition" of bacchanal and nativity, anticipates Malraux's deadening of the affective response as described by Joseph Frank: "Scholarship can—and should—help to understand the metaphysical sources of style; but if we really could feel like the first spectators of an African fetish or a Byzantine Christ, it would be impossible . . . to endure their existence in the museum."[2] For existence to be possible within the Museum, both Ruskin and Malraux understand that art has to be severed from not only soil but expectation and response. As opposed to the circumferential space or food that the Centre would import with a kind of dreadful lust, the eccentric soil of context and function should, it would appear, be left with its roots of presumably dead "honour" intact— a dead, circumferential "honour" that is far removed from the triptych's central (or middle) panel of transitional absence.

Yet characteristically, appearances deceive. The shadow is neither substance nor figural prediction. If eccentric soil is to be left behind with dying roots, circumferential design may become not only central but vital. In the Museum, where "superabundance" threatens to summon "disorder," there is nevertheless an order that is occasionally—and necessarily—transgressed in the search for what is revealed by the potentially "jarring" comparison implicit in "opponent form": "We will, as before, glance round the rooms in the order of the catalogue, sometimes breaking the line to go in quest of such pictures as may be desirable to compare at once with that under consideration" [XIV, 92]. But if the line is broken for purposes of comparison, if the linear, even catalogued order is forsaken for the information harshly revealed by the Middle of absent transition, it nevertheless exists. And Ruskin—as we shall clearly see—is most certain of its precise design.

For one thing, the interior design that informs the structure of the Museum is a design that is without easily defined limits. Symmetry is subordinate to extent. Without an ending (as Ruskin would in fact have his world), galleries are perhaps without beginnings. Definition—or better, linear limitation—has become anathema. If both panorama and plenitude require pasteboard, Ruskinian line does not, and, as we shall see, never has. Essentially, the Museum's "inside" is—or rather should be—an extended reconstruction of the Middle that is now absent of transition ("dead satin" having become a kind of necessary point of origin for the Transformations of an elaborating and negotiable Maze), where an unserial or divided presence is most painfully apparent when the triptych's first bacchanalian panel predicts the third's nativity, in a form of infernal typology: "while a National Gallery should be stately and lovely, it should not be limited by symmetries of plan. It should look like,

[2] Frank, *The Widening Gyre*, p. 71.

in a word, what it is—a gallery, capable of being extended without any limit in any convenient direction" (xix, 226). Perhaps signaling a significant change, it is as if Newman's irritating Maze were now to be cultivated from "within" rather than mastered (logo)-concentrically from "above." Further, it is as if the National Gallery, as opposed to the Thesean labyrinth, were without need of an exit. The "eastern edge" is anticipated, but it is closer to being an asymmetrical geometry than a rectilinear door to the "outside."

Still, merely because the "Museum-like order" (xxxiv, 249)[3] is as labyrinthine as territory that, irritating Newman, also, in the geometric form of fretwork, once irritated Ruskin, does not mean that even now it is incapable of being as deadly as we shall soon find it "vital." The South Kensington Museum, for example, is a labyrinth of horror, whose Ariadne is a policeman:

> and augur no good from any changes [from the design of the British Museum] of arrangement likely to take place in concurrence with Kensington, where, the same day that I had been meditating by the old shark, I lost myself in a Cretan labyrinth of military ironmongery, advertisements of spring blinds, model fish-farming, and plaster bathing nymphs with a year's smut on all the noses of them; and had to put myself in charge of a policeman to get out again [xxxiv, 248-49].

What is evident in the South Kensington's "Cretan labyrinth" is the disorder that may result from "superabundance," when what is needed are clues that are not necessarily "dream-gifted." Forsian chance, which, as we shall see, is the "gifted" chance of Ruskin's Atropos, who is a kind of threadless Ariadne of the immediate, should not be the "order" of either acquisition or exploration for the Museum: "You can only have a confused museum of objects acquired by chance, out of which the student must learn what he can discover by chance" (xix, 223).

With Ruskin's Museum—and his "Museum-like order" that would tame disorderly "superabundance" as it threatens to become repletion—there will be recognition amidst necessary surprise, and that recognition will not be the result of chance. If there is, in this world without beginnings and endings that would be capable of

---

[3] The phrase should itself perhaps be placed in context. Talking about order, Ruskin is talking about letter writing. The emphasis is on serial order that will mnemonically "fill" the transitional absence of a long night: "The only chance of getting these letters themselves into fairly consistent and Museum-like order is by writing a word or two always the first thing in the morning till I get them done; so, I shall at least remember what I was about the day before" (xxxiv, 249).

infinite extent, surprise around the next labyrinthine turn—the surprise of a kind of fallen transcendence that is part of the need for perpetual retinal readjustment—there should also be some sense of the serial. "Dead satin" should be neither "dead" nor "satin." Absent transition must become a present series. It is necessary for the triptych's central panel of immorality to be reconstructed in order to become as transitively "vital" as a labyrinth of Lucent Verdure—a labyrinth that would, in fact, by extending the serial central or Middle, make Strange Chords almost familiar.

What irritates Newman about the labyrinth is that within it he cannot jump toward the synthesis that is implicit in the synoptic juxtapositions of the True Centre. But it is precisely that inability which soothes Ruskin in a central space that might otherwise be condemned. Arranging paintings, Turner arranges with a sense of the consecutive that fails to irritate those who would not have their bacchanals side by side with their nativities: "Among the many peculiarities which distinguished the late J.M.W. Turner from other landscape painters, not the least notable, in my apprehension, were his earnest desire to arrange his works in connected groups, and his evident intention, with respect to each drawing, that it should be considered as expressing part of a continuous system of thought" (XIII, 9).

Ruskin's architecture of the Centre would imitate Turner's "continuous system of thought." Following chronology, the design Ruskin would suggest, economical enough to return upon itself, is of course the labyrinth in which serial and orderly procedures, like Ariadne's thread, would make more sense out of superabundance than does South Kensington's Policeman. Again, what is significant is that both the necessary detachment and separation at the Centre from the eccentric Roots of Honour, as well as the superabundance that is penultimately close to the final condition of Illth, are countered—at least for a while—by the familiar emphasis on the "continuous": "The whole gallery would thus become of great length, but might be adapted to any form of ground-plan by disposing the whole in a labyrinthine chain, returning upon itself. Its chronological arrangement would necessitate its being continuous, rather than divided into many branches or sections" (XII, 413).

Slow travel through the almost infinite Middle of the Maze, far from irritating Ruskin, is instead a kind of linear pastoral in motion. It is as if circumferential extension—suburban line—had tamed both the superabundance and spacelessness of the Centre. The "jarring" of central "parallel juxtaposition" is cushioned by an overlay of contrary design: series comes to the Centre, and the eccentric

Roots of Honour come to a new home—a home that is in fact a "vast storehouse" which would exhibit as well as store. A gallery capable of infinite extent requires attention to the economics of space, and Ruskin would turn that central interior into a version of circumferential line returning upon itself in a connected series which would save space, while sacrificing something that approaches what we will come to know as the Daedalean splendour of the House that Jack built:

> Though the idea of a single line of pictures, seen by light from above, involves externally, as well as internally, the sacrifice of the ordinary elements of architectural splendour, I am certain the exterior even of this long and low gallery could be rendered not only impressive, but a most interesting school of art. I would dispose it in long arcades; if the space were limited, returning upon itself like a labyrinth. . . . Courts should be left between its returns, with porches at the outer angles, leading one into each division of the building appropriated to a particular school; so as to save the visitor from the trouble of hunting for his field of study through the length of the labyrinth [XIII, 179].

Ruskin's museum has the irregular charm of a Gothic facade. Capable of being extended at will, even "returning upon itself" with a serpentine intricacy that is a spatial anticipation of a later language, it perpetually accommodates present tense necessities, and in that happily myopic accommodation tames what is, with its "fimetic" potential in that vast storehouse of aesthetic detachment, the quintessential Architecture of the Index.

The Centre, importing the virtually endless labyrinthine line of the Circumference, brings "cautious sequence" and "sweet transition" to what otherwise might be the triptych's transitional absence of "dead satin," or the dead, central rivers of the Cloaca Maxima. Plenitude, which might become the superabundance of "parallel juxtaposition," of Chords that are too Strange for rational tolerance, is transformed instead into a kind of diffused and serial condition before the Repletion (next to IIIth) that leads to the terrible sameness of the Travel Diary's blank page—a condition before, in fact, the penultimate "all" has become the homogeneous "nothing at all" of White Silence.

For a while, the vortex spirals with the implication of excessive interrelation over its abyssal bottom, as if attempting to delay a fall, when no bridge can be built, and labyrinthine design weaves through concentricity and the centrally "opponent form" of a terrible juxtaposition that is like infernal typology, as if attempting to maintain an architecture that is just reasonable enough, which is to say reasonable enough to accommodate apparent "error" and dissymmetry, to remain standing, if "shattered" at least temporarily.

B. The Art of the Provinces: Suburban Efficacy

An avaricious imagination dies of Repletion that, after its fashion, is pure. Density of concentration, once an achieved Centre (or Centre of achievement), has become a "slime-pit" that is "fimetic." And the Juggling Man, having stood "hurdle-deep" amidst the "bloody carcases" of slain sheep, has become the juggling man of a polygonal consciousness—two or three selves, listening to the screaming of peacocks as those multiple aspects of the self suffer from the consequences of attempting to accommodate the Repletion that, killing the avaricious imagination, may first drive it mad.

The overtaxed or maddened imagination is a city of stone, with the design and "tendency" of yellow quartz translated into a morality play for a future Theatre of Blindness—a city of stone whose water is either a river of dead fish or a Cloaca Maxima. But beyond the geological morality of nearly centripetal apexes of mastery, there is—as will be evident—the necessary consideration of sanity on cold dawns, and even existence: sanity that might permit existence and an imagination that might even finally transform the Repletion of central city space into something that is, penultimately, less than the Illth of "too much." Or perhaps, instead of Central Museums importing the labyrinthine designs of the Circumference for purposes of sanely "sweet transition," the Centre might be turned unparenthetically inside out. There might, of necessity, be an "immoral" centrifugal tendency toward an "apex" that is of an eccentric epicycle, like the synoptically decentred marginalia of *Modern Painters II*. Yet all this is conditional.

Still, excess bordering on Illth—a penultimately peripheral vision, say, extending until it becomes an infernal, rather than felicitous, Circumference—though capable of demanding more than a narrowly confortable comprehension can handle, is almost always admired. There is that initial bias for concentrated plenitude, a bias now tempered by a newly acquired instinct for survival. The Centre—even if it might be tamed by a circumferential importation undiminished by the Middle Man's sleight of hand subtraction—is an "inside," now too full to do anything other than export itself to an "outside" of possible pastoral. Certainly, it is not the fruit of central industry that is admired any more than the experience: "I cannot but more and more reverence the fierce courage and industry, the gloomy endurance, and infinite mechanical ingenuity of the great centres, as one reverences the fervid labours of a wasp's nest, though the end of all is only a noxious lump of clay" (xxviii, 267).

But Ruskin, introducing a centrifugal "tendency" (albeit submerged at this point) that may be more apparently rational than moral, is introducing a movement, or geological countertendency, that will lead, in an act of return and unwinding, toward both original space and food—toward, in fact, the extensive and horizontal spaces of survival. With a stomach as empty as his central vision is spaceless, Ruskin's city dweller turns to an original spaciousness that has been politically disastrously subordinated to the city's territory of thickly (and, finally, immorally) teeming privilege: "All efforts, whether of the Government or the landed proprietors of England, for the help or instruction of our rural population, have been made under two false suppositions: the first that country life was henceforward to be subordinate to that of towns, the second that the landlord was, for a great part of the year, to live in the town, and thence direct management of his estate" (xxx, 93).

"False suppositions" must be made true performance. The introduction of extensive, suburban space would correct the political imbalance between Centre and Circumference. Further, aesthetics are (or should be) synchronized with politics, art with the manipulation of power: Ruskinian designs are, after all, intricately and intimately interrelated. And politics should be as attractively moral, which is to say ultimately pragmatic, as either geology or the right kind of art. Yet art, no longer moral in cases of extreme density, but rather the product of that dying, avaricious imagination, which is the imagination of Repletion, is as mad or infernal as that of the Juggling Man whose consciousness faces the inevitable consequences of becoming "polygonal." The "true Cloaca Maxima," we know, is worthy of "modern progress in the Fimetic Arts" (xxxvii, 408). And those "Fimetic Arts" are a product of an "infectious insanity" that would turn a True Centre into a central "mephitic cancer":

> extending the inquiry beyond England, to the causes of failure in the art of foreign countries, I have especially to signalize the French contempt for the "Art de Province," and the infectious insanity for centralization, throughout Europe, which collects

necessarily all the vicious elements of any country's life into one mephitic cancer in its centre   [XXXIII, 397].

Central exhibition, close to the "unfine grotesque" of advertisement, is far from creation. And if great art is centripetally, if not morally, drawn, with that "infectious insanity for centralization," toward the "mephitic cancer" of, say, a nation's capital, in order to be exhibited in a central Museum, it is nevertheless most emphatically produced on the Circumference. That "French contempt for the 'Art de Province' " is itself, Ruskin is certain, contemptible, even dangerous. Great art comes from where there is both original food and unimported space, as if grown from those Roots of Honour:

> All great art, in the great times of art, is *provincial*, showing its energy in the capital, but educated, and chiefly productive, in its own country town. The best works of Correggio are at Parma, but he lived in his patronymic village; the best works of Cagliari at Venice, but he learned to paint at Verona; the best works of Angelico are at Rome, but he lived at Fésole. . . . And, with still greater necessity of moral law, the cities which exercise forming power on style, are themselves principal. There is no Attic style, but there is a Doric and Corinthian one. There is no Roman style, but there is an Umbrian, Tuscan, Lombard, and Venetian one. . . . There is no London or Edinburgh style, but there is a Kentish and Northumbrian one   [XXXIII, 397].

Following the centripetal example of the European, the British artist moves toward an equivalent "mephitic cancer," which, detached from the provincial space of the Circumference, translates and reduces art to an homogenized condition of dung in a city whose essential architecture, as the expression of its densely crowded spirit, is nothing less than a "National Cloaca":

> —the tendency to centralization, which has been fatal to art in all times, is, at *this* time, pernicious in totally unprecedented degree, because the capitals of Europe are all of monstrous and degraded architecture. An artist in former ages might be corrupted by the manners, but he was exalted by the splendour, of the capital; and perished amidst magnificence of palaces: but now—the Board of Works is capable of no higher skill than drainage, and the British artist floats placidly down the maximum current of the National Cloaca, to his Dunciad rest,

content, virtually, that his life should be spent at one end of
a cigar, and his fame expire at the other   [xxxiii, 397].

Yet this architecture of sewage, which is the architecture of pernicious centralization, instead of relieving the corrupt Repletion of
rootless centricity, compounds it. The British artist's incipient and
unprovincial corruption is reenforced by an architecture that has
also, at last, been similarly corrupted (bad architects having become
worse plumbers), as design mirrors the gestures of debased man-
ners.

C. The Garland of Thoughts:
A Case for Fanciful Extension

We recall Ruskin's yellow quartz, bought in Keswick, which speaks
of "moral and immoral tendencies"—centripetal and centrifugal
movements. The same problem, or better, the possibility of opposite
movements is hinted at in another passage that, less explicit, employs what proves to be suggestive diction: "And think that from
the earliest dawn of Greek life that cone has been the centre of
tradition and passion as relating to the gods of strength and darkness (Proserpina's city is in the mid-island, but in full sight of Etna),
and you may fancy what a wild dream of incredible, labyrinthine
wonder, it is to me" (xxiii, xxxv). Ruskin's response to a "centre
of tradition and passion" is something other than passionate.
Rather, it is, significantly, a response of "wonder," which is "labyrinthine" and about which the reader is invited to "fancy." The
designs of the object eliciting response and the response itself are
opposed to the deliberations of a geologist confronting a moral
dilemma. The "passion," central, is placed against a "wonder" that
is at least close to "fancy"—a "fancy" that, as we shall see, is in turn
as "labyrinthine" as the irritating Maze over which originally Newman's True Centre triumphs. The procedures of the fanciful labyrinth—of a "wonder" that is, like the Museum's "diffused interest,"
a lesser and more dispersed emotion than concentrated passion—
are mathematical, like the shattered and multiple observations of
St. Peter's, as contrasted to the simultaneity of a synoptic grasp, as
of Strange Chords, that is strictly aesthetic: "aesthetic observation,
even if weak, takes in the whole at a glance; but mathematical study
proceeds from part to part" (xxiii, 211-12).

Yet now the Centre no longer masters the Maze. And the mathematical—even fanciful—procedure of calculated progression is
not to be dismissed, even by nonmathematicians. With a "wild

dream" that is "incredible," there comes a new awareness and respect for what surrounds the Centre, the way a garland of speculation might circle a central ideal: "The power . . . of thus fully
perceiving any natural object depends on our being able to group
and fasten all our fancies about it as a centre, making a garland of
thoughts for it, in which each separate thought is subdued and
shortened of its own strength, in order to fit it for harmony with
others; the intensity of our enjoyment depending, first, on its own
beauty, and then on the richness of the garland" (v, 359). Still, in
Ruskin's chronologically early bouquet, the Centre coordinates that
serial and circumferential speculation, offering a consolidating
gravity. But the suburbs of thought—the area of the garland—must
be taken into account, almost as if they were dying fish that, if not
properly watched, would also be diminished in transit to the Centre
by the Middle Man's sleight of hand subtraction. The garland of
Ruskin's bouquet of perception is nothing if not rich—as rich and
varied, in fact, as a fanciful labyrinth of "incredible . . . wonder."

Ruskin's opposing (and occasionally overlapping) designs, translated to personae—a limited cast of characters—become the difference between the energetic wanderer in the Maze, who, as a
man of thought, perceives serially, with a sense of mathematical
accumulation, and the immobile habitué of the fixed (and possibly
True) Centre, who, more artist than thinker, passively perceives—
or receives—those Strange Chords of demanding inclusion. The
difference is precisely the difference between the serial perceptions
within the Maze—perceptions that may irritate some in their aggressive multiplicity but save Ruskin's version of St. Peter's—and
the broad, panoramic act of reception that approaches a condition
of passive, central simultaneity:

> The first thing that a thinking and knowing man sees in the
> course of the day, he will not easily quit. It is not his way to
> quit anything without getting to the bottom of it, if possible.
> But the artist is bound to receive all things on the broad, white,
> lucid field of his soul, not to grasp at one. For instance, as the
> knowing and thinking man watches the sunrise, he sees some-
> thing in the colour of a ray, or the change of a cloud, that is
> new to him; and this he follows out forthwith into a labyrinth
> of optical and pneumatical laws. . . . But the painter must catch
> all the rays, all the colours that come, and see them all truly,
> all in their real relations and succession. . . . The thoughtful
> man is gone far away to seek; but the perceiving man must sit
> still, and open his heart to receive. The thoughtful man is

knitting and sharpening himself into a two-edged sword, wherewith to pierce. The perceiving man is stretching himself into a four-cornered sheet, wherewith to catch. And all the breadth to which he can expand himself, and all the whiteness into which he can blanch himself, will not be enough to receive what God has to give him [XI, 52].

But even within the mental gymnastics of an essentially passively perceiving artist, there are, in Ruskin's allegory of the creative act, a variety of imaginative operations—some more active than others. There is apparently, in the very midst of passivity, as if at the core of a "white emptiness" that is a preliminary version of White Silence, something quite different from the mere receptivity of the artistically inclusive vision. Somewhat paradoxically, like the thinking man, whose artistry is limited to the serial negotiation of the labyrinth that concentrates perception to the surgical precision of a "two-edged sword, wherewith to pierce," which is like the double axe of a single labyrinth that will itself eventually double, the artist, employing the faculty of the "Imagination Penetrative," is neither altogether passive nor interested in receiving perception that might be as generalized as the "true" vision from the True Centre. Instead, avoiding the thinking man's labyrinth while employing his tracking energy, the artist gets to the heart of the matter—a specific Centre that, more interior than elevated, is also an origin, a Root of Honour, without, presumably, being the thinking and knowing man's "bottom":

It [the Imagination Penetrative] never stops at crusts or ashes, or outward images of any kind; it ploughs them all aside, and plunges into the very central fiery heart; nothing else will content its spirituality; whatever semblances and various outward shows and phases its subjects may possess go for nothing; it gets within all fence, cuts down to the root, and drinks the very vital sap of that it deals with . . . its function and gift are the getting at the root, its nature and dignity depend on its holding things always by the heart. Take its hand from off the beating of that, and it will prophesy no longer; it looks not in the eyes, it judges not by the voice; it describes not by outward features; all that it affirms, judges, or describes, from within [IV, 250-51].

Yet unlike the surgical activity of the thinking man, with his scalpel that is, in fact, a double-edged sword, the possessor and employer of the Imagination Penetrative is not involved in activity that is entirely rational: "There is no reasoning in it; it works not by algebra, nor by integral calculus; it is a piercing pholas-like mind's tongue, that works and tastes into the very rock heart" (IV, 251). In Ruskinian anatomy, the heart (at times it is the head or mind) is central, rather than the omphalos, and the energetically creative journey to the Centre is one that permits some of the same synthesizing acts that the artist—in his blanched and passive role, receiving information with the "white emptiness" of a "four-cornered sheet"—achieves by virtue of his inactivity:

> . . . every sentence, as it has been thought out from the heart, opens for us a way down to the heart, leads us to the centre, and then leaves us to gather what we may. It is the Open Sesame of a huge obscure, endless cave, with inexhaustible treasures of pure gold scattered in it; the wandering about and gathering the pieces may be left to any of us, all can accomplish that; but the first opening of the invisible door in the rock is of the imagination only [IV, 252].

The Fancy, as Ruskin conceives of it, is a circumferential labyrinth (one is, after all, invited to "fancy" about "labyrinthine wonder")— a circumferential labyrinth, at this early stage before the pathos of the Labyrinthine Penultimate, that suggests the rational, even mathematical design of a thinking man whose thought about optical and pneumatical laws is as intricate as the negotiation of a Maze. But the Imagination, essentially passive only in the sense that it does not commute between Suburb and Centre, penetrates as incisively and ruthlessly as entirely mathematical thought. It is as if the original and coalescing altitude of the bird's-eye view, which is also the view not *of* but *from* St. Mark's, were to be exchanged for a location that would be either underneath or interior; it is further as if what had been "above" were translated into an interior dimension, with Fancy, swirling with labyrinthine wonder and complexity, on the "outside": "The fancy sees the outside and is able to give a portrait of the outside, clear, brilliant, and full of detail. The imagination sees the heart and inner nature, and makes them felt, but is often obscure, mysterious, and interrupted, in its giving of outer detail" [IV, 253].

The difference between being "inside" and being "outside" is, among other things, the difference in the number of vantage points. Inside, at the condensed and submerged heart, the "aesthetic observation" of the Imagination, like the elevated Turin Gardens, requires only a single focus to take in "the whole at a glance"; while on the "outside," the Fancy, tracking through an intricate design of mathematical logic that has the potential to lead both to "analogies" and caught "resemblances," requires multiple vantage points (as if one were to view St. Peter's from a Gothically fallen position and condition) to replace an incipiently angelic elevation. And with that multiplicity of circumferential vantage points, there is a sense of space, like "vacancies" that are "kindly," which contrasts felicitously with the superabundance of a potentially replete Centre.

Those circumferential "vacancies," which are quite different from the openness of "white emptiness" that is the receptive vacuity of an artist who would not follow the labyrinthine logic of pneumatical laws, provide room to breathe, which, with Ruskin, is also room to see. There is an oxygen of multiple or serial "single points," which permits the civilized observation of a world without the almost inhuman, angelic demands that are elicited by the synoptic perception of Strange Chords. But with the Fancy, there is not the oxygen of "slow travel." Instead, the activity of the Circumference is quick, agile:

> . . . the imagination being at the heart of things, poises herself there, and is still, quiet and brooding, comprehending all around her with her fixed look; but the fancy staying at the outside of things cannot see them all at once; but runs hither and thither, and round and about to see more and more, bounding merrily from point to point, and glittering here and there, but necessarily always settling, if she settle at all, on a point only, never embracing the whole. And from these single points she can strike out analogies and catch resemblances, which, so far as the point she looks at is concerned, are true, but would be false, if she could see through to the other side. This, however, she cares not to do; the point of contact is enough for her, and even if there be a gap left between the two things and they do not quite touch, she will spring from one to the other like an electric spark, and be seen brightest in her leaping   [IV, 258].

Space, the dimension perceived first (and first perceived by the Cock-Robinson-Crusoe child), is translated into time. The fanciful and circumferential labyrinth shapes time in a different way but with the same idiosyncratic force as a Centre that is either elevated or interior. Just as the Centre is spatially more demanding than its suburbs (demanding, finally, a price that brings economics to nothing less than sanity), so the infernally angelic concentration of time to a single, central point—not the "single points" of circumferential multiplicity—is more demanding than the serial, tracking time that imitates the turns of mathematical and labyrinthine pneumatical laws, a tracking time, occasionally fanciful, that nevertheless possesses the oxygen of conjunctive "vacancies": "Now these differences between the imagination and the fancy hold not only in the way they lay hold of separate conceptions, but even the points they occupy of time; for the fancy loves to run hither and thither in time, and to follow long chains of circumstances from link to link in the middle that implies the rest and fastens there" (IV, 258-59).

Describing the difference between Moritz Retzsch and Turner, Ruskin describes the initial difference between the "outside" and the "inside," his early perception, with implied valuation, of the Maze and the Centre—a serial Fancy, which "loves to run hither and thither in time," following "long chains of circumstances from link to link," and an imagination that perceives with the apparent centripetal mastery of the simultaneous. With "vacancies" in a middle that connects historical extensions, which are the suburbs of time, Retzsch illustrates with a sense of temporal panorama that requires a series of retinal adjustments. The lines of history, both "awful" and "strange" when condensed, become the fanciful components of illustration. The eye perceives the extension of time, the environment of the present tense: "In Retzsch's illustrations to Schiller's *Kampf mit dem Drachen*, we have an instance, miserably feeble indeed, but characteristic, and suited to our present purpose, of the detailing, finishing action of the fancy. The dragon is drawn from head to tail. . . . We have him, from the beginning of his career to the end" (IV, 259). Tracking through the Maze, the Fancy maneuvers through a variety of tenses. Shaping time, the Maze turns duration into an intricate—if, in the case of Retzsch, debased—line that proceeds "from head to tail."

Still, having the dragon by the tail, as well as the head—"beginning . . . to the end"—Retsch, enamored of extension, fails to get to the Centre. Simply, he does not get into the dark heart of the dragon. Yet Turner, who would, with "awful lines," condense the panoramic expanse of the Sienese narrative painters (or even Retzsch) into a central moment, a central focal point, holds the dragon in a moment of the middle:

> Now take up Turner's, Jason, Liber Studiorum, and observe how the imagination can concentrate all this, and infinitely more, into one moment. . . . No more claws, nor teeth, nor manes, nor stinging tails. We have the dragon, like everything else, by the middle. We need see no more of him. All his horror is in fearful, slow griding upheaval of the single coil. Spark

after spark of it, ring after ring, is sliding into the light, the slow glitter steals along step by step, broader and broader, a lighting of funeral lamps one by one, quicker and quicker; a moment more, and he is out upon us, all crash and blaze, among those broken trunks;—but he is nothing then to what he is now [IV, 259-60].

An extended serial time, composed of a "then" that is both past and future, is reduced to a present "now"—a "now" that nevertheless incorporates the temporal extension of the "awful lines of time." The dragon, itself serpentine if not labyrinthine (as it later will be), is perceived in its centricity.

The concentration of line (a dragon's or a serpent's, though not yet the "colubrine chains" of the labyrinth that would mediate between Centre and Circumference), at a point that is a privileged present, as opposed to the multiple pictures (pictures requiring, like the architecture of St. Peter's, the discriminations of retinal adjustment) of either Retzsch or, say, Sienese narrative paintings—that ability, in either or any case, to bring extension to a point requires, for endurance as much as conception, a man of no small magnitude. Strange Chords are not easily perceived. The optical system that seizes the central point in order to seize the whole must be able to endure superabundance. For Repletion, as perhaps in the case of the exaggerated condition of that Central Judge of "the United States in particular and the world in general" whose worldly focal point is in fact his own autobiographical vantage point, is a focal point become vantage point that may prove too much, in its compacted state, for even an egocentrically tenuous sanity that does not find safety in madness. But for the great man, that privileged present is stable, immobile. Both Strange Chords and Awful Lines are perceived with the passivity of "white emptiness," a "four cornered sheet," where extension is reduced to no series of "kindly vacancies" but to the point of a highly charged (and dangerous) union. Between heads and tails, beginnings and endings, the great man is secure not only in his greatness but in his sane centrality. And central endurance itself continues to be a sign of greatness anywhere:

. . . the one [great man] knows too much of the past and future, and of all things beside and around that which immediately affects him, to be in any wise shaken by it. . . . The smaller man, with the same degree of sensibility, is at once carried off his feet; he wants to do something he did not want to do before; he views all the universe in a new light through his tears; he is gay or enthusiastic, melancholy or passionate, as things come and go to him. Therefore the high creative poet might even be thought, to a great extent, impassive (as shallow people think Dante stern), receiving indeed all feelings to the full, but having a great centre of reflection and knowledge in which he stands serene, and watches the feeling, as it were, from afar off   [v, 210].

Yet despite the stability of a Centre that, like a cathedral supported by opposed flying buttresses, achieves some of its poise by being "between," Ruskin can conceive of a situation in which the magnitude of even a great man, a man born to endure central stress, cannot accommodate penultimate Repletion, as it tends toward that condition of Illth which is the excessive presence become absence of White Silence. If the Imagination, "knowing too much," also sees "too far, too darkly, too solemnly" (iv, 257), Ruskin begins to understand that, for those who are not entirely angelic, "too much" can, in fact, be just that. And at this point, Repletion, if not Illth, may be rescued by extension, and Imagination by the Fancy: "There is, however, a limit to the power of all human imagination. When the relations to be observed are *absolutely* necessary, and highly complicated, the mind cannot grasp them; and the result is a total deprivation of all power of imagination associative in such matter. For this reason, no human mind has ever conceived a new animal . . . the intellect utterly fails under the load, and is reduced to mere composition . . . there is no action of imagination (iv, 236-37).

In a letter to his father, Ruskin confesses that panorama, "vast breadth," can, at times, only be handled by a serial division that, transforming the simultaneous into the serial (like the function of his "paste-board"), is similar to the capacities and performances of his version of Fantasy. Essentially, what is "all at once" must be divided in order to be dealt with: "There is also something burdensome in the vast breadth of the subject at present. It is all weighing on my brains at once, and I cannot devote my full mind to any part of it. As soon as I have it all down on paper—out of danger, as it were, and well in sight—I can take up any part and finish it" (x, xxxvii). What Ruskin is suggesting is a means of combating the dangers of the avaricious Imagination. Dispersal becomes survival—at least before the centrifugation of patho-eccentricity, which is a saving grace that makes an already attenuated existence problematic at best.

Yet something other than dispersal is required, something other than dispersal and "paste-board" exclusion. Presumably necessary, survival is perhaps not enough. What is needed is a kind of amalgamation—an overlay of designs (and the responses to those designs) that will offer a reconciliation between the Maze of the energetic tracker, who zealously follows the unwinding peregrinations of the often mathematical logic, and either the artist's dense (or blank as a "four-cornered sheet") Centre, which is a Centre of passive immobility, or the imaginative heart of synthesis, which is arrived at by an exclusively aggressive, straight-forward penetration that finds a point of passive mastery, unhindered by the hesitations of meandering thought or movement. Reconciliation can be psychic balance. The new stability would be central, or in a condition of "between" that is close to an efficacious Middle, only by being partially central:

> It is thus evident that a curiously balanced condition of the powers of mind is necessary to induce full admiration of any natural scene. Let those powers be themselves inert, and the mind vacant of knowledge, and destitute of sensibility; and the external object becomes little more to us than it is to birds or insects; we fall into the temper of the clown. On the other hand, let the reasoning powers be shrewd in excess, the knowledge vast, or sensibility intense, and it will go hard but that the visible object will suggest so much that it shall be soon itself forgotten   [v, 357].

Still, playing with designs (and Ruskin's "play" is emphatically a game of life), he solves no problems. But at the least, manipulating, he suggests the necessity of the circumferential "garland of thoughts." Despite central obsessions—and at first the Centre of Cock-Robinson-Crusoe conceit is nothing less than the topography of the self or landscape autobiography (though later it will become the horizontal territory of the mad Judge of the World)—a fanciful labyrinth, composed of flowers (of "vital" hawthorn that, as we shall see, will bloom before it will fall like a wilted rose), has been included in Ruskin's bouquet. If at first the inclusion of the Circumference (anticipating the later Transformations of the Maze) seems almost generous, as though Ruskin were in a verbal "play" that would exchange "great chords of errorless curves" for both the cords of strained nerves and Strange Chords, that inclusion is shortly to become more increasingly necessary that merely magnanimous— or clever:

. . . that the great composers, no less deep in feeling, are in the fixed habit of regarding as much the relations and positions, as the separate nature, of things; that they reap and thresh in the sheaf, never pluck ear to rub in the hand; fish with net, not line, and sweep their prey together within *great chords of errorless curve*;—that nothing ever bears to them a separate or isolated aspect, but leads or links a change of aspects—that to them it is not merely the surface, nor the substance of anything that is of import; but its *circumference* . . . [italics mine, VII, 234].

Finally, or with the midpoint finality of Part One, one might say that the "garland of thoughts" had come into its own. One might further say that the delicately imbalanced "bouquet" was a preparation for a transformation that might enable one to make the Thesean and serial journey from the condemned Centre of sewage to the no less serial Circumference of multiple perspectives, though the Circumference, in Ruskin's case, may itself be a pre-Circumferential territory of penultimate Repletion that can only delay final madness by distortions that are versions of a "line returning upon itself." Just as Repletion would be rescued by linear extension and the Imagination by serial fancy, so there are indications that the Centre has been—and, for a while, will continue to be—rescued by the "kindly vacancies" of the Circumference and what might be called the syntax of the labyrinth, which, instead of "killing" time and space with travel that is "too fast," will animate and extend those available dimensions, giving them new life. Since the quickest route between two points is a straight "length without breadth," Ruskin, in any case preferring the stuttering delay of the penultimate to immaculate ultimacy, would finally involve himself with the curvilinear.[4]

[4] Nevertheless, first things are not penultimate but first. And what is first, with Ruskin, is straight—or almost so:

Now, bringing these universal and eternal facts down to this narrow, straight, and present piece of business we have in hand, the first thing we have to learn to draw is an extremely narrow, and an extremely direct, line. Only, observe, true and vital direction does not mean that, without any defection or warp by antagonist force, we can fly, or walk, or creep at once to our mark; but that, whatever the antagonist force may be, we so know and mean our mark, that we shall at last precisely arrive at it, just as surely, and it may be in some cases more quickly, than if we have been unaffected by lateral or opposing force. And this higher order of contending and victorious rightness, which in our present business is best represented by the track of an arrow, or rifle-shot, affected in its course both by gravity and the wind, is the more beautiful rightness or directness of the two, and the one which all fine art sets itself principally

It is as though the lines and language of return (hardly "error-less") would render the Strange Chords of attempted mastery, which may become part of an even stranger antiphon than that of conventional Antiphonal Contention, both less strange and potentially maddening by a kind of spiraling familiarity. And that familiarity would be the recognition with a difference—perhaps, as we shall "see," a blindly "crocodilian" difference (the screams of peacocks above competing with, rather than completing, the latent silence of buried crocodiles below)—that might be effected by the superimposition, if not substitution, of a design that is newly employed over one that is original with the concentricities of conceit. Orthodox geometries anticipate later distortions that will produce a temporary heterodox solution—an anamorphically centrifugal solution that will fall just "short" of salvation.

---

to achieve. But its quite first step must nevertheless be in the simple production of the mathematical Right line, as far as the hand can draw it; joining two points, that is to say, with a straight visible track, which shall as nearly as possible fulfil the mathematical definition of a line, "length without breadth"   [xxviii, 442].

Part Two

Lucent Verdure and
Asymmetrical Decompositions

DIPTYCH

To Theseus: Finding No Minotaur

Thread the chaos, pattern the despair.
　Shadows loom and worry you:
Dead hope, and empty heaven, and now bare.
　Meadows—fearful! but all perspective true.

To Penelope: Weaving in Autumn

True perspective all, but fearful! meadows
　Bare now, and heaven empty, and hope dead.
You worry and loom shadows,
　Despair the pattern, chaos the thread.

　　　　　　—Richard Ringler

When a man rides a long time through wild regions he feels the desire for a city. Finally he comes to Isidora, a city where the buildings have spiral staircases encrusted with spiral seashells, where perfect telescopes and violins are made, where the foreigner hesitating between two women always encounters a third, where cockfights degenerate into bloody brawls among the bettors. He was thinking of all these things when he desired a city. Isidora, therefore, is the city of his dreams: with one difference. The dreamed-of city contained him as a young man; he arrives at Isidora in his old age. In the square there is the wall where the old men sit and watch the young go by; he is seated in a row with them. Desires are already memories.

—Italo Calvino, *Invisible Cities*

Chapter Six

Labyrinths of Presence, Labyrinths of Absence: Initial Experiences of the Superimposition of Contrasting Designs

A. The Theatre of Blindness:
Items, Queries, Laws, the Bestiary, and
Originally Invisible Dramatis Personae

Item: "The morning always dark; no vestige of dawn ever coming to comfort me. Fire and candle only. Now, one does not *want* dawn in summer—it is too early—but just now, the one precious thing and eye of day taken out of it.—Blind, Blind, Blind, for ever . . ." (*Diaries*, p. 877).

Item: the water offers a way that is like a "street which is called Straight"; the path may be curved, but is it necessary without an error that can be recovered?

Query: should it be? (Should *Laura* be a fallen mistress?) And, if there is a fallen path, is there also a high road composed of "Right Lines"?

Item: guides who are even blind to themselves need special guidance on that road of Life, which is as "Straight," though unmarked, as a central city's waterway. Even the road, which is like a "straight visible track," is as difficult to trace as if it were among morasses and mounds of desert:

> . . . the word Strait, applied to the entrance into Life, and the word Narrow, applied to the road of Life, do not mean that the road is so fenced that few can travel it, however much they wish (like the entrance to the pit of a theatre), for that, for each person, it is at first so stringent, so difficult, and so dull, being between close hedges, that few *will* enter it, though all *may*. In a second sense, and an equally vital one, it is not merely a Strait, or narrow, but a straight, or right road; only, in this rightness of it, not at all traced by hedges, wall, or telegraph wire, or even marked by posts higher than winter's

snow; but, on the contrary, often difficult to trace among morasses and mounds of desert, even by skilful sight; and by blind
persons, entirely untenable unless by help of a guide, director,
rector, or rex: which you may conjecture to be the reason why,
when St. Paul's eyes were to be opened, out of the darkness
which meant only the consciousness of utter mistake, to seeing
what way he should go, his director was ordered to come to
him in the 'street which is called Straight' [xxviii, 441-42].

Item:

This famous place is a subterranean Passage in manner of
a Street, which by a thousand Intricacies and Windings, as it
were by mere Chance, and without the least Regularity, per-
vades the whole Cavity or Inside of a little Hill at the foot of
Mount Ida, southwards, three miles from Gortyna. The Entrance into this Labyrinth is by a natural Opening, seven or
eight Paces broad, but so low that even a middle-siz'd Man
can't pass through without stooping.

The flooring of this Entrance is very rugged and unequal;
the Ceiling flat and even, terminated by divers Beds of Stone,
laid horizontally one upon another.

The first thing you come at is a kind of Cavern exceeding
rustick, and gently sloping: in this there is nothing extraordinary, but as you move forward the place is perfectly sur-
prizing; nothing but Turnings and crooked By-ways. The principal Alley, which is less perplexing than the rest, in length
about 1200 Paces, leads to the further end of the Labyrinth,
and concludes in two large beautiful Apartments, where
Strangers rest themselves with pleasure. Tho' this Alley divides
itself, as its Extremity, into two or three Branches, yet the
dangerous part of the Labyrinth is not there, but rather at its
Entrance, about thirty paces from the Cavern on the left hand.
If a Man strikes into any other Path, after he has gone a good
way, he is so bewildered among a thousand Twistings, Twin-
ings, Sinuousities, Crinkle-Crankles and Turn-again Lanes,
that he could scarce ever get out again without the utmost
danger of being lost [G. P. de Tournefort, *Voyage du Levant*,
1717, trans. J. Ozell, 1718].

Item: the labyrinth is a series of stages (and performances for
originally invisible dramatis personae) in a blind theatre.

Item: "left, right, right, left, left, left, left." And is that a dialogue
between the contrasting mirrors of the brain's hemispheres, or

eccentric directions for the blind march in darkness mentioned by Lucian?

Query: does Ariadne dance on Daedalus' *Choros*?

Item: blind tails of flamboyant eyes (knowing either too much or Nothing at all) may lead from eyes that are cruelly tearless to frozen tears of a February dawn, when there will be no more "wandering of the feet in the labyrinth like this."

Item: Muffled Rumblings and Torn Presences: the ripped surface of an archaeology approaching silence. And after the discourse of conventional geometries, there remains the aesthetics of "pretty pieces" and the antiphonal logic of madness. After conventional, rectilinear perspective studies, there remain the anamorphic distortions of line and language that may fulfill and temporarily solve the problems of the Strange Chords of attempted mastery.

Item/bestiary: there are, we know, in Ruskin's bestiary that is also an aviary, peacocks, strutting in their unmitigated arrogance (the beauty of their plumage countered terribly by their screeches), with fanning tails of a reflexive blindness like madness that cannot even see as retrospectively as "*rose*mary" (can they see as prospectively as "Laura"?)—peacocks, whose cry of triumph, as if heard by suitably labyrinthine ears in the curious and dim illumination of the "lyric glow of illness" (the "lyric glow," perhaps, of the embers of "charred meaning") that is penultimate to the concluding madness and silence of a blank page.

Item/bestiary: consider the dancing cranes, their awkward turns, the stomping of their feet, and the defensive space of Troy.

Item/bestiary: And the cats, there are the cats as well, who might stalk those peacocks, and that one particular large, black cat, leaping for "contention" from in back of a mirror where one might find ripped immanence, hear the muffled rumblings of a torn presence—a mirror that itself reflects a letter writer who would, on occasions, "purr" his letter "catcataeceously," signing himself simply "Cat."

Item/bestiary: further and closer to the ground, with only dim aspirations for altitude, Ruskin's bestiary includes snakes, snakes traveling with capricious sinuousity, with either God's speed, which may be slow travel, or the Devil's. And then there are the crocodiles, with their sacred bacon that is potentially profane.

Item/footnote: "1) Edouard Monod-Herzen, *Principes de morphologie générale*, Vol. I, p. 119, Gauthier-Villars, Paris, 1927. 'Shells offer countless examples of spiral surfaces, on which the joining lines of the successive whorls are spiral helices.' The geometry of a peacock's tail is more aerial: 'The eyes in a peacock's spread tail are situated at the intersecting point of a double cluster of spirals, that are apparently Archimedean spirals.' (Vol. I, p. 58)." Footnote to Gaston Bachelard's *The Poetics of Space*, trans. Maria Jolas (New York, 1964), p. 105.

Query/bestiary: do the tears of crocodiles freeze in the labyrinth?

Item/bestiary: "Outside or inside edge does not, however, I suppose matter to the snake, the fulcrum being according to the lie of the ground, on the concave or convex side of the curve, and the whole strength of the body is alive in the alternative curves" (XXVI, 317).

Item: "I do not know if children generally have strong associative fancy about words; but when I was a child, that word 'Crocodile' always seemed to me very terrific, and I would even hastily, in any book, turn a leaf in which it was printed with a capital C. If anybody had but told me the meaning of it—'a creature that is afraid of crocuses!' " (XXVII, 484).

Item/bestiary: Then there is Herodotus, who will speak of double stories of double labyrinths that will, penultimately, be antiphonal in nature:

> For in the eyes of some of the Egyptians, the crocodiles are sacred; but by others they are held for enemies. And it is they who dwell by the Lake Moeris, who think them greatly sacred. Every one of these lake people has care of his own crocodile, taught to be obedient to the lifting of finger. And they put jewels of enamel and gold into their ears, and bracelets on their forefeet, and feed them with the sacred shew-bread daily, and attend upon them, that they may live beautiful lives; and, when they die, bury them, embalmed, in holy tombs. . . . But they of the city of Elephantine eat their crocodiles, holding them nowise sacred. Neither do they call them crocodiles, but "champsae"; it is the Ionians who call them "crocodiles," because they think them like the little crocodiles that live in the dry stone walls   [Herodotus, ii, 69; Ruskin, XXVII, 484].

Item/bestiary: And the dragon—or crocodile—may not at first be blind to others or itself: "The word 'Dragon' means 'the Seeing Creature,' and I believe the Greeks had the same notion in their other word for a serpent, 'ophis.' There were many other creeping and crawling and rampant things; the live stem and the ivy were serpentine enough, blindly; but here was a creeping thing that saw!" (XXVII, 483).

The Law of Curvature: "all mountain forms not cloven into absolute precipice, nor covered by straight slopes of shales, are more or less governed by these great curves, it being one of the aims of Nature in all her work to produce them" (xv, 178).

Item/bestiary: "our dragon does not fail us, both Carpaccio and Tintoret having the deepest convictions on that subject;—as all strong men *must* have; for the Dragon is too true a creature, to all such, spiritually. That it is an indisputably living and venomous creature, materially, has been the marvel of the world, innocent and guilty, not knowing what to think of the terrible worm, and not whether to worship it, as the Rod of their lawgiver, or to abhor it as the visible symbol of the everlasting Disobedience" (xxvii, 483).

Query: Do double stories tell of double stories in three dimensions? And do different tails tell different tales? And what of the place of the double axes?

Item: "Take the two reverses together, and you have 'blind mouths'" (xviii, 72).

Query: "Have you so much as watched a spider making his cobweb, or if you have yet had the leisure to do that, in the toil of your own cob-web making, did you ever *think* of how he threw his first thread across the corner?" (xxvii, 398).

Query: Does the conjunction of pebble and mussel make for the threads of the exit? The threads of entrapment? Or merely Strange Chords? And how are the knight's nerves? His strained intellect?

Item: Consider "the labyrinth of life itself, and more and more interwoven occupation . . . and of the time wasted in blind lanes of it" (xxii, 452).

Item: "so I suppose you want to see the Theseus, or the stuffed birds, or the crabs and spider . . . or the parched alligator-skins; and you imagine these contemplations likely to improve, and sanctify, that is to say, recreate, your minds" (xxvii, 398).

Item/the cast: there are, in Contrasting Mirrors of the "naked contention" of the mind, "double, or even treble" selves, and the play of symbolical personages in the labyrinthine consciousness of the Theatre of Blindness, where Ophelia can say "*Rose*mary, that's for remembrance," and an untransformed Adèle or Rose can have her threads severed, as if by an angry Atropos, who may do the same to Ariadne, even if she is careful.

Item/the cast: there is Daedalus; there is Theseus, as well as Ariadne, who is like Rose, in her postcircumferential location; then there is Daedalus again, whose initial villainy becomes a problem of solution, a problem without which salvation is impossible—no matter how temporary. And there will be the Maze—the penultimate Maze, its aesthetics, as well as the distortions and breaking of the circle, which, as Cock-Robinson-Crusoe centricity becomes increasingly anathematic and perfectly balanced sentences fall into the serpentine syntax of the labyrinth, is ever more apparent.

Query: is Atropos the goddess or fate of curvilinear immediacy? How blank is her tablet, and if entirely so, for how long will it be immaculate?

The Law of Curvature: "This variation is itself twofold in all good curves.

"A. There is, first, a steady change through the whole line, from less to more curvature, or more to less, so that *no* part of the line is a segment of a circle, or can be drawn by compasses in any way whatever. . . .

"B. Not only does every good curve vary in general tendency, but it is modulated, as it proceeds, by myriads of subordinate curves" (xv, 178-79).

Close to Ruskin's beginning, even while concerned with both the orthodox geometries of Cock-Robinson-Crusoe concentricity and the straight lines of "converging orthogonals" that, anticipating St. Paul's "street which is called Straight" (as rectilinear, in fact, as later waterways), provide the underlying design for his perspective studies—studies that are themselves prospective diagrams for his exploration of the third dimension—Ruskin expresses an incipient interest in the curvilinear. As early as *Modern Painters II*, he notes the beauty of spirals:

> The simplest of the beautiful curves are the conic, and the various spirals; but it is difficult to trace any ground of superiority or inferiority among the infinite numbers of higher curves. I believe that almost all are beautiful in their own nature, and that their comparative beauty depends on the constant quantities involved in their equations   [IV, 106].

Taken together, those orthodox geometries and the more eccentric (and later, fully developed) geometries or irregular lines that "return," like the design of Ruskinian Museums, upon themselves, with only loose circularity, suggest the later possibility of a kind of superimposition. It is as if an early and entirely errorless perfection of (logo)-concentricity might be saved or rescued from its impossible to maintain condition of synoptic mastery by the imperfect, or asymmetrical, just as altitudinous Centres are "rescued" by fallen Circumferences. It is further precisely as if those perfect geometries and their altitudinously True Centre were located on a palimpsest that had superimposed over their remains the eccentric curvilinearity of an unpredictable Maze that, experienced from neither "above" nor "outside" but from "within," might delay an inevitable process of decomposition.[1]

Yet at times it may appear, depending upon the vigor of the palimpsestic erasure and retracing, as if superimposition had become substitution, as remembered rectilinearity, which has its own validity, gives way to curvilinearity (the shaping Hampton Court Maze as prototype of later recreation is, after all, itself remembered in such a way that the memory may be more important than the initial, model experience)—and all this before the paratactical break up into the shattered ruins of a kind of "musical mosaic" and the ultimacy of White Silence, with the double labyrinths at the circumferential edge anticipated by the single, recollected labyrinth of Lucent Verdure at Hampton Court. One might finally say that, along with palimpsestic superimposition/substitution, there were also, close to the end, a form of multiplication to accommodate, at least temporarily, the spatial requirements of Repletion before the reversal of Illth.

The model for the lines of irregular return,[2] or return with a difference, is the *Helix virgata*, the discussion of which in "Letter 63" of *Fors* is like the song about Ariadne and Theseus: "the gradual involution of the ballad . . . is a pretty good vocal imitation of the deepening labyrinth" (xxvii, 402). The description of the *Helix virgata* is itself no less a syntactical imitation of that "deepening labyrinth," explored in the immediate consciousness of a present tense that might be examined, as it will penultimately, through a magnifying glass:

> Yes; the Holy Ghost of Life, not yet finally departed, can still give fair colours even to an empty shell. Evangelical friends,— worms, as you have long called yourselves, here is a deeper

[1] Ruskin is, in fact, entirely aware of the efficacy of antithetical superimposition: "Superimposition, wisely practiced, is of two kinds, directly contrary to each other, of weight on lightness, and of lightness on weight; while the superimposition of weight on weight, or lightness on lightness, is nearly always wrong" (ix, 241). Superimposition that is not antithetical predicts a condition of "superabundance" that is itself preliminary to Repletion and finally Illth.

[2] Discussing the turf labyrinths of "Troy Town" games, as well as certain aspects of military engineering, Jackson Knight discusses the etymological sources of those "turns": "There are of course 'Troys' and 'Troy' names in Italy. The names long ago received an approximately right explanation, by reference to a root meaning primarily 'turn' . . . . Meanwhile, a suggestion was made for a maze in Wales called Caer Droia. 'Caer' is 'camp'; 'Droia' was referred to a Celtic root TRO, meaning 'turn' in many slightly varying senses. This applied well to the turns of the maze, like the Latin word 'tro-are' " (*Vergil*, p. 229).

expression of humility suggested possible: may not some of you be only painted shells of worms,—alive, yet empty?

18. Assuming my shell to be Helix virgata, I take down my magnificent French—(let me see if I can write its title without a mistake)—"Manuel de Conchyliologie et de Paléontologie Conchyliologique," or, in English, "Manual of Shell-taking and Old-body-talking in a Shell-talking manner." Eight hundred largest octavo—more like a folio—pages of close print, with four thousand and odd (nearly five thousand) exquisite engravings of shells; and among them I look for the creatures elegantly, but inaccurately, called by modern naturalists Gasteropods; in English, Bellyfeet (meaning, of course, to say Belly-walkers, for they haven't got any feet); and among these I find, with much pains, one that is rather like mine, of which I am told that it belongs to the sixteenth sort in the second tribe of the second family of the first sub-order of the second order of the Belly-walkers, and that it is called "Adeorbis subcarinatus,"—Adeorbis by Mr. Wood, and subcarinatus by Mr. Montagu; but I am not told where it is found, nor what sort of creature lives in it, nor any single thing whatever about it, except that it is "sufficiently depressed" ("assez déprimée"), and "deeply enough navelled" ("assez profondément ombliquée,"—but how on earth can I tell when a shell is navelled to a depth, in the author's opinion, satisfactory?), and that the turns (taken by the family) are "little numerous" ("Peu nombreux"). On the whole, I am not disposed to think my shell is here described, and put my splendid book in its place again.

19. I next tried my English Cuvier, in sixteen octavo volumes; in which I find no notice whatever taken of these minor snails, except a list of thirty-three species, finishing with an etc.; out of which I mark "Cretacea," "Terrestris," and "Nivea," as perhaps likely to fit mine; and then I come, by order of Atropos, on this amazing account of the domestic arrangements of a little French snail, "Helix decollata" (Guillotined snail?) with references to "Cm. Chemn. cxxxvi. 1254-1257," a species which "has the singular habit of successively fracturing the whorls at the top (origin, that is,—snails building their houses from heaven towards earth), of the spire, so that at a particular epoch, of all the whorls of the spire originally possessed by this bulimus, not a single one remains." Bulimus,—what's a bulimus? Helix is certainly a screw, and bulimus—in my Riddle's dictionary—is said to be "empty-bellied." Then this French

snail, revolutionary in the manner of a screw, appears to be a belly-walker with an empty belly, and no neck,—who literally "breaks up" his establishment every year! Query—breaks? or melts? Confraction, or confusion?[3] [xviii, 552-53].

The twisting and eccentric language describing the *Helix virgata* is close to Ruskin's own drawings of the shells, which, in their "irregularities," are the result of "conditions of perspective":

> I drew the three advancing stages of the common snail's houses, thus sent me, forthwith; and Mr. Burgess swiftly and rightly engraves them. Note that the apparent irregularities in the spirals are conditions of perspective, necessarily affecting the deeply projecting forms; note also that each whorl is partly hidden by the subsequent one, built with its edge lapping over it; and finally, that there is really, I believe, a modification, to some extent, and enlargement, of the inner whorls; until the domestic creature is satisfied with its length of cave, and expresses its rest in accomplished labour and full age, by putting that binding lip round its border, and term to its hope [xxviii, 555].

In the same way that eccentric geometries follow the orthodox, so regular perspective is followed, in both line and language, by a distortion—or "modification"—that anticipates, as we shall see, the distortion or "anamorphosis" of Ruskin's penultimate syntax of the labyrinth.

Interested in the inaugural anamorphic "modification" of the spirals of the *Helix virgata*, Ruskin is interested in the labyrinthine. The curvilinear prepares for the Transformations of the Maze in its various manifestations and its various stages. But the labyrinths are themselves not the same; there are significant differences between them. One might say that the labyrinths of "right angles"— or "Greek fret"—are further preparations for those more felicitous

---

[3] The connection between weaving and shells has a curious fiction/ history. There is, as Gaston Bachelard points out, "a certain eighteenth century volume that purports to be a textbook for the instruction of a young knight, and in which we find the following 'description' of an open mussel attached to a pebble: 'With its cords and stakes it could be mistaken for a tent.' Naturally, the author doesn't fail to mention the fact that these tiny cords can be woven into fabric, and it is true that at one time thread actually was made from the mooring-cords of mussels" (*The Poetics of Space*, p. 120). Any relation between the *Helix virgata* and the weaving that is to become so important with Ariadne, Atropos (and even Arachne) is only, perhaps, intriguing.

labyrinths without angles that are geometrically "right." Incorporating the sweeping lines of return, those essentially efficacious labyrinths also advance in a way that is both aesthetically and morally correct. Sequence, the performance at various stages, is important.

Just as there is the "perfect" before the "imperfect," or the "irregularities . . . of perspective," so the rectilinear fret is before the curvilinear labyrinth: "Of course frets and returning lines were used in ornamentation when there were no labyrinths—probably long before the labyrinth. A symbol is scarcely ever invented just when it is needed" [xxvii, 404-5]. And Ruskin's attitudes toward the straight-lined return of the fret, which might be considered an elevated return uninformed by the Law of Curvature, and the labyrinth of the fallen serpentine line, are attitudes, one assumes, for "double, or even treble" selves at different altitudes. Still, the essential, undivided Ruskin makes a distinction between the "right-angled" fret, which is looked upon with suspicion, and the preferred labyrinth of sweeping line and flawed curves.

Yet despite his continual concern (a concern that finally involves survival itself), Ruskin's remarks on the curvilinear—though those lines are informed by the great design of Nature—can be surprisingly offhand: "Again, the free sweep of a pen at the finish of a large letter has a tendency to throw itself into a spiral. There is no particular intelligence, or spiritual emotion, in the production of this line. A worm draws it with his coil, a fern with its bud, and a periwinkle with his shell" [xxvii, 405].

And even though there is the embryonic notion, already expressed in "Circumferential Considerations," of the curvilinear or labyrinthine as a solution to, among other things, the synoptic demands of (logo)-concentricity and altitude, a form of curved central descent, as of a vortical labyrinth of absence, can be no less hellish than the excessive demands of central mastery. What is at one time "off-hand," can at another time be something infernal, to be wrestled with—not "off-hand" but with the two hands of "naked contention." The mechanical spiral, almost dismissed because of a lack of "spiritual emotion," has the capacity, in a Fall that is without the Gothic humility which is a form of nobility, to be a labyrinthine handful:

> That Hell, which so many people think the only place Dante gives any account of (yet seldom know his account even of that), was, he tells you, divided into upper, midmost, and nether pits. You usually lose sight of this main division of it,

in the more complex one of the nine circles; . . . Here it is in labyrinthine form, putting the three dimensions at right angles to each other, and drawing a spiral round them. I show you it in a spiral line, because the idea of descent is in Dante's mind, spiral (as of a worm's or serpent's coil throughout); . . . and Minos accordingly indicates which circle any sinner is to be sent to, in a most graphically labyrinthine manner, by twisting his tail round himself so many times, necessarily thus marking the level   [xxvii, 411].

But what is to be noted by Ruskin's schematic illustration of the spiral is precisely that the "labyrinthine form" has been rendered in "three dimensions at right angles to each other," around which a mechanical spiral has been drawn. Even labyrinthine precision is a malediction and it is important to note that this is a precision that has been brought about by the rectilinearity of "right angles." Descending toward the bottom of "nether pits," the vortical labyrinth of absence, which is a spiral organized about straight lines joined at angles of ninety degrees, is anticipated in the early *The Seven Lamps of Architecture* (1849), where, as "Guilloche," or a "vile concatenation of straight lines," it is attacked as ornament which is an imitation of a form that has departed from natural models. Ruskin's response to that mechanically original Labyrinth of the Fret, which is also the labyrinth of straight lines, suggests the necessity of the impulse toward the asymmetrical curvilinearity of "eccentric geometries"—"geometries" that are not merely arcing versions of concentricity:

> The first so-called ornament, then, which I would attack is that Greek fret, not I believe, usually known by the Italian name Guilloche, which is exactly a case in point. It so happens that in crystals of bismuth, formed by the unagitated cooling of the melted metal, there occurs a natural resemblance of it almost perfect. But crystals of bismuth not only are of unusual occurrence in everyday life, but their form is, as far as I know, unique among minerals; and not only unique, but only attainable by an artificial process, the metal itself never being found pure. I do not remember any other substance or arrangement which presents a resemblance to this Greek ornament; and I think that I may trust my remembrance as including most of the arrangements which occur in the outward forms of common and familiar things. On this ground, then, I allege that ornament to be ugly; or, in the literal sense of the word, monstrous; different from anything which it is the nature of man

to admire: and I think an uncarved fillet of plinth preferable
to one covered with this vile concatenation of straight lines:*
. . .

* All this is true; but I had not enough observed when I wrote, the use of
the Greek fret in contrast to curved forms; as especially on vases, and in the
borders of drapery itself. The use of it large, as on the base of Sanmicheli's
otherwise very noble design of the Casa Grimani, is always a sign of failing
instinct of beauty.   [1880. viii, 143-44].

The original architect of Ruskin's "fatal labyrinth," which is an
early (and almost unrecognizable) version of the concluding Theatre of Blindness—especially, or specifically, with its "right angles"—is Daedalus about whom, as Jack the builder of houses, Ruskin has much to say. Just as there is an initial distaste for the
mechanical spiral of "labyrinthine form," so there is at least an early
suspicion concerning the inventiveness of Daedalus, who is an executive craftsman of elevated centricity, of altitudinal mastery:

Take Daedalus, his [the Greek's] great type of the practically
executive craftsman, and the inventor of the expedients in
craftsmanship (as distinguished from Prometheus, the insti-
tutor of moral order in art). Daedalus invents,—he, or his
nephew,

The potter's wheel, and all work in clay;
The saw, and all work in wood;
The masts and sails of ships, and all modes of motion;
    (wings only proving too dangerous!)
The entire art of minute ornament;
And the deceptive life of statues.

By his personal toil, he involves the fatal labyrinth for Minos
[xx, 352].

Even the Daedalean lines of "labyrinthine sequence," which are
involved in the taming or attempted "rehabilitation" of the Centre,
are viewed with a similar suspicion—a suspicion that surrounds
"noblest things" with a shadow that is, in fact, "lurid": "Then from
the tomb of your own Edward the Confessor, to the farthest shrine
of the opposite Arabian and Indian world, I must show how the
glittering and iridescent dominion of Daedalus prevails; and his
ingenuity in division, interposition, and labyrinthine sequence,
more precisely still. . . . His ingenuity plays around the framework

of all the noblest things; and yet the brightness of it has a lurid shadow" (xx, 352-53).[4]

It is as if the quality of light—"the glittering and iridescent dominion" as well as that "brightness" which is surrounded by "lurid shadow"—and the labyrinthine were together combined in a kind of morality play to be performed in a shadow box. More often than not, the light of Daedalus "glitters" as though reflected from the highly polished and perfect surface of an ingenius, but predictable and regular (and, in that sense, "prophetic") style—a style that is without an interior, organic form organized about lines of unpremeditated integrity:

> And this peril of the influence of Daedalus is twofold; first, in leading us to delight in glitterings and semblances of things, more than in their form, or truth;—admire the harlequin's jacket more than the hero's strength; and love the gilding of the missal more than its words;—but farther and worse, the ingenuity of Daedalus may even become bestial, and instinct for mechanical labour only:—(you will find this distinct in the intensely Daedal work of the Japanese); rebellious, finally, against the laws of nature, and honour, and building labyrinths for monsters,—not combs for bees   [xx, 353-54].

Daedalean light, it would appear, is often a reflected light, rather than one that penetrates the form. And reflecting, perhaps with a burning reflection of mirrored intensity, it seems capable of blinding one not only to oneself but to the morality implicit in organic form. Ruskin's "harlequin's jacket," unsupported by substantial shoulders, might reflect the immoral sheen of a "deadly satin."

Yet later, filtered through the "golden stains of time," the Daedalean light has mellowed; it no longer blinds one to oneself, or Ruskin to Daedalus. In "Letter 23" of *Fors*, which is "The Labyrinth" letter, Daedalus is not seen as merely a mechanical and life-denying

---

[4] Daedalus' ingenuity, revealed in his "glittering and iridescent dominion," predicts the madness of others. With an oblique approach that is in fact straight to the point, Foucault notes:

> Tamed, madness preserves all the appearance of its reign. It now takes part in the measures of reason and in the labor of truth. It plays on the surface of things and in the glitter of daylight, over all the workings of appearances, over the ambiguity of reality and illusion, over all that indeterminate web, ever woven and broken, which both unites and separates truth and appearance. It hides and manifests, it utters truth and falsehood, it is light and shadow. It shimmers, a central and indulgent figure, always precarious in this baroque age   [*Madness and Civilization*, p. 36].

architect of, among other things, the Cretan labyrinth.[5] Just as "labyrinthine sequence" would "rehabilitate" (or resurrect) the fallen Centre, so time, as seen through the eyes of Ruskin, whose "earned" altitude always possesses a sense of ground-level origins, has resurrected Daedalus' reputation. Though there remains an attitude of qualification about him, it is no longer the qualification of brilliantly reflected light or "lurid shadow." Transformed by golden time, he has become a rather beneficent Jack, instead of an ingenious Master of perfectly shaped death:

> Lastly, in our nursery rhyme, observe that the name of Jack, the builder, stands excellently for Daedalus, retaining the idea of him down to the phrase, "Jack-of-all Trades". . . . To-day I can only tell you he is distinctly the power of finest human, as opposed to divine, workmanship or craftsmanship. What-ever food there is, and whatever evil, in the labour of the hands, separated from that of the soul, is exemplified by his history and performance. In the deepest sense, he was to the Greeks, Jack of all trades, yet Master of none; the real Master of every trade being always God. His own special work or craft was inlaying or dovetailing, and especially of black and white   [xxvii, 403-4].

Nevertheless, Daedalus persists as an architect of workmanship that is "cunning," a cunning involution that may be like the recti-linear labyrinth of right angles that, "returning upon itself" or "repeating itself," is memorialized as that "Greek fret" which was once as despised as Daedalus himself: "And this house which he built was his finest piece of involution, or cunning workmanship; and the memory of it is kept by the Greeks for ever afterwards, in that running border of theirs, involved in repeating itself, called the Greek fret" (xxvii, 404).

---

[5] As an architect of the Labyrinth, Daedalus, as we know, is also Jack, the builder of a house, which also happens to be the Labyrinth, as if one might wish not so much to escape as abide in that Labyrinth. The Thesean slaying of the Minotaur might be a kind of housecleaning. On the cathedral door of Lucca:

> you are to note, first, that the grave announcement, "This is the labyrinth which the Cretan Dedalus built," may possibly be made more interesting even to some of your children, if reduced from medieval sublimity, into your popular leg-end—"This is the house that Jack built." The cow with the crumpled horn will remind them of the creature who, in the midst of this labyrinth, lived as a spider in the centre of his web; and the "maiden all forlorn" may stand for Ariadne—. . . while the gradual involution of the ballad, and necessity of clear-mindedness as well as clear utterance on the part of its singer, is a pretty vocal imitation of the deepening labyrinth   [xxvii, 402].

Yet Ruskin's attitude toward that "Greek fret" remains somewhat ambiguous. The early and easy dismissal of the fret and its recti-linearity, as a labyrinth of absence (or false presence), is replaced by a depth of meaning that is not reductively defined. There is a posture toward the fret both "then" and "now" that, while not entirely opposed, never, finally, seems to coalesce. There is, in fact, a kind of "split synthesis" between the appearance "above" and the meaning "below," which comes close to anticipating those double labyrinths of Antiphonal Contention and the Theatre of Blindness we shall arrive at penultimately:

> You cannot pass a china-shop, for instance, nor an uphol-sterer's, without seeing, on some mug or plate, or curtain, or chair, the pattern known as the "Greek fret," simple or com-plex. I once held it in especial dislike, as the chief means by which bad architects tried to make their buildings look classical; and as ugly in itself. Which it is: and it has an ugly meaning also, but a deep one, which I did not then know   [xxvii, 400].

If it is ugly, that Greek fret still performs a "definite and noble service in decorative work, as black has among its colours; much more, has it a significance, very precious, though very solemn, when you read it" (xxvii, 400).

But the ambiguity that surrounds both Daedalus and his "right angled" fretwork is not an ingredient found in what might be called an ideal Ruskinian self, whose response to the architecture of Daedalus is that of a personage who is "the type of human, or humane power." Itself a problem, the Maze, it would tentatively appear, is only effective as a solution to its own implicit problems, as well as those of Strange Chords/cords and (infernally) True Centres, if it can be mastered by the experience from "within"— even if that interior mastery must be, of myopic necessity, only immediate or "makeshift," as a series of temporary, conjunctive solutions. In any case, after the Daedalean problem of straight lines, perfect "right angles," and the "Greek fret," there is, in a later stage of the Transformations of the Maze, Ruskin's heroic Theseus, who, among other things—and opposed to Daedalus—makes "roads passable that were infested by robbers or wild beasts":

> Theseus, as I said before, is the great settler or law-giver of the Athenian state; but he is so eminently as the Peace-maker, causing men to live in fellowship who before lived separate, and making roads passable that were infested by robbers or wild beasts. He is the exterminator of every bestial and

savage element, and the type of human, or humane power, which power you will find in this, and all my other books on policy, summed in the terms, "Gentleness and Justice" [XXVII, 408-9].

Ruskin urges the reader of *Fors* to go to a Museum of the unadulterated Centre to regard the statue of this entirely admirable, path-clearing Theseus—despite the notion of "liberal historians" that Theseus, who may not even be " 'a utility fixed and embodied in a material object,' "[6] is not so much an ideal to be aspired toward as a kind of debased Everyman, whose fallen condition is without even the potential of Greek solution or Gothic salvation:

> And the reason I do want you, for once, to go to the British Museum and to look at that broad chest of Theseus, is that the Greeks imagined it to have something better than a Lion's Heart beneath its breadth—a hero's heart, duly trained in every pulse.
> 7. They imagined it so. Your modern extremely wise and liberal historians will tell you it never was so:—that no real Theseus ever existed then; and that none can exist now, or, rather, that everybody is a Theseus and a little more [XXVII, 399].

Just as Daedalus will construct paths of vertiginous and mystifying intricacy—an intricacy that, like the most difficult of Ruskin's own elaborate syntax with its branching "nodal points of failure," would defy expectations of the Exit—so Theseus, with his "hero's heart, duly trained in every pulse," will overcome the obstacles, as if informed by a kind of divine grace.[7] Far from being a debased

---

[6] Developing the significance of myth and symbol at the expense of a more conventional Utilitarian view of the world, Ruskin continues:

> All the more strange then, all the more instructive, as the disembodied Cincinnatus of the Roman, so this disembodied Theseus of the Ionian; though certainly Mr. Stuart Mill could not consider him, even in that ponderous block of marble imagery, a "utility fixed and embodied in a material object." Not even a disembodied utility—not even a ghost—if he never lived. An idea only; yet one that has ruled all minds of men to this hour, from the hour of its first being born, a dream into this practical and solid world [XXVII, 399].

[7] Perhaps making a delicate distinction between the labyrinth and the maze, or suggesting a problem that is its own solution, the editors, touching on the function of church labyrinths and the *Chemin de Jérusalem*, indicate that engraved labyrinths on churches are symbols of grace that can save man from a sinful maze, as if by "recovering" error: "[On the subject of labyrinths thus engraved on many Christian churches—symbolical of the Divine grace which alone can extricate men from the mazes of sin and error—see *Les Labyrinthes d'Eglises: Labyrinthe de la Cathédrale d'Amiens*, by Edmond Soyez, Amiens, 1896]" (XXVII, n. 402).

and perhaps useless Everyman, Ruskin's Theseus remains a present-tense ruler of influence, a ruler, in fact, who may be able to detect even the paths of winds that blow on faces and through the feathers of ostriches: "Ruled and still rules, in a thousand ways, which you know no more than the paths by which the winds have come that blow in your face. But you never pass a day without being brought, somehow, under the power of Theseus" (xxvii, 400).

Yet the "power of Theseus" is one that has initially been aided by the demystifying thread of Ariadne, with Ariadne as a kind of Clotho, just as Ariadne is to become, in a different way, similar to Rose. And Ruskin's version of the love between Theseus and Ariadne is the only acceptable one for the Ruskinian Theseus, who has his Ariadne "deserting" Theseus because her "thread of life," intact for him in the Labyrinth, will not hold for her. There is the "conclusive" stroke of the Third Fors. It is as if, analogously, Atropos, Ruskin's guardian of chance and his Third Fors, had severed, in an act of sorocide, the thread of Clotho's path of life:[8] "he [Theseus] being both the founder of the first city whose history you are to know, and the first true Ruler of beasts; for his mystic contest with the Minotaur is the fable through which the Greeks taught what they knew of the more terrible and mysterious relations between the lower creatures and man; and the desertion of him by Ariadne (for indeed he never deserted her, but she him,—involuntarily, poor sweet maid,—Death calling her in Diana's name) is the conclusive stroke of the Third Fors" (xxvii, 387).

[8] Briefly, as Cook and Wedderburn point out, in Ruskin's orthodox (it is not always so) mythology, it is Clotho who is the fate "which has the power over the clue, thread, or connecting energy—that is, the conduct of life; Lachesis, the fate which ordains the chances that warp it; and Atropos, the inflexible, who cuts the thread for ever" (xxvii, xxi). Certainly, the "power of clue, thread, or connecting energy" is suggestive of Ariadne's serial aid to Theseus.

Further, in passing, one might also note the danger Ruskin finds in threads that, anticipating a spider's work, are only initially attractive. As perfect on the outside as the architecture of Daedalus, Arachne's spinning is dismissed (as Arachne is herself by Athena) with undisguised distaste by the son of an importer of wine, perhaps for her somewhat remote connection with Bacchus: "Arachne, in the outer aspect of her work, had none [faults]; but in the inner power of it, it was fault altogether."

Earlier, we wonder why Arachne's work was bordered with ivy-leaves.

"Because ivy-leaves, in their wanton running about everywhere, were the emblem of the wild god, Bacchus; and were put there to express impertinence to Athena [Minerva], and wilful insult to her trim-leaved olive of peace" (xx, 376).

Consequently, "she is changed by Athena into the meanest of animals, the most loathsomely venomous, whose work [the cobweb], instead of being an honour to the palace of kings, is to be a disgrace to the room of the simplest cottager" (xx, 377).

But of course there is no surrogate sorocide, and Clotho, with her threads, while closer to Ariadne than Arachne (and her threads of danger), is not subject to the "conclusive" end of the Homeric Ariadne (*Odyssey*, xi). Spinning, Clotho might have provided a thread, if not scissors, for Ariadne. At any rate, if Ruskin is, in this stage of the transforming Maze, in some sense Theseus, he needs his own version of Ariadne (beyond the Homeric) for a kind of guidance that may prove even more useful to him than that of the shaping Athena (though, in the end, this may prove subject to change), the Rose-like St. Ursula, or St. George. And for this guidance, he turns, not to the first fate, but to the third, Atropos, his "careful and prudent mistress" (xxviii, 443), who manages matters "like the daintiest and watchfullest housewife for me,—everything in its place, and under my hand" (xxviii, 551). Essentially, it is Atropos who informs Ruskin's life—and, on a lesser and more personalized scale, the design of his books, which, reflexively, are versions of the pattern of his life. The Master, feeling the burdens of Strange Chords and the eventual altitudinous vertigo of True Centres, would indeed be "makeshift"; in a profound sense, he would be irresponsible: "I rather like the Third Fors to take the order of them [the "many things I have to say"] into her hands, out of mine" (xxvii, 323).

The relationships of originally invisible characters and their mythological performances, occurring in the Antiphonal landscape "between" Centre and Circumference—a territory which is like a stage-set for a Theatre of Blindness that, perhaps blind to its own significance, itself seems to be the result of the superimposition of secondary and eccentric geometries over those initial geometries that are rectilinear and concentric—are relationships that are as complicated, even labyrinthine, as Cook and Wedderburn find the "spinning" indeterminacy of Ruskin's multivocal meanings: "These crossings and interlacings in Ruskin's meanings, intricate even as the warp and woof in the web of fate, are very characteristic of him" (xxvii, xxii).

It is perhaps enough to say for now that there is a design, which is often the intermediate design of a spiraling thread, that involves these essentially mythological characters and their performances in the drama of Ruskin's consciousness. And that, further, the thread of intricate meanings is at least either the guiding lifeline of serial continuity, or, instead, as a heterodox version of concentricity, a labyrinth within a labyrinth, like a spider's web, which may indeed involve the fate of a character (either actually or mythologically larger than life and death) and the possibility or impossibility of the Exit—beyond which there may be either survival or the nothing-at-all of White Silence.

With Ruskin, the design of the Maze and the experience within that design—the apparently temporary existence inside its fortunate constriction of "narrow caution" (and with Ruskin, constriction, if not guided from "above" or holding the potential of "extrication," is usually a condition of claustrophobia)—offers a way out that relieves centrally originating Repletion. And that centrifugal leaving process yields Ruskin an unwinding sense of the provincial Exit, a sense impelled by an involuntariness that is close to heavenly, along an intricately Thesean path between Centre and Circumference, the "pretty" guides of which may begin as Ariadne, coupled with, if not his "*Rose*mary," perhaps "Laura," and almost end, penultimately as Atropos.

Here is Ruskin's description of the invisible or "imaginary maze" (as well as its obstacles) that is also a language which might describe the "anamorphic" turns—the "apparent irregularities" being "conditions of perspective"—of the *Helix virgata*, in which one might even, for a while, live: "I oughtn't to be teased to talk any more at my time in life, but should be left to paint snail-shells—and live in a big one" (xxxvii, 4):

> Now, in the pictures of this imaginary maze, you are to note that both the Cretan and the Luccese designs agree in being composed of a single path or track, coiled, and recoiled, on itself. Take a piece of flexible chain and lay it down, considering the chain itself as the path: and, without an interruption, it will trace any of the three figures. (The two Cretan ones are indeed the same in design, except in being, one square and the other round.) And recollect, upon this, that the word "Labyrinth" properly means "rope-walk," or "coil-of rope-walk," its first syllable being probably also the same as our English name "Laura," "the path," and its method perfectly given by Chaucer in the single line—"And, for the house is crenkled to and fro." And on this note, farther, first, that *had* the walls been real, instead of ghostly, there would have been no difficulty whatever in getting either out or in, for you could go no other way. But if the walls were spectral, and yet the transgression of them made your final entrance or return impossible, Ariadne's clue was needful indeed.
>
> Note, secondly, that the question seems not at all to have been about getting in; but getting out again. The clue, at all events, could be helpful only after you had carried it in; and

if the spider, or other monster in mid-web, ate you, the help in your clue, for return, would be insignificant. So that this thread of Ariadne's implied that even victory over the monster would be in vain, unless you could disentangle yourself from his web also   [xxvii, 407-8].

Yet if "the initial question seems not at all to have been getting in; but getting out again," one might still consider the defensive engineering of the exclusive labyrinth, like Troy, that would keep the "outside" Out. Still, that is for a later, even pragmatically penultimate, Transformation of the Maze.

B. Lurid Shadow, Lucent Verdure:
Early Manifestations of the Centripetal Maze

We recall that brief excursion of Newman into horticulture and landscape architecture—Newman, enamored of synthesis and elevated Centres that would permit organization, who would have his labyrinthine landscape, as his knowledge, transformed into the equivalent of a synoptic text that might, conceivably, be mastered by a centripetal, elevated Index. When he is without either map or prior topographical knowledge, Newman is irritated by complex specificity. He takes no pleasure in exploration. To explore is to be more lost than found. And losing his way in fallen intricacy, Newman loses control of potential synthesis and generalization: "It matters not whether our field of operation be wide or limited; in every case, to command it is to mount above it. Who has not felt the irritation of mind and impatience created by a deep, rich country, visited for the first time, with winding lanes, and high hedges, and green steeps, and tangled woods, and everything smiling indeed, but in a maze?" (Discourse 6, Section 7, *The Idea of a University*)

And we further recall that Ruskin, pleased by the plenitude of an infinitely various Nature, is nevertheless uncomfortable at the prospect of no prospect—of being "shut up into hurdled fold or hedged fields" that are, after all, like Newman's irritating "winding lanes and high hedges." At first, or after his Herne Hill confinement from where there is no "extrication," he would be farsighted more often than not. Optically, he would ride the straight lines of converging orthogonals toward the horizons of orthodox transcendence. At this early time—a time of beneficent, Cock-Robinson-Crusoe concentricity and the straight lines of any rectilinearity that would avoid the "right angles" of the fret—he prefers distance to the proximate, transparency to opacity. Before the "failing distance" of a "killed" time and space, it is almost as if he would exchange wholesale virtually any neatly hedged or fenced foreground for the desired background that might be perceived best by a version of the poet Philip Larkin's "long perspectives,"[9] which are, disconcertingly, like Ruskin's own "long shadow" of death:

> Truly, though our element is time,
> We are not suited to the long perspectives
> Open at each instant of our lives.
> They link us to our losses.

As a "practiced" and obsessive traveler, he would, it seems, exchange the proximate landscape of England for the vistas of the Alps, the peaks of which are like the "thrones in heaven" (xxxv, 116). The difference between fenced foregrounds and open backgrounds is, at this early point, essentially and too easily the difference between a despised myopia (after a childhood spent in the act of examining what is at first happily close and then simply too close for optical and psychic comfort) and a prized, distant vision of the transcendental Exit.

Yet, in fact, the hedges of immediacy, giving proximate landscape the intricate and often curvilinear design of a twisted, anamorphically perceived *Helix virgata*, are later (in both mnemonic experience and the experience of re-creation) more to be admired than despised. Ruskin's later "road of Life," which is also his later syntax, is perhaps more narrow than merely straight. At any rate, the straight line, which is the line of St. Paul's "street," becomes suspect. At least potentially, those curvilinear lines of narrow immediacy assuage. Linear intricacy, eliminating the inclusive burden of peripheral vision, also eliminates the dimension of "long perspectives" for someone who, not wanting to witness the ingestion of " 'blind mouths,' " much less the performance of his own death, his own shadow become substance (even in a Theatre of perhaps necessary Blindness, as a kind of final act), would create, among other strategies, designs of "optical fictions" in order to defend against that encroaching vision of the end.

Calculated myopia, like a narrow focus employed against Parallel Advance, becomes a version of pastoral vision. Loss of self—with Ruskin, often an optical extinction of farsightedness that is, at the least, an avoidance of the first person, the autobiographical im-

---

[9] The lines are from "Reference Back" in Larkin's *The Whitsun Weddings* (London, 1964) and are quoted in Frank Kermode's *The Sense of an Ending* (New York, 1966), which was originally called, when delivered as a series of lectures, *The Long Perspectives*.

pulse—is not always desirable. For self-annulment in a distant focal point is also the infernal perception of the "long shadow," the day of final diary subtraction when no numbered days will be left, when time, like a traveled distant landscape, has come to an end.[10] Further, distant vision can be as excessively ambitious as the "mephitic" (xxxiii, 397) vision of central fire, the sight both "of" and "from" the Index, or the visual encompassment of the Centre from the elevated gardens of Turin. Farsightedness directed beyond the Circumference, as if in fact "over" the Edge, toward an infinitude, which is not "cross-referenced" like an ambitious Index or Arachne's weave, does not so much lose the self as murder it, with the awareness or announcement of the coming of the diary's last page. It is as untenable an optical procedure as the lengthy, unsquinting perception of central Repletion.

In any case, between the Centre and Circumference (or at least "as if" between those locations), there are the cramped and intricate hedges and fences of occasional irritation that may, in fact, be designs of frequent optical appeasement. "After" madness, the trip beyond the Edge—or to choose the appropriate preposition with a care that has geographical significance, "between" attacks of madness—those formerly despised hedges of enforced myopia ("despised" when transcendence—as the only possible condition of existence—was found merely in the uncomplicated distance that is not a view of the "long perspective") become the horticulture of a new version of pastoral:

> So after this seventh year, I am going out into the highways and hedges but now no more with expostulation, I have wearied myself in the fire enough; and now, under wild roses and traveller's joy of the lane hedges, will take what rest may be, in my pilgrimage   [xxix, 294].

Seeking "rest" as well as roses that are "wild" (and "roses" that are, simply, postcircumferentially out of reach) Ruskin's traveler seeks the irresponsibility, after attempted mastery, of a myopic, linear manipulation that is without both the long shadows of "long perspectives" and the burdens of a terrifyingly inclusive panorama for an overdeveloped peripheral vision ("interrelation" having here become an enveloping circle that will itself become, in a final twist, a Möbius strip or Klein bottle that renegotiates "outsides" and "insides" in an act that is proleptic of the penultimate interface).

Still, Ruskin has gone to the hedges before the requirements for

---

[10] See *The Diaries*, p. 833, as well as *The Failing Distance*, p. 114.

the horticultural pastoral of both myopia and narrow vision send his soon-to-be-joyous traveler amidst "lane hedges." Originally, he goes both before he has made a historical, if "fatal," case for the medieval landscape of hierarchical boundary[11]—a landscape of the hedge and fence—and before he has experienced the mephitic fires of a Centre that is pernicious in its demands.

Originally, he goes neither to write art history nor to recuperate from the central perception of those Strange Chords of potential madness. Rather, from his childish position of Cock-Robinson-Crusoe centricity, which is a geometrical position without fire, he goes to the hedges more for vigorous play than idle "rest."

As a child, visiting the Hampton Court Maze's hedges of "vital hawthorn" (xxvii, 407), Ruskin involves himself in a formative experience that will become a model of consciousness for later re-creations as recreations which are also interior, mnemonic revisitations—a model that will prove far more felicitous in its metamorphoses than the later versions of his initial experience of the reflexive, Cock-Robinson-Crusoe Centre. Running, at least parenthetically, in recalled moonlight through "intricate alleys of lucent verdure," Ruskin is preparing for a later pastoral design that will be located "between" the "mephitic cancer" of a Centre that is inevitably pernicious and a Circumference that, permitting the optical release of an extensive view, deals with the dangerously sublime responsibility of farsighted men on the Edge—a responsibility that is focused, as if with "long perspectives," on the extensive, rather than "cross-referenced *ad infinitum*," infinite.

But before the sublime proves vertiginous—with Ruskin, the failure of the eye, his "blindness," is almost the same as the failure of his mind—there is the significant activity (one is tempted to say "central" activity) of close maneuverings, in the company of Adèle Domecq,[12] within the proximate intricacy of "lucent verdure"—the

---

[11] In the "Of Medieval Landscape:—First, the Fields" chapter of *Modern Painters III*, Ruskin notes a "fatal change," which is "expressed in the medieval landscape by the eminently pleasurable and horticultural character of everything; by the fences, hedges, castle walls . . ." (v, 249).

[12] Not only is the Hampton Court Maze important in Ruskin's early (and then remembered) life but so, as has been suggested, is Adèle, with whom Ruskin at seventeen fell in (unrequited) love. The "lucent verdure" passage from *Praeterita* is a textual location of compound significance—a labyrinthine passage, as of superimposed design, of central importance. An entry from Ruskin's diary on the anniversary of the day he learned of Adèle's marriage helps to define her importance to Ruskin:

> *March 12th.* I would have sealed this for a black and void day for ever; but if it has not been, and will not be, such for her, it cannot be to me. It may be—

shaping memory of which, as selectively recorded in *Praeterita*, will, perhaps reflexively or mnemonically,[13] last a lifetime, or, more accurately, the time of Ruskin's sanity. Or, one might say that that single, recollected labyrinth of Lucent Verdure will last until the condition of penultimate repletion, when, with no lateral place to go, there is the vertical, doubling of the labyrinth. Here, at any rate, is Ruskin's "Dantesque" experience in the Lucent Verdure of the Hampton Court Maze and its more apparent consequences:

> My runs with cousin Mary in the maze, (once as in Dantesque alleys of lucent verdure in the moon, with Adèle and Elise) always had something of an enchanted and Faery-Queen glamour in them: and I went on designing more and more complicated mazes in the blank leaves of my lesson books—wasting, I suppose, nearly as much time that way as in the trisection of the angle.
>
> Howbeit, afterways, the coins of Cnossus, and characters of Daedalus, Theseus, and the Minotaur, became intelligible to me as to few: and I have unprinted MSS. about them, intended for expansion in *Ariadne Florentina*, and other labyrinthine volumes   [xxxv, 247].[14]

---

for she cast away her truest heart—as true at least as ever man gave—and that is a cost which may be repented of. I will pray to night it may not be. I went up Vesuvius to day—up the Atrio del Cavallo at least—and lay among the ashes in the sun, with gay guides; they little thought of the dark ashes my spirit was lying in. It was a bright day and I worked hard to keep my thoughts among the black lava and along the pleasant shore. They went a little, however, back to that evening in Ch. Ch. when I first knew of it—oddly enough the 12th— and when staggering down the dark passage through the howling wind, to Childs' room, and sat there with him working through long interminable problems, for what seemed an infinite time, without error, without thought, all confusion and horror in eyes and brain. How well I remember how my feet silpped on the smooth pebbles as I staggered on, and the stars danced among the dismal clouds above me like fire-flies   [*Diaries*, p. 165].

[13] *Praeterita* is an autobiography. But it is an idiosyncratic autobiography as Ruskin would have it. Perhaps it should be read both forward and backward. For its inaccuracies, see *The Ruskin Family Letters*, edited by Burd.

[14] W. H. Matthews's description of the Hampton Court Maze, in his *Mazes & Labyrinths*, is as follows:

The Hampton Court maze was constructed in 1690 and in all probability displaced an older maze, a relic of Wolsey's time. The maze is situated close to the Bushy Park entrance. Defoe speaks of it as a "labyrinth," and tells us that the "Wilderness," of which it forms part, replaced the old orchard of the palace.

It is of no great complexity, but . . . is of a neat and symmetrical pattern, with quite sufficient of the puzzle about it to sustain interest and to cause amusement but without a needless and tedious excess of intricacy. The area

Spiraling backward toward a slightly differrent perspective, we must return, as though to a *Helix virgata* viewed from a new vantage point, to material that is familiar with a difference. If the recollected lines of Hampton Court's Lucent Verdure comprise the model for the later transformations of Ruskin's Maze, the model for Hampton Court is the labyrinth of Daedalus, who, in the process of building his house, becomes Ruskin's Jack of All Trades: "Jack's ghostly labyrinth has set the pattern of almost everything linear and com-

---

occupied by it is rather more than a quarter of an acre—not a great amount of space, but enough to accommodate about half a mile of total pathway. The longest side of the maze measures 222 ft.. . . . .
. . . .
The gate almost opposite the entrance should normally be closed. It is for the purpose of affording the gardener or attendant direct access to the "goal" and its approaches, or occasionally for facilitating the release of impatient visitors; if left open it spoils the fun. The goal is provided with two bench seats, each shaded by a leafy-tree.

The hedge was at first composed entirely of hornbeam, but, like most of its kind, it has required renewal at various points from time to time, and this has not always been carried out with appropriate material. The result . . . is a patchwork of privet, hornbeam, yew, holly, hawthorn and sycamore. It is nevertheless questionable whether the lack of uniformity in this respect causes any grief to the bulk of its visitors   [pp. 128-29].

An experience, other than Ruskin's within that Hampton Court Maze is described, as quoted by Matthews, in the *British Magazine* for 1747:

REFLECTIONS ON WALKING IN THE MAZE
AT HAMPTON COURT

What is this mighty labyrinth—the earth,
But a wild maze the moment of our birth?
Still as we life pursue the maze extends,
Nor find we where each winding purlieu ends;
Crooked and vague each step of life we tread,—
Unseen the danger, we escape the dream!
But with delight we through the labyrinth range,
Confused we turn, and view each artful change—
Bewildered, through each wilder meander bend
Our wandering steps, anxious to gain the end;
Unknown and intricate, we still pursue
A certain path, uncertain of the clue;
Like hoodwinked fools, perplex'd we grope our way
And during life's short course we blindly stray,
Puzzled in mazes and perplex'd with fears;
Unknown alike both heaven and earth appears.
Till at the last, to banish our surprise,
Grim Death unbinds the napkin from our eyes.
Then shall Gay truth and wisdom stand confest
And death will shew us *Life* was but a jest   [p. 199].

plex, since; and the pretty spectre of it blooms at this hour, in vital hawthorn for you, every spring, at Hampton Court" (xxvii, 407).

Nevertheless, despite the later bloom, the original sources of that shape of "vital hawthorn" are, we recall, tinged with a kind of corruption—a corruption that, after the attempted mastery of panoramically Strange Chords has led toward central Repletion, is associated with the difficult-to-maintain (and perhaps, finally, "immoral") True Centre, as it descends along the lines of the vortical labyrinth of absence toward the no less central, though considerably lower, "slime-pit"/"nether-pits." But then with Ruskin, very little is simply sacred: cathedrals—like ideas or designs that incarnate metaphysical attitudes—are supported by buttresses that only "fly" by obvious opposition. And the labyrinth, if not infernal (and, descending along a mathematically constructed spiral toward hell, it occasionally may be), has the potential, as we know, to be as mechanical as the rectilinearity of "right-angled" fretwork, which, at the most, is a version of those suburban or Renaissance "frosts of death." It is as if the house that Jack built were a Greek mausoleum constructed to a point of hideous perfection. We recall, in this spiraling recapitulation that is, itself, close to being a language (with a difference) of return, that the early, "penumbral" Daedalus of *Aratra Pentelici* casts, with the characteristic morality of Ruskinian light, a "lurid shadow" on what is noble—a shadow that transforms the "linear and complex" into a design that is nothing more than a game for the ingenius: "I must show you how the glittering and iridescent dominion of Daedalus prevails; and his ingenuity in division, interposition, and labyrinthine sequence, more widely still. . . . His ingenuity plays around the framework of all the noblest things; and yet the brightness of it has a lurid shadow" (xx, 353).

Casting a shadow that is "lurid," as opposed to a light that is "lucent," the power of Daedalus' art, as Ruskin initially perceives it, is nothing less than "cruel and venomous" (xx, 353). His appeal, we have learned, is not to substance but to an intricacy of form that is mechanical filigree—a monstrous (and threadless) labyrinth. Ingenuity becomes thoughtful bestiality, a characteristic that is as enslaving as the perfect repetition of Victorian bead-making—that entirely specialized (and monotonously linear) performance which is opposite to the vertiginous perception of maddening "interrelation."[15] The price of Daedalean sanity is as high as his perfectly

---

[15] Foucault describes the maddening "interrelation" at the end of the Gothic world, as a time when conventional symbolism begins to "unravel," only to be replaced by an excessively woven presence of branching meanings that becomes the madness, or absence, of the condition of final Illth. Uncannily, Foucault's description of this

centered "altitude." And the "peril of the influence of Daedalus" is, as we recall, not only in the "admiration of the harlequin's jacket more than the hero's strength," but in an "ingenuity," directed from above, that may "even become bestial, an instinct for mechanical labour only, strangely involved with a feverish and ghastly cruelty."

Geometric and perfect, Daedalus' labyrinth is as dehumanized and impersonal as later Gothic tracery is organic and empathetically vital, like hedges of hawthorn.[16] The difference in kinds of intricate

---

process, vortical before centrifuged, might also be of Ruskin's own penultimate language:

> The dawn of madness on the horizon of the Renaissance is first perceptible in the decay of Gothic symbolism; as if that world, whose network of spiritual meanings was so close-knit, had begun to unravel, showing faces whose meaning was no longer clear except in the forms of madness. The Gothic forms persist for a time, but little by little they grow silent, cease to speak, to remind, to teach anything but their own fantastic presence, transcending all possible language (though still familiar to the eye). Freed from wisdom and from the teaching that organized it, the image begins to gravitate about its own madness.
>
> Paradoxically, this liberation derives from a proliferation of meaning, from a self-multiplication of significance, weaving relationships so numerous, so intertwined, so rich, that they can no longer be deciphered except in the esoterism of knowledge. Things themselves become so burdened with attributes, signs, allusions, that they finally lose their own form. Meaning is no longer read in an immediate perception, the figure no longer speaks for itself; between the knowledge that animates it and the form into which it is transposed, a gap widens. It is free for the dream. One book bears witness to meaning's proliferation at the end of the Gothic world, the *Speculum humanae salvationis*, which, beyond all the correspondences established by the patristic tradition, elaborates between the Old and the New Testament, a symbolism not only on the order of prophesy, but deriving from an equivalence of imagery. The Passion of Christ is not prefigured only by the sacrifice of Abraham; it is surrounded by all the glories of torture and its innumerable dreams; Tubal the blacksmith and Isaiah's wheel take their places around the cross, forming beyond all the lessons of the sacrifice of the fantastic tableau of savagery, of tormented bodies, and of suffering. Thus the image is burdened with supplementary meanings, and forced to express them. And dream, madness, the unreasonable can also slip into this excess of meaning   [*Madness and Civilization*, pp. 18-19].

[16] It should perhaps be stressed here again that the Maze as stylized geometry—the Maze as "Greek fret"—is discussed by Ruskin first in *The Seven Lamps of Architecture* (viii, 143), and then later, in *Fors Clavigera* (xxvii, 400). The attitude is fundamentally, with final modification, one of antagonism toward a rectilinear, dehumanized labyrinth that fails to admit both the life and morality of unpredictably curved Gothic imperfection—the fallen and mysterious condition of life itself. Further, it might be recalled that the "central position" is tolerable, "finally," which is to say for a while of childishness, only to the Cock-Robinson-Crusoe child, who, with his conceit, is one of those curiously "geometrical animals" (xxxv, 37) suggestive of a metamorphosis into the incarnation of a kind of mathematics which Ruskin, with his qualified bias against geometry, could hardly have looked back upon with more favor than indulgence.

filigree is the difference not only between varieties of light—"lurid shadow" and "lucent verdure"—but between altitudes: an angelic perfection that is human death and a fallen imperfection that is, if not eternal imperfection, at least vital for a mortal while. It is as if, in the process of making distinctions that are also judgments, Ruskin would not have Newman's irritating Maze mastered by a True Centre that was close to death for, say, Pater's Sebastian van Storck. Further, it is as if that True Centre, which may well be an important part of Greek topography—a place, perhaps, to be both seen and to see from—is a position too elevated to permit easy breathing. And the fall into the Maze of "lucent verdure" is as fundamentally fortunate as it may potentially prove to be irritating to some in its unmechanical and unindexed imperfection. But then, with Ruskin, unsymmetrical abrasions are the vital frictions of life.

In Ruskin's Theatre of Blindness—a Theatre that, including everything "linear and complex," as well as what is daemonically between the Centre and Circumference, is also an ironic location for a kind of morality play of light—the hero of the ghostly model for Hampton Court is not, as we know, the almost daemonically Daedalean Jack, a master of virtually all trades, who, despite his inclusive abilities, is best known for an architecture, like the Minotaur-dominated London, that is more difficult to get out of than to enter—an architectural structure whose entrance, at least in the early stages of the Transformations of the Maze, is more enticing or inevitable than its exit is apparent;[17] instead, we understand the hero to be Theseus, who, as if rising "above" the labyrinthine occasion, does so, in fact, "below."

Thesean mastery, which is not the mastery of altitude or Christian "extrication" from the "mazes of sin and error," is the serial mastery of endurance and process centrifugally extended in what will become a curvilinear time (with the Maze giving shape to that time) capable of defying the implications of long shadows—a process of

[17] A point worth emphasizing. Ruskin's problem, presumably, has never been one of entering but of leaving. The Ruskinian claustrophobe is rarely happy "within." At the least, he requires psychic space. Consequently, he can be read, with considerable justice, as a writer of sought exits, a writer whose energies are employed in the construction, or location, of transcendental space—the search, say, for a window, if not a door: "the question seems not at all to have been about getting in, but getting out again" (xxvii, 408). Yet we may be beginning to wonder whether he, as opposed to his Theseus, wants, in the penultimate (if not the end), to get out after all.

It may be pointed out, in passing, that the entrance into the Hampton Court Maze is the "middle" of an arc, while the exit, as one leaves (if, in fact one either wants to, or does), is on the far left-hand side of that arc.

temporal endurance within proximate space, "returning upon it-self," like a consciousness involved in self-interrogation. Still, as with the awareness of Ariadne's thread, there is the important sense of the exit, the feeling that, in a future tense which may always remain future, "nothing but process" (xxv, 216) will lead to the open space of the Circumference. That that "process," when it becomes "nothing" in open space, will also become the White Si-lence of madness is, at this point, only dimly perceived.

If the Maze before transformation is initially born corrupt by a perfect Daedalean death—the death of a mechanical perfection that may be either angelic or merely ingenius but which, at any rate, does not acknowledge the fall "into" the labyrinth—that Maze is historically humanized for Ruskin (it has, after all, already been autobiographically made ecstatically human in recollected Lucent Verdure) in the significant lecture, "Design in the Florentine School," from *Ariadne Florentina*, which is the bridge between per-fect death and moonlit ecstasy. The Florentine Maze, designed by no Greek blueprints of predicted geometric perfection, is nothing less than life itself—the mediating labyrinth between Centre and Circumference that is a preliminary version of the Theatre of Blindness:

> . . . the labyrinth of life itself, and more and more interwoven
> occupation, become too manifold, and too difficult for me; and
> of the time wasted in blind lanes of it, perhaps that spent in
> analysis or recommendation of the art to which men's present
> conduct makes them insensible, has chiefly cast away [xxii,
> 452].

The spiraling, labyrinthine design of "life itself," as if an increas-ingly spinning "interwoven occupation"—occasionally and perhaps inevitably an "idle arabesque" (xxii, 451) that, returning upon itself as its own antiphonal response, is a series of "blind lanes" for a man who is in the act of becoming more blind to himself than aware of the prospective Exit as anything but a potentially dead end—is also a design which accommodates the fall into a Gothic imperfection that would, at the same time, make allowances for a juggling ex-istence of elongated sanity. Going forward, that labyrinthine design of "life itself," in a serialized version of superimposition, also re-treats, perhaps in order to recover previous errors of necessary irregularity. More succinctly, it is a design that succeeds finally in its failure—as though Hampton Court's left-hand, arcing Exit could not be found. At the least, the fall into the advancing and retreating threads of "interwoven occupation" is fortunately vital, like a fall into the moonlit hedges of Lucent Verdure. The contradictory, inclusive movement, one of "labyrinthine intricacy" that gives coherence and transition to what it encompasses—"through which the grace of order may give continual clue"—connects Hampton Court to a flourishing, serial performance on either page or parchment that incarnates more life than corruption, more irritating "recovery" than grievous "error," though "error" capable of redemption, admitting imperfection, may delay madness:

> The entire body of ornamental design, connected with writing, in the Middle Ages seems as if it were a sensible symbol, to the eye and brain, of the methods of error and recovery, the minglings of crooked with straight, and perverse with progressive, which constitute the great problem of human morals and fate; and when I chose the title for the collected series [*Ariadne Florentina*] of these lectures, I hoped to have justified it by careful analysis of the methods of labyrinthine ornament, which, made sacred by Theseian traditions, and beginning, in imitation of physical truth, with the spiral waves of the waters of Babylon as the Assyrian carved them, entangled in their returns the eyes of men, on Greek vase and Christian manuscript—till they closed in the arabesques which sprang round the last luxury of Venice and Rome   [xxii, 451].

We have perhaps come to understand that Ruskinian life is "itself" the equivalent of his adroit movement in the intricacies of "vital hawthorn"—though without the recalled ecstasy of confined, or guided, maneuvering within Lucent Verdure, which is, among other things, the efficacious, if fallen, experience of "life itself" as presumably seen with the "sight" of mnemonic revisitation. But whether composed of a darkened stage of "blind lanes," or directed toward a circumferential Exit, the "interwoven occupation" of "life itself" is apparently a labyrinth.

But in fact, whether immediate or recollected, life does not have to be a labyrinth. Or rather, it may "have to be," but it is not always labyrinthine. Indeed, it can be nothing at all. Going to the hedges in order to trim them is to approach the death of the abyss, an entirely unfortunate fall, or topographical vacuum of the desert. Life without a design like the Maze at Hampton Court is existence without rules, religion without the rigorous gardening to define a vitality that would otherwise be unchecked. Touching upon Church history, which might well be a recapitulation of autobiography, Ruskin, in a counterpoint between original text and later footnote that is in fact reaffirmation, explains the consequences of trampling the shaping hedges of obligatory irritation: "the struggle which, however necessary, was attended with infinite calamity to the Church. . . . It [the Protestant Reformation] poured new life into the Church, but it did not form or define her anew. In some sort it rather broke down her hedges, so that all they who passed by might pluck off her grapes . . . .

. . . .
⊦ *Rather* so, certainly! Life had been before a labyrinth, but became then, a desert" (xi, 122).

Life without hedges, without the shaping impulse of what at worst is a design of mere mechanical ingenuity and at best is a design that incarnates, at least mnemonically, ecstatic experience, is a desert, like that desert of the "straight way," which, composed of "morasses and mounds of desert," is difficult to trace "even by skilful sight." As a topographical "nothing," it is like the ultimate reduction of Newman's instincts away from specific irritation toward the synoptic grasp of generalization—a reduction of the labyrinth, which is a plenitudinous design (before penultimate Repletion) of "everything linear and complex," to a condition of simplicity that horrifies Ruskin by an almost unvirtuous unity and coherence so austere that it is like the blind White Silence of a page of madness. Excessive presence, having become absence, returns as the presence of madness.

At any rate, the labyrinth, "wearisome," an "idle arabesque," and worse, a "Greek fret" of mechanical, Daedalean death, is also "life itself"—even that labyrinth of an often pernicious urban Centre, in which a dangerously dense unity has the capacity to delight rather than dominate to death: "All was at unity with itself, and the city lay under its guarding hills, one labyrinth of delight" (xii, 311). Either overlying concentricity, like that superimposition of the antithetical which anticipates the simultaneous, or incorporated within both the privilege and infernal density of an immobile Centre, as if imported from the Circumference and then contorted in an act of condensation, the serial design of the Maze has, it would seem, the potential to breed not the mephitic pestilence of the "slime-pit" but rather a condition of "unified" delight, which, perhaps based upon the recollection of the ecstasy of Lucent Verdure,[18] is as necessarily split as a perception of even complementary tenses must be.

---

[18] The notion of Ruskinian ecstasy autonomously in the present tense is close to being an ephemeral fiction; the stains of time, we know, are golden (just as the right kind of past-tense "verdure" is "lucent"), and what might be called the "ecstatic past" is cast in a light that is perhaps both "lucent" and "golden."

But if not always a delight, the Maze at least brings circumferential line to the Centre, the humanized pastoral of sequence to angelic (and dreaded) simultaneity. The recognized necessity of perpetual optical adjustment to a vision of replete homogeneity becomes part of a solution to the burden or problem of central putrefaction—a problem of organization about dense centricity that dissolves with the superimposed design of "life itself," which is a version of the coiling manipulation that occurs within Lucent Verdure, or perhaps, as we shall see, among moonlit streets, where there is no "street which is called Straight." Ruskin's mastery would now be not only "makeshift" but unmasterful; he would have his Strange Chords at least familiar. Or put differently, like Theseus (and unlike Daedalus), he would attempt a qualified mastery, with the aid of low threads, in a fallen interior that holds no more than a memory of his high-flying, trans-European *vol d'oiseau*, which may have been an anticipation of heavenly elevation, if not in fact Christian "extrication."

Yet memory, for one who, close to the end, takes the censored, autobiographical *Praeterita* for the oxygen of existence (the composition of self as the re-creation of semifictional biography), may be, for a while, almost enough. The experience within the Gothically fallen Lucent Verdure of the Hampton Court Maze is one that both elicits an ecstatic response, which is a form of fortunately distanced, mnemonic experience, and anticipates the final doubling of the labyrinth into the "marred music" of Antiphonal Contention. In any case, still impelled by that primary will toward the plenitude of "numerical superiority," Ruskin involves himself in the superimposition of the felicitous and complex design of centrifugal peregrination over the orthodox geometry of concentricity in an act that would bring the almost infinite, circumferential extension of a single line to a space of limitation.

Essentially, one might say that for Ruskin, at least metaphorically, or as a trauma that might be "read" reflexively, all serial "richness" or plenitude is a metamorphosis originating in the presumed (if mnemonically distorted) activities at Hampton Court. But in the transposition from those hedges to an art form other than horticulture and topiary, which with Ruskin is the significant transposition from the shaping experience within the labyrinth to the possible creation of one, Ruskin's early imitation of Sir Walter Scott's "curliewurlies and whigmaleeries" may come closer than the Lucent Verdure of Hampton Court, experienced both in immediacy and recollection, to setting Ruskin's later "pattern of almost everything linear and complex."

Scott's design, with an intricate richness that is more assuaging than irritating, is both involved in the serial procedures of Maze-shaped time—significantly a time turning in upon itself as if wishing to avoid the end, the point where death's "long shadow" becomes substance—and detached from any historical category as confining as centuries:

> . . . all carving came nearly alike to me, so only that it was rich. I carved only for "curliewurlies and whigmarleeries," and was as happy in the fifteenth century as in the tenth. Although already I had begun to draw traceries carefully, and the tab-ernacle work connected with them, for crockets, bosses, or decorated moldings, I used only such rude and confused lines as I had learned to imitate from Prout, and left their places blank in my sketches, to be filled up "out of my head" at home. But richness, the aspect of much work on the building, was essential to my pleasure   [xxxv, 622-23].

Ruskin's version of Scott's "curliewurlies and whigmaleeries" per-mits Ruskin to be "inside" time (as though fallen fortunately into Lucent Verdure) on terms that are almost entirely his own. Further, it suggests a process of maneuvering that has little to do with me-chanical models, but is instead a design of the present tense that joins inspiration to performance with no interval of calculation between. Finally, it would seem that rectilinear time, the early time of orthodox geometries, was in the process of being transformed to a coiling time of immediacy that is perhaps best suited to myopia, if not in fact blindness, in its proximate curvilinearity—this, even as the youthful Ruskin is exploring the distances diagrammed in the straight lines of his elaborate perspective studies.

Unpremeditated spaces are left blank. The elaboration of the Maze is necessarily an act of the present tense. Prophecy, seeing far, perceives the "long shadow" of its own death. And an interior plenitude, filling blank places, comes from "out of my head," almost as if previous patterns for intricacy were fiction, a fraudulent his-tory that immediate ingenuity, operating close to consciousness, would counter. Yet models persist. Despite these present-tense con-cerns, the past holds hard shapes. Ruskin's nascent biography of Scott, in *Fors Clavigera*, is an early draft of the autobiographical *Praeterita*, and Scott's "curliewurlies and whigmaleeries" anticipate Ruskin's own idiosyncratic predilection for vital complexity—a lin-ear complication that, if it is "life itself," is also close to being either excessive or merely foolish. Ruskin's design of life, which is also his Maze of ecstatic recollection, is not always a wise map. Incarnating "error and recovery," the ability to transfigure error in a fallen design that holds within itself the potential for its own resurrection, those labyrinthine lines also speak of a movement that, going everywhere in limited space, goes nowhere of final significance. Farsightedness, rectilinear time, and "long shadows" along streets that might be called "Straight" are all to be avoided, like concluding punctuation to language that would always, if it had its coiling way, be in the act of return.

Filigree, one version of the transforming Maze, is neither wiser nor more vital than the "Greek fret." Yet wisdom, often the product of an extraordinary sense of "interrelation," is often a burden that is not bearable for long. And filigree, a shape of playful, if flamboyant, pastoral, like recalled hedges in moonlight, is a defense—perhaps later, a penultimate defense—against the incipient madness that comes after the breakdown of the attempted mastery of Strange Chords. Still, the transformed Maze as filigree is treated as no more than an appendage—an additional, even embarrassed, passage to *Praeterita* that is, despite its inherent foolishness, nevertheless marked "Keep":

> One great part of the pleasure, depended on an idiosyncrasy
> which extremely wise people do not share—my love of all sorts
> of filigree and embroidery, from hoarfrost to the high clouds.
> The intricacies of virgin silver, of arborescent gold, the weaving
> of birds'-nests, the netting of lace, the basket capitals of By-
> zantium, and most of all the tabernacle work of the French
> flamboyant school, possessed from the first, and possess still,
> a charm for me of which the force was entirely unbroken for
> ten years after the first sight of Rouen; and the fastidious
> structural knowledge of later time does not always repay the
> partial loss of it   [xxxv, 157 n. 3].

Yet Ruskin, despite a tentative admission that is also an appendage marked "Keep," is determined to make his obsession something other than wholly idiosyncratic. Aware of a bias for what he calls foolish intricacy, he sees another kind of complexity—or "intricacy of involution"—as a type of art that, if it admits "error," like the "entire body of ornamental design, connected with writing, in the Middle Ages" (xxii, 451), also suggests the "recovery" of a "living art." And that "living art," losing itself in "error" in order to find itself in "recovery," as if falling to rise, is animated by tracing the "labyrinthine wanderings of a clue," which, we shall soon see, is like artful living in a central city.

In any case, here is Ruskin transforming idiosyncracy into a mythology that even includes "the Greek mind in its best times"— a mythology with elaborate implications touching all art that, unlike Daedalus' predictably dead Maze of mechanical geometry, lives not merely *with* errors but *because* of them:

> You are doubtless all aware that from the earliest times, a system of interwoven ornament has been peculiarly characteristic of northern design, reaching greatest intensity of fancy in the Irish manuscripts represented by the Book of Kells.
> . . . This delight in the embroidering, intricacy of involution,— the labyrinthine wanderings of a clue, continually lost, continually recovered, belongs—though in a more chastised and delicate phase—as much to Indian, to Arabian, to Egyptian, and to Byzantine work, as to that of Norway, and Ireland;—nay, it existed just as strongly in the Greek mind in its best times. . . . But in all living art this love of involved and recurrent line exists,—and exists essentially—it exists just as much in music as in sculpture, and the continually lost and recovered threads and streams of melody in a perfect fugue, correspond precisely in their sweet science of bewildering succession, to the loveliest traceries over the gold of an early missal, or to the fantasies of the stone work   [XIX, 258, 259].

Still the "art" of "involved and recurrent line," no matter how "living" or mythologically "vital," is perhaps not an ultimate justification for a love that can at least be treated as an idiosyncratic appendage that defies amputation. But the foolishness of the Maze has been intentionally overstated. With Ruskin, vertiginous filigree, if occasionally unwise, is almost always more than the autobiographically indulgent doodling of line meandering "out of my head," the entirely subjective and centripetal filling of a blank space with the casual peregrinations of a self in search of either magnification or reflection. "Living art" is living intricacy; flamboyant architecture is a version of a plenitudinous nature whose filigree is an expression of "Omnipotent kindness":

> On fine days, when the grass was dry, I used to lie down on it, and draw the blades as they grew . . . until every square foot of meadow, or mossy back, became an infinite picture and possession to me. . . . The love of complexity and quantity before noticed as influencing my preference of flamboyant to purer architecture, was here satisfied, without qualifying sense of wasted labour, by what I felt to be the constant working of

Omnipotent kindness in the fabric of the food-giving tissues of the earth; nor less, morning after morning, did I rejoice in the traceries and the painted glass of the sky at sunrise [xxxv, 429].

In Ruskinian space, less is rarely more—unless that "less" is a "kindly vacancy," which is the occasional Ruskinian agoraphile's plenitude. More, at least before the more characteristic repletion of claustrophobia—the "too much" that is the functional less than nothing of Illth—imitates a natural order that abhors vacuums. Drawing, filling emptiness, is an act of virtually infinite possession— a possession that is, fundamentally, the infinite transformation of a Maze that comes closer to "kindness" than either irritation or foolishness.

If the seed for Ruskin's transforming Maze is sown at Hampton Court—that seed becoming "vital hawthorn"—the labyrinthine ger- mination, given a plenitudinous justification by an almost infinite nature, is a generative explosion that creates new worlds of stylized metamorphosis. Curiously, despite obvious antecedents (an early autobiography of preoccupation with "mere quantity" and "nu- merical superiority"), the discovery of those new worlds in their various manifestations occurs with the force of revelation, almost as if, having forgotten (or not yet having made autobiographically significant) the Lucent Verdure of Hampton Court, he had under- gone an aesthetic conversion—though with Ruskin, the aesthetic has moral implications—to the coiling or centripetal winding of the "linear and complex":

> But I had never cared for ornamental design until 1850 or '51 I chanced at a bookseller's in a back alley, on a little four- teenth-century Hours of the Virgin, not of refined work, but extremely rich, grotesque, and full of pure colour.
>
> The new worlds which every leaf of this book opened to me, and the joy I had, counting their letters and unravelling their arabesques as if they had all been beaten gold. . . . my love of toil and of treasure, alike getting their thirst gratified in them. For again and again I must repeat it, my nature is a worker's and a miser's; and I rejoice, and rejoice still, in the mere quan- tity of chiselling in marble, and stitches in embroidery [xxxv, 490-91].[19]

[19] Ruskin is dealing in "portable" cathedrals: "For truly a well-illuminated missal is a fairy cathedral full of painted windows, bound together to carry in one's pocket, with the music and the blessing of all its prayers besides" (xxxv, 491).

The implication of this passage is dramatically opposed to the later postcentricity of an essentially centrifugal process of unwinding. And it suggests consequences that can be stressed too much. Still, even with the creation or exploration of "new worlds," which is an "unravelling [of] their arabesques," it is nevertheless as though Ruskin were a Theseus on the way in—a slow-traveling Theseus, having for the moment forgotten Ariadne and in search of no exit at all. Further, it is as if, with his "love of toil and treasure," he were assuaged not by prospects of the circumferential outside except insofar as the Circumference is transformed into a serial centricity—the serial centricity of a concentrated thread that coils and winds like the "nothing but process" of "vital" life itself. The act of "unravelling" is predicated upon the delight of an initial raveling; there is no pastoral or circumferential unwinding, which is what we shall find later, without there being at first a centripetal winding. And Ruskin's initial "unravelling," going nowhere, is closer to a process of winding toward central interiors than centrifugal exploration of "new worlds."

The autobiographical beginnings of the experience of the Maze, both as the directly apprehended occurrence and the mnemonically ecstatic recollection that itself recalls the Daedalean labyrinth of a perfect geometric death beyond "error," prepare for the revelatory discovery of a manuscript in either 1850 or 1851 which involves the consciousness in a centripetal process that Ruskin terms "unravelling"—a process that calls attention to the myopic, if not blind, immediacy of spatial proximity and the present tense.

An unraveling "nothing but process" is a "nothing" that is change—like a language of return, with a perpetual difference. And the recalled ecstasy in the Hampton Court Maze is in the inevitability of its changing surprise, which is not the response sought by those who would exercise the farsightedness of prophecy along the rectilinear lines of a "street which is called Straight." Gothic peace, beyond the manipulation of "vital hawthorn," is also beyond life. And Daedalus' labyrinth, unfallen into Lucent Verdure, in a perfection that apes the condition of the angels, is as infernal as it is deadly. At this time, peace is a Greek life in a "triglyph furrow" that is also a kind of death, just as Gothic pacification is nothing but a prefiguration of death. Peace, at this stage of the Transformations of the Maze, is for the farsighted who would prophetically view the luminous calm of their own end. Yet the "vital hawthorn" at Hampton Court is as insistently alive as "change" itself:

The vital principle is not the love of *Knowledge*, but the love of *Change*. It is that strange *disquietude* of the Gothic spirit that is its greatness; that restlessness of the dreaming mind, that wanders hither and thither among the niches, and flickers feverishly around the pinnacles, and frets and fades in laby-rinthine knots and shadows along the wall and roof, and yet is not satisfied.

The Greek could stay in his triglyph furrow, and be at peace; but the work of the Gothic heart is fretwork still, and it can neither rest in, nor from, its labour, but must pass on, sleep-lessly, until its love of change shall be pacified for ever in the change that must come alike on them that wake and them that sleep [x, 214].

The continual retinal readjustment or "change" that comes from maneuvering within the Lucent Verdure of curvilinear space—a space that hides its beginning from its end—underscores the nec-essarily "vital" attention to the fallen life of the present tense, which is a tense that denies the elevated and demanding "gift" of the "long perspective's" prophecy or farsightedness. That "vital" pres-ent tense is the myopic tense of the Maze not from "above" but from "within"—the Maze-shaped tense of a Theseus who, if he is able to salvage past "error" by future "recovery," understands that his life coils with a thread or clue of immediacy, perhaps guided by the imminence of Atropos as much as either the serial thread-work of Ariadne or the "extrication" of Christian grace. The Gothic disposition behind the necessarily fallen affections for intricate line, which has the partial validation of a plenitudinous nature, is part of a topography of consciousness that, composed entirely of fore-grounds which are like rebeginnings in the serial and myopic mid-dle, is deliberately without a perception of the end. Disposition and chosen optics are connected; the lens is the mind. Amidst Lucent Verdure, there is a kind of transcendence of immediacy. And the distant vision stylized and diagrammed in Ruskin's *The Elements of Perspective* (1859) gives way, after the failure of distance, to a cal-culated (and momentarily life-preserving) myopia, as rectilinear space yields to the curvilinear imitation of Hampton Court.

Finally, the Gothic disposition behind the intricate experience and perpetual transformations of the vital Maze does not admit a finish line. The final pacification will ultimately make "change" changeless, but the "long perspective" will not incorporate the sub-stance that casts the "long shadow" until then. Instead, exploding with flamboyant and potentially centrifugal line, the spirit of the

Circumference, which is incipiently Gothic in that it is a serial territory that is neither elevated nor privileged, attempts to negate
the vestiges of a deadly, perhaps geometrically perfect, central altitude. And True Centres, impossible to endure for long, are themselves locations of the Index, where the chords are strange and the
"cross-references" are *"ad infinitum."* As opposed to the Strange
Chords of attempted mastery and orthodox, if overly ambitious,
geometries, "labyrinthine knots," expressing the "strange disquietude of the Gothic spirit," will peregrinate "hither and thither," as
if to avoid the end with "slow travel" returning upon itself. Those
"labyrinthine knots," colored by Lucent Verdure and superimposed
upon contrasting centripetal concentricity, become the incarnation
of available life, which is as irregular as an anamorphically perceived *Helix virgata.*

Gothic filigree and Lucent Verdure would rescue Jack's rectilinear, Greek labyrinth, its "lurid shadow" that is also "long," from a
fate precisely as unfortunate as an altitudinous and geometrically
hubristic death. The superimposition of heterodox designs, or
eccentric, anamorphically perceived geometries over orthodox geometries that are (logo)-concentric and rectilinear, occurs at a
ground level that, as though for a "Naked foot/That shines like
snow," is the Gothic altitude of convention for a fallen man who
may rise again—at least in the recovered "error"[20] of a transforming
memory.

[20] A life and death matter, labyrinthine "error and recovery" (xxii, 451) in Ruskin
also speak of madness and sanity. "Error," capable of "recovery," admits the necessary imperfection of the irrational, and with that accommodation delays the arrival
of Ruskin's "error" that, "blind to itself," is finally beyond the "recovery" that is only
"makeshift" mastery. Somewhat analogously, Foucault observes the madness which
is the persistence of a "notable error," without exit or "extrication," that imprisons
the self in the "circle of an erroneous consciousness":

> Error is the other element always present with the dream, in the classical def-
> inition of insanity. The madman, in the seventeenth and eighteenth centuries,
> is not so much the victim of an illusion, of a hallucination of his senses, or a
> movement of his mind. He is not *abused*; he *deceives himself.* If it is true that on
> the one hand the madman's mind is led on by the oneiric arbitrariness of
> images, on the other, and at the same time, he imprisons himself in the circle
> of an erroneous consciousness: "We call madman," Sauvages was to say, "those
> who are actually deprived of reason or who persist in some notable error; it
> is the constant *error* of the soul manifest in its imagination, in its judgments,
> and in its desires, which constitutes the characteristics of this category   [*Mad-
> ness and Civilization*, p. 104].

Chapter Seven

Capricious Sinuousities:
Venice and the City
as Mind

A. White Clues: Instincts for the Exit

The act of "unravelling their arabesques" is, we know, the para-doxical, centripetal raveling of "slow travel"—the joy of the laby-rinthine "nothing but process," which is, at this stage of the Trans-formations of the Maze, an intricately inevitable motion that leisurely winds toward the central interior of potential Repletion. Still, integrated within concentricity, the Maze, like a Museum, would domesticate that Centre, making it habitable by its slowly extensive and slackly serial procedure, while, at the same time, transforming the terror of the rectilinear "long shadow" into the figment of someone else's imagination by a kind of "transcendental myopia" (or, perhaps inverted, an enforced immanence of dim perception) that approaches blindness. The winding entrance into the Maze predicts the Thesean necessity of an unwinding Exit, which may be an end, a new beginning, or the ambiguous null-set's absence/presence of White Silence.

Presumably, the notion of a conventional ending is anathema in Ruskinian design. The final period would become the series of addenda of Stendhal's *De l'amour*—or closer to home, the tacked-on "Notes and Correspondences" that begins to follow the letters of *Fors Clavigera*. Textual conclusion is the prophecy of death. To write the final period is to feel the substance, the rectilinear weight, of death's "long shadow." Syntactical periods in the middle of a text, lacking force, become nothing more than transitional punc-tuation—strong commas or anticipations of new capitals. In the labyrinth, the language of conjunctions is a necessity. There is always a curvilinear expectation of origins, of syntactical rebegin-nings that are very much like a new turn within "Dantesque alleys" of Lucent Verdure. Syntax aspires toward the self-perpetuation of futurity. And in the end, with *Praeterita*, there is a new beginning, which is also an old beginning, with fresh paper taking up where old life has left off.

But before that end or rebeginning, with its "language of return," the possibility of future autobiography is something to be accomplished by an aspiration, however dimly perceived, that goes beyond the Maze's next turn, which is the origin of a new sentence. Even early, though after the experience within Hampton Court, there is the impulse for "an escape forward": "Escape, Hope, Infinity, by whatever conventionalism sought, the desire is the same in all, the instinct constant" (IV, 83). Still, it is possible to view the landscape of Hope (a postcircumferential Promise[d] Land), if it is to be an end in itself, with qualms.

Like "clues" that are "labyrinthine wanderings," the Hampton Court dance in the moonlight, which is the assuagement (especially in recollection) of a linear involvement that is both fortunately fallen and necessarily myopic, seems to require a way out that may, after all, only be a fiction of the Exit. There is at least the sense of another kind of light far beyond the next turn of Lucent Verdure and Gothic immediacy. Perhaps prophecy is not inevitably an elevated Greek perfection that sees its own death. And if not, what is presumably needed, after the experience within the Maze, is precisely that "conventionalism" which is a constant "instinct" for the Exit—an instinct for the centrifugal, Thesean "escape forward" that must include, even in its sense of futurity, the curvilinear "nothing but process" of present tense negotiations.

In the intermediate stages of the Transformations of the Maze, the end, which is where and when the "long shadow" will be traced to its source, would itself be transformed, by an act of imaginative will, into at least an instinctive search for an Exit. Any myopic "advance" of filigree toward a conditional futurity that Ruskin might enjoy is a partial solution to the central density resulting from the Parallel Advance and Strange Chords of an extraordinary peripheral vision that would master what it can barely include. Labyrinthine "clues," which might be called serial clues of the conjunction, become a centrifugal answer to True Centres that may, in fact, be "mephitic cancers."

The Parallel Advance prepares for, if it does not necessitate, a labyrinthine leave-taking. The way out, the way toward those problematic spaces that are "of" the future and "beyond" the Maze, must be as narrow and curvilinear as flamboyant line—that line of cautiously narrow convolution, which, unraveling in the present for the sake of the future, is the essence of the Lucent Verdure of recollected pastoral that mnemonically precludes horizontal and peripheral responsibilities. To exit with centrifugal filigree is not only to be myopic but to wear blinders as well; the vision on the way "out" is as narrow as it is nearsighted. As long as he can feel the thread, Theseus might just as well be blind. And a Thesean Ruskin, when and if the thread has been cut and the "clues" either lost entirely or submerged, may be blind even to himself. Ariadne's thread may become Arachne's web and the serial clues of immediacy may not be prophetic enough. In an early incarnation, before the doubling of labyrinths, the Theatre of Blindness may be an essentially present-tense version of the mnemonic pastoral of Lucent Verdure. But for now, that is speculation dependent upon, among other things, the eventual condition of thread and clues.

Maps suggest the mastery of Strange Chords—the elevated grasp of a situation from a Centre that is "true" before it is "mephitic." To have a map that will lead toward the Exit is to dominate experience rather than be dominated by it. Further, it is to achieve the geometric and mechanical altitude of Jack—an altitude in which the unfailing or perfect Daedalean death is implicit. Nevertheless, one might assume that with a map, the playful involvement in the process of the present might predict a later present that would be something other than a dead end. And, in fact, Ruskin was as attracted to maps as he was to attempted mastery.[1] But the Gothic disposition, which is Ruskin's curvilinear disposition of "vital" life, is without the fatal elevation of maps. The height of cathedral towers is a necessary product of an essentially fallen and irregular condition. Now, at this stage of labyrinthine metamorphosis, the mastery of maps (as well as bird's-eye views) would be banished, along with the extensive inclusion of the rectilinear field; the straight lines of altitude, width, and distance anticipate more despair than hope. Salvation, if it is to come, will be incarnated in the solution of the labyrinthine "clues" of immediacy.

Like maps, the vantage points of altitude—once as privileged as "the rectitude of the verticals" (I, 238)—would attempt to master central cities. Problems are compounded. To be lost in Lucent

---

[1] As the editors of the Library Edition point out, quoting W. G. Collingwood, the map-as-itinerary held an important place in Ruskin's affections, as did the map-as-travel diary. Plans and recollections are combined on sheets of six inches:

> When a boy of sixteen he made for himself a set of geological maps in preparation for his journey of 1835; and throughout his life he collected maps wherever he went. "He kept them in a special set of drawers in his study, some mounted on spent diagram-cards from his lectures, and some dropping to pieces with wear and tear. . . . The Ordnance Survey is fully represented, but too much was put into these beautiful six-inch sheets, he has coloured them fancifully and vigorously, to get clear divisions of important parts." To a map-lover such as Ruskin the ordinary map was an abomination. It was too full and too empty [xxvii, lxxi].

Verdure is one thing; to be lost in the mixed or superimposed "geometries" of a labyrinthine central city, without even a sense of the Exit, is quite another. The tight complexity of Venice, which, in *The Stones of Venice*, is an early, objectified version of a kind of urban autobiography—the central city as Cock-Robinson-Crusoe self—is momentarily mastered, as we know, by the altitude of St. Mark's, an altitude that brings synoptic coherence to the narrow irritation of streets that are not called "Straight." Apparently, without the necessary evil of altitude, the traveler would be lost in the myopic curvilinearity of the Centre, rather than either assuaged or found. Nevertheless, the farsightedness of Greek perfection must be avoided in order to salvage existence and sanity.

Yet "within" the concentricity of Venice, as if "within" the fallen pastoral of the recollection of Lucent Verdure, there is a solution to both the problems of maps and the altitudes of the bird's-eye view. There is an alternative to St. Mark's ambiguous mastery that predicts its own downfall—an alternative that is even lower than the happily fallen "vital hawthorn" at Hampton Court. The farsighted map (or map of the overview), which is the perception of the bird's eye that is close to an angel's, has felicitously descended to the level of the fortunate imperfection inherent in Gothic myopia. With the later Transformations of the Maze, the Exit that might be achieved by either St. Mark's altitude or maps from "above" has instead become dependent upon a nearsighted, labyrinthine "clue" of conjunction "within" that brings mastery especially to pedestrians. Amidst the apparently contradictory design—or design of superimposition—of labyrinthine concentricity, one can be "found" enough to be able to endure one's lost, if not entirely "blind," condition. Merely the "sense" of the Exit makes the fallen and myopic condition at least as endurable as an "error" that will eventually find "recovery."

Here, in any case, is Ruskin's Venetian traveler, who might well be, as we shall see, moving through the "involution of alleys" of Ruskin's own troubled consciousness—maneuvering "through," but more importantly "from," the city's claustrophobic and plenitudinous centricity, with his "fallen map" that speaks of a kind of salvation via the solution of pedestrian "clues." As though instructed by not entirely "blind guides," he finds himself propelled by feet that can never walk on the perfectly "Straight" way of water:

> . . . to those, however, who seek it [SS. Apostoli] on foot, it becomes geographically interesting from the extraordinary involution of the alleys leading to it from the Rialto. In Venice,

the straight road is usually by water, and the long road by land; but the difference of distance appears, in this case, altogether inexplicable. Twenty or thirty strokes of the oar will bring a gondola from the foot of the Rialto to that of Ponte SS. Apostoli; but the unwise pedestrian, who has not noticed the white clue beneath his feet, may think himself fortunate if, after a quarter of an hour's wandering among the houses behind the Fondaco de' Tedeschi, he finds himself anywhere in the neighborhood of the point he seeks. With much patience, however, and modest following of the guidance of the marble thread, he will at last emerge   [x, 295-96].

Engaged in intricate performance, that traveler, no less than Ruskin himself, is in love with filigree and embroidery, as well as "interesting" geography—an affection that we know "extremely wise men do not share." But in that condition of fallen "foolishness," which is also a kind of humility, there resides, as if incarnate, the traveler's survival that is dependent upon the conditional futurity of a sense of the Exit. Yet in passing, it might be noted that the Ruskinian traveler's survival is not always Ruskin's. Writing *The Stones of Venice*, shortly after his marriage to Effie Gray, Ruskin might well be said to be married more to a Venice that is like his New Jerusalem, "prepared as a bride," than to Effie—more to the central Rialto than to Effie, who is little more than a "farthest extremity,"[2] in

---

[2] See John D. Rosenberg's *The Darkening Glass*, p. 80. The syntax of Ruskin's urban or architectural marriage can be seen in his labyrinthine description of St. Mark's Edenic, yet serpentine facade, which virtually, ending where it begins, at the Cross, is a "continuous chain of language and of life" that he does not seem anxious to leave:

> —sculpture fantastic and involved, of palm leaves and lilies, and grapes and pomegranates, and birds clinging and fluttering among the branches, all twined together into an endless network of buds and plumes; and in the midst of it, the solemn forms of angels, sceptred, and robed to the feet, and leaning to each other across the fates, their figures indistinct among the gleaming of the golden ground through the leaves beside them, interrupted and dim, like the morning light as it faded back among the branches of Eden, when first its fates were angel-guarded long ago. And round the walls of the porches there are set pillars of variegated stones, jasper and porphyry, and deep-green serpentine spotted with flakes of snow, and marbles, that half refuse and half yield to the sunshine, Cleopatra-like, "their bluest veins to kiss"—the shadow, as it steals back from them, revealing line after line of azure undulation, as a receding tide leaves the waved sand; their capitals rich with interwoven tracery, rooted knots of herbage, and drifting leaves of acanthus and vine, and mystical signs, all beginning and ending in the Cross; and above them, in the broad archivolts, a continuous chain of language and of life—   [x, 82-83].

It is as if St. Mark's facade would be the architecture of an idealized city, its streets and buildings—New Jerusalem as a Maze that would be transformed no more.

which case the sense of the Exit is a centrifugal fiction. That intricate performance, which is fallen "foolishness," will become, despite the allegiance to the central Rialto-bride, when transformed from "marble" and consciousness into a verbal process of serial conjunction, Ruskin's own temporary style of survival in the face of penultimately replete Strange Chords and the excessive "nothing" of Illth that lies ominously, in its White Silence, beyond.

The exact nature of the key to the deciphering of the "extraordinary involution of the alleys," which is contrasted to the "straight road" of the water, is explained, fittingly enough, in a "footnote" which makes a case for the hitherto "unwise pedestrian" to pay attention to something very much like a foolishly necessary filigree. Serpentine intricacy, transformed into a "clue" of "white marble," speaks of the future, connecting Circumference with the Centre, the "farthest extremity" of Venice with the Rialto:

> Two threads of white marble, each about an inch wide, inlaid in dark grey pavement, indicate the road to the Rialto from the farthest extremity of the north quarter of Venice. The peasant or traveller, lost in the intricacy of the pathway in this portion of the city, cannot fail, which thenceforward he has nothing to do but to follow, though their capricious sinuousities will try his patience not a little   [x, 296].

With characteristic Gothic disposition, Ruskin, making a strength out of an apparent weakness, wisdom out of fallen foolishness, is preparing for a form of pastoral—a pastoral of "capricious sinuousities" that is like those other "Dantesque alleys" at Hampton Court. Yet there is a difference. The "capricious sinuousities" of "two threads" offer more than the recollected experience of serial plenitude and myopic delight within Lucent Verdure. Located or "found," they offer, along with a kind of pedestrian mastery, the possibility of an Exit as well as the inevitability of the entrance. The future tenses of prophecy are joined to the Maze's already existing memory and myopic immediacy. With "clues" of "white marble" at ground level, the Maze has now become a design of low (and therefore "high") grace, whose serial prediction is coherence at a pedestrian Gothic altitude, and whose better, if one is to survive, instincts, like those implicit in the labyrinthine Museum, are "for the arrangement of pure line, in labyrinthine intricacy, through which the grace of order may be a continual clue" (xxii, 451).

The physical involvement in the fallen "capricious sinuousities" of the "continual" clue-yielding white marble is fundamentally a circumferential involvement that is imitated from "within" at the potentially "mephitic" True Centre. At first, as with Museums, it seems as if the "inside" might be "tamed" by following the act of Ruskin's ambitious and avaricious parenthesis and turning the "outside in." At first, it is as if a breath of fresh air might be imported in the form of a new line of possible salvation. For without those playful "capricious sinuousities," which are to become lines of centrifugally linear pastoral, central plenitude leads to a perception of the penultimate and intricately related Strange Chords. And the Repletion of that attempted mastery is nothing less than the inevitable preparation for the naked night watch, the screaming peacocks, and that mirror behind which, after the departure of the black cat, lies the terrible vacuity of White Silence, as of ripped immanence, the muteness arrived at by white stones.

But eventually it would appear that fresh air cannot be imported, that fresh air, having gone stale "within," must be found amidst the "provincial" location of originally fresh air. The circumferential source of flamboyant line, which is like both the sacrament of Athena's breath or oxygen and the "vital" life that has been lost in centripetal motion, is energetically sought, as though even the centrifugal process toward the "outside" could temporarily resurrect a "pedestrian" line. After the labyrinthine winding process—the coiling attempt at central domestication—there is the labyrinthine process of unwinding, the Ariadne-guided movement for the Exit. And the consequences of that movement, which is like the tracing of the spiraling *Helix virgata* from interior origins to the surface of the exterior shell, cannot be known until arrival. We know that "the labyrinth of life itself," an "interwoven occupation," may well be composed, finally, of "blind lanes" (xxII, 452) that are dead ends. Yet, the centrifugal sense of the Exit, even if the Exit proves to be a "farthest extremity" that is a "blind," dead end, might be written about by a bewildered, occasionally lost traveler in a curvilinear syntax incorporating both Ruskin's circumferential instincts and his myopia: in order for that problematically lost traveler/writer to be "found," like an "error" that has been "recovered," the future must be anticipated, but it cannot, in any case, be seen. Before Ruskin is unfortunately blind to himself, he is fortunately blind, by virtue of his recollected fall into the Maze of Lucent Verdure, to a future that must nevertheless be sensed.

Almost always himself antiphonal, like his "choral landscape," Ruskin, lost as traveler/writer, is almost found, like an "error" of admitted irrationality that can almost be recovered in a necessary condition of imperfect sanity. Blind, he can almost see. Or at least he can sense the point that will, tentatively, enable him to find himself—although that location, somewhere within the present-tense, labyrinthine Theatre of Blindness, might be as "spinning" as the infernally central squirrel-cage of London which has served only as centrifugal impetus. The "spinning" origin may, in fact, predict the pirouetting just before the end, when Ariadne's spun thread is penultimately severed.

B. Colubrine Chains:
The Maze of Consciousness

Ruskin's Venice is a mind. More accurately, it is his own mind, and, as has been suggested, *The Stones of Venice* is a kind of urban autobiography of consciousness—an anticipation of the autobiography of the censored self, *Praeterita*. Similar designs, in different locations, perform similar functions. Urban planning is a way of organizing the mind. But the failing architecture of the House of Usher—its deconstruction—is a way of going mad. Topographical maps, taken too seriously, as if something more than the aerial view of a bird's flight, predict insanity. And thought, having advanced with parallel extension, creates problems of overpopulation, the central density of that squirrel-cage turning forever on its own axis. Like either an overcrowded city or an Index that delivers "cross-references *ad infinitum*," the mind's problem is both the "press of coincident thought" (*Diaries*, p. 1121), which is an act of perception, and the unwinding of what has been panoramically perceived, which is the necessarily serial act of expression that is like following "continual clues." He writes a favorite correspondent, Susan Beever: "I was greatly flattered and petted by a saying in one of your last letters, about the difficulty I had in unpacking my mind. That is true; one of my chief troubles at present is with the quantity of things I want to say at once" (xxxvii, 111).

Simply, there is no parallel exit from a mind burdened with the "quantity of things I want to say at once"—a quantity that is either a version of overpopulation or especially dense and vertical architecture. With something to express, Ruskin cannot commute "all at once" what he has to say to a blank page that is like suburban space. Although the simultaneous perception of the eyes is at least a possibility, words, it would seem, are as serial as threads of white marble, whose only sense of either the future or something other than themselves is a clue that is "continual." If perception, albeit a theoretical and highly demanding perception that is impossible either in the case of "reading" St. Peter's or language on a page, may be "all at once," expression—the unpacking or "unravelling" of what has been perceived—occurs, most likely, with a serial narrowness.

And since Ruskin's mind, in the later stages of the Transformations of the Maze, is an overcrowded city in need of fresh air and new space, it is also a place where the circumferential movement of Fancy occurs, which, as a process of thought, proceeds step by step, or "point by point," as if by "continual clue," instead of "all at once," like the perception of panoramic sight of the demanding amalgamations of a central Imagination moving toward either Strange Chords or a stultifying sameness. The Fancy, pirouetting on the outskirts of the mind, running circumferentially "hither and thither, and round and about to see more and more, bounding merrily from point to point, and glittering here and there, but necessarily never settling, if she settle at all, on a point only, never embracing the whole" (IV, 258)—that Fancy, "necessarily never settling," perhaps impelled by an urge toward transcendental discriminations, imitates the serial act of departing expression from a mind approaching the replete homogeneity of insanity.

The lines of Fancy, "bounding merrily," are pastoral lines of the Exit that would centrifugally release the pressures of a highly concentrated Imagination, just as the superimposed Maze of contrary designs, bringing extensive series to simultaneity, would attempt to tame the central demands of excessive privilege and responsibility: the fallen, step by step lines of the "white clues" of conjunction, whose mastery is necessarily and happily "pedestrian," are also lines, like Ariadne's thread, that make the central "inside" at least temporarily bearable by making the circumferential "outside" a Thesean possibility. But the path of apparent survival to the "farthest extremity" of the "outside," which is the path that seriously follows the "capricious sinuousities" of white marble, makes no immediate attempt to accommodate the panoramic perception of the enveloping Circumference.

In any case, perception is not expression; arrival is not leavetaking; centripetal winding only predicts centrifugal unwinding; and writing, which is the externalizing search for an Exit that is a blank page to be filled before it is the impossible-to-fill blank page of final Illth and White Silence, is the elaboration and extension of simultaneous centricity to the condition of the serial slack of a line of syntax, whose conjunctions impel the traveler/writer with the urgency of "white clues." The "wide circumference" toward which Ruskin's language travels—as sensing the Exit, he moves toward the "farthest extremity"—can be panoramically perceived but only sinuously expressed: "this morning so full of so useful thoughts that I can't set down one, they push each other round in my head. As a man gets older, he takes in all knowledge at a wide circumference, but can only speak it from his little mouth in the middle like an echinus: and his mouth is no bigger than it used to be" (*Diaries*, p. 869).

Just as Ruskin would fill empty space with the equivalent of Scott's "curliewurlies" that come, as we recall, "out of my head" (xxxv, 623), so those "curliewurlies"—Hampton Court brought to the blank page—are the only lines that can get "out" of a head with a mouth no bigger than that of an echinus, or from the tip of a pen whose diameter is only slightly smaller. What was once parallel extension, now on the way "out" toward the fresh air of a blank page, has been reduced to the serial procedure of intricate line. Shortly, we shall come across the language of the Exit, incarnating the style of the tightrope, which is also, somewhat paradoxically, the language of return with a difference. That language, holding the capacity to release infernal pressure, becomes an imitation of the recollected and ecstatic shaping experience in Hampton Court—a mnemonic experience that has perhaps been given the reflexive significance of an imaginative autobiographer. The Rus-kinian syntax of both exit and return, without the elevation of synoptic generalization, becomes proximate, sinuous and "pedes-trian," only incorporating the peripheral by touching upon its "point to point" and step-by-step multiplicity, as though the trav-eler/writer were viewing St. Peter's or Rome without visiting express points of "lionisation." A process of rational and necessary division of perception itself becomes the serial expression of the echinus's mouth. And the echinus's mouth, through which Ruskin would find expression, is as narrow as the spiraling line of the shell of the *Helix virgata* in which Ruskin might himself live.

Following something less formal and predictable than either itin-erary or map, Ruskin, led more by circumstance than premedita-tion, seeks a ground-level Exit from an imperfectly Gothic altitude that is, at first "curiously," more a lowly serpentine movement to-ward solution, if not salvation, than one that is either avian or angelic. The farsightedness of rectilinearity and altitude is, we know, Jack's suicide, the "fall" of the house that he has built, which is not as sturdy as a shell that spirals like either the "defensive exit" of the snail or the slithering "advance" of a snake: "The opening of the second volume of *Deucalion* with a lecture on Serpents may seem at first a curiously serpentine mode of advance toward the fulfillment of my promise. . . . But I am obliged now in all things to follow in great part the leadings of circumstance" (xxvi, 295-96). Those "leadings of circumstance" are directed toward the "farthest extremity" of circumferential emptiness.

"Advancing" with serpentine motion toward an Exit that may justifiably be called Ariadne's, with a curvilinearity that might be called the earthly Athena's[3] (though we must remember that Atro-

---

[3] Ruskin notes the motion of "serpentine advance" that is, in fact, an imitation of his own style: "A snail and a worm go on their bellies as much as a serpent, but the essential motion of a serpent is undulation,—not up and down, but from side to side." He asks either himself or the reader (though at this time there may be no difference): "Why should not it go straight the shortest way?" (xxvi, 316). Here Ruskin is wondering about not only his own style, but the way of "white marble."

Athena, it should be pointed out, is herself both vertically and laterally antiphonal, as if the incarnation of her own superimposition. She is associated with both the air (or oxygen), as a bird, and the earth, as the snake. Yet even the snake has antiphonal qualities beyond its seemingly digressive, "side to side" movement. It is both a symbol of evil as well as an agent of healing. But before all else, Ruskin is fascinated by the nature of the "syntax" of the "serpentine advance," which is a syntax of "error" and "recovery" that, for a while, accommodates both imperfection and the irrational, an accommodation that is itself not only "rational" but "perfectly necessary":

> Why that horror? We all feel it, yet how imaginative it is, how disproportioned to the real strength of the creature! There is more poison in an ill-kept drain,—in a pool of dishwashings at a cottage door,—than in the deadliest asp of Nile. . . . But that horror is of the myth, not of the creature. There are myriads lower than this, and more loathsome, in the scale of being; the links between dead matter and animation drift everywhere unseen. But it is the strength of the base element that is so dreadful in the serpent; it is the very omnipotence of the earth. That rivulet of smooth-silver—how does it flow, think you? It literally rows on the earth, with every scale for an oar; it bites the dust with the ridges of its body. Watch it, when it moves slowly;—A wave, but without wind! a current, but with no fall! all the body moving at the same instant, yet some of it to one side, some to another, or some forward, and the rest of the coil backwards; but all with the same calm will and equal way—no contraction, no extension; one soundless, causeless march of sequent rings, and spectral procession of spotted dust, with dissolution in its fangs, dislocation in its coils. Startle it;—the winding stream will become a twisted arrow;—the wave of poisoned life will lash through the grass like a cast lance. . . . It is a divine hieroglyph of the demoniac power of the earth,—of the entirely earthly nature. As the bird is the clothed power of the air, so this is the closed power of the dust; as the bird the symbol of the spirit of life, so this is the grasp and sting of death [xix, 362-63].

Yet, as with the superimposition of contraries,

> there is a power in the earth to take away corruption, and to purify (hence the very fact of burial, and many uses of earth, only lately known); and in this sense, the serpent is a healing spirit,—the representative of Aesculapius and of Hygieia; and is a sacred earth-type in the temple of the Dew;—being there especially a symbol of the native earth of Athens; so that its departure from

pos, with her shears, is always above[4] and, further, that the Exit may have a diameter no wider than the point of a pen), Ruskin reduces expressed thought to the linear progress-as-egress of a snake that may be a metamorphosis of both Theseus and Ruskin (or a Thesean Ruskin as traveler/writer), on the centrifugal way out of the Maze. Perhaps, though it is doubtful, the snake, Theseus, or Ruskin, may travel with "Devil-speed instead of God-speed."[5] Still, that "speed" *should* be "slow travel." And if, as we shall see, the logic of that necessarily low syntax, which, though not "extricated" by Christian grace, is also high, follows the peregrinations of the serpent (which is like the tracing of pedestrian "clues" from the central Rialto), so Ruskin, as though magnifying or making his models life-size, would have the entire body of his work imitate the binding of threads that have achieved the strength of serpentine "chains":

> I would rather indeed have made this the matter of a detached essay, but my distinct books are far too numerous already; and if I could only complete them to my mind, would in the end rather see all of them fitted into one colubrine chain of consistent strength, than allowed to stand in any broken or diverse relations   [xxvi, 296].

The chainlike logic of the snake, thin, capable of fitting through openings as small as the mouth of an echinus—labyrinthine openings that are like doors leading from a centrally "mephitic" perception of the simultaneous—is essentially a "nothing but process" of immediacy. At first, it seems to be a movement almost entirely within an uncalculated present tense that possesses only the history and prophecy that can be found in the "error and recovery" of Gothic design. But Ruskin, employing the same pattern, uses multiple tenses, rewriting (or reexperiencing) original effect. And the

---

the temple was a sign to the Athenians that they were to leave their homes. And then, lastly, as there is a strength and healing in the earth, no less than in the air, so there is conceived to be a wisdom of earth no less than a wisdom of the spirit; and when its deadly power is killed, its guiding power becomes true; so that the Python serpent is killed at Delphi, where yet the oracle is from the breath of the earth   [xix, 364].

[4] Atropos, that "daintiest and watchfullest housewife," is also the more sinister Jael-Atropos, who is "Fortune, the Nail-Bearer."

[5] In "Gothic work," which is not the whole story, Ruskin has the serpent as the devil, and we recall, as he says in *Fors*, that "in this very tale of Theseus, as Chaucer tells it,—having got hold, by ill luck only of the later and calumnious notion that Theseus deserted his savior-mistress, he wishes him Devil-speed instead of Godspeed" (xxvii, 405-6).

later Ruskinian mind, as the present-tense Theatre of Blindness, which in this case is the antiphonal consciousness between Centre and Circumference, is an imitation of that fallen design of Lucent Verdure at Hampton Court, which, in its curvilinear intricacy, is felicitously recalled in the golden-stained light of memory. The sense, if not sight, of the Exit "finds" the traveler/writer in a condition that might otherwise be hopelessly "lost." But if the Exit must be sought, it must be done so without any established notion of a "beforehand" that is more than "clues" of white marble or "veins of the mine as they branch" both "here and there":

> . . . the labour of seeking must often be methodless, following the veins of the mine as they branch, or trying for them where they are broken. And the mine, which would now open into the souls of men, as they govern the mysteries of their handicrafts, being rent into many dark and divided ways, it is not possible to map our work beforehand, or resolve on its directions. We will not attempt to bind ourselves to any methodical treatment of our subject, but will get at the truths of it here and there, as they seem extricable [XIX, 59].

In the act of exploring a mine that is both like a mind and Venice itself—the veins of ore being equivalent not only to the "serpentine mode of advance" of a lecture but also to a consciousness that attempts to deal with Repletion in the same way as either "clues" of white marble amidst central architecture or a "colubrine chain" holding together and making sense of an ambitious work—the end of that act, which, were it more orthodox, would be predictable by an uncharacteristically "methodical treatment," is, in fact, unpredictable. If the Exit, which may only be preliminary to the end, is sensed, that end, it is becoming apparent, is either blind or an "act" that Ruskin would have disappear.

Yet before it is at least blind, the path of that end travels both "here" and "there," from "side to side," like a snake. And since the finding of the "there" is a process that would occur most felicitously with a nearsighted Ruskin wearing blinders (dispelling shadows not only "long" but "wide"), the peripheral, as opposed to that distantly rectilinear "there," can only be discovered by extensively employing the horizontality implicit in "capricious sinuousities." Further, perhaps one can say that death's encroaching shadow is "long," while the shadow of madness is essentially wide, and that, with Ruskin, the unguarded perception of both leads to penultimate Repletion and final madness. But concerned now, if not always, with the "here"[6]—with what is as close at hand (or foot) as the next unexplored turn of a labyrinth that is like the unprophetic experience of self-perpetuating "life itself"—Ruskin, in order to get to a "there" that may be a location of the "farthest extremity," as well as the fresh air that is more important than food, can only do so by attending to the "here" beneath the foot.

Atropos is immediately above, and Ariadne's thread, which promises a circumferential "there" that might also be a location for a spiritual Rose, is at no more than the "extremity" of a long arm's length. The "here" is a preliminary "there." The "colubrine chain" of the traveler/writer's "serpentine advance," which, at times represents a kind of weaving, is also the "spinning" digression of "capricious sinuousities," and at best a link-by-link process. But the "warp and woof" of the Maze of Ruskin's consciousness may, in the future, include a perceived thread of autobiography and history more intricate than lines of Lucent Verdure, the thread of Ariadne, the "clues" of white marble, or a "colubrine chain." Then (and "there"), filigree—or more specifically, "inlaid threads"—would be wisdom incarnate: "Now I hope some day to trace out a few threads of this history. . . . I cannot disentangle for you even the simplest of the inlaid threads of this tapestry of the fates of men that here lies beneath us" (xix, 434).[7] If the threads of fate are to be eventually

---

[6] There is, as has been indicated, another Ruskin, the significant Ruskin of *The Failing Distance*, who would sacrifice any pedestrian or fallen foreground for an elevated distance. Basically, this is an early, farsighted Ruskin who is involved in a transcendence of distance rather than a myopic transcendence of perpetual surprise. Briefly, the distinction has something to do with the difference between a loss of self-consciousness and the *Helix virgata* loss of sight of death's long shadow, which, presumably, would be replaced, at least for a "spinning" while, by the curvilinear labyrinth of "life itself."

[7] Still, the "fates of men" are often, as suggested in "Athena Keramitis" from *The Queen of the Air*, the apparent fates of a "lacertine breed"—the "clues" of which can be found even on sacred paper, as once the original "clue" could be found amidst innocent vegetation:

In the Psalter of S. Louis itself, half of its letters are twisted snakes; there is scarcely a wreathed ornament, employed in Christian dress, or architecture, which cannot be traced back to the serpent's coil; and there is rarely a piece of monkish decorated writing in the world, that is not tainted with some ill-meant vileness of grotesque—nay, the very leaves of the twisted ivy-pattern of the fourteenth century can be followed back to wreaths for the foreheads of bacchanalian gods. And truly, it seems to me, as I gather in my mind the evidences of insane religion, degraded art, merciless war, sullen toil, detestable pleasure, and vain or vile hope, in which the nations of the world have lived since first they could bear records of themselves—it seems to me, I say, as if the race itself were still half-serpent, not extricated yet from its clay; a lacertine

disentangled, if the end is not to be dead and blind, perhaps Ruskin's "mine" should be a marble quarry.

C. The Gothic Anomaly: Peripheral Shadows
of Madness and Narrow Caution

The "curiously serpentine" advance/exit that Ruskin effects is one that, adapted to the narrow mouth of the echinus, vitiates the panoramic extension of Repletion simultaneously perceived. The wanting breadth of vision leaves one first virtually breathless (as if there were oxygen only in the "farthest extremity" of the horizon) and then finally witless in the same way that Ruskin's imitation of Scott's "curliewurlies" would turn the rectilinearity of the "long shadow" into nothing but an avoidable thought. Its narrowness is ironically, after the ambitious perception and winding process that would condescend to "narrow caution" (x, 191), a fall away from both angelic perfection and Jack's altitudinous and optical death— a fall toward the irregularity of "error and recovery" that is mere mortal existence chronicled most effectively in a language of turn and return, like a traveler/writer, recording his experiences, who is "lost" in order to be "found."

Ruskin's initial attitude toward the expressive narrowness offered at last by the unwinding toward the Echinus Exit by thread or pen is no more enthusiastic than his early (after he has left the confinement of the Herne Hill garden) response to the foreground, which, despite the sacrifice of the foreground for the distance, becomes the necessary "here" of the later Transformations of the Maze. The narrowness of "colubrine" structures, which are serpentine structures after the fall from Daedalean pride, would appear to be a threat of limitation to the initial unqualified good of plenitude, which is innocently blind to a penultimate Repletion that can itself anticipate—or "see"—the inevitable excesses of a vacuous Illth. At first, what is narrow—with a world as empty or unexplored as a blank page that cannot, in the madness of post-Repletion, be written—is viewed as something less than worthy. And narrowness as an "un-Gothically" elevated and perfectly safe condition, which is to say a condition/dimension that has not yet fallen into the significance of the mnemonic experience of Lucent Verdure, is a concept that, for a while, persists without a sense of necessity that will become apparent.

---

breed of bitterness—the glory of it emaciate with cruel hunger, and blotted with venomous stain: and the track of it, on the leaf a glittering slime, and in the sand a useless furrow   [xix, 365].

Later, the narrow curvilinearity of Lucent Verdure will be thought of as a lost paradise to be recalled by an affective, involuntary memory, and perpetually imitated, if not entirely resurrected, in the Transformations of the Maze, which, ironically, are versions of serpentine intricacy. It is as if the "colubrine chains" of the serpent would not only "locate" the traveler/writer but attempt to "find" the Paradise Lost of Hampton Court. Whether that Paradise Lost can be found in the "furthest extremity" of the Exit in the same way it can be recalled in Origins is, for now, problematical. The possibility of a Paradise Regained, which may become a kind of Promise(d) Land, may also be "lost" or disappear in the final page of White Silence that is a tragic parody of the innocently inaugural blank page, which is itself the starting point (or garden) where the serpent of solution and salvation is as hidden as are the serpentine problems to come.

In the same way that, earlier, the ambitious and amalgamating Imagination is contrasted with the Fancy, which is a quasi-imaginative process that knows its own limitations, so later, even after the "mephitic" experience of the Centre, in a lecture on Brunelleschi (1874), Ruskin, with judgment implicit in tone, will contrast "aesthetic observation" with an uninspired "mathematical study" that is a slim, serial procedure, moving "part to part," as if seeking Ariadne's Echinus-like Exit: "aesthetic observation, even if weak, takes in the whole at a glance; but mathematical study proceeds from part to part, and may pause at an unimportant part" (XXIII, 211-12). Nevertheless, with Ruskin, digression, which is apparent evasion, is often finally central thought, becoming a new heart of the matter, and the "unimportant part" becomes a matter of life and death, in the same way that fallen altitude can provide the breath of life in the promise of the right kind of elevation beyond the Exit.

And if mathematical study is, at first glance, somehow unworthy in the exclusiveness of its vision, the problems inherent in aesthetic observation, which are essentially the familiar problems of the Centre, swiftly result in a higher valuation being placed on the mathematics of limitation—mathematics that would proceed, like the fanciful "point to point," or "part to part," as if much could be conquered by a kind of serial, Thesean division of necessarily limited perception. Just as the recollection or imitation of the curvilinear experience of the Hampton Court Maze would temper the terror of death's "long shadow," so, eliminating peripheral vision by the "narrow caution" of the traveler/writer's "blinders" as he moves myopically toward the Echinus Exit, that same fallen curvilinearity would also temper the horizontal panorama first perceived with the Parallel Advance—the original panorama in which there are, incipiently, both Strange Chords that will attempt an impossible mastery and the shadows of eventual madness.

The inclusion of aesthetic observation, taking in "the whole at a glance"—the glance, precisely, of the "wide circumference," which is the opposite of circumferential sight, if it is not released, if it is without an adequate sense of Ariadne's unwinding Exit, even if that Exit is only the size of the mouth of an echinus—breeds a "grotesque" perception of Illth. The implicit metaphor is almost unavoidably gastronomic, intestinal, and labyrinthine: too much perceived without adequate expression—expression that does not "stutter"—leads to the obstruction of infernally replete plenitude which is the penultimate "nothing but process" of going mad even as one attempts to go to that "extremity" which is "farthest" from the centrally "mephitic" "Cloaca Maxima." Still, there may remain, in circumferentially concluding madness, "one leg [of] dung" (*Diaries*, p. 1001). Beyond bodily hygiene, Repletion, which translates to a Ruskinian claustrophobia, yields an idiosyncratic aesthetics of insanity: "chiefly, with respect to Florentine art at this period, the greatest subjects on which it was occupied involved the exercise of the aesthetic faculty in what I ventured in my last lecture [delivered in 1874] to call an insane degree of intensity; that is to say, to the point of actually seeing and hearing sights and sounds which had apparently no external cause" (xxiii, 212). Simply, aesthetic observation, which is the perception of the "wide circumference" "all at once," is the condensed central perception of simultaneity that finally has the capacity—in Ruskin's case, the inevitable capacity—to possess, or be possessed by, an "insane degree of intensity."

With Ruskin, history is often ambitious autobiography. Unsurprisingly, that intensity which is insane is as autobiographical as it is historical; it is not only reached in Florentine art at the time of Brunelleschi, but by Ruskin himself, who, in the manuscript of the Brunelleschi lecture, links Florentine intensity with his own visionary dreams—that "acute inflammatory illness at Matlock."[8] Discussing another history—Milman's *History of Latin Christianity*—Ruskin also discerns both autobiographical substantiation and amplification:

[8] "In 1871, partly in consequence of chagrin at the Revolution in Paris, and partly in great personal sorrow, I was struck by acute inflammatory illness at Matlock, and reduced to a state of extreme weakness; lying at one time unconscious for some hours, those about me having no hope of my life" (xxii, 444).

The last sentence—equally, and violently, foolish and false—
I must put well out of the reader's way. Whatever these phenomena [i.e. religious visions at the time of St. Gregory] were,
they were not poetry. They might have been insanity, or the
reports of them may be folly, but they were neither troubadour
romances nor Newdigate prize poems. Those who told them,
believed what they had seen,—those who heard them, what
they had heard; and whether sane or insane, some part of the
related phenomena is absolutely true, and may be ascertained
to be so by any one who can bear the trial. And this I know
simply because I have been forced myself to bear it not once
or twice, and have experienced the two forms of state, quick-
ening of the senses both of sight and hearing, and the conditions of spectral vision and audit, which belong to certain
states of brain excitement [xxxiii, 198].[9]

If Venice is Ruskin's mind, architectural design is writing, a house
is a book, and a Gothic self, like a successful Walter Scott (as if led
at ground level through Hampton Court), has no more than a
"clue" of what lies in the future. Nearsighted, if not blind, Scott
cannot predict the end. If his art succeeds, his prophecy fails; the
proposed end is instead a discursive middle. And his initially classical, or "regular," architecture is, in the process, transformed into
a book, like a building, that is a "Gothic anomaly" accommodating
the present-tense meanderings of a consciousness close to a myopic
and curvilinear ground level. Significantly, Ruskin quotes from an
introduction to "The Fortunes of Nigel"—an introduction written
in the fallen, unprinted immediacy of Scott's own hand:

"But to confess to you the truth the books and passages in
which I have succeeded have uniformly been written with the
greatest rapidity and when I have seen some . . . my regular
mansion turns out to be a Gothic anomaly and the work is
done long before I have attained the end I proposed" [xxix,
264].

Scott's classically "regular mansion," like the house-as-Noun Substantive, which is a verbless study in reflexive autonomy—that early,
anathematic "word-house" from *The Poetry of Architecture*—is predictable. But, dependent upon an unmapped process of "unravelling," the "Gothic anomaly," like a syntax of consciousness (and

---

[9] For a discussion of some of the same problems from another approach see my
"Assaults: Spectral Vision and Audit," from *The Failing Distance*, pp. 136-44.

a language that, arriving at the end, will "return to itself") is not the result of prophecy. Unlike that early architecture/syntax of the Noun Substantive, the structure of the "Gothic anomaly," which is not located on a "street which is called Straight," does not cast the "long shadows" of inevitability: "he who sees one end should feel that, from the given data, he can arrive at no conclusion respecting the other" (I, 187). Further, the "Gothic anomaly," succeeding with an unplotted rapidity that undercuts propositions with the transcendence of immediacy, is not a structure for the perfect sheen of editorial process. The second time around is a time for maps and floor plans.

With Scott—and later with Ruskin—speed, whether the Devil's or God's, replaces "slow travel." And the unpremeditated writer is a traveler without itinerary or maps, who is also an architect without blueprints. It is as though, at this stage of the Transformations of the Maze, the centricity of the Rialto must be left before Repletion becomes the excessive presence as absence of Illth: the "farthest extremity" must be swiftly, if serpentinely, attained. There is a certain urgency of the Exit that speeds up the serial elaboration of "capricious sinuousities." (And there is always Atropos, with shears or nail above, if un-Christian "extrication" proves more necessary than Ariadne's thread below.) Refusing to (rather than failing to) rise to the angelically orthodox position of either Jack's deadly altitude or Newman's True Centre, Scott, pointing the swift, if centrifugally "spinning," way toward both the expressive Exit, which is not necessarily the end, and Ruskin's own penultimate style, finds his guiding angel fallen (one might say "pedestrian"), though not "daemonic":

> Alas, he did not half know how truly he had right, to plead sorcery, feeling the witchcraft, yet not believing in it, nor knowing that it was indeed an angel that 'guided,' not a daemon . . . that misled his hand, as it wrote in gladness the fast-becoming fancies. For, truly in that involuntary vision was the true 'design,' and Scott's work differs from all other fiction by its exquisiteness of art, precisely because he did not "know what was coming" [XXIX, 265].

A combination of the serial conjunctions of Ariadne and Ruskin's paratactic Atropos of present-tense chance, Scott's fallen angel, whom Ruskin takes to heart, is an angel of the Maze, trailing threads behind a glorious design—threads like clues of white marble—that speak of both the coherence of immediacy and an unpredictable,

serpentine advance. If Scott did not "know what was coming," someone else did. The unwinding or "unravelling" of Scott's "true 'design,' " which would be Newman's false Centre, is as involuntary
as a mnemonic imagination whose gift of dream involves an angelic
imagination. And if a "lost" paradise can be remembered and imitated in remembrance, perhaps as the Exit is sought, its regaining
can at least be imaginatively conceived: there may be the hope of
origins in the end, the promise of what has been lost, and Ariadne's
way would seem to be related to the "recovery" that Rose La Touche
might have offered Ruskin in his "error."

Ruskin's notion of modern greatness—and perhaps previous greatness—comes no more from premeditation than elevation. Rather,
that perception of greatness is a perception resulting from a narrow
sense of organic immediacy—the transcendentally intricate proximity of a labyrinth of "curliewurlies" uninfluenced by Daedalus'
symmetrical and hubristic elevation. The movement toward greatness occurs in a "vital present" (v, 127) whose potential greatness,
necessarily fallen, is in its fortunately imperfect and unpredictable
life.

The "vital present" is the tense of a low, meandering design of
intricate immediacy—no True Centre of premeditation but a True
Design of "involuntary vision"—that is the recollected shape of
Hampton Court's Maze of "vital hawthorn," which has taken on
the reflexive significance of present meaning imposed upon previous experience. And greatness is composed of both a shape and
tense of serpentine vitality that is either a way out, a way toward
the exits of the "farthest extremity," or a method of myopic survival—a way of maintaining precarious sanity (of keeping the peacocks from the ears) in the face of shadows both rectilinearly longer
and peripherally wider than "narrow caution" would permit.

Yet before the exit to the "farthest extremity," if not the expressive and vital process that connects the dense Rialto with that
"extremity," there are the angels—and the druggists. Or, more
accurately, there is a heaven whose involuntary tense is without the
apothecary guile of, say, Jack's perfect and deadly premeditation:

> . . . as I have a thousand times before asserted—though
> hitherto always in vain,—no great composition was ever pro-
> duced by composing nor by arranging chapters and dividing
> volumes; but only with the same heavenly involuntariness in
> which a bird builds her nest. And among the other virtues of

the great classic masters, this of enchanted design is of all the least visible to the present apothecary mind" [xxix, 265].[10]

Curiously, in Ruskin's hierarchy in which angels fall to the pedestrian altitude of mere "clues," the "clues" of immediate transcendence, it is the overtly apparent druggists who prophesy, as if from the altitude of Newman's True Centre where Mazes may be mastered. And it is the True Design, which is the design of heavenly enchantment, that is invisible. In any case, although leery of heights, even after (or because of) a bird's-eye trip over Europe, Ruskin would nevertheless have his birds fly rather than fan their blind tails at ground level—and scream.

The "enchanted design," like Ariadne's thread that might have pointed the way to Rose's postcircumferential Promise(d) Land, at least points to cautiously narrow Exits without apparent shadows or "long perspectives." And Scott's "Gothic anomaly," which is also Ruskin's, is an architecture that is not a "regular mansion" but one of "heavenly involuntariness" constructed from the "unindexed" Maze of a storehouse memory. On paper, Scott's "anomaly," with the discursive energy of expressive "fast-coming fancies," eases what in Ruskin is the "press of coincident thought"—the more than panoramic encompassment of the "wide circumference." Translated to Ruskin, that ease becomes the pastoral and "enchanted design" that, if not paradisiacal, offers at least temporary sanity in "involuntary" release. And the enchantment of Scott's Gothic design, which is a first-time design without the blueprints of regularity, is necessarily an imperfectly perfect enchantment, taking process for anticipation of the "farthest extremity" of the "outside," and the "vital present" as all the intimation of prophecy one can reasonably—or sanely—aspire toward. Always now, the shadows— both wide and far—would be avoided.

We have perhaps come to understand that the Parallel Advance is not the arabesquelike "unraveling" of the Exit, and that neither horizontal and peripheral perception, which may be the uncircumferential perception of the "wide circumference," nor depth perception, which is the future tense made visible, is the linear and serial expression manifested in the transforming Maze: that there is no accurate verbal equivalent to the Parallel Advance, and that an inaccurate equivalent—elevated prediction, say, or even the lofty and youthful (as of Cock-Robinson-Crusoe geometric centricity) "apothecary" tone of *Modern Painters II*, with elaborate tables of

[10] It may be noted that Ruskin will write, rather than build, *The Eagle's Nest*, which explores the "Relation of Natural Science to Art" (xxii, 115-287).

contents and paragraph summaries in the margins—is to be avoided, at the cost of one's wits.[11] The early, elaborate "Table of Contents" is replaced by a less elevated, "involuntary" wandering that will, with its assumed myopic transcendence of immediacy, reduce broad perception to the narrow width and fallen line of often playful, and even "capricious sinuousities." As we shall see, if Venice is a mind, architecture—flamboyant architecture—is a model for an increasingly idiosyncratic syntax. And the stones of Venice—the stones of white marble, that is, which anticipate the stones or archaeology, of White Silence—are closer to being the stones of pedestrian continuity (with line as a fallen version of pastoral) than the stones of implicitly elevated prophecy, like a towering St. Mark's.

What is sought, before the inevitability of the "long shadow," before it comes into short perspective, which may be an autobiographical version of the closing Storm-Cloud of the Nineteenth Century (with Ruskin, meteorology is often autobiography), and with a mind as densely populated as a central city that has ambitiously imported the "wide circumference"—what is sought, almost ultimately, is an architecture of words, a verbal "Gothic anomaly" to be built by an impulse that is at least an approximation of Thesean advance, an "involuntary" advance below, as of pedestrian "white clues," that is impelled by elements more heavenly than infernal, more angelic than "daemonic." For apothecary, or (logo)-concentric, prophecy—the hubristic prediction and synthesis from the Index (an unrevised Jack/Daedalus being both a builder of mechanical houses, perhaps like St. Peter's, and Mazes of "right angles," as well as being the perfect Renaissance druggist)—leads not only into the history of the irredeemable labyrinth of feverish and insane Florentine intensity about the time of Brunelleschi, but to more personal fevers and less historical insanity. Even when "unravelled" and expressed with a kind of "heavenly involuntariness" that is decidedly not the building of a peacock's nest, the encroaching peripheral shadows of the maddening "wide circumference," shortly to overlap, bring with them the cries of those infernal peacocks, along with a cat soon to be dead—a cat from behind a mirror that may also be a contrasting mirror of consciousness, that is, at least in feverish fact, seen as the Devil incarnate.

---

[11] Robert Hewison, following Landow, makes a convincing case for Ruskin's later resurrection of, or "return" to, the argument of *Modern Painters II*—a case that does not, however, include the volume's dogmatic, epicyclical tone of "Evangelical trappings." (*John Ruskin*, p. 211.)

Scott's "Gothic anomaly," which is Ruskin's lost Hampton Court recollected in Lucent Verdure and transformed into a labyrinthine architecture of language, is, in the later Transformations of the Maze, among other things, a sanctuary, that is a kind of halfway house for a traveler/writer between vast mnemonic storehouses "behind" and a "regular mansion" dangerously "above" and "in front" (perhaps built by Jack precariously close to the Exit). And that "regular mansion" may be like nothing so much as a version of Bedlam—the Hospital of St. Mary at Bethlehem done in the Greek style of the rectilinear fret of "right angles"—a style that, for Ruskin, is more wrong than "right." In any case, next to a Bedlam that may itself be as replete as a dangerously overpopulated Centre, Ruskin would take the "Gothic anomaly" of, say, the *Helix virgata* for architectural and syntactical shelter, replacing True Centres and Strange Chords with designs that are both "true" and "enchanted" in their eccentric geometries. And in that anamorphic eccentricity, which is like concentricity twisted by a centrifuge, there may reside sanity—or at least a sanity within a temporary sanctuary composed of a shell's spiraling and "aedicular" architecture.

But Ruskin may not have an "architectural" choice. If he would take that *Helix virgata* for shelter, he may instead find himself, if not in St. Mary's designed in perfect "right angles," then enclosed in the final Theatre of Blindness, with its antiphonal double labyrinths of the three-dimensional Maze, which is in fact his own highly idiosyncratic architecture, his own "Gothic anomaly" that is indeed an imprisoning asylum for the "erroneous consciousness" ultimately without either an Exit or "extrication" other than White Silence.

Yet Ruskin's way toward madness is not St. Paul's way to the Kingdom of God, though, curiously, Redemption, whether heterodox or not, is in either case close to a promise that might be kept. Unrectilinear, Ruskin's peregrination is one of characteristic centrifugal digression that, at the point of verbal dissolution, is transfigured in an agonized attempt at an articulation that would be a fallen "error's" still fallen "recovery," as if the "recovery" of a lost tongue could aid in a landscape's elevation, and this, in a highly idiosyncratic version of the anonymous, universally repressed lexicon of pathos and "*folie*" mentioned by Foucault that would include, above all, "those words deprived of language whose muffled rumbling, for an attentive ear, rises up from the depths of history, the obstinate murmur of a language which speaks by itself, uttered by no one and answered by no one"[12]—after which, with Ruskin, there is only the return to White Silence beyond even the fiction of Redemption, and the occasional revisitations of sanity.

[12] Michel Foucault, *Histoire de la folie*, Preface to the original edition (Plon, 1961). I have used Shoshana Felman's eloquent translation.

Chapter Eight

The Excavations of Silence: Double Labyrinths and the Architecture of Reluctant Nihilism

A. The Threads of Thought:
Unsystematic Intimations of the Centrifuged Style

At first, which is to say before apparent problem has necessitated attempted solution, the Hampton Court Maze is a model for a fundamentally insignificant syntax of orthodox convolution: a *Helix virgata*, say, undistorted by anamorphic perspective, or a pre-planned labyrinth that has, syntactically, none of the "mystery of dazzling light" that it describes. At first, not far from the Ruskinian child's Cock-Robinson-Crusoe Centre of conventional and concentric geometries, that innocent and essentially untransformed Maze, which may be a located Paradise of the present tense "lost" in an unselfconsciously assumed immanence, is a shape for a syntax which, uninformed by that ambiguously fallen altitude of "heavenly involuntariness," would imitate the perfectly regular "design" of Jack—that design which is notably lacking in both enchantment and ultimately livable truth.

Describing not "vital hawthorn" but nevertheless the labyrinthine "play" of light and shadow among foliage—"the labyrinth and the mystery of dazzling light and dream-like shadow"—an example of Ruskin's early syntax, elaborately extended and, at the same time, retarded only by semicolons and commas, whirls with a deliberate, though not rectilinear, intricacy. The effect is one of drawn-out, serial lucidity and pretty, impressionistic word-painting, or even word-building. As a passage more purple than green, as if a drug-gist had designed, with the control of premeditation, a labyrinth, here is the syntax of anthologized fame, with a diction of depth and penetration that comes close to transcending the limitations of a promising but stylistically shallow (and innocent) imitation. One might say that two dimensions were aspiring toward the earned bulk of three—that a stage-set for an incipient Theatre of Blindness, as the labyrinthine/serpentine territory between Centre and Circumference, would become the "fallen" architecture of planes and transparency from an early version of the three-dimensional Maze:

> . . . it [foliage] is always *transparent* with crumbling lights in it *letting you through to the sky.* . . . then, under these, you get deep passages of broken irregular gloom, passing into *transparent*, green-lighted, misty hollows; the twisted stems glancing through them in their pale and entangled *infinity*, and the shafted sunbeams, rained from above, running along the lustrous leaves for an instant; then *lost*, then caught again on some emerald bank or knotted root, to be sent up with a *faint reflex* on the white undersides of dim groups of drooping foliage, the shadows of the upper boughs running in grey network down the glossy stems, and resting in quiet chequers upon the glittering earth; but all *penetrable* and *transparent*, and, in proportion, inextricable and incomprehensible, except where across the *labyrinth* and the mystery of the dazzling light and dream-like shadow, falls, close to us, some solitary spray, some wreath   [III, 590, italics mine].

Imitating subject with syntax, Ruskin's early verbal maneuvering is no more than an embryonic, perhaps stillborn, example of the Maze transformed into style. If it is a version of young death, it is hardly tragic. There is no urgency for the Exit. And Jack's perfect death, predicting the mechanical end as if with a syntax of Noun Substantives or floor plans of something like Scott's "regular mansion," is Ruskin's own beginning beyond the geometric Cock-Robinson-Crusoe Centre. Nevertheless, this is before the perception of the "wide circumference" has necessitated an unpremeditated and imperfect unwinding that is like a *Helix virgata* perceived anamorphically—an unwinding impelled by an equivocal "above" that, both pedestrian and heavenly, is certainly no True Centre, though perhaps shaped by Scott's True Design.

Later, beyond flattened impressionability and with the architectonics of his own "enchanted design" etched in his consciousness as a paradigm of linear felicity, Ruskin, understanding the correlation between Hampton Court and Scott's "Gothic anomaly," recreates both of them as he develops his own, highly idiosyncratic verbal Maze—a Maze of depth and achieved experience (rather than flat innocence) that becomes, at least for a while, Ariadne's conjunctive style of the Exit. Ruskin, as if leaving the central Rialto

for the "farthest extremity," would effect a serial escape from in-
sanely intense Repletion as it approaches the Edge of Illth, beyond
which a vertiginous plenitude, having become "too much," has de-
clined to a condition of absence that is, at the same time, a silent
madness of blind presence.

Understanding that greatness does not often come from prediction—after all, Scott's "regular mansion," despite its blueprints, is
never successfully built, although Jack's St. Peter's, if indeed that
is the house which Jack finally builds, is—Ruskin learns to avoid
the synthesizing authorial position he had assumed in the second
volume of *Modern Painters*. That early position is not so much a
position of earned elevation—a place where generalization is possible (if unpleasant as a locus of endurance)—as it is a position of
arrogant naiveté, of dogmatic innocence. For that reader of early
Ruskin, the Centre is not so much elevated as paginally peripheral:
the margins, like epicycles of knowledge, contain reductive summaries of paragraphs. But those summaries of the specific in the
form of the general made small are not even the result of having
achieved Newman's altitude. Instead, according to Ruskin, it comes
from an altitude that is almost a parody of his later experience of
"capricious sinuousities" within the Maze. The later myopia and
wearing of blinders in the Maze, both of which occur after the
inclusive vision has taken in at a glance the soon to be "overlapping"
"wide circumference," have been anticipated by an early "sectarian
narrowness" (IV, xlvi), which, before the perceptions of the Parallel
Advance, is not the same thing as a necessarily "narrow caution."

Systems, which are Newman's altitudinal syntheses elaborated
upon—taken to Jack's height from where the end can be predicted—shape Scott's unsuccessfully constructed "regular mansion." Finally, Scott, as well as Ruskin (and we must remember that
we are dealing with Ruskin's version of Scott, which is incipient
Ruskinian autobiography) cannot successfully build or write with
a predetermined synthesis that would organize twisting vitality toward a systematic and geometric organization beyond the vitality
of life itself. Systems—the manipulation of classifications, which is
also the manipulation of self—are better suited for minerals, dead
stones, than Venice's white marble of continuity that is more actively
manipulating than passively manipulated. And Ruskin's style of the
Maze, removed from the stately naiveté of "dazzling light and
dream-gifted shadow," is, curiously, as immediately alive in its recollected Lucent Verdure, as the initial Daedalean Maze is dead in
its right-angled and elevated pride. In *Modern Painters III*, after a
lengthy digression that is in fact *The Stones of Venice*, Ruskin re-

nounces the system-mongering of apothecary prophecy and "lurid shadows" for the myopia of an entirely Atroposian improvisation:

> I do not intend, however, now to pursue the inquiry in a method so laboriously systematic; for the subject may, it seems to me, be more usefully treated by pursuing the different questions which arise out of it just as they occur to us, without too great scrupulousness in marking connections, or insisting on sequences. Much time is wasted by human beings, in general, on establishment of systems; and it often takes more labour to master the intricacies of an artificial connection, than to remember the separate facts which are so carefully connected. I suspect that system-makers, in general, are not of much more use, each in his own domain, than, in that of Pomono, the old women who tie cherries upon sticks, for the more convenient portableness of the same   [v, 18].

The "all-embracing prospect of life as a whole"[1] that Pater, after Arnold's "wide prospect," calls for even as his Sebastian van Storck dies when forced to encompass something very much like Ruskin's (logo)-concentric "wide circumference" (and Sebastian's problem is perception, not the necessarily more serial expression of the echinus-exit)—that compensatory "all-embracing prospect," in the face of the divided specialization of the nineteenth-century assembly line, is a "prospect" that can only be adequately treated by a systematic organization that is extraordinary. But organization qua system is as deadly as the self-vivisection of bead-making on the assembly line.[2] Pater's "all-embracing prospect" is close to Ruskin's "wide circumference" that has become a variety of "large views." And those "views" are observed with a distaste usually reserved for Jack's geometrically perfect architecture, his house, his deadly Maze: "scientific men are too fond, or too vain of their systems, and waste the student's time in endeavouring to give him large views; when there is not one student, no, nor one man in a thousand, who can feel the beauty of a system, or even take it clearly into his head; but nearly all men can understand, and most will be interested in, the facts which bear on daily life" (xvi, 111-12). The system's "interesting connections" have something to do with the "fearless connection" of Strange Chords. Of course, neither Jack nor Turner is everyman. Yet the suspicion arises that any man— Ruskin, as Makeshift Master, as well as that "one man in a thou-

---

[1] Walter Pater, *Miscellaneous Studies* (London, 1910), p. 12.
[2] See "The Nature of Gothic" chapter in *The Stones of Venice, passim.*

sand"—is finally, in some important meaning, Everyman. And Gothic sympathy is for the plurality that is unprophetically unsystematic.[3] But Jack's House, even with its "large views," is, in no sense, inclusive enough to be a public house.

Ruskin's version of Scott's "Gothic anomaly"—Ruskin's most extreme example—becomes a style that is the result of a present tense of consciousness that is more significant than merely impressionable: the stakes, which are now those of sanity and survival, have become greater than before. Appropriately, Ruskin employs an unpremeditated style of "surprise" (rather than one of "recognition") that can be reduced to formulaic summary no more easily than that "vital" and curvilinear Maze can be abridged to mastered, or even generalized, simplicity. The syntax of the Anomaly, which is probably the stylistic incarnation of "The Nature of Gothic" in its most essential form, has no existence as the epicyclic True Centre of summarized marginalia. Further, as if systematically defying both systems and aphoristic condensation, the syntax of the Anomaly also defies easy translation. As the final Transformation of the Maze, that highly allusive and obscurely associative style (or styles, as the late example of the intricately serial Ariadne competes with the penultimate syntactical design of Atropos) attempts to return, in a language that "returns upon itself," to the "lost" experience of the autobiographical origins of Lucent Verdure—that labyrinth of light which is itself recalled, from a Theatre of Blindness, through the "golden stains" of remembered time.

But the dance in the moonlight of Hampton Court, which was originally Ruskin's parenthetical dance with Adèle Domecq, with whom he was more than infatuated, has, like the spiraling of the single line of the *Helix virgata*, become the "intentionally progressive," yet solipsistic, dance of Morgiana in *The Arabian Nights*—in this case, a singularly autonomous dance, in a condition of lonely plurality, of the one for both the one and the many: "I beg the reader to observe that any further gamboling on my part, awkward or untimely, as it may have seemed, has been quite as serious and intentionally progressive, as Morgiana's dance round the captain of the Forty Thieves" (xxviii, 512). The captain is the focal point— the cancerous, or mephitic, Centre that must be negated by hyp-

---

[3] The problem of systems is of course not simple. Ruskin looks back at *Modern Painters II*, which had once displeased him in its rigorous organization, and finally discovers that "I find now the main value of the book to be exactly in the systematic scheme of it which I had despised" (xxii, 512). As almost always, Ruskin, a man of Antiphonal Contention, is at least "biped."

notic peregrination. Syntactical re-creation as recreation, if no longer ecstatic in its self-conscious effort to recapture a serpentinely edenic situation that has been lost, is still a kind of play, although that play is more desperately "bitter" than the fun that may be found in the entirely evasive landscapes of occasional and exclusive pastoral. There is a "stern final purpose" among the solitary pirouettes of the syntax of the Anomaly just as there is a sense of ultimacy in the conjunctive Maze of "white clues." Here is Ruskin on the epistolary Anomaly that is *Fors Clavigera*:

> *Fors* is a *letter*, and written as a letter should be written, frankly, and as the mood or topic chances; so far as I finish and retouch it, which of late I have done more and more, it ceases to be what it should be, and becomes a serious treatise, which I never meant to undertake. True, the play of it (and much of it is a kind of bitter play) has always, as I told you before, a stern final purpose as Morgiana's dance; but the gesture of the moment must be as the moment takes me   [xxix, 197].[4]

The dance is "bitter play" without a partner (and there will be no recollections, either forged or actual of Rose La Touche as even an untouched partner, or [re]visitations with Adèle Domecq to the Lucent Verdure of Hampton Court), but he will dance instead, with "stern final purpose," as though that "purpose" were a substitute partner. Yet the "final purpose," like a chance encounter, must be arrived at "as the humour takes me." And the line between bitterness and "play," sternness and "humour," is as winding as it is fine—and potentially a "fine grotesque." It is as if, wearing a "Harlequin's mask," Ruskin were gingerly traveling along the serpentine interface that will finally negotiate the double labyrinths

---

[4] Especially in *Fors*, Ruskin is generously philosophical about "errors" that should not be recovered. Time is the uncorrected error of God's speed:

> I must submit to all and sundry chances of error, for, to prevent them, would involve a complete final reading of the whole, with one's eye and mind on the look-out for letters and stops all along, for which I rarely allow myself time, and which, had I a month to spare, would yet be a piece of work ill spent, in merely catching three t's instead of two in a "lettter." The name of the Welsh valley is wrong, too; but I won't venture on correction of that, which I feel to be hopeless; the reader must, however, be kind enough to transfer the "and," now the sixth word in the upper line of the note at page 509, and make it the fourth word, instead; to put a note of interrogation at the end of the clause in the eighteenth line of page 508, and to insert an s, changing "death" into "deaths," in the eleventh line of page 504; the death in Sheffield being that commended to the Episcopic attention of York, and that in London to the Episcopic attention of London   [xxvii, 511].

of his Theatre of Blindness, though now with jokes on that fine line's one side and madness on the other.

But those sides, shaped by a sinuous curvilinearity, are not defined with certainty. Peregrination is digression. And digression is an almost necessary form of transgression, which is itself close to the metamorphosis of a comedian into a madman. That the "Harlequin's mask" may become self-portraiture, or that the mask dropped may reveal a catlike self quite mad, is the inevitable danger of the style of the tightrope—the danger being in the transgression/ metamorphosis, rather than the "fall" from pedestrian height. Yet the ambiguity of categories, of sides, which is part of the curvilinear difficulty, is also part of Ruskin's informing architectonics behind the syntax of his—and Scott's—"Gothic anomaly":

> . . . our Bishops in St. George's Company will be constituted in order founded on that appointed by the first Bishop of Israel, namely, that their Primate, or Supreme Watchman, shall appoint under him "out of all the people, able men, such as fear God, men of Truth, hating covetousness, and place such over them to be rulers (or, at the *least*, observers) of thousands, rulers of hundreds, rulers of fifties, and rulers of tens;" and that in these episcopic centurions, captains of fifty, and captains of ten, there will be required clear account of the individual persons they are set over;—even a baby being considered as a decimal quantity not to be left out of their account by the decimal Bishops,—in which episcopacy, however, it is not improbable that a queenly power may be associated, with Norman caps for mitres, and for symbol of authority, instead of the crozier (or cross, for disentangling lost sheep of souls from among the brambles), the broom, for sweeping diligently till they find lost silver of souls among the dust.
>
> You think I jest, still, do you? Anything but that; only if I took off the Harlequin's mask for a moment, you would say I was simply mad. Be it so, however, for this time [xxviii, 513].

Of all the styles available to Ruskin, it is his Third Style,[5] which unravels, as if in a spinning (or "un-spinning") dance, in the syntax of the "Gothic anomaly" (or the architectural syntax of the present-tense Theatre of Blindness) that comes closest to the "Dantesque," rather than Daedalean, moonlit alleys of Hampton Court:

[5] See "The Syntax of Consciousness: Broken Sentences," *The Failing Distance*, pp. 86-126, for amplification, "with an anamorphic difference," of some of these same points.

I have always had three different ways of writing: one with the single view of making myself understood, in which I necessarily omit a great deal of what comes into my head; another in which I say what I think ought to be said, in what I suppose to be the best words I can find for it; (which is in reality an affected style—be it good or bad;) and my third way of writing is to say all that comes into my head for my own pleasure, in the first words that come, retouching them afterwards into (approximate) grammar. These notes for the Art Journal were so written; and I like them myself, of course; but ask the reader's pardon for their confusedness   [xix, 408].

If Ruskin is not guided by low-flying, even pedestrian angels through the verbal Maze of the Third Style (and that he is not is far from certain), he is, at the least, led by the play of a kind of humor that arrives, as we shall see, only as that "humour comes upon me." And that "humour," appearing of its own volition, is contrasted in *Fors Clavigera* to the gravity of "system-mongering." Peddling systems, we know, is Jack's perfect (and perfectly suicidal) way to his own Daedalean death—a useful enterprise when either the lifeless consequences of orthodox geometry or death's "long shadow" is sought. It is as though Arnold's "high seriousness"—as high as the (logo)-concentric altitude of Jack, Newman, or Pater's optically "all-embracing" Sebastian—were translated by Ruskin into a low play, which, neither a bad joke nor a false dance step, is as serious as survival itself.

At his best, which is bad for the advertised reluctance of the autobiographer, Ruskin indulges himself. And that indulgence is the "nothing but process," between inspiration and madness, that yields a pleasure of its own, a kind of desperately extended "play" that is, in fact, a game of existence. Even if there were not that "stern final purpose," the dance would not be interrupted. And if Ruskin had a partner, he would not permit anyone to cut in (unless, as we shall see, it were Atropos, with her nail or shears). Releasing the backwaters of imaginative Repletion—the centripetal "vortices" of the "wide circumference" internalized, and without hope of orthodox and expressive unwinding—the Third Style employs that tense furthest (as in "extremities") from what might be called central "apothecary prophecy." And the thread Ruskin follows is a "thread of thought" rather than one of white marble, though the two are perhaps one:

. . . none of this work can be done but as a kind of play, irregularly, and as the humour comes upon me. For if I set myself at it gravely, there is too much to be dealt with; my mind gets fatigued in half-an-hour, and no good can be done; the only way in which any advance can be made is by keeping my mornings entirely quiet, and free of care, by opening of letters or newspapers; and then letting myself follow any thread of thought or point of inquiry that chances to occur first, and writing as the thoughts come,—whatever their disorder: all their connection and cooperation being dependent on the real harmony of my purpose, and the consistency of the ascertainable facts, which are the only ones I teach; and I can no more, now, polish or neatly arrange my work than I can guide it   [xxviii, 461].

Ruskin avoids the "too much to be dealt with"—an adequate description of the sewage of the Cloaca Maxima that has been taken in from a "wide circumference"—by a style that, with no more width for expression than the myopic, if not blind, mouth of the Echinus, refuses to consider the inclusively peripheral. He can "no more, now, polish or neatly arrange" his work than he can "guide it." But that sighted "guiding," which, with "polish," might have been a premeditated "blind march" through the intricate fretwork of a rectilinear labyrinth that, serially extending similes, would be like a city of right angles or a masterful mind on the verge of "perfect" breakdown, is in the hands or eyes of a guide—either Ariadne or Atropos—who would exchange the orthodox geometries of the True Centre (and even Strange Chords) for the eccentrically "true" and "enchanted design" of digressive and transgressing (though not panoramic) curvilinearity. The Ruskinian "Gothic anomaly" replaces Jack's deadly rectilinearity, which is the informing architectural line of an errorless "regular mansion" that might be constructed from the masonry of Noun Substantives.

More angelic, if fallen, than daemonic, the Third Style, wandering with not only serial myopia but blinders that might well be appropriate for those with small, perhaps, "unbishoply" mouths, is the meandering syntax of a thread that has become the pastoral of happy exclusion.[6] Incorporating the wide curves of a roving consciousness, the travelogue is nevertheless edited. If the dehumanized immobility of Daedalean "fretwork" is like perfect rest

---

[6] We recall not only that "The most unbishoply character a man can have is . . . to be Blind," but also that "The most unpastoral is, instead of feeding, to want to be fed,—to be a Mouth" (xviii, 72). When the "Mouth" becomes cannibalistic, even self-cannibalistic, it is the mouth of a blind bishop, a pastor whose once pastoral landscape has become topographical autobiography as Cloaca Maxima, as if he had in fact become his own source of fertilization.

either beyond or above the vitality of the Hampton Court Maze, an indulgent Ruskin, whose wandering is the essence of existence, rests before both the end and the edge. Specifically, irregular change, which in the Maze is the transcendence of immediacy discovered in surprise (a kind of counterfeit immanence in that Ruskin's fundamentally informed claustrophobic existence becomes as momentarily possible in narrow curvilinearity as it is in parenthetical intimacy), is a vacation—a version of elaborate pastoral, like trimmed hedges winding in moonlight: "it seems to me that the involuntary wandering of the brain is sometimes almost a rest to it, and at the worst a far less strain than any resolute rational occupation" (xxxv, xxxvi). Wandering mapless (though with the pedestrian intelligence of "white clues") toward the Circumference, which inevitably and unfortunately will lead toward the Edge of Illth and the White Silence beyond, the brain's penultimate "thread of thought" extends, in "colubrine" design, the densely "mephitic" burden—the "insane intensity"—of perceived and experienced Repletion, which is finally the qualified acknowledgment of the consequences of the response to shadows that are as wide as they are long.

Attempting to attain the "farthest extremity" of salvation/solution, Ruskin may now also be moving toward centrifugal dissolution and exhaustion—a broadly encompassing "error" that cannot satisfactorily be "recovered." And those "lurid" shadows—the shadows of both depth and panorama, which signify the encroaching darkness of death's "long shadow" as well as the peripheral and inclusive width of the shadows of incipient madness—are, in this late stage of the Transformations of the Maze, in the process of being surrounded by a perfectly undistorted circle of orthodox, Daedalean geometry. It is beginning to look as if the Centre that Ruskin, who may be now less Thesean than before, would escape from is all too similar to the Circumference he is headed toward. Perhaps the Centre is reflected in a convex mirror. For now, although perhaps not penultimately, it is as though Jack's deadly concentricity were both In and Out—though not in the meandering, returning-upon-itself "process" of the present-tense Theatre of Blindness that is Between, with the Lucent Verdure of Hampton Court Maze both temporally "behind" and mnemonically "present."

As he centrifugally travels toward the Circumference, it appears that even the eccentric geometry of the shell of the *Helix virgata*, which might be a "remaining place" for him, is becoming the perfect circle he would often avoid—either that, or the transforming Maze is becoming increasingly defensive, as the shaping Centre loses some of its terror and the instinct for the Exit diminishes. Yet all this remains to be "seen," like the sight of the problematical dragon.

A Promise(d) Land, as either a paradise lost or an invisible land that is indeed promised, the Circumference—in one of its rectilinear aspects—is a borderland, where, as we know, the lofty paragraphic summaries of *Modern Painters II* reside, like a "rude brick campanile, of the commonest Lombardic type" (x, 17) outside the "text" of Venice, with the altitude of three dimensions reduced to the fact and necessity of paper, or marginalia aspiring toward the condition of an eccentrically True Centre. And Ruskin moves, as traveler/writer, toward the "farthest extremity" of borders, with a qualified sense of at once an inaugurally urgent requirement and the "stuttering" hesitation of second thoughts that might recover initial "errors," in a syntactical peregrination of "nothing but process" that is Thesean wandering translated into both exploration and temporary vacation. As if ignoring any apparent impulse toward the coherence that might be found in unity-of-being, which for Ruskin would be a potentially infernal claustrophobic confrontation, he will invert the process of the Middle Man who, despite subtraction for his own gain, imports the products or resources of the Circumference into the Mephitic Centre in almost the same way that Ruskin reluctantly receives the eventually replete information of the Parallel Advance. Inverting the "vortices" of "instinctive drainage," which is a reversal tending toward centrifugal and expressive intricacy, is Ruskin's version of the "Gothic anomaly." General organization, anticipating specific syntax, will become as unpremeditated as the originally innocent Circumference before its importation to the Centre. And like a Circumference—like a "wide circumference"—that anticipatory organization will encompass, even if only through a width as limited in expression as the mouth of an Echinus, more than the "sectarian narrowness" of *Modern Painters II*: "I purpose . . . henceforward to trouble myself little with sticks or twine, but to arrange my chapters with a view to convenient reference, rather than to any careful division of subjects, and to follow out, in any by-ways that may be open, on right hand or left, whatever question it seems useful at any moment to settle" (v, 18).

The organization proposed in *Modern Painters III* becomes, in approximate fact, the later organization of *Fors Clavigera*, where structure also imitates the style of the Exit, which is further a style of stress that would, by the elaborations of penultimate peregrination, begin to avoid the "farthest extremity" of the circumferential edge, beyond which there is perhaps "nothing" but Illth's blank page and the Dream of blind and silent absence—a dream, nonetheless, that will itself be invaded by the presence of a metamorphosed contention, as between a Devil (who dies less easily than a cat) and the barrage of artillery that, signaling both the contention and its conclusion, will punctuate White Silence. Despite "Devilspeed" or "God-speed," there are second thoughts implicit in the backtracking of the curvilinear. But the "process" continues.

And that "process," now only anticipating "nothing" and including the spiraling second thoughts of return and the expressive unwinding of reversed "vortices," whirling on the "by-ways" of transgression and transformation, is the opposite of Jack's Daedalean and immobile altitude and predictably central deadliness. The anamorphic or unpredictably distorted unwinding is, in fact, as organically "vital" as life itself, which may incorporate not only the movements of "capricious sinuousities" toward either "right hand, or left," like the progress of the serpent, but also the backward and forward motions of Gothic "error and recovery." It is as though, in Ruskin's morality play of light, a shadowy Maze of "sin and error"—or a Theatre of (approaching) Blindness—might indeed be recovered, in the illuminative retrospect of a golden-stained Lucent Verdure, by the "extrications" of a Divine Grace.[7]

Like the gesture of life, the curvilinear (and both determined and hesitant) movement from the Rialto, which is a gesture that would find fresh air to breathe, is a movement with qualified expectation, as if a paradise lost, before plenitude has become Repletion, might somehow be regained. In the end, there will be the White Silence of the Travel Diary's blank page, though that blank page will not be like an innocent garden or a fresh start. It is easier

---

[7] See note 1 of "The Labyrinth," xxvii, 398. We may recall that, interestingly, the twenty-third "letter" of *Fors* is devoted not to an ecstatic redaction of the Lucent Verdure of the Hampton Court Maze, but, at least partially, to the Thesean endurance within the Maze—and not as a version of pastoral—with Ruskin coming characteristically close to playing the part of Theseus. Spiraling concentricity leads to the later ramifications of a Dantean Hell—"and Minos accordingly indicates which circle any sinner is to be sent to, in a most graphically labyrinthine manner, but twisting his tail round himself so many times, necessarily thus marking the level" (xxvii, 410)—a Dantean Hell in striking contrast to Ruskin's early ecstatic dance, with no "stern final purpose," in the "Dantesque alleys" of Hampton Court. Like Theseus, Ruskin would slay the Minotaurean heart of the Maze, its Centre, in order successfully to retrace his steps to the Circumference of the "farthest extremity"— that Minotaurean version of centricity, after all, being the "type of embodiment of the two essentially bestial sins of Anger and Lust" (xxvii, 412-13). The movement through the labyrinth, far from the recollections of Lucent Verdure, can be an infernal trip from Hell. Certainly, it can be a trip of survival.

to begin than re-begin. Further, it is easier to lose than regain, especially when what has been lost may be the experience of a faulty, if precious, memory—unless, of course, that memory is a fiction summoned by requirement.

Writing *Fors*, Ruskin wanders. But, unlike the maneuvers of Theseus, Ruskin's wandering is at times apparently almost purposeless, with the style of Ariadne's Exit submerged to a kind of reflexive, though desultory, enjoyment of Atropos' unpremeditated present. Farsightedness, even of the Exit, which is not necessarily the end (though in the conjunctive movement toward the Exit there may be increasing questions about the distinctions), is perceived as the rectilinear optics of death. If not for St. Paul, streets, we know, can for others be too "Straight." In any case, the irritation of friends, who, wanting to go straight to the "point," are instead brought to a Forsian version of Hampton Court—Ruskin's lost pastoral that, as a necessary model for present imitation, achieves greater significance in its mnemonic recovery than it had in its initial "presence"—can be close to that other irritation, the irritation of Newman, who would master the art of prediction as well as synthesis. Still, Ruskin's meandering is the continual planting of roots in "new ground"—a re-beginning manqué with roots which may well become curvilinear hawthorn that is "vital" in its predictably inevitable unpredictability. The red, or pink, blossom of hawthorn will appear where Atroposian chance will have it (and beyond Ruskin, that hawthorn will bloom for both Pater and Proust, though without the aid of the Third Fors):

> A friend, in whose judgment I greatly trust, remonstrated sorrowfully with me, the other day, on the desultory character of *Fors*; and pleaded with me for the writing of an arranged book instead.
>
> But he might as well plead with a birch-tree growing out of a crag, to arrange its boughs beforehand. The winds and floods will arrange them according to their wild liking; all that the tree has to do, or can do, is to grow gaily, if it may be; sadly, if gaity be impossible; and let the black jags and scars rend the rose-white of its trunk where Fors shall choose.
>
> But I can well conceive how irritating it must be to any one chancing to take special interest in any one part of my subject— the life of Scott for instance,—to find me, or lose me, wandering away from it for a year or two; and sending roots into new ground in every direction: or (for my friend taxed me with this graver error also) needlessly re-rooting myself in the old   [xxviii, 254].

The apparently desultory performance in the Maze of *Fors Clavigera* is, in fact, a desparate form of gardening—as if replanting a version of Hampton Court he might, instead of going mad, resurrect, in a language of return, an experience in a paradisiacal landscape that has been lost, like a past tense he would recall with intense nostalgia. With Ruskin, homesickness is that original sickness for the garden. "Re-rooting" would be the "recovery" of past "error," which is part of the necessarily hesitant and "serpentine"/ "colubrine" advance of life itself incarnated in vital syntax. And that syntax retains its conjunctive vitality as long as the mind remains sane, or uninterrupted by the ripped immanence of "torn presences"; as such, it is a syntax of the unpremeditated consciousness that would centrifugally ease the eddying backwaters (or perhaps more accurately, that central sewage of the Cloaca Maxima) before the penultimate peregrinations and elaborations near the Exit, where syntax threatens to become parataxis. And all the time "above," there is not merely Daedalus, but the nail-bearing Jael-Atropos.

If Newman, no acrophobic, is elevated from the "irritation" of a landscape very much like that of Hampton Court to his felicitous True Centre, where synthesis soothes the exacerbation of "colubrine," and perhaps Thesean, vitality, Ruskin, avoiding altitude and having fallen into the recollection of Lucent Verdure, at crucial times begins to avoid what may only be the fictional salvation of Ariadne's Exit. It is possible, now, that salvation might be anything but the "solution" of "white clues." We understand that Newman's "irritation" is Ruskin's "play," although that "play" is not entirely happy. Considerable sections of *Fors Clavigera*, as well as early sections of *The Cestus of Aglaia*, are essentially reflexive performances— the presumably irresponsible autobiography of apparently casual self-indulgence that would seek a lost self in the language of return.

Yet the centrifugal "play" is "bitter" and the indulgence of self is something far more serious than a digressive holiday.[8] Instead, there is the fight against the triumphant screams of peacocks, cold dawns, and a black cat that may be the reflection of Ruskin's own madness, a reflection that is not blind to itself. If Ruskin appears self-indulgent, creating "irritation" among friends by heterodox gardening in the organization and syntax of his Maze, he is not

---

[8] Leo Bersani shrewdly points out: "Art may be the best argument we have for the pleasures of centrifugal play" (*Balzac to Beckett: Center and Circumference in French Fiction* [New York, 1970], p. 23). But Ruskin's "centrifugal play," "bitter," is short-lived. Perhaps Ruskin's art may be the best argument we have for the possibility of a centrifugal (not postcircumferential) sanity—albeit temporary.

entirely to blame. After all, writing at least partly to the singular and idiosyncratic audience of the self, for a release from the "mephitic" Centre that "unravels" (or dances) in the form of "bitter play," and not exclusively for either irritated friends, or the more than somewhat baffled "Workmen and Labourers of Great Britain," he is writing for the tenuous existence of the Thesean tightrope-walker, whose wire is, of dangerous necessity, less than taut, less than "Straight."

But if the wire is slack, the strain, paradoxically, is not. Attempted mastery—and attendant responsibility—is not only a Strange Chord perceived from a True Centre but a straight line pulled to a breaking point, like the "Strained Cord" of an intellectual nerve about to snap. Still, whether the quintessential Ruskin can entirely accept the responsibility for the authorship of the digressive, curvilinear "bitter play," which is a kind of syntactical myopia that would be blind to the rectilinearity of attempted mastery, is far from certain. Given that "Florentine intensity," which is virtually insane, of both Ruskin's masterful attempts and his sense of interrelation and responsibility, it is almost as if Ruskin would become anonymous—or if not that, a new self who is a version of an old self that never existed. He might create a kind of autobiographical fiction of the beginning.

Changing location may adumbrate a change of identities. In the fire and water (or burning sewage) of the Centre for too long, Ruskin goes to the hedges for comfort—perhaps the hedges of "vital hawthorn," which would be a mnemonic trip to Lucent Verdure. Responsible "to," or, more accurately, "for" others, to the point where stress meets breakdown—that cold dawn of moral contention and mental anguish—Ruskin, with "stern," if not "final," purpose, would "play" at the abdication of his temporarily "true" position. We recall he will only be a Makeshift Master. He will manufacture the fiction of a second childhood beyond vortical interrelation/responsibility, where the attempted mastery of Strange Chords is invisible. And if his first childhood is located in the innocence of Cock-Robinson-Crusoe centricity, his second childhood, innocent only in the happy loss of memory, will be necessarily circumferential.

Briefly, with an epistolary style—perhaps a fourth way of writing (style and tone being here not so much a "bitter play" as a pleasant picnic with terrifying implications)—that apes childish letters which a precocious Ruskin never wrote the first time around, he carries on an extended, girlish correspondence with the illustrator of little girls, Kate Greenaway, from what might be called a curvilinear hedgerow of irresponsibility.[9] As an oasis of abdication, childish or "girlish" play replaces the final dance on the wire that threatens to become increasingly tight as stress creates unbearable tension. Perhaps, informed by his "Law of Curvature," his second childhood, circling back, will supersede his problematical first. And under the extreme duress of the attempted mastery of Strange Chords, Ruskin, who already has "guides," will further search for fathers (if not indeed "masters"), like Carlyle (his "Papa") and John Brown, whose combined authority, at least as long as they live, will ease the pressures of his own. If the "strange," a category for the overreaching, is not made familiar (and attempted mastery does not become a fact of accommodation), surprise will be only as temporarily efficacious as that predictably labyrinthine wonder within the curvilinear.

But second-childishness is only an interlude—a happy interlude of doubleness and disequilibrium. Operating more seriously, as we shall see, in the syntactical intricacies of the Third Style than in the calculated naiveté of a style of exclusive innocence, Ruskin, as death's "long shadow" approaches a final completion that is beyond even the purview of the "wide circumference," is a man who would become the lonely father to his more sociable "childhood"—or, more specifically, whose language would return from the present-tense labyrinth of the Theatre of Blindness to the "enchanted design" of the Hampton Court Maze, as seen in the overshadowed light of the "blind memory" of Lucent Verdure. And without either map or index, that language of qualified "play" will itself not be childish, though responsibility will still be delegated—yet not so much to an original "Papa," who, with Ruskin now in the surrogate role himself, may no longer be found, as to a "prudent mistress," whose paradoxical "bidding" of chance will be his own immediate

---

[9] An appropriate example is the letter in which the feet and shoes of the pedestrian "compete" with mussel shells that, if Ruskin does not find as architecturally inviting as snail shells, nevertheless once provided for someone else, mooring-cords that Ariadne could have transformed into a lifeline. At any rate, the concern and tone is characteristic of this correspondence from the "hedgerow":

December 27, '82

Dear Miss Greenaway,—Friday will do delightfully for me, even better than to-day, having been tired with Xmas letters and work.

This is a lovely little book—all through. The New and Old Years are chiefly delightful to me. But I wish some of the children had bare feet—and that the shoes of the others weren't *quite* so like mussel-shells.

The drawing on my letter, however, is perfect! shoes and all—eyes and lips—unspeakable.—Ever your grateful and devoted

J. Ruskin

performance: "This disappointment I accept thankfully as the or-
dinancy of my careful and prudent mistress, Atropos,—the Third
Fors; and am indeed quickly enough apprehensive of her lesson
in it. She wishes, I doubt not, to recognize that I was foolish in
designing the intrusion of technical advice into my political letters. . . . .
. . . .
I must needs do her bidding" (xxviii, 433).

Ruskin does "her bidding" with the enthusiasm of one who, more
than familiar with the instructive tone of dogmatic paternalism,
fears central structures and the attendant organization of prophecy.
Atropos, the allegorized Third Fors, is mistress in fact of the most
extreme form of the Third Style, providing relief with a syntax
(as long as it can maintain itself as a syntax of conjunctions) that,
like a form of desperate "play" or restless "rest," is a dark mas-
querade of "heavenly involuntariness." Often, toward the end (and
before the time of the mirror), there is the "Harlequin's mask."
Like Ariadne, though perhaps without Ariadne's confidence that
the Circumference of "promise" will—or should—be attained,
Atropos at least signals the direction toward the Exit of expression:
"It has chanced, by help of the Third Fors (as again and again in
the course of these letters the thing to my purpose has been brought
before me just when I needed it) . . ." (xxvii, 360).

"Unravelling" on the penultimate way to the "farthest extremity,"
Ruskin is more than pleased to submit to a responsibility outside
himself in a way that no permanently (rather than "makeshift")
Central Man would find either necessary or possible. Divested, by
a kind of legerdemain, of responsibility and that corresponding
vision of replete "interrelation," which is the vortical vision of "insane intensity" not unusual at the time of Brunelleschi, Ruskin, at
least partially sane before the "nothing" beyond the edge of Illth,
retains what remains of that tenuous sanity by virtue of his submission. It is the submission of fallen Gothic altitude—a descent
as if to the ground level of low foliage and Lucent Verdure, where
Theseus' Ariadne is metamorphosed into Ruskin's more elevated
Atropos and the (white) clues of immediacy may yield neither an
Exit nor a future. Still, before the blindness that is blind to itself,
this remains to be "seen," and, for the moment, Ruskin finds his
fallen condition Atroposian, which is to say fortunately hierarchical:
"It chanced by the appointment of the Third Fors, to which, you
know, I am bound in these letters uncomplainingly to submit"
(xxvii, 270).

Led, instead of leading, and on the way toward the "farthest extremity" of a potentially dangerous Circumference, rather than (re)turning reflexively and centripetally within a squirrel-cage that is either a mind or London, if not in fact the Venice of autobiographical consciousness, Ruskin attempts to release received Repletion along shadowy corridors of "capricious sinuousities" that lie not only "below" but "ahead," in a future of dubious extent. Simply, the problem is now, not that there is "too much to be dealt with" (xxviii, 461), but that "too much" has already been dealt with. One might say that the double axe of Crete (*labrys*) predicts the doubling of labyrinths—that the Maze of consciousness above, which is unavoidably like an intestinal tract below, tending toward the "mephitic," requires room for an equivalent Maze of "serpentine" expression outside, an adjacent "serpentine" analogue that, as syntax becomes parataxis, may itself, as we shall see, double into verbal ruins above and the "archaeology of silence"[10] below. The (logo)-concentric "wide-circumference," virtually ingested and, in the process, contorted into the shape of a labyrinth, must be turned inside out. The "threads of thought," before what might be called the implosive self-destruction of the labyrinthine consciousness, must find paginal release—a blank space that is perhaps closer to what might be offered by Atropos, who, after all, holds not only shears but an initially blank writing tablet: "I am almost giddy (though perfectly well)," he writes his mother in 1869, "with the quantity of things in my head—trains of thought beginning and branching to infinity, crossing each other, and all tempting and wanting to be worked out" (xix, lxiv).

Describing "trains of thought," like either "threads of thought" or threads (presumably not from the mooring-cords of mussels) in a tapestry or mosaic, that cross each other with an intricacy and complexity which is close to the vertiginous "*ad infinitum*" of potential Ruskinian indexing, Ruskin is also describing his early and undiminished "love of all sorts of filigree and embroidering, from hoarfrost to the high clouds. The intricacies of virgin silver, of aborescent gold, the weaving of birds'-nests . . . and most of all the tabernacle work of the French schools" (xxxv, 157n). Even a plenitude that eventually unravels in the flamboyance of penultimate peregrination recalls a condition before terrible beauty, when Repletion was closer to a plenum met of benign, if implicitly claus-

---

[10] The phrase is essentially Foucault's, employed in the Preface of the original edition (Plon, 1961) to *Histoire de la folie*.

trophobic, "superabundance" than the eventual vacuum that horrifies. We remember the horizontally "full" results of the received Parallell Advance: "three or four things coming into my head *calling to be done*" (*Diaries*, p. 868); "Head full of thoughts" (*Diaries*, p. 869); "No rest even in sleep; head full of thoughts . . ." (*Diaries*, p. 871).

Fullness "inside" at first requires a comparative and appropriate emptiness of potential "outside"—this before both the imitation of labyrinthine consciousness in elaborate syntax and then the final blank page of Illth (less than "nothing" having come of both a disconfirmed "nothing" and substantiated excess) that is a sign of madness no longer contested. If Atropos, with her well-developed transcendence (or even "extrication") of immediacy, is a later version of the uncompetitively thread-bearing Ariadne, who is neither Arachne nor Athena, then Ruskin, happily retreating (and falling) into a censored memory of Lucent Verdure, when the labyrinth was the horticulture of fortunate pastoral, is a Theseus, perhaps with "Harlequin's mask," "on the way out" who has reluctantly come to understand that paradise exists best, if at all, as a memory of what has been lost. The "farthest extremity" of potential composes a kind of land of promise about which it might be assumed that one can regain, if not in fact resurrect, something paradisiacal that has been lost.

Yet there persists the incipient sense that Ruskin would have that "farthest extremity" farther still, in a future that is already dubious, as if to avoid the disconfirmation of confrontation, the failure of prophecy. Despite the somewhat tentative instincts for the exit, as well as a purpose that would be both "stern" and "final," future tenses may be most serviceable as disguised tenses of the memory of "nothing but process." That the memory may be faulty is almost another matter—a matter, at least in part, for a Promise(d) Land that functions best as an imaginative landscape for psychic exploration.

A Promise(d) Land—a territory of the past as well as the future—may be a Paradise both creatively remembered and conveniently forgotten. Its presence is in its absence.

B. Paratactical Texts of Ripped Immanence: From Ariadne to the Shears and Penultimate Tablet of Atropos

As he releases the mephitic sewage of the Cloaca Maxima, which is an "unheavenly" or infernal memory so full that it is on the border of amnesia, Ruskin, in significant portions of *Fors*, is not only unwinding the private threads of his thought in public but is doing so in an almost exhibitionistic tense (and tone) of consciousness that is more immediate than even a conventional diary or a personal letter. Curiously, the more immediate the tense, the less claustrophobic it appears. A magnifying glass may be in order. Or one may say that the closer he is to his subject, the farther he is from it as though, nearsighted, he were, calculatingly, wearing glasses for the farsighted. At times, he seems blind to the intimacy of his material. In any case, the closer Ruskin stands in relation to his text—the more "myopic" his stance—the less "right-angled" premeditation and responsibility he feels. The burdens of the attempted mastery inherent in both Strange Chords and the rectilinearity of a street (or Venetian canal) that is called "Straight" are eased, if not entirely eliminated.

The syntactical gravity of central elevation (or even the eccentric condensations on the margins of *Modern Painters II*) weighs more heavily than a verbal proximity that is modeled after the style of Ariadne's ground-level thread: the foreground of the Maze, which is all the Ruskinian traveler/writer knows, is a landscape of immediacy that perpetually transcends itself in the "surprise" of the next turn. The future within curvilinearity is, essentially, a tense without a future, a tense without the prospects of either death or disconfirmation. Further, the Maze may also, for a time, be able to deny Ruskin information about himself, his precarious sanity, as if the contrary superimposition of curvilinear myopia over (logo)-concentric farsightedness had created a kind of countered or opposed blindness that would temporarily prevent the recognition of madness.

We recall the early and curiously prescient, or "returning," passage from the inaugural *The Poetry of Architecture* (1837-38) that joins initial buildings with both penultimate syntax and travel/perception—the "Gothic anomaly" being also the Gothic analogy: "The house must not be a noun substantive, it must not stand by itself, it must be part and parcel of a proportioned whole: it must not be seen all at once; and he who sees one end should feel that, from the given data, he can arrive at no conclusion respecting the other" (I, 187). Like the "right" kind of architecture, the syntactical travel of the Third Style, as "overseen" by either Ariadne or Atropos (though, despite certain similarities, the similarities of eventualities, they are no more versions of each other than syntax is a version of later parataxis) is not composed of the predictable and autonomous Noun Substantive, which is what prefabricated housing is to the irregularly aedicular architecture of the "Gothic anomaly." For many reasons, one must be "blind" to the circumferential Promise(d) Land. Prophecy is itself a prediction of disappointment—or worse.

If predictability, though in many cases inevitable, is anathema (even perhaps the predictability of the passage from *The Poetry of Architecture*), more than the serpentine syntax of the Third Style has nevertheless been unwittingly anticipated. Architecture, syntax, and motion are incarnated in those "enchanted designs" that are necessarily lower than Scott's "regular mansions." The writer, who is an un-Daedalean architect, is also a pedestrian traveler. Unlike the fundamentally intransitive and autonomous author of the text as Noun Substantive, the Ruskinian traveler/writer has no intention of remaining motionless in the Maze. There is still a kind of vestigially Thesean instinct for the Exit. Yet impelled by replete stress and the need for the release of expression, the Third Style is a spiraling syntax that, close to an exit that is in fact the collapse of the architecture of reluctant nihilism, may be too anxiously fast for its own good. Curvilinear speed may create the same vertigo as altitude.

That narrow, serpentine "travel" is not only like moving from the central Rialto to the "farthest extremity" of Venice—a city that we know is like a mind, its "white clues" like the threads of intricate thought that accommodate "error" and "recovery" in a motion and style of myopic immediacy that avoids angelic elevation—it is also like visiting Rome the right way, with the appropriate "slow travel" that would negate any tendencies toward replete condensation and juxtaposition. Like the returning (with a difference) *Helix virgata*, we recall not only the admonitions concerning architecture that have syntactical application, but also early travel advice that acts as a kind of figural fulfillment:

> In the city, if you take a carriage and drive to express points of lionisation, I believe that most people of good taste would expect little and find less. The Capitol is a melancholy rubbishy square of average Palladian—modern; the Forum, a good group of smashed columns. . . . But if, instead of driving, with excited expectation, to particular points, you saunter leisurely up one street and down another, yielding to every impulse, peeping into every corner, and keeping your observation active, the impression is exceedingly changed. There is not a fragment, a stone, or a chimney, ancient or modern, that is not in itself a study, not an inch of ground that can be passed over

without its claim of admiration and offer of instruction, and you return home in hopeless conviction that were you to substitute years for the days of your appointed stay, they would not be enough for the estimation or examination of Rome [I, 380-81].

Avoiding "express points of lionisation," and instead "yielding to every impulse, peering into every corner, and keeping your observation active," what is sought, both in Rome and syntax, is not the straight-lined recognition of "particular points" so much as the curvilinear exploration of "right hand, or left," as if there were "not a fragment, a stone, or a chimney, ancient or modern, that is not itself a study." In a passage from *The Cestus of Aglaia*, Ruskin avoids rectilinear confrontation with work, in order to "saunter leisurely" in a digressive syntax of "capricious" consciousness that approaches the final Transformation of the Maze:

> I cannot get to my work in this paper, somehow; the web of these old enigmas entangles me again and again. That rough syllable which begins the name of Griselda, "Gries," "the stone"; the roar of the long fall of the Toccia seems to mix with the sound of it, bringing thoughts of the great Alpine patience; mute snow wreathed by grey rock, till avalanche time comes— patience of mute tormented races till the time of the Grey league came; at last impatient. (Note that, hitherto, it has hewn its way to much: the Rhine-foam of the Via Mala seeming to have done its work better.) But it is a noble colour that Grison Grey;—dawn colour—graceful for a faded silk to ride in, and wonderful, in paper, for getting a glow upon, if you begin wisely, as you may some day perhaps see by those Turner sketches at Kensington, if ever anybody can see them.
> But we *will* get to work now . . .   [XIX, 87-88].

More and more, Ruskin "plays" before he works, if in fact he does not "play" in order to work. Or further, as the failing distance of perspective studies coils into the condensed serialization of the curvilinear, like the contorted ingestion of the "wide circumference," the suspicion increases that the "play" may be in the originally innocent "nothing but process" of becoming more important than the work planned. One might say that the location and significance of the "before" and "after" were undergoing an inversion of even the hesitant sequence of the *Helix virgata*, which modifies progress with return. Toward the end, which has hitherto suggested the Exit, the Origin, in a most un-Thesean fashion, threatens to become of greater significance than that end which may itself, concentrically enclosed, be located within a final circumferential frame, rather than exist as a threshold to a further "outside" of once desired emptiness.

After a period of advertised "play," there "*will*" indeed be a kind of work. But at this point, work, without the following of the "threads" (whether Arachne's thread of at least weblike hesitation or Ariadne's thread of propelling conjunction)[11] of a "play" that may even be "bitter," is unthinkable—or rather thinkable only as a kind of blind madness, for the "blind guides" of the canal, who cannot even "see" the straightforward waterways of confirmed rectilinearity.

Increasingly, the penultimate becomes important, almost as though it would aspire toward the concluding condition of ultimacy. But then, with Ruskin, the false ending may in fact be true. At times, now, the "before," prompted by the prospect of the "after" (where shadows, both long and wide, meet the blank page of "naked contention"), would become more than merely preliminary. It is as if a "Preface" without apothecary prophecy that might be disconfirmed, like a Promise(d) Land that will fail to keep its promise, would exchange places with an "Appendix" that, itself like a Paradise lost, would be "present" enough to fill, or fulfill, without rectilinear summary. The "language of return" would begin—or re-begin—informed more by memory than prediction.

Significantly, that present tense of microscopic (and enlarged) immediacy which traces the "colubrine" turns of consciousness in the elaborate syntax of the Third Style is not a tense of narrow exclusion. Instead, while employing the felicitous syntax of release, albeit a syntax of the labyrinth, that tense, too sinuously close for the True Centre's synoptic grasp of context, nevertheless involves itself in exploring digressively peripheral areas beyond the present. In fact, limiting the aperture of his vision, Ruskin "plays" with the temporal panorama of history: magnifying the present, he finds the spiraling depths of the past. E. T. Cook, one of the dedicated editors of the Library Edition, has ambitiously undertaken the archaeology beneath that *Cestus* passage of considerable richness. Ruskin's excursion, close to consciousness—to "right hand, or left" (or the right and left hemispheres of the brain), involving Gothic "error" and "recovery"—proves to be a labyrinthine excursion that

[11] Hillis Miller makes an intriguing case for the affiliation of Ariadne and Arachne in *Troilus and Cressida*. See "Ariachne's Broken Woof," *The Georgia Review* (spring 1977). With Ruskin, as we shall see, Ariadne will almost become both Arachne and Atropos.

makes consciousness historically/politically, as well as territorially/ geologically, inclusive:

> *Gris*elda brings into his head memories of the Tosa (or Toccia) falls beneath the Gries glacier (he may have visited the falls from Demo d'Ossola in 1845); then he passes to think of the long oppression of Raetia under petty tyrants (of which record remains in the many ruined feudal castles which stud that part of Switzerland). Their rule was at last shaken off by the formation of the Grison Confederation, in which one of the constituents was the Grey League (Graue Bund): hence the name of the present canton, Graubünden (*Fr.* Grisons). The name (though possibly referring to several counts, Grafen, whom the League comprised) is popularly derived from the grey home-spun coats of those by whom it was formed: (see the passage quoted by Ruskin in Vol. xiii, p. 516). The thought of the Grison country brings to his mind its central defile, the Via Mala, the grandeur of which had impressed him so many years ago . . . and he doubts incidentally whether the men of Graubünden have hewn their way in the world so decisively as a foaming river. Then the color of Grison Grey recalls to him at one moment Tennyson's Enid ("Earl, entreat her by my love, Albeit I give no reason but my wish, That she ride with me in her faded silk"—"The Marriage of Geraint"); and at the next, Turner's brilliant water-colour sketches on grey paper (see Vol. xiii, p. 385), which allusion, lastly, leads him to a lament at the little interest taken in sketches . . . then shown at the South Kensington Museum   [xix, 87n].

The syntactical incarnation of the Maze is not always as dense or obscure as it is in the *Cestus* passage. Throughout *Fors Clavigera*, the Third Style, apparently whirling—the speed of the turning pirouettes increasing—toward a circumferential Exit (an Exit that, itself involving the collapse of the Theatre of Blindness, should perhaps not be found; for, as we may now be beginning to understand, the Ariadne who will initially provide Theseus' solution, his "salvation," may ultimately in fact be Ruskin's chilling personification of those open spaces that inspire the horror beyond the *horror vacui*, his demigoddess of Illth, of plenitude become absence)—that Third Style, it must be remembered, is a counterpoint to another which, closer to reportage, does not seem impelled by the need to fill all available space with flamboyant line, to blacken even the white margins of a page with the errant tracery of "right hand, or left." Directed reportage is necessary for the balance and serial continuance of the Third Style, which, if unconstricted by other necessities, would become mere indulgence without what may be the fictional "stern final purpose" of the "farthest extremity." Still, occasionally, an inspired passage appears that seems to be led by no thread, angelic or daemonic, and that leads neither to the Exit nor to an "indexed" part of a tapestry in which the dense weave holds the history of the world (as well as the design of coiled entrails).

Instead, that passage will appear to proceed by virtue of its own syntactical energy. Operating in the unmapped (and unindexed) labyrinth of a consciousness that is like a storehouse, museum, or memory organized by "heavenly involuntariness," that antiphonally lateral, serpentine style will supply its own impetus in the form of a series of present participles that, kinetically, perhaps with the vitality of both "presence" and their present-tense immediacy, will extend the release of a condition of Repletion that will "prematurely" end (again, with what may be the fiction of the Promise(d) Land's finality "beyond") in a state of exhaustion, like a solitary dancer who has pirouetted too long in a multicursal Maze, and who may, in fact, be too tired to be either irritated or insane:

Read, before the next *Fors*, that epistle of Jude with intense care. It sums all the Epistles coming, by the order of the *Fors* which grouped the Biblebooks just before the Apocalypse; and it precisely describes your worst—in verity, your only,—Enemies of this day; the *twice* dead people,—plucked up by the *roots*, having once been rooted in the Holy Faith of Christendom; but now, *filthy* dreamers of the Gospel of Dirt, in perpetual foul dream of what man was, instead of reverence for what he is; carried about of winds of vanity (pitiful apothecaries' apprentices), speaking evil of things they know not; but in the things they know naturally as brute beasts, in these, corrupting themselves; going in the way of Cain—(brother kingdom at war with brother. France and Germany, Austria and Italy)—running after the error of Belaam for reward (the Bishop of Manchester—whom I finally challenged, personally and formally, through my Oxford Secretary, two months ago, not daring to answer me a word,—knowing that the city he rules over is in every business act of it in mortal sin, and conniving,—to keep smooth with it—he!—and the Bishop of Peterborough, "neutral," in sleek consent to the son of Zippor's prayer—"Neither curse them at all, nor bless them at all"), and perishing in the gainsaying of Kore, going down quick into volcanic petroleum pit, in the gathering themselves against Lawgiver and Priest, saying, "Wherefore lift ye up yourselves above the congregation of the Lord? the days of Kinghood and Priesthood are ended!" [xxix, 95-96].

Or again, in *Fors*, after having reestablished what he calls "the Position of William"—

> Sweet William, carrying generally more absinth in his brains than wit, has little to say for himself, having, indeed, wasted too much of his sweetness lately, tainted disagreeably with petroleum, on the desert air of Paris. And the people who are to get their five per cent out of him, and roll him and suck him,—the sugarcane of a William that he is,—how should they but think the arrangement a glorious one for the nation? [xxvii, 136].

—after having dealt for the moment with William, whose "Position" of precarious economy, of interest and capital, will resurface symphonically several times through later letters, Ruskin macaronically turns to homes that are sweet before they are bitter, in the "bitter play" of both kaleidoscopically vacillating tones and widely ranging allusions that give the impression that Ruskin's resounding, oracular voice (a voice driven to strange resonance, like that of the prophet of Israel, under the stress of Assyrian collapse) is coming not only omnisciently from everywhere but in allusions that also make the reader uncertain of his own peculiar textual location— or even, for that matter, the language ("pourtrayed," "petroleuse") that is being employed. Beginning with sweet homes, he swiftly winds up, with a kind of economy entirely different from that of Sweet William and his "Position," in quasi apocalypse—in flames, the banners of flames (oriflamme) that might be held aloft by "the helmed Pucelle," whose own home, the forests of Domremy, is only sweet if there are no fires, but who will herself, nevertheless, end up in flame:

> Did you chance, my friends, any of you, to see, the other day, the 83rd number of the *Graphic*, with the picture of the Queen's concert in it? All the fine ladies sitting so trimly, and looking so sweet, and doing the whole duty of woman—wearing their fine clothes, gracefully; and the pretty singer, white-throated, warbling "Home, sweet home" to them, so morally, and melodiously. Here was yet to be our ideal of virtuous life, thought the *Graphic*. Surely, we are safe back with our virtues

in satin slippers and lace veils;—and our Kingdom of Heaven is come again, *with* observation, and crown diamonds of the dazzlingest. Cherubim and Seraphim in toilettes de Paris— (bleu-de-ciel—vert d'olivier-de—Noé—mauve de colombe-fu-sillée) dancing to Coote and Tinney's band; and vulgar Hell reserved for the canaille, as heretofore! Vulgar Hell shall be didactically pourtrayed, accordingly (see page 17),—Wicked-ness going its way to *its* poor Home—bitter-sweet. Ouvrier and pétroleuse—prisoners at last—glaring wild on their way to die.

Alas! of these divided races, of whom one was appointed to teach and guide the other, which has indeed sinned deepest— the unteaching, or the untaught?—which now are guiltiest— these, who perish, or those—who forget?

Ouvrier and pétroleuse; they are gone their way—to their death. But for these, the Virgin of France shall yet unfold the oriflamme above their graves, and lay her blanch lilies on their dust. Yes, and for these, great Charles shall rouse his Roland, and bid him put ghostly trump to lip, and breathe a point of war; and the helmed Pucelle shall answer with a wood-note of Domremy;—yes, and for these the Louis they mocked, like his master, shall raise his holy hands, and pray God's peace   [XXVII, 137-38].

If Ruskin's horizontal surface perspective includes areas that break the observing self into a polygonal consciousness, it is only the felicitious and internalized circumferential line of the trans-forming Maze that keeps the observer-turned-reporter in, more or less, one piece—a single reporter engaged in a series of perceptions and, more importantly, expressions that are like the retinal ad-justments within the Hampton Court Maze. Public play becomes, as we shall see, a private (if not entirely integrated) play, perhaps to be performed in that Maze-like Theatre of Blindness that is half-patterned on the labyrinthine pastoral of recollected Lucent Ver-dure. And, as such, that private play will shortly become more desperately concerned with solution/salvation or resurrection/ "extrication" than meandering turned "bitter" wandering. The Third Style employed in *Fors Clavigera*, addressed to the working men of Great Britain, is not much different from the Third Style of *The Diaries/The Brantwood Diary*, which is addressed to a version of himself, either as immediate writer or later reader.

In a late diary entry, Ruskin privately suggests the dangers of the Third Style—those occasionally peripheral ambitions. He con-trasts his own version of Scott's "regular mansion," *Praeterita*, which, though by no means dead or mechanical in a Daedalean sense, is nevertheless a syntactical architecture of calculated, farseeing premeditation, as well as premeditated recollection, with his own potential for the extravagant and myopically Atroposian "Gothic anomaly"—that desultory wandering, as if in a Hampton Court without end, of a Third Style, whose final, digressive ambitions may not be merely for the "farthest extremity" of margins, which may be a version of Ariadne's dancing place, but also for Ruskin's location of postcircumferential madness that has the capacity to be both as other-wordy (one word perpetually summoning another) and otherworldly as the "next planet or nebula":

> The thirty-six chapters of *Praeterita* being already arranged to the end, require extreme care in packing their contents, so as to keep what I have called the essentials only; but not the cardinal ones, so as to fix the reader's attention, without the severest reduction of what I write at first "garrulously." Merely, for example, I have written this morning of brought up diary, from date 1st October to this present word, straight off before breakfast, and it is now 5 minutes past nine, morning, of Tuesday the [blank]th of October. But if I wrote a parenthesis of that length every now and then, the entire book would overlap into the next planet or nebula; and if I began putting notes to explain or confirm, I should probably write a new book on the trotting of Centaurs and Lapithae, or the riding of Bellerophon, or the crawling of the tortoise of Aegina, or the flying of Harry the Fifth's tennis balls . . .   [*Diaries*, p. 1136].

Play, even if it contains the likelihood of being "bitter," can become apparent burlesque. Wandering on "right hand, or left" is at times almost low comedy (though, as we know, fallen altitude, the altitude of the serpent, has its ironic virtue). The style of the Exit—Ariadne's Exit, not Christian "extrication" or Atropos' shears/nail—may become a joke, but the joke is finally closer to terrible tears than laughter, as the defined Exit becomes the debris of the architecture of reluctant nihilism that is in fact the decomposition of the Labyrinthine Penultimate. Still, Ruskin's description of his serial, associated peregrinations becomes an obvious—and because obvious, not entirely successful—version of his sly play:

> Were I to yield, as I was wont to in the first series of these letters, without scruple, to the eddies of thought which turned the main stream of my discourse into apparently irrelevant, and certain unprogressive inlets, I should in this place proceed

to show how true-love is inconsistent with railways, with joint-stocks banks, with the landed interest, with parliamentary interest, and grouse shooting, with lawn tennis, with monthly magazines, spring fashions, and Christmas cards. But I am resolute now to explain myself in one place before becoming enigmatic in another [xxix, 445].

But the occasional comedy of the Third Style, as the Exit's "capricious sinuousities" of expressive release are sought—this against the backwaters of the central Cloaca Maxima—is not only a version of ambiguously informed tears; it is also a preparation for tragic collapse, the collapse of an exhausted dancer, whose ultimately "stern final purpose" is the penultimate "nothing but process" of the curvilinear pirouette. It might be said that the centrifugal traveler/writer of "slow travel" has become the circular—if not of "squirrelian revolution"—dancer/writer of "Devil speed." The noise, whether of laughter or weeping, will become silence. And the Exit will be understood to be an entrance into that "farthest extremity" where White Silence is not a relief or a pastoral of absent sound even after plenitudinous language has become verbal repletion. The prospect for the ultimacy of Illth, which is the ultimacy of silence and blindness, where notable "error" is beyond the "recovery" of returning/retracing lines, would be exchanged for the penultimate process, or dance, of the present tense that can only be perpetuated as long as exhaustion can be avoided—after which point one drops to the floor or collapses on an immaculate bed, like a final blank page, that has not been slept in for at least a night. Still, as long as one is in the labyrinthine "nothing but process" of going mad, one is not entirely mad. And the postcircumferential Promise(d) Land of dubious, if not yet disconfirming, futurity will not be able either to keep or break a promise that is now "in the process" of being seen as more infernal than paradisiacal.

Reading portions of Ruskin's discourse with himself, which is dialogue pretending to be a monologue that will nevertheless conclude, beyond even the dialogical, in silence, one is watching a turning mind that is, in turn, in pirouettes of blind self-consciousness, watching itself, in that blind darkness, "through" a reflexive looking glass of the mind, going mad—and this during an apparently interminable nightwatch.[12] If the laughter of "bitter play,"

---

[12] One thinks of the "perilous mirror" of Foucault that joins self-consciousness with madness: "presumptuously identified with the object of his delirium, the madman recognizes himself as in a mirror in this madness whose absurd pretensions he has denounced; his solid sovereignty as a subject dissolves in this object he has

interrupted by tears that are warm before they are cold, seems to go on for too long, it is a noise nevertheless more desirable than the contrasting, as if superimposed, cacophonous screaming of peacocks that promise, after their antiphonal chorus, the ultimacy of silence. The myopic Third Style of the Exit, winding centrifugally through the curvilinear topography of consciousness, will finally give way to an entrance, surrounded by the debris of the failed architecture of the penultimate Theatre of Blindness, not into a promised landscape of either the "farthest extremity" or "farthest reaches" that might be pastoral after the "slime-pit of central corruption" but to a state of exhaustion and madness, and, in February of 1878, to the *Dream*—an oneiric entrance that will lead to the blank page, or abyss, of White Silence beyond the temporary salvation/solution of elaborated "process" that is closer to the arresting of a disease than a final cure.

Later, in 1881—in what is essentially after the last Transformation of the Maze, a memory after the last imitative recollection of Lucent Verdure, and in the form of the "multicursal" labyrinth with nodes of options and "queries" that are in fact blind alleys, rather than the earlier "unicursal" ("once-run") labyrinthine language of solution/salvation as "nothing but process"—there is the language of a kind of gastronomic transcendentalism, whose vertiginous surface of meta-presence gives way to an inward-turning, vortical syntax that spirals, as if informed by an unreversed "instinctive draingage," toward the bottom, as in a labyrinth of absence, where there is at least "one leg [in] dung," in an act of virtual self-consumption. It is a vortical syntax (the vortical vision of interrelation having turned infernal, as in a labyrinthine descent, organized about "right angles," to Dante's "nether pits") that is in fact a reversal of the centrifuged style that leads to the earlier parataxis of double Mazes and the Labyrinthine Penultimate.[13] But in 1878,

---

demystified by accepting it. He is now pitilessly observed by himself. And in the silence of those who represent reason, and who have done nothing but hold up the perilous mirror, he recognizes himself as objectively mad" (*Madness and Civilization*, p. 264). Ruskin's "perilous mirror" is both of the mind and the hiding place of the cat, the "Evil One," on the dawn of the blank page.

[13] The passage, remarkable, is the incarnation of the Third Style, dealing with both intimacy and transcendence, like the "capricious sinuousities" of a Maze that is always changing direction in proximate space. Digression as transgression becomes essential metamorphosis. And the "returning upon itself" reflexivity of self-cannibalization, as of "unbishoply" "blind mouths" (xviii, 72), becomes a kind of final transformation of the Maze, as that Maze is, in the end, presumably, a digestive tract leading to—or perhaps "sauntering" to—at least "one leg [of] dung," as a "mephitic" recreation of the Cloaca Maxima of the centralized sewage of Venice.

the associative and serial procedure of the Maze is more allusively esoteric than gastronomically transforming. Still, ranging widely, Ruskin is also exploring intimately, coming closer to the essential topography of his consciousness than to the threshold of his mouth (even his echinus-mouth of sinuous expression). It is as if that

---

If there is the attempted paradisiacal imitation of Lucent Verdure, as well as the memory of that experience as an ecstatic experience itself, there is also, among the by now disintegrating if not entirely decomposed, transformations of the Maze, an infernal (perhaps merely intestinal) counterpart:

September 23rd. Friday. Joan home y[esterday], and Lollie. Feast of sucking pig. (Q[uery]: what had Tobit for dinner—the father?)

I, a spot in their feast of charity! But carry my wine best, being the servant of the 'gluttonous man, and winebibber.'

Q[uery]—happy thought!—when and how often *did* Christ enjoy himself and —the company—with any of his apostles who took after him? St. Martin, suppose, or—St. Crumpet—Crumpin! Frenchman not liking me cold—will he like me hot?

I *opened* just now (down to coffee in good time) at the entry for 23rd Oct. last year—page 153, A, B—and must mind what I'm at. This morning, thought of *Sortes Virgilianae*, and the sign of angle-dial of paper, turned accidentally in folio yesterday, to *Infelix sedebit*, but *hiding* the anatomical part to the left.

Q[uery]. Where, and who, sits infelix—Unhappy? or unlucky? "Lead me, as he leads his flocks" &c.—Wild *deer*—Chamois—Fawn at Lucerne. Aig[uille] *d'Argentière*—(Silver *How*?). Set Alic to find diary of day when I went up—I and Couttet—alone in the early morning, on aiguille *Bouchard* (not Argentière) and saw the three flocks of wild *deer*, not goats.

"The High hills are a refuge for the wild *goats*, and the (Brantwood) rocks for the conies."

Scapegoat—Melville's sermon on the *two* Goats. "*Aha*; the TWO *goats* are now in the hands of their enemies." . . .

His [Mr. Melville] last call upon me when I was at dinner. I came to him in the drawing room, intimated to him I *was* at dinner. "Go to your dinner," he said, benevolent, contemptuous—and left; and I never saw him seriously again, unless perhaps, for some chance form of call, or knock-head-together in street.

"Revenons à nos moutons"—goats, I should say, Moses and *his* horns. Zedekiah the son of Chenaanah, and *his* horns of iron or iron clad—or iron cast.

"With these shalt thou push the *Syrians* till thou have *consumed* them"—i.e. Caffres, New Zealanders, Afghans, &c. and the Gallant Colonel and my lady Clara (*Gallant*-galantes) Coloneless—shall have their pipe, and pot, of Champagne, in peace, and punkah fans of Japanese design, on the hills of the Himalaya.

"I will lift up mine eyes unto the hills from whence cometh my—income and coolies."

"Revenons—Revenons—à nos moutons," and Lambs that are slain, and made Chops of, and cutlets. Human *grillades*.

(N.B.) Happy thought No. 1. "Vous y grillerez Cicéron, et le bon Socrate, le divin Platon." (N.C.) Happy thought No. 2. If Aristophanes had run away with Xantippe, would Socrates have forgiven him? Perhaps—Perhaps! See Socrates' last love message to Xantippe, while "on old Aegina's rock &c.—the God of

problematical "farthest extremity" had become the closest, interior point of both the mine of a mind "above" and coiled entrails "below," like double labyrinths (as if for double axes), one on top of the other, with an expressive, if indeterminate, equivalent paginally "outside," both explicit and implicit, in the form of a double labyrinth of syntax become parataxis "above," and the crocodilian "archaeology of silence" unexcavated "below."

On February 17, the *Dream* has been syntactically approaching obviously for three days, beginning with a "Madonna for a Valentine—Fors gave me her from the Beatra Vigri— . . ." (*Brantwood Diary*, p. 91), and the Devil, not yet a cat at dawn, has made an appearance, before the "naked contention," along with Ophelia ("little Ophelia—who bewept to her grave did go, larded all with sweet flowers"), who is a type for Rose La Touche, just as Ruskin is Hamlet, when he is not Theseus:[14]

> February 17.—Sunday. Stopped upstairs behind Kate to pray, a little—after "seeing my way" at last at 1/2 past three this morning—with beata Vigris help—and Ophelias.—Let in— that out—Departed, never more

---

(matrimonial) gladness, sent his *parting* smile." But—Q[uery]. Happy thought No. 3 (both of these given me last night with a few more). Did Socrates ever forgive him the *Clouds*? and *if* he had written the *Clouds after* having run off with Xantippe! Or instead of *writing* the *Clouds*, gone on Back-biting *behind* the clouds! fog—of the Acheron.

St. Ulpha's Frogs, and Dionysus's—same beasts—virtually, and the *one leg dung* of the first specter—what was the other leg of?

(Part of iron—part of clay. Stone cut out without hands; see Amiens.) . . .

Enough, for this morning, anyhow. But see to left page.

Not quite enough, neither. Remember, yesterday afternoon, invented possible or probable title of next part of "Our Fathers have told us"; "The Font of Cluse" or "Bells of Cluse"—i.e. Springs at Magland and Baptism (see *Fors*). Arve stream at Cluse, and Turner's 'Bains' at foot of Church on Rock in Splugen. This may be of course said to be not in *his* mind—but in mind! It would be good for nothing, if it were intended by him to the full. Its power is in being "the word of God" to *me* through—"The Bagpipe singing in the Nose"—(See context of *that*)—Bagpipe—blown by Angels, by Angelico, by Devil in rich man's ear (Holbein). The Two modern Bagpipes! Gladstone and D'Israeli! blown into by the Devil at Britannia's (Cockney Britannia of the *Market's*) ear; see proposed Statue of *her*—long ago   [*Diaries*, pp. 1000-2].

For a brief analysis of the passage, see *The Failing Distance*, p. 117.

[14] Helen Gill Viljoen has brilliantly annotated the entries of *The Brantwood Diary*. Especially impressive is her tracking down of the incredibly allusive and inclusive references in the two entries here quoted—the entry for the seventeenth and the final entry of the twenty-second, both of which would seem to be more than merely "against" interpretation. See "1878 Supplementary Notes," pp. 104-32.

The devil put a verse into my head just now—"let us not be desirous of *vain* glory." I am NOT oh Devil. I want useful Glory.—"provoking one another"—Oh Devil—cunning Devil— do you think I want to provoke Beata Vigri and little Ophelia then—?

I will—pro—voke—Somebody else, God willing "to day" and to purpose.

And Bishop Laertes,—you had as lief take your fingers from my throat—The Devil will not take my soul, yet a while—Also— look you—and also looking other [things may be at YOUR throat before long]. (Thou pray'st not well—even by your own account and the Devil will not answer you therefore [)] and least said is soonest mended—for—if up when the scuffle comes—the foils should be Sheffield whettles—it is dangerous work—Laertes—'very'—as Mr. Jingle said, even the public press & Mr. Jingle will advise you of that.

Public press Mr. Jingle, in then! and St. George of England both.

Advise you of that.

"Forty thousand brothers" Yes, and sisters too, and I have a few—in Heaven—besides little Ophelia—who bewept to her grave did go, larded all with sweet flowers.

Walking about the room, and thinking—after writing the opposite page I pick up little Lily's "nice little nest with birds in it" and put it away in my drawer of precious things, with Wisies violets.

Putting it into the drawer I come on my mothers watch in the case I used to be so fond of. What o'clock is it?

Six minutes to 12—and a few seconds over—as far as I can see with my magnifying glass—my old eyes wont.—Oh yes the second-hand— — (Second! life) twenty one seconds.—Time— Twice and a half time or so. I[']m wasting it—Devil puts me in mind of Iachimo—Imogene dear—& the mole cinq spot- ted—we'll beat him, wont we? [*Brantwood Diary*, pp. 92-94].

Penultimately (the Exit as decomposing edge/entrance being a centrifugally ultimate condition he would "finally" avoid as long as possible, even as he would delay the centripetal and vortical "self-cannibalization" of 1881, if only by the extended, *Helix virgata* lan- guage of return ["*revenons à nos moutons*"], with perhaps "one leg [of] dung" dipped into the Cloaca Maxima), there is still that last entry before the 1878 edge—beyond which lies the *Dream* of ex- cessive presence become absence, the delirium of his first bout with insanity, the visionary aspects of which are partially described in two later diary entries: in an entry from January 21, 1880, he will describe an infernal Antiphonal Contention immediately after the 1878 textual edge—the metamorphosed contention of the *Dream*, which will finally be no longer between himself and the Devil, but between Lady Burne-Jones (Georgie) and the Devil:

> I lying awake since five, thinking over the great dream, which I am ashamed to find is beginning to pass from me—and that too, in one of its most wonderful parts—the great contest between the Devil and—Georgie! (who represented throughout the adverse queenly or even archangelic power,) for the Kingdom of the world. I dreamed that every seven thousand years it had to be run for in a chariot race—and that the Devil won always, because he knew some way of overlapping at the end of the last round, and counted the turns so that he always must win. This is the part that has got dim to me; but I thought that the secret had somehow become known to Georgie and that she raced him, and won   [*Brantwood Diary*, pp. 220-21].

As if in control of the final Circumference towards which Ruskin, as dancer/writer, is presumably headed, the Devil always wins, "because he knew some way of overlapping at the end of the last round." At any rate, beyond that concluding overlapping of circularity, which, unlike the whimsical overlapping of an "entire book . . . into the next planet or nebula," is a demonic version of both the superimposition of contrary designs and circumferential enclosure, in an entry from February 5th, 1883, the visionary aspects of the dream are again recalled—this time in a more deadly, if less geometric fashion:

> The notion of guns, in the first dream—was quite constant, through great part of the dream—(1878) I was shot, myself, twenty times over, and was attendant on a desperate artillery man who fired batteries of ball and grape into opera-houses and shot whole audiences dead at a discharge. I have greatly forgotten the long and complex tortures of this fancy (Ash Wednesday, 1883) but observe generally that all the grand and melancholy mountain visions, and the idea of a Kingdom possible to me, and lost, beyond the great imaginary mountains from which I was at last restored in mercy to "my own Coniston" in humiliation and thankfulness, belong to the first dream   [*Brantwood Diary*, pp. 298-99].

In any case, before both the framing recollections of the Dream of contention and the "contending" Dream itself, in the approach toward penultimacy, the Devil, who first put a verse into Ruskin's head on February 17, 1878, will be awaited on the night of Good Friday, February 22. And that contention, with Ruskin's "mind racked with ecstasy and anguish," his naked "body benumbed with the bitter cold of a freezing February night"—that Antiphonal Contention, which will be transformed into the recollected shooting of whole audiences in the *Dream*, will then, on the twenty-second, be with that same poetizing Devil, finally changed into a "large black cat" that is not much different from his own occasional identity.

But before the contention, in the final diary entry before the walking and the *Dream*, the pacing of naked feet that shine like snow—before that triumphant and defeated collapse at dawn in the last entry of the Travel Diary toward Nothing, words wander wildly, allusively, as if language, like even a Maze transformed into a "multicursal" design of problematic negotiation, might, in its attempted tracing and retracing, which is the work of the obsessive highwire artist, might keep the night from coming, the night and that almost fatal contention on a cold, grey dawn. The "play" is now more extravagant than anything prompted by mere bitterness. Yet the pen, as long as it wanders, as if following "white clues" through a topography of consciousness that will inevitably lead to the "farthest extremity" of a blank page (a blank page of White Silence beyond the possibility of even an eccentric syntax hovering like a net of language above the abyss of the page's column of potential marginalia) offers a form of curvilinear, serial survival— an unwinding centrifugal solution, albeit temporary, to the (logo)-concentricity of orthodox geometries, which have been made unnaturally dense by those centripetal tendencies "of the modern system of centralization" (xxiv, 412) that has all but destroyed that central city, Venice, which is Ruskin's decomposing mind.

As long as the pen wanders, like Ruskin sauntering through St. Peter's or Morgiana dancing (as that penultimate Ruskin will himself dance), in a kind of perpetual and perpetuating (though not self-cannibalizing) transcendence, the peacocks will not win and the naked contention will not occur. But the way out, which, in the earlier stages of the Transformations of the Maze, had always appeared more difficult than the centripetal way in, has become not so much a way toward an efficacious, perhaps irregular, "Circumference" (the Devil, after all, understands the process of "overlapping" the concluding "round"), as an entrance—literally, a diary entrance into the *Dream*, which is a "fall" to a bed that is like a blank page, as if Morgiana, caught in the repetitions of pirouettes that will lead to a version of the "Piranesi effect," had dropped from vertiginous exhaustion.

Just as Theseus has his Ariadne (or almost—if he wants her), Ruskin would almost have his Rose. Who deserts whom is problematical, and Ruskin we know, chooses that his Theseus be deserted by Ariadne (in death). How Ruskin responded to the "growth" of Rose cannot be gone into here. Perhaps Ruskin's Theseus (if at this point Ruskin still *has* a Theseus) has failed to find an entirely pleasing Ariadne, even as Ruskin has lost (whether he would or not) his Rose—either that (or in the more conventional telling of the story) a Ruskinian Theseus has deserted Ariadne, who is like a Rose in the postcircumferential Promise(d) Land who has arrived before Ruskin. Now serial survival, as the "unicursal" Maze has become "multicursal," will not be survival at all—or not for long. Precisely, it is as if Atropos, the Third Fors, with her nail or shears, in this place that may be of "double axes," had become the "Blind Guide" who had in fact "seen" something, as in a vision, like a "celestial light"; or if Atropos were not the "seeing" "Blind Guide," perhaps Arachne has been, at the last moment, sought, in order to spin a web of faulty syntax—or better, parataxis—from which Ruskin (even a claustrophobic Ruskin, understanding that beyond the Exit lies a madness that is as silent as it is blind) will not wish to escape.[15] If the labyrinth is as enticing as Ruskin finds the movement of the serpent, it is also as defensive as Troy itself.

[15] Earlier, in *The Cestus of Aglaia*, the claustrophobic Ruskin will not find the incipient web so appealing: "I cannot get to my work in this paper, somehow; the web of these old enigmas entangles me again and again" (xix, 87). Yet earlier still, there are no problems. The "noble grotesque," . . . "which belongs to the effort of the mind to unweave the riddle" (v, 133) that has been posed, or woven, more in the theory of perception than the fact of experience/endurance, solves "old enigmas" that cannot, of course, be very old.

Still, syntactical/logical obstruction, or *aporia*, is predicted by familiar travel. Serial breakdown, or the difficulty of the way, is anticipated by the traveler approaching Venice, which becomes Ruskin's consciousness. Perhaps the sinuous approach to Venice is the writing of dark autobiography. We recall the traveler whose procedures are models of syntax in difficulty, if not points of failure:

> . . . let the traveller follow in his boat at evening the windings of some unfrequented channel far into the midst of a melancholy plain; . . . and so wait, until the bright investiture and sweet warmth of the sunset are withdrawn from the waters, and the black desert of their shore lies in its nakedness beneath the night, pathless, comfortless, infirm, lost in dark languor and fearful silence [x, 13].

Allegorical travel as progress through right life is also allegory for Ruskin's syntax that will, in the "labyrinth of life itself," face "blind lanes," leaving him "pathless,

As the serial, though by now self-defeating, Labyrinthine Penultimate becomes the paratactical penultimate (and as "nothing but process" becomes first "nothing" and then both more and less than "nothing"), the shifting, close-to-musical tones of the Travel Diary's last used page, in the form of a series of addresses initiated by a "To" that is doubtless itself stimulated by the "too" of Repletion and Illth, announce, scold, and whine, almost like woodwinds that, with disintegrating reeds, will become atonal before silent. That final shifting syntax, which will not go on for long, which will not in fact survive the exhausted collapse near the Exit that is itself the result of a disintegrating architecture, is, as the text becomes more immediate and enlarged out of context, like a magnifying glass held over a watch ("Six minutes to 12—and a few seconds over— as far as I can see with my magnifying glass"), more abstractly mosaic, like either the labyrinthine marble pavement executed in

---

comfortless, infirm, lost in dark languor and fearful silence." Even attempting to follow a rectilinear course, life, as Ruskinian syntax immediately before breakdown, is "difficult to trace among morasses and mounds of desert." Again, the allegory of travel, informed by loss and surprise, is perhaps worth the repetition of recognition:

> . . . the word Strait, applied to the entrance into Life, and the word Narrow, applied to the road of Life, do not mean that the road is so fenced that few can travel it, however much they wish (like the entrance to the pit of a theatre), but that, for each person, it is at first so stringent, so difficult, and so dull, being between closed hedges, that few *will* enter it, though all *may*. In a second sense, and an equally vital one, it is not merely Strait, or narrow, but a straight, or right road; only, in this rightness of it, not at all marked by posts higher than winter's snow; but on the contrary, often difficult to trace among morasses and mounds of desert, even by skilful sight; and by blind persons, entirely untenable unless by help of a guide, directed, or rex, which you may conjecture to be the reason why, when St. Paul's eyes were to be opened, out of the darkness which meant only the consciousness of utter mistake, to seeing what way he should go, his director was ordered to come to him in the "street which is called Straight" [xxviii, 441-42].

Syntax at a point of failure, or what Hillis Miller in a slightly different context calls the "double blind" that is "at once the failure to reach the center of the labyrinth and in fact the reaching of a false center, everywhere and nowhere, attainable by any thread or path" ("Ariadne's Thread: Repetition and the Narrative Line," *Critical Inquiry* [autumn 1976]; 72) is both Arachne's web of graceless, unChristian "unextrication"—"if the spider, or other monster in mid-web, ate you, the help in your clue for return, would be insignificant. So that this thread of Ariadne's implied that even victory over the monster would be vain, unless you could disentangle yourself from his web also" (xxvii, 408)—and what Freud, as we shall see, speaking of dreams, calls the "dream's navel, the spot where it reaches down into the unknown." The inability of the tracking imagination to accept the unknowability of the unknown prepares for the collapse of a writer turned returning dancer, whose pirouettes will lead to vertiginous blindness and collapse, as onto a bed that has not been slept in, which is itself like a blank page.

opus alexandrinum or the "marred music" of a Strange Chord/Cord
of impossible mastery (the music being the result of jangled nerves),
than linear and overtly associative, as with the recalled Lucent Verdure of perpetual conjunction. Having run out of possible serial
metamorphoses, the conjunctive aspect of the transforming Maze,
which is "multicursal" before doubling into three dimensions, will
eventually collapse, like a breathless Morgiana (or, finally, an exhausted Ruskin), to the stultified condition of Dead Satin—the juxtaposition of a triptych with the middle panel of transitional sanity
missing. The "slow travel" of the serpent, moving from "side to
side" (xxvi, 316), will have become a mnemonic fiction, replaced
by the circular speed of pirouettes close by the Circumference that
the Devil will overlap.

And what will be left, with the propelling and associative conjunctive links of "clues" submerged, if not entirely lost, with Ariadne having given way to Atropos, with syntax having become
parataxis (the implied and disruptive silence "between" anticipating
the silence of the end), is a text of Medusa-like beauty, of a shattered
immanence that might lie behind a broken mirror, a musical
(though not harmonious) language next to silence, composed of
something close to Foucault's notion of "words deprived of language whose muffled rumbling, for an attentive ear, rises up from
the depths of history, the obstinate murmur of a language which
stifles itself, sticks in the throat, collapses before having attained
formulation and turns, without incident, to the silence from which
it had never been freed."[16] It is a text of immediacy, like the "too
fast" travel which "kill[s] space and kill[s]" time, that races blindly
before the crash. Everything whirls together, in a binding and
blending within a "magnified" present tense that is, just before
disintegration, beautifully infernal. Having escaped from the endless revolutions of the squirrel-cage Centre, Ruskin, no longer Theseus, will become Morgiana, pirouetting in revolutions that will
have an end only in exhaustion.

Yet once there had been the Thesean hope for the successful end
to curvilinear advance: "No more wandering of the feet in labyrinth
like this, and the eyes, once cruelly tearless, now blind with frozen
tears" (xxvii, 413). But the inescapability of a "turn" returning can
be discerned even through the blindness of frozen tears. There is
no Exit but exhaustion and madness, blindness and silence. The

---

[16] Michel Foucault, *Histoire de la folie* (Plon, 1961), Preface of the original edition,
as quoted in Shoshana Felman's "Madness and Philosophy *or* Literature's Reason,"
Yale French Studies, no. 52, ed. by Marie-Rose Logan, p. 212.

Strange Chords/Cords of attempted mastery, after the temporary salvation of the recollection and imitation of Lucent Verdure that has now become the problematic Theatre of Blindness, have reappeared, perhaps shaped by the *Helix virgata* spiral of returning lines with a difference. And they have reappeared as Chords/Cords of a marred and Medusa-like beauty, with the snakes of "serpentine advance" themselves transformed into something more compelling than hopeful, neither in a paradise that has been lost nor in the "colubrine chains" that might lead to a land of promised or wished for regain/"recovery."

Yet in the Ruskinian bestiary, which is his zoo/museum as text, the reptiles are not only in the hair, waving like Thesean plumes, but underground. Just as the present tense can be magnified, so can the serpent. And the magnified serpent is the crocodile of a second, subterranean labyrinth of the Egyptians. If labyrinths are not only efficaciously placed over (logo)-concentric geometries but also superimposed upon each other, as if a serpent of the Fall can become "sacred" in layers, this buried labyrinth is appropriate territory for the excavations of an "archaeology of silence" that will at best yield "muffled rumblings": "Not but that the real and artful labyrinth might have been, for all we know. A very real one indeed, was built by twelve brotherly kings in Egypt, in two stories, one for men to live in, the other for crocodiles;—and the upper story was visible and wonderful to all eyes, in authentic times" (xxvII, 407).[17] Invisible now, for blind eyes and "frozen tears," if not for "blind mouths,"[18] the savagely sacred labyrinth of crocodiles is like a lost

---

[17] An appropriately archaeological footnote is presented by the editors of the Library Edition. The "buried" footnote appears as follows:

[Herodotus, ii. 147, 148: "The Egyptians set up over them twelve kings, who made agreement . . . to live in perfect friendship. . . . Moreover they resolved to join together and leave a memorial of themselves; and they caused to be made a labyrinth. . . . This I saw myself, and I found it greater than words can say. . . . There are in it two kinds of chambers, one below the ground and the other above. The upper set of chambers we ourselves saw, going through them, and we tell of them having seen with our own eyes; but the chambers underground we heard about only, for the Egyptians who had charge of them were not willing on any account to show them, saying that here were the sepulchres of the kings who had first built this labyrinth of the sacred crocodiles"] [xxvII, 407].

If words fail Herodotus in the seen labyrinth, both words and eyes "fail" Ruskin—though the "failure," as we shall see, may be verbally eloquent—in the antiphonal response of the submerged crocodilian labyrinth.

[18] "Unbishoply," "blind mouths" might entertain exotic gastronomics, brought on by an acute awareness of both pollution and economics:

language, or silence that, if recovered or given voice, would complete the syntax become parataxis shaped by the apparently incipiently antiphonal Maze at Hampton Court, joining madness to hypothetical reason in what is at best indeterminate meaning.

Perhaps before their final silence, submerged cries of crocodiles are in "naked contention" with the peacocks, producing a cacophonous antiphon in "choral space," like that between the two "storied" languages of a double labyrinth—a double labyrinth of three dimensions that is like the bicamerality of a mind, with the brain's right and left hemispheres in antiphonal conversation with each other (although now the right hemisphere may be damaged, as the labyrinthine syntax of recollected Lucent Verdure begins to break down).[19] Or the double labyrinth of the mind may be like the relation between consciousness and unconsciousness of a mind that may itself double the lateral bicamerality, as if the "mine" of a mind were split in two (or multiplied) by those original double axes, at a geological "apex" that, if "morally" central, is in fact penultimately precircumferential. Ruskinian integration, if desired (and it may not be), seems barely possible.

But then again, the labyrinthine language of the crocodile is finally buried "out of sound" for the Ruskin who, in his increasingly

---

—and though fish can't live in our rivers, the muddy waters are just of the consistence crocodiles like: and, at Manchester and Rochdale, I have observed the surfaces of the streams smoking, so that we need be under no concern as to temperature. I should think you might produce in them quite "streaky" crocodile,—fat and flesh concordant,—St. George becoming a bacon purveyor, as well as seller, and laying down his dragon in salt (indeed it appears, by an experiment made in Egypt itself, that the oldest of human words is Bacon; potted crocodile will doubtless, also, from countries unrestrained by religious prejudices, be imported, as the English demand increases, at lower quotations; and for what you are going to receive, the Lord makes you truly thankful [xxvii, 504].

[19] It is curious to note a point that Martin Gardner makes in his *The Shattered Mind: The Person after Brain Damage* (New York, 1975), p. 356: "studies indicated that the right hemisphere is dominant for other than visual functions—notably, for tasks in the tactile or somato-sensory realm. Patients with right-hemisphere lesions displayed difficulty in learning mazes presented to them when they were blindfolded." Further, it might be mentioned, in connection with the severence of cords and the "doubling brain," the experiments that Gardner describes as a means of controlling epilepsy: "the left hemisphere was surgically separated from the right hemisphere by the cutting of the connections between the two, most particularly the inch-long, quarter-inch-thick bundle of fibres called the corpus callosum. With this operation (usually called a commisurotomy or callosectomy) the patient effectively became 'two brains inside one body' " (p. 357). Of course, this is only metaphorically applicable to Ruskin's "dis-integration" and the corpus callosum as Strange Cord.

interior Theatre of Blindness, which is evolving into the enclosed space of the three-dimensional Maze, is becoming "blind to himself"; still, for a moment, there may remain the inspired fiction of a kind of counterpoint between the paratactical remains (or ruins) of the now shattered, if not forgotten, syntax of Lucent Verdure (a syntax of precise, though luxuriant, sinuousity) and the would-be completing silent conjunctions of the crocodilian labyrinth that is—words having failed in Herodotus' text—as "below" interpretation as the paratactical antiphon is itself "beyond." Yet though the counterpoint is potentially there, the syntax of the Maze of Lucent Verdure may be no more than a single, if implicitly "multicursal," anticipation of the vertical doubleness to come—or it may, at almost the last moment, be something more. If penultimate language as univocal meaning fails, perhaps there is a success of hidden implication. Perhaps, further, there is a kind of ventriloquy involved, if not the "teachings" of spiritualism,[20] with voices, like two-dimensional labyrinths that have taken on the "intercommunicating planes" of the labyrinth of three dimensions, as though Ruskin were not quite himself—or not only himself.

It is just possible that those peacocks, their tails of blind eyes fanning like the fluttering of recently failed eyes (not yet frozen with tears) of "Blind Guides," have found a most "unbishoply" language which is, after all, the mad triumph of blindness that is blind to itself. Or perhaps those terrifying, blasphemous screams are in contention with the buried, silent language of sacred crocodiles for the ears of a dichotomic listener, who, himself doubling, simultaneously receives different messages. In any case, there is the undeniable beauty of the peacock's flamboyant tails—tails that, in their paradisiacal elegance, are not constructed for reptilian advance, the contorted (as in "narrow caution") curvilinear movement through either the ecstatic (or at least ecstatically remembered) Maze of Lucent Verdure, or the subterranean labyrinth of Herodotus' text. There is that beauty of blind tails, as well as the peacock's strutting conceit before the blank page of "torn" or ripped immanence, with its terrible nakedness, like Ruskin's own, which is of original (and perhaps ultimate) moral/bestial contention that is next to a divine immediacy. Perhaps the peacocks would replace Ruskin before that mirror of the mind, or looking-through glass, on that dawn of February twenty-second, 1878; and maybe for a moment—just a moment—even a "catcataceous" Ruskin

---

[20] Ruskin's interest in spiritualism stemmed from his relationship with Mrs. Cowper-Temple, whose house, Broadlands, was the place for a seance which brought news, in 1875, from a dead Rose.

would have it so. (Then again, in the doubling of reflection, which is also the double blindness of contrasting mirrors, as if maddening reflection might be returned to the vantage point of a labyrinthine node's twin blind alleys—nothing and everything returning to nothing and everything—there may be a man who is half a man, or a beast who is half a beast—or a man confronting the demonic reflection of the double characteristics of the offspring of Queen Pasiphae.)

Conceivably, close to the "tail-end" of "multicursal" (retraced) stories of double labyrinths in three dimensions, Ophelia is, after all, only writing a "rather pretty bit" to Hamlet, giving him directions—or, like Ariadne, maybe she is attempting, at the last possible moment, to give the thread of salvation to her Hamlet/Theseus, whose plumes (more likely those of ostriches than peacocks, though one cannot discount the ruffled feathers of the dancing crane) wave in the winds of unmapped, labyrinthine confusion. Or perhaps Ophelia is like an Ariadne whose thread has been cut, or perhaps similarly, they are both like Rose, whose thread, as if by an angry Atropos (or an Atropos understanding certain of Ruskin's darker portions of his consciousness),[21] had been severed in December 1875; for, as Ruskin would have it, "all the bitter catastrophe" in *Hamlet* occurs "because she [Ophelia] fails Hamlet at the critical moment, and is not, and cannot in her nature be, a guide to him when he needs her most" (xxviii, 114). But then Ruskin, if neither Hamlet nor Theseus, may not want a guide to the Promise(d) Land, where the almost certain promise is of a disconfirmation that is the fulfillment of madness. With Ruskin, initial desertion, as well as the "difficulty of the syntactical way," delays final disconfirmation. And perhaps, after investigation, the shape of the dear doge's cap is all that can—or would—eventually be known, with anything approaching certainty.

But if there are other voices, there are, for Ruskin, who has

---

[21] Ruskin writes Charles Eliot Norton, *Letters of John Ruskin to Charles Eliot Norton*, edited by C. E. Norton, 2 vols. (Boston, 1904), 1; 138: "she has been scolding me frightfully, and says 'How could one love you, if you were a Pagan? *She was a marvellous little thing when she was younger* [italics mine], but . . . there came on some over excitement of the brain, causing occasional loss of consciousness, and now she often seems only half herself, as if partly dreaming." As Ruskin "doubles," Rose, as if by contrary design, is halved. Rose's growing older is a form of postcircumferential Ruskinian disconfirmation. The youth of Adèle Domecq was traumatically "frozen" by her marriage to another in 1840, leaving Ruskin, at Oxford, coughing blood. But Rose's vanishing youth—"she was a marvelous little thing when she was younger"—is only "frozen" by Atropos' shears, and perhaps Ruskin's own "frozen tears" of labyrinthine blindness.

turned from traveler/writer to dancer/writer, pirouetting ever faster, no apparent dance partners (it is not for him, after all, that Ariadne does her dance on the ironically Daedalean *Choros*). And if, outside the Maze, there is the spectre of the lonely dancing crane—a solitary reminder of the Thesean Geranos (Crane) dance on the isle of Delos, with ropes employed like "familiar" umbilical cords—in the final, disintegrating Transformation of the Maze, from which there is no rational escape, there is only one dancer, if the sympathetic reader who may participate in Ruskin's unexegetical performance is not included. Ruskin is, in fact, like Morgiana, without hope of, or desire for, partners. Yet now it may be that his "stern final purpose" is no longer the attainment of the Promise(d) Land beyond the Circumference, which would, at one time, have been conceived of as a landscape for both the past and future, to be "lost" and "regained," as of a landscape whose "error" is a version of fallen reason or madness to be "recovered" in the threads of a returning syntax. Instead, as a dancer whose only partner can be the "uncritical" reader who is content to experience the pathos of the performance, Ruskin would settle for that territory of enclosed, "curvilinear" survival, in which the cutting of cords will be delayed for as long as possible—almost as if Ruskin would have a second childhood without the severed umbilical cord of a second birth.

Rose La Touche, who knows something about backs, though Ruskin will himself not *look* back—"I have not looked back, nor took my hand from the Jason plough"—is not available,[22] and Adèle Domecq, that original partner in the Lucent Verdure of Hampton Court, has long since departed, despite her vital mnemonic presence amidst "Dantesque alleys" that anticipates the coming (and going) of another Beatrice. And probably, it is too early (and too late) for Kathleen Olander and Jessica Sykes.[23] There are double Mazes and perhaps double axes, but, with Ruskin, there is only the single dancer. Penultimately, he dances along the tenuous threads of curvilinearity alone. Yet there will be reflections of a compounded multiplicity.

The pirouettes are of course exercises in solipsism, and Ruskin's ventriloquy is perhaps a lateral dialogue with himself, as if the brain's right and left hemispheres, still joined by a version of

[22] For the most recent and complete account of the relation between Ruskin and Rose La Touche, see *John Ruskin and Rose La Touche: Her Unpublished Diaries of 1861 and 1867*, introduced and edited by Van Akin Burd (London, 1980).

[23] Cf. *The Gulf of Years, Letters of John Ruskin to Kathleen Olander*, edited by R. Unwin (London, 1953); and J.A.C. Sykes, *Mark Alston, an Impression* (London, 1908).

Strange Chords, were in exclusive conversation with each other. But then—and all importantly—there is the antiphonal counterpoint no longer between the Centre and the Circumference, but within the interior Theatre of Blindness that is the analogous vertical space which is between Herodotus' excavated labyrinth "above," as a visible fulfillment of the dimly recollected "ruins" of Lucent Verdure ("left, right, right, left, left, left, left" is presumably the key to the Hampton Court Maze)[24] and the buried labyrinth of sacred crocodiles "below." Still, dance, dialogue, and the antiphon end in exhaustion, vertigo, and the shattered plural "music" of Strange Chords, as well as strained cords—maybe two pairs of mucous membranes—stretched too tightly, like a tightrope about to snap.

With Ruskin's language of reluctantly nihilistic architecture, as of a design of delayed but inevitable decomposition, it is as if, instead of the House of Usher falling, the archaeological house of Sir John Soane in Lincoln Inn's Field, with its self-conscious pastiche of debris (its underground room containing an Egyptian sarcophagus that is not, presumably, for the sacred crocodile) were falling into a state of authentic debris, like the labyrinthine Troy, that would require a meta-archaeologist, or psychologist, for reassemblage to the condition of meaning: an archaeologist/psychologist for a museum/mind to be constructed out of ruins that have indeed returned, like that *Helix virgata* return with a difference— "Not only does every good curve vary in general tendency, but it is modulated, as it proceeds, by myriads of subordinate curves"— along different lines.

The Law of Curvature anticipates the language of return—and a kind of reflection, the distorted reflection of a shattered mirror that doubles blindness. And penultimately, in the final stage of the Transformation of the Maze, before white marble has become White Silence, syntax becomes parataxis. If Ruskin's echoing and fragmented language, like Soane's house fallen into authentic debris, in some sense "returns," or rather is "returned to" from an at best problematical "excavation of silence" as toward the complementary "remains" of coherence and conjunctive safety and transitional sanity, that language cannot be finally restored any more than an unfallen landscape of Lucent Verdure can be regained. Reconstruction, let alone an abhorred restoration, would be further paratactical decomposition. The syntactical thread has been cut, if not the cord for a second birth. Alone, the dancer is

[24] Matthews, *Mazes & Labyrinths*, p. 191.

in the Maze with an Exit itself at the point of disintegration—the far-left corner, as he "sees" it, of an inverted arc—that he apparently no longer desires, as if, deserting guides before they desert him, he would be the first to break the promises of both a restored language and landscape that would only yield further disconfirmation.

Far from being the "best argument we have for the pleasures of centrifugal play," the art of Ruskin's final text of the Travel Diary, which is his Theatre of Blindness at/on the last stage of the Transformation of the multiplying and decomposing Maze, is beyond the possibility of Amiel's centripetally sane "reimplication"; labyrinthine consolidation, though there is the less disastrous vortical self-cannibalization of September 23, 1881, is apparently only the Circumference's inner side of a "bitter" fiction adjacent to the Promise(d) Land. But the textual spaces of emptiness, which can only be completed by the lower, crocodilian aspect of the vertical antiphon, seem to require a last attempt at orthodox coherence.

If only for a moment, the reader, facing the incoherent, searches for the point/s of failure precisely where the conjunctive thread has been cut, as if either by Atropos, or one side of an anonymously wielded double axe. For a moment of hubris met of terrible empathy, he would, in his affinity toward the text, attempt to employ the conjunctive thread of his own logic. Then, the reader, despite his "instincts for an Exit of meaning," must draw back, as if in his own act of desertion, realizing the possible efficacy of an aesthetics, if not mastery, of absence—as in the musical silences, say, of Anton von Webern, which help provide their own perhaps alogical counterpoint between sound and what, as in Ruskin's case, is buried below the apprehension of ears that are themselves as labyrinthine as ostrich feathers blowing in the winds of confusion.[25]

What must perhaps finally be understood is that if the dance partner is missing, so, in some sense, must the reader be (if the two are not already, in fact, the same)—at least in his own problematical role of archaeologist/psychologist, who, in the dubious restoration

[25] That there are problems inherent in talking about the language that returns from silence, the language of madness, and even the language that interrogates itself in order to delay its going mad, is not itself entirely mysterious. A lexicon of madness may itself subvert its subject. Derrida asks: "is not an archaeology, even of silence, a logic, that is, an organized language, a project, an order, a sentence, a syntax, a work? Would not the archaeology of silence be the most efficacious and subtle restoration, the *repetition*, in the most irreducibly ambiguous meaning of the word, of the act perpetuated against madness—and be so at the very moment when this act is denounced?" ("Cogito and the History of Madness," *Writing and Difference*, translated by Alan Bass [Chicago, 1978], p. 35).

of "returning" debris or in a univocal act of aggressively interpretive "reading," would excavate the labyrinthine ruins of the sacred crocodile.[26] One could say that the reader's "absence" (or interpretative desertion) is the text's "presence"—the ripped immanence of a wounded page, the terrible beauty of paratactical remains, or even a remaining place. Or, more to the point, the reader, involved in this "archaeology of silence," is to be present in an emotional participation that is necessarily without elucidation. Like Ruskin's moral area "between" that is the theoretical faculty's dialectical territory between eye and mind,[27] so the antiphonal choral space exists, but without the conventional efficacy of synthesis. Only an untranslatable interior language can negotiate that space. The labyrinth's textual sacrosanct third dimension of double tiers must be acknowledged, felt, like the Gothic space of symbiotic reciprocity, but not explored in search of a single solution (or reading) that will inevitably prove false, if not misguided in its enterprise. Even the meanings of multivocality may be no more than excessive echoes as replete as that condition of surplus which itself leads to the White Silence after double "blind lanes." One experiences the pathos, without examining the remains of a problematic, if not discredited, logos that now defies exegesis.

Surviving, if severed, even as arts seem to conspire, there is the antiphonal music for double labyrinths and a doubling mind—the frozen architectural music for frozen tears, the woven texture that, capable of being unraveled at any time, has become a kind of mosaic of deconstructed sound for a locus of double axes. It is as though, with the paradigmatic labyrinth of his inner ear, the reader, no longer reading "into," listens, and, like the dragon (ophis),[28] sees

---

[26] As we approach what Ruskin called "The Dream," it is perhaps helpful to be aware of a passage of Sigmund Freud that deals with centricity, labyrinthine "networks," and indeterminate interpretation:

> There is often a passage in even the most thoroughly interpreted dream which has to be left obscure; this is because we become aware during the work of interpretation that at that point there is a tangle of dream-thoughts which cannot be unravelled and which moreover adds nothing to our knowledge of the content of the dream. This is the dream's navel, the spot where it reaches down into the unknown. The dream-thoughts to which we are led by interpretation cannot, from the nature of things, have any definite endings; they are bound to branch out in every direction into the intricate network of our world of thought" [*The Interpretation of Dreams, The Standard Edition of the Complete Psychological Works of Sigmund Freud*, translated by James Strachey, Vol. 5 (London, 1953), 525].

[27] Cf. Hewison, *John Ruskin*, p. 211.

[28] "The word 'Dragon' means 'the Seeing Creature', and I believe the Greeks had

the "living hieroglyph" of an "inner language"[29] of counterpoint and indeterminate meaning that is, or has been, blind to itself.

And if, after the mastery of Strange Chords/Cords is no longer attempted (and after the attendant separation of self from orthodox and [logo]-concentric geometries), there is an aesthetics of the "remains" of the Labyrinthine Penultimate and its anamorphic distortions, which leads to the "frozen music" of a Strange Chord— that *"lyric glow of illness"* described by Foucault,[30] which, as Exit/diary entrance to the blank page of ultimacy, may also be at the "root of charred meaning"[31] ("charred meaning" as the embers of the heat from the aftermath of the *"lyric glow"* that is itself like a recollection of the light of Lucent Verdure)—that aesthetics of "marred music"[32] may well be demonstrated toward the conclusion of the Travel Diary's Nothing but a Dream, in a penultimate and paratactical voice that is punctuated at first by the intermediate silence of the buried, crocodilian half of the double labyrinth "below," and then by the ultimate finality of the White Silence of a blank page. Lying terrifyingly beyond both "torn presences"[33] and a mirror of consciousness that may have been shattered in the

---

the same notion in their other word for a serpent, 'ophis'. There were many other creeping and crawling, and rampant things; the live stem and the ivy were serpentine enough, blindly; but here was a creeping thing that saw!" (xxvii, 483).

[29] Ruskin's "inner language" for an "inner ear" is connected with a language that does, in fact, see: "the dead hieroglyph may have meant this or that—the living hieroglyph means always the same; but remember, it is just as much a hieroglyph as the other; nay, more,—a 'sacred or reserved sculpture', *a thing with an inner language* [italics mine]. The serpent crest of the king's crown, or of the god's, on the pillars of Egypt, is a mystery; but the serpent itself, gliding past the pillar's foot, is it less a mystery? Is there, indeed, no tongue, except the mute forked flash from its lips, in that running brook of horror on the ground?" (xix, 361-62).

[30] *Histoire de la folie* (Paris, 1972), "Appendice I," p. 582.

[31] The term is Foucault's taken from the *Histoire de la folie*, Preface to the original edition (Plon, 1961).

[32] The phrase is taken from John Rosenberg's sympathetic footnote, dealing with Ruskin's "intricate orchestration of . . . thought [as it] becomes unintelligible" (*The Darkening Glass*, p. 172). Ruskin's "music," like the Gothic line of error and recovery, is lost in order to be recovered, in the lines of *Helix virgata* return. If Ruskin would later, in 1881, return to the point of *La Farce du Maître Patelin*, which is a point of sheep—"Revenons—Revenons—à nos moutons"—he further understands, we remember, that "in all living art this love of involved and recurrent line exists,—and exists essentially—it exists just as much in music as in sculpture, and the continually lost and recovered threads and streams of melody in a perfect succession, to the liveliest traceries over the gold of an early missal, or to the fancies of stone work" (xix, 259).

[33] Again, the term is Foucault's, this time borrowed from *Histoire de la folie* (Paris, 1972), "Appendice I," p. 537.

violent "contention" with the naked "roots" of a demonic, or bestial self, the Illth of White Silence is the final punctuation of the Travel Diary.

And that bestial self, no longer a categorical, "catcataceous" cat, looking back perhaps in the blind doubleness of reflection, as if in the Contrasting Mirrors of his own dark mind, may be observing instead, with the eyes of a bull, a Ruskin, who, at his most intense point of madness, may no longer be unaware of the antiphonal multiplicity of himself—"all the dark sides and in all the dark places" (xxxvii, 247). That "double, or even treble" self will leave behind the paratactical remains (ruins cast in the light of Lucent Verdure) of an entirely problematic text—a partial yet multivocal text given anamorphic shape by the aesthetics of the double-tiered Maze of the Labyrinthine Penultimate—that is closer to being a language of turn and return from silence (a language that "stifles itself, sticks in the throat, collapses before having attained formulation and returns") than a rectilinear and (logo)-concentric language heading felicitously toward an Exit that is, in fact, a blind end. Almost finally, the deserting or deserted reader is left with a profound sense of unresolved Antiphonal Contention—both horizontally between Centre and Circumference, and vertically, within the "shattered majesty" (x, 191) of the Theatre of Blindness, between the paratactical remains "above" that are virtually "blind" to themselves in their self-referential, yet equivocal, meaning, and the latent silence, as of the "muffled rumblings" "below"—as if, next to the end, there were neither synthesis for a kind of "multicursal" dialogue nor mutual exclusion for the dichotomic listener of split-levels.

In a sudden reversal of its previously enticing role that would at once encourage entrance and obstruct leaving, the Maze, transformed to the doubling point just before nihilistic deconstruction, is as defensive as Troy, even in its Homeric blindness—with Ruskin, in shifting mythological personages, for a moment more like a reluctant Hector in the end, whose Maze-defying ghost later appears to Aeneas (xxix, 457), than either Theseus on the way "out," or Achilles, already "out," waiting to circle the labyrinth's Circumference three times—presumably with no reason, devilish or otherwise, for "overlapping at the end," unless to underscore the significance of that newly fearful Circumference, which is the compounded circularity of (un)contrary superimposition that is the last vestige of a now discredited (logo)-concentricity, perfect circles having given way to imperfect spirals that may inspire an asymmetrical pathos of myopia.

Perhaps Ruskin, with Ariadne's thread originating from beyond the Circumference but now severed, like Rose's life, would be "inside" as long as possible, attached to another kind of thread, a labyrinthine umbilical cord emanating from an elaborately mythical Centre of "Dew" and "Earth," as though from a womb of the shapingly maternal and "owl-eyed" ("Glaukopis") (xix, 306) Athena, sighted even in darkness (one of those "living hieroglyphs" of multiplicity that Hillis Miller finds "branching" from a Ruskinian "single entity"), who is "the power which shaped you into your shape, and by which you love, and hate, when you have received that shape" (xix, 351)—a Centre of Air/Oxygen that is further like the un-"mephitic" genesis of the spiraling line of the *Helix virgata.*

Perhaps, as a final glimmer of glory, the Maze of the "very centre of the mother city," a former mephitic locus of "squirrelian revolutions," may penultimately, at next to the last, centrifugal moment, have been efficaciously, if temporarily, "shaped" by an act of Athena's returning will, into that "New Jerusalem, prepared as . . . [the] bride" (xxviii, 137) that Rose, now "beyond," never was. It is as though, with the superimposition of efficaciously contrary designs, Athena's centricity, speaking of an unfallen condition both of language and landscape, had, for a moment, given new memory to the Maze at Hampton Court—as though, further, Athena, in her retrospective energy for origins rather than endings, were the only guide, sighted or otherwise, not to desert Ruskin, or, more importantly, whom Ruskin would not have desert him, though the coherence will not hold and the bride, if not in fact deserted, will not wait. Still, in that ephemeral New Jerusalem which, like Ruskin's Venice, is more bridelike than Effie Gray, there will be the obfuscating, Trojan "blind lanes" of the "labyrinth of life itself" that are, after all, finally only a circumferential, dead end before the blank page's White Silence of excessive presence become the absence of "dazzling whiteness."

Here, in any case, is the "choral topography" of penultimate Antiphonal Contention. And, recapitulating with that *Helix virgata* difference, it is not only a territory mediating laterally between Centre and Circumference, with the White Silence of the blank page beyond, as if led to by white stones, but, more significantly, a vertical Antiphonal Contention of essential unmediation, of difference, as that "archaeology of silence" yields nothing but silence for renegotiation.[34] The early horizontal transitional absence of the triptych's Dead Satin has found a vertical fulfillment that defies the

[34] Foucault's "History," as we have seen, is also prediction with a Ruskinian difference. Foucault's architecture of imprisonment is not Ruskin's Theatre of Blindness, but Ruskin's doomed dialogue, ending in White Silence, is close to Foucault's:

mediation of at least an "outer," "centred," and entirely rational language. That previously impacted language of centrifugal, penultimate Repletion, with nowhere to go before the "overlapping" Circumference (after which excessive presence becomes the absence of Illth), has exploded; and doing so, it has, in the maddening meta-presence that will first become debris, doubled that single recollected labyrinth of Lucent Verdure (which has already in fact turned "multicursal") into the more spacious "ruins," as of "shattered majesty," of the Theatre of Blindness' double-tiered, three-dimensional Maze, whose planes are connected not by the equivalent of the Museum's transitional series but only by a kind of labyrinthine interface, a Möbius strip or Klein bottle of interior dialogue[35] in the ineffective guise of monologue, as of discourse between a "double, or even treble self"—an "inner language," as dialogical, if not finally alogical, as it is antiphonal, that is informed by a returning silence which predicts the White Silence beyond. And with the metaphorical double labyrinths of a replete consciousness, there is the centrifugal parataxis "above" that is, even as Ruskin blindly "sees" the shattered and multiple reflections of himself, blind to its own disjunctive meaning (a blind interior language of indeterminate meaning and implicit madness), partially informed by Ophelia's "*Rose*mary, that's for remembrance" (this, after once "vital hawthorn" bloom has become postcircumferential and ghostly) and the "buried" silence, as of the "muffled rumblings" of crocodiles, of potential or latent completion "below," which has been accepted as inevitable, if not entirely adequate, response.

Vertically, as if in a condition of contrary "contention" that would

---

Confinement, prisons, dungeons, even tortures, engaged in a mute dialogue between reason and unreason—the dialogue of struggle. This dialogue itself was now disengaged; silence was absolute; there was no longer any common language between madness and reason; the language of delirium can be answered only by an absence of language, for delirium is not a fragment of dialogue with reason, it is not a language at all; it refers, in an ultimately silent awareness, only to transgression   [*Madness and Civilization*, p. 262].

[35] We recall the relatively early pronouncement of the Ruskin in *Modern Painters III*: "the more I see of useful truths, the more I find that, like human beings, they are eminently biped; and although, as far as apprehended by human intelligence, they are usually seen in a crane-like posture, standing on one leg, whenever they are usually to be stated so as to maintain themselves against all attack it is quite necessary they should stand on two, and have their complete balance on opposite fulcra" (v, 169). But if the crane is now the postlabyrinthine Crane of the Isle of Delos, the "biped stance" is no more than a wistful recollection of original dialogue, before the twisting permutations into a kind of moebius logic that would require something more ambitious than either the "biped" or bifold—this, as polygonal consciousness moves towards the syntactical ruins that are beyond even the fictions of dialectic accommodation.

be nostalgically, if not potentially (as an "error" that cannot quite be rationally "recovered"), more complementary than a combat that is either "naked" or moral, and within the space of architectonic superimposition of Blindness over Silence that has been anticipated by the salutary laminations of labyrinthine design over farsighted (logo)-concentric geometries, as of the encompassed "wide circumference," there resides, as between those tiers of the three-dimensional Maze, the once-sighted (and now, almost blindly visionary) "inner language" of pathos that, having first seen Strange Chords and then "that running brook of horror on the ground," has now been poignantly and ecstatically (mis)-shaped by the decomposing energy/enervation of the architecture of the reluctant nihilism that is the Labyrinthine Penultimate—an uncanny "inner language" of myopic (patho)-eccentricity that, combining the syntax become parataxis with what is mystifyingly implicit in the uncompleting absence of disjunctive silence, is of a ripped immanence and "torn presence" divided against itself, like a self-inflicted wound suffered in "honourable defeat" (x, 191), whose legacy may at least be the pastoral recollection, or "traces" of immanence, of a run through "Dantesque alleys of lucent verdure in the Moon[light]":

Recollected all about message from Rosie to me as I was drawing on the scaffolding in St. Georges Chapel—My saying I would serve her to the death—

Tonight—(last night)—lying awake—came—Ada with the Golden Hair.

—Can the devil *speak truth* (confer letter to Francie about her little feet.)

If that thou beest a devil &c. connected with, (Made wanton— &c. the night with her)

To Burne-Jones.—Oh, my Black Prince—and they take you for one of the firm of Brown—&c.—See Brown, &c. away on Lago Maggiore—

Tintoret—<Sempre si fa il Mare Maggiore>

To Connie—Oh Connie—did'nt we quarrel among the Alpine Roses, and make it up again by the moonlight.

—And was'nt I naughty sometimes!—and do you recollect bidding me go *before* you, at Verona? Ask Rosie to make your back better. She knows something about backs.

—To Madge. Oh, Madge—so do *you* don't you, but why do you ever play with darling old Vulgar Baxter—see opposite

darling old vulgar Baxter—(and our American cousin—)—: Baxter did so spoil that loveliest part of yours—Madge,—when you made somebody so jealous, and had to go away again—you naughty lamb of a Madge.

To Joseph Severn—Keats—Endymion—quenched in the Chaste beams—yes—oh yes—Proserpina mine. I have not looked back, nor took my hand from the Jason plough.

And when Gold and Gems adorn the plough! Oh—you dear Blake—and so mad too—

Do you know what Titians good for *now* you stupid thing?

I did'nt know where to go on—but don't think I should stop.—And Andrea Gritti—then? quite unholy is he, you stupid? And Dandolo then, I suppose? and the Blind Guide that had celestial light? Yes—and you barefoot Scotch lassies—Diddie and all of you dears— —if only you *would* go barefoot a bit, in the streets So pretty—so pretty.
Naked foot,
That shines like snow—and falls on earth—or gold—as mute.

Oh—dear doge Selvo, I want to know the shape of your cap, terribly. I dont know which is best—yours—or Gritti's.—Tell me all about it—Raphael dear—from the angle then and pleas[e] angel of the lagoons from the Paradise—tell me what my own sweet Tintoret meant by those—Yes

"Send for the lady to the Sagittary."

(And praise be to thee—oh God. We praise thee Oh God, we acknowledge thee to be the Lord.)

Finished, and my letter from 'Piero' my Venetian gondolier put it in, here, and all. I am going to lock up with the Horses of St. Marks. ¼ to one (20 minutes[)] by my Father's watch—22nd February 1878*

* I couldn't find the key and then remembered I had not thanked the dear Greek Princess—nor Athena of the Dew—and Athena [of the Earth] February,—to April—the Dream [heading of a blank page,[36] *Brantwood Diary*, pp. 100-102].

---

[36] The silence of the blank page is appropriate. If words fail Herodotus, contention with the "Evil One" can only be expressed in failing words that become White Silence: "and every time I did the wrong I heard the voice of the Demon—that is the peacock—give forth a loud croak of triumph. And it was more terrible than words can express" (xxxviii, 172).

Further, the blank page at night is "reason dazzled" at dawn: "Dazzlement is night in broad daylight, the darkness that rules at the very heart of what is excessive in light's radiance. Dazzled reason opens its eyes upon the sun and sees *nothing*, that is, *does not see*; in dazzlement, the recession of objects towards the depths of night has as an immediate correlative the suppression of vision itself; at the moment when it sees objects disappear into the secret night of light, sight itself sees itself in the moment of its disappearance" (Foucault, *Madness and Civilization*, p. 108).

Appendices

For a moment, facing "nothing," one considers the nature of the diary's blank page that is something like an osmotic, semi-transparent membrane, with negotiations between that tenuous boundary which separates the tightrope act of sanity from White Silence, negotiations and renegotiations between that condition of White Silence and the later excursions into the mnemonic pastoral of retraced immanence of *Praeterita*, along with the more various, though less sustained, postcentrifugal, occasional returns to a sanity of highly problematical integration, as though to a territory of temporary Redemption, where "error" might be recovered in periods that are increasingly brief. One perhaps recalls Ruskin's "equation in the second degree," in which there is "at least one positive and one negative answer" (XVI, 187). The answers would seem to be "separated" by that vulnerable membrane, which may be a "point of failure" that will also be a returning point of at least momentary success, at the edge of the Labyrinthine Penultimate.

But then again, the blank page, upon closer examination, may be a palimpsest. Even oscillating sequence, in an oeuvre that is dependent for its extended survival upon the conjunctive presence of an elaborated series, may appear, after the apparent fact of hazardous density, benignly simultaneous. One is almost always aware of the sanity beneath the layer of insanity, the reason beneath the folly: the orthodox structures of (logo)-concentricity beneath the architecture of a reluctant, if inevitable, nihilism. Still, if the blank page conjures acts of superimposition that have been as dangerously demanding as they are also efficacious, there is always the sense of the erasure—the possibility of the return to a condition of marred whiteness, to the almost blank page.

For a moment, one considers the nature of the maddened postcir-cumferential dream landscape of Illth, or false presence as meta-presence that, for a while, covers "nothing" with "too much"—a landscape of ruined surplus or excessive meaning become refuse that tends to dispose of itself almost as if in the vortical syntax of self-cannibalization (bypassing reintegration) of the September 23, 1881, diary entry that would pretend to return to the point of *La Farce du Maître Patelin ("Revenons à nos moutons")*, but would instead first turn the "outside" "in," and then the "in" further "inside" into Nothingness. We are no longer at Ruskin's "equation of the second degree" for the (at least) polygonal consciousness. Instead, we are entirely in the territory of the "negative answer," whose only plus, less than the mathematician's null-set, is in fact a minus category that is, by turns, a category of the imagination's death and silent madness after that penultimate "lyrical explosion."[1]

And considering the nihilistic condition of an "existence" of "non-presence," one briefly considers the variegated history of space that begins with a potentially horrifying absence to be filled with a be-neficent plenitude until that plenitude becomes a "superabundant" obstacle of Repletion, at which branching "nodal point" "vacancies" can be "kindly" for an "avaricious imagination" to lie down in, in order to recuperate temporarily, if not be finally cured—an "ava-ricious imagination" that might otherwise be its own "point of fail-

---

[1] These "appendices of presumed ultimacy" are textual landscapes of the false presence of Illth that become less than the Travel Diary's "nothing." But that "noth-ing" with Ruskin is, as we know, filled with the madness of the *Dream* of devilish contention and circumferential "overlapping." This false presence, when it has been filled with the plenitude of the oneiric, perhaps becomes, as Foucault would have it, the *"culmination of the void,"* as in a labyrinth of descent and absence, which may further become a nightmare in the "dazzlement" of broad daylight that is the antithesis to the daydream of "lucent verdure" in moonlight. Again, Foucault's "history" is provocatively prefigurative, as the false presence of Illth becomes the true presence of madness:

Madness is precisely at the point of contact between the oneiric and the erroneous; it traverses, in its variations, the surface on which they meet, the surface which both joins and separates them. . . . But while error is merely non-truth, while the dream neither affirms nor judges, madness fills the void of error with images, and links hallucinations by affirmation of the false. In a sense, it is thus plenitude, joining to the figures of night the powers of day, to the forms of fantasy the activity of the waking mind; it links the dark content with the forms of light. But is not such plenitude actually *the culmination of the void?* [Foucault, *Madness and Civilization*, p. 106].

ure," or "honorable [self-] defeat." But "kindly vacancies" are infernal when missing as in the transitional absence of a series—or a broken "colubrine chain"—which becomes harsh juxtaposition that may be, at its most demanding, the pseudoscopic inversion of foreground and background, as well as the antiphonal "choral space" of vertical unmediation. And that "choral space," which occupies the Theatre of Blindness, anticipates the postcircumferential landscape, and its attendant nonlanguage ("And it was more terrible than words can express") beyond the (logo)-concentric "recovery" or an originally necessary "error" that has finally become a decentred and myopic pathos, perhaps on the "eastern edge."

Points of failure, as of blind alleys in the "multicursal" Maze, become the broken promises that might otherwise have restored the language of silence to uttered (or written) syntax and the landscape of Lucent Verdure to blind eyes. But the abyss of Illth, as a space of false presence, is finally only a Promise(d) Land, where promises are not to be kept (though by whom may be the ultimate "query")—a lost paradise set out to be regained that is only revealed in the process that is never further than that condition of loss or excessive presence/absence, the absence of false presence vertiginously superimposed upon the abyss for the writer/dancer, as sometime tightrope walker, whose only net is a wire, and whose only wire, to be traced and retraced, is a net that is like a spider's web of language that would ultimately defy "extrication" in its attempt to master absence.

III

Further, for a moment, one considers the question of earth met of absence. If digging and archaeological excavation/explication are not, beyond a certain point, desirable activities, perhaps the reluctantly approached postcircumferential landscape of Illth and White Silence that is also of broken promises presumably beyond Redemption would prove to be an infernally ideal location, in its excessive presence, for an excavatory "nothing but process" even more inexhaustibly suited, if less apparent to the blind eye, than the lanes near Ferry Hincksey that are themselves "blind lanes," or "points of failure," for a "blind march"—Ruskin's spades of folly at least partially redeemed by a labyrinthine and asymmetrical pathos.

Since only Illth lies beyond the circumferential Promise(d) Land, Ruskin, with "play" that is not entirely "bitter," suggests the need for a postcircumferential play-ground as garden, perhaps a version of the Isle of Delos—as if the lost paradise could indeed be reclaimed as a land with room for, among other things, the partners of dancers. But the recovered (or constructed) Eden would be a series of "floating gardens" beyond both the constrictions of the Centre and, as a fictional heterocosm, beyond the disconfirmation of possibility—the disconfirmation, say, of the performance of St. George's Guild:

> To prevent overcrowding would be the first work of a rightly educational State system. To see that baby, boy—and man, had everywhere their Play-grounds.
>
> Imagine all the energies and resources we now spend for war, spent in energetic, adventurous, lovingly national colonisation—fighting with ice, with desert, and with sea. Binding sand, breaking ice, building floating gardens—instead of ships of the line.   [xxxvii, 67].

Yet one wonders whether, even in these "Play-grounds," these "floating gardens," St. George, if not Theseus, might not be needed. For here,

> in England, is our great spiritual fact for ever interpreted to us—the Assumption of the Dragon. No St. George any more to be heard of us; no mere dragon-slaying possible: this child, born on St. George's Day [Turner] can only make manifest the dragon, not slay him, sea-serpent as he is: whom the English Andromeda, not fearing, takes for her lord. The fairy English Queen once thought to command the waves, but it is the sea-dragon now who commands her valleys; of old the Angel of the Sea   [vii, 408].

But the original serpent might "of new" be the "Angel of the Sea," an Angel not "of" the lagoon but "for" gardens that "float." And there may be the recollection of the fortunate "colubrine chains" of reptilian advance, as well as the awareness of the sacrosanct qualities of the three-dimensional labyrinth of sacred crocodiles.

But the Ruskinian reptile—"a running brook of horror," "a wave but without a wind" (xix, 362)—is Medusa-like. And the "Angel of the Sea" may just as well be the demonic "sea-dragon," in which case, St. George, if not his Guild, might be summoned (though not found) to protect the imaginatively conceived pastoral of a "Promise(d) Land" that floats. Here, amidst the concluding, antiphonal doubleness, is the doubleness, and more, of a species from a paradise that is lost (even as a land of Promise is a land where promises are broken, like cut cords)—and, because lost, remembered:

> The forms of the serpent and lizard exhibit always every element of beauty and horror in strange combination: the horror, which in an imitation is felt only as a pleasurable excitement, has rendered them favourite subjects in all periods of art; and the unity of both lizard and serpent in the ideal dragon, the most picturesque and powerful of all animal forms, and of peculiar symbolical interest to the Christian mind, is perhaps the principal of all the materials of medieval picturesque sculpture. By the best sculptors it is always used with this symbolic meaning, by the cinque cento sculptors as an ornament merely. The best and most natural representations of mere viper or snake are to be found interlaced among their confused groups of meaningless objects. The real power and horror of the snakehead has, however, been rarely reached   [IX, 276-77].

V

There are the "angels of the lagoon" and the "Angel of the Sea," who might be swimming toward "floating gardens" somewhere off the "isle of Anglesea," where, it is just possible, there may be the "remaining places" of the unfailing architecture of "many monas"— a heavenly "Gothic anomaly".

But the Third Fors helped me, to-day, by half effacing the "n" in the word Mona, in the tenth-century MS. I was deciphering; and making me look at the word, till I began to think of it, and wondered. You may as well learn the old meaning of that pretty name of the isle of Anglesea. "In my Father's house," says Christ, "are many monas,"—remaining places— "if it were not so, I would have told you." (John xiv, 2)

Alas, had He but told us more clearly that it *was* so!

I have the profoundest sympathy with St. Thomas, and would fain put all his questions over again, and twice as many more. "We know not whither Thou goest." That Father's house,—where is it? These "remaining-places," how are they to be prepared for us?—how are we to be prepared for them? [xxvii, 489].

VI

And Rosamond, though not *Ros marina*, is in her mazy Bower, which is a "remaining place" at least for a time, while that other Rose, who knew something about backs ("Ask Rosie to make your back better. *She* knows something about backs."), is in a "remaining place" forever, sending "back," occasionally, a sprig of "sacred vervain" (xxix, 31).